PENGUIN

Pekin

Luigi Barzini was born in 1874 at Orvieto. In 1898 he joined a Roman paper as a caricaturist and writer, but after a few months was taken on by the *Corriere della Sera* in Milan as its London correspondent. This was the beginning of a brilliant and varied career as a foreign correspondent. He covered the international expedition against the Boxers in China in 1900; in 1903 he went to Russia, and he went on to Tokyo at the outbreak of the Russo-Japanese war. He was the only European journalist present at the decisive battle of Mukden, and the book he wrote of his front-line experiences was used in nearly every army school at the time, as the only authoritative account of a battle fought in 'a modern style'. He reported from San Francisco on the earthquake, and in 1907 returned to China to take part in the Peking to Paris race. He was present at early attempts to fly aeroplanes, and he interviewed the Wright brothers in America. He followed the Libyan war and the Balkan war, and during the 1914–18 war was a special correspondent on many military fronts. In 1921 he founded the *Corriere d'America*, an English-language paper in New York, which he edited until 1933. He then returned to Italy and was editor of the Naples *Mattino* for two years, after which he became a senator and joined the *Popolo d'Italia*. During the Second World War he wrote reports from the Russian front. He died in Milan in 1947.

Luigi Barzini Jr, who has written the new introduction to this book, is the author of *The Italians* (1964) and *From Caesar to the Mafia* (1971). He has worked on the *Corriere della Sera*, *Il Globo*, and *Libera Stampa*. He was elected to Parliament in 1958 as deputy of the Italian Liberal Party from Milan, and served for fourteen years. He has discovered much new material and many photographs about the Peking to Paris race, which are incorporated in this edition.

LUIGI BARZINI

PEKING TO PARIS

A Journey across two Continents in 1907

Translated by L. P. de Castelvecchio

WITH AN INTRODUCTION BY
LUIGI BARZINI JR

PENGUIN BOOKS

Penguin Books Ltd, Harmondsworth, Middlesex, England
Viking Penguin Inc., 40 West 23rd Street, New York, New York 10010, U.S.A.
Penguin Books Australia Ltd, Ringwood, Victoria, Australia
Penguin Books Canada Limited, 2801 John Street, Markham, Ontario, Canada L3R 1B4
Penguin Books (N.Z.) Ltd, 182–190 Wairau Road, Auckland 10, New Zealand

First published in 1908
Revised edition first published by Alcove Press Ltd 1972
Published in Penguin Books 1986

Made and printed in Great Britain by
Cox & Wyman Ltd, Reading

Typeset in 9 on 11 pt Times by
Rowland Phototypesetting Ltd
Bury St Edmunds, Suffolk

CONTENTS

CONTENTS   vii

LIST OF PLATES

All pictures supplied courtesy of the author's family

INTRODUCTION

by Luigi Barzini Jr

Until a few years ago there were few respectable Italian families that did not own a copy of *Peking to Paris*. By the late 1930s there must have been many hundred thousands of copies of the book in print. For myself I have always looked upon it with particular affection. It was almost my twin. We were both born in the same year. The book was published in Italy (as well as ten or eleven other countries and almost as many languages at the same time) a few months after the end of the voyage, not long before my birth. It had been reprinted regularly until, I believe, 1929.[*]

Like many more famous and durable books, it was at first bought and read by mature people (who were, at the time, preoccupied with the future of automobilism and world communications); then, as the years went by, by younger and younger readers. By the late 1920s it had become one of the traditional gifts bestowed on diligent schoolboys who passed their examinations. Still today many middle-aged or old people's faces light up when they hear my name and ask: '*Peking to Paris*?' Most of them recall the memorable incidents: the Russian telegraph operator who sent Barzini's dispatch vertically; the Latin-speaking wheelwright in the Siberian village; and the disenchanted close of the last chapter: '*Sic transit gloria . . .*' (The only words Pope Paul VI said to me at an audience given some time ago to writers, actors, film directors, and journalists, almost predictably were about *Peking to Paris*. He said,

---

[*] Incidentally, this great success did not make my father rich and our family life less penurious. He was given an advance for the book, which the publisher assured him was generous, and never imagined the book would become a stable household fixture, like Pellegrino Artusi's 19th-century Italian cookbook, called *L'arte di mangiar bene*, which was given to every bride for generations.

using the *pluralis majestatis*: 'When we were young, we read with great pleasure your father's memorable book . . .')

Why, then, did this particular book become so solidly embedded in Italian hearts? It is, to be sure, the truthful, colourful, and readable account of a difficult and uncomfortable voyage in which, however, nothing really unexpected, shocking, or disastrous happened. There is no real cliffhanging suspense whatever. As the reader starts the first chapter, he already knows that none of the protagonists will die, the car will not quite break down, it will arrive in Paris in sixty days (the Italian title artlessly gives it all away, *Da Pechino a Parigi in sessanta giorni o la metà del mondo vista da un'automobile*), and will beat its nearest competitors by almost three weeks. It should have been less popular than other travel books of the time, written by explorers, missionaries, and big-game hunters, containing fascinating descriptions of more inaccessible and mysterious countries, hair-raising tales of attacks by bloodthirsty animals or hostile savage tribes, of mutinies of native bearers or being captured by pirates, of horrible diseases, torture and death.

The first explanation that comes to one's mind is that not very often had such a good writer been on a voyage of the kind to see and describe, in such terse and evocative prose, incidents which would have gone unnoticed by less perceptive men. Luigi Barzini was famous as a 'painter with words', a precious talent in an age in which published photographs were rare, small, and foggy, and there was no television. *Corriere della Sera* subscribers, when reading his transparent prose, used admiringly to say: '*Per Bacco*, it's like being there . . .' His narrative and descriptive genius were fully employed in *reportage* which was (reality once more imitating fiction) disturbingly like Jules Verne's novels, perhaps more similar to *Le tour du monde en 80 jours* than to others. (This my father was surely aware of when he added the words 'half the world' and 'sixty days' to the original title.) And there was no suspense in Jules Verne's novels, either. One knew Phileas Phogg would win his wager in the end.

One must also admit that any book about the transcontinental automobile race, however written, would have had an immediate success in 1907. There was a natural craving all over the world for such reports. The automobile was not yet ten years old. It was still a magical and romantic machine. Its ultimate possibilities had not yet been imagined, let alone explored. It had never been tried in long, arduous, transcontinental voyages, over deserts, plains, forests, mountain passes, with only primitive tracks to follow.

A book about the competition would not contain the account of a single and isolated expedition, with the enumeration of the supplies, the recruiting of guides and interpreters, the negotiations with local authorities, the laborious choice of itinerary, the meticulous listing of scientific data gathered, animals killed, which usually made such dreary reading, together with the tale of a few hardships and dangers, but the infinitely more exciting *compte rendu* of a race, perhaps the most extraordinary race yet held, an international competition among men, industries, and diverse conceptions of the ideal machine of the future (light, middle-weight, or heavy). To be sure, the field of competitors at Peking was not as widely representative as one could wish. Britain, the United States, and Germany, the mightiest engineering and industrial powers, had not participated. The cars were only French, Dutch, and Italian. Yet nobody could deny it was a competition of nations.

Furthermore, the publicity surrounding the event had been deafening. The purse had been dramatically put up by *Le Matin*, one of the powerful French daily newspapers; it kept up a cannonade of front page stories for months, all about the probable competitors, the preparations, the geographical and meteorological conditions, the experts' forecasts, and, in the end, the vicissitudes of the race. One or two of the participants were journalists or part-time journalists, who sent regular stories to their newspapers. After the race started Luigi Barzini's daily dispatches appeared not only in the Milan *Corriere della Sera* but also in the London *Daily Telegraph*.* London and Paris being the centres from which lesser papers got their news second-hand, Barzini's and *Le Matin*'s dispatches ricocheted within hours to the far corners of the world. Surely the first book which would have come out with the complete story, however written, would have made a killing.

Why, then, did this one book become so solidly embedded in European bookshops? Why was it reprinted, sold, and read long after the automobile had become as unglamorous as the sewing machine? There are many purely provincial reasons for the phenomenon. The moment was psychologically right. The event was an Italian triumph of sorts after years of humiliating deceptions and defeats. It seemed to confirm qualities (mechanical capacity, moral determination, adventurous spirit) which foreigners, who thought of us mostly as 'mandolin

---

* The Italian paper covered general expenses, the British agreed to pay for the telegraph tolls. My father exceeded the sum he had been instructed to spend for the whole voyage with his first cable, but was immediately instructed from London to go on filing as abundantly as he had started, such being the interest shown by the public.

strummers', refused to believe we possessed. The cast was perfect. The author was a famous and beloved figure for the younger generation. At a time when Italian prose was a decorative and almost incomprehensible wrought-iron masterpiece, encrusted with jewel-like adjectives and archaic verbs, Barzini wrote simply, clearly, absorbingly.

The cast was almost too perfect.

There was Ettore Guizzardi, the moustachioed and silent mechanical wizard, who could take the whole automobile apart and put it together again in a matter of hours anywhere, in the Gobi desert or the Ural mountains, even after having driven all day and night. Ettore had become an orphan at an early age when his father, a railroad worker, had been killed in a train accident not far from the estate of Prince Scipione Borghese in the Castelli Romani. The prince had taken the ragged and barefooted little boy in, gave him an education, discovered his mechanical genius, and, as Ettore grew older, sent him to institutes and workshops where he could learn all about that new invention, the automobile. He had become the family's head chauffeur and mechanic, in charge of the princely automobiles, and travelled everywhere with Don Scipione. In later life, Ettore entered the state railroad organization, rose to the rank of station master, and died a very old man, only a few years ago, the last of the Peking/Paris three. His role in the story was was that of the feudal family retainer, translated into contemporary terms.

Then there was the Prince, the protagonist, a fascinating and contradictory character. He was born at Migliarino, Pisa, one of the family's estates, on 11 February 1871. His grandfather's brother Don Camillo had been the husband of Paolina Bonaparte (who gave him no heirs); his grandfather Don Francesco had married a Rochefoucauld; Don Scipione's maternal grandmother was Russian, a von Benckendorff; his mother was Hungarian, an Appony; his wife, a de Ferrari, was half-Russian, the daughter of an Annenkov. Don Scipione spoke French, Russian, German, English as fluently as Italian or Roman patois. There was, in fact, very little Italian blood in this Italian hero, the man who proudly flew the little green, white and red flag across Asia and Europe, making his countrymen's heart flutter with pride.

When Don Scipione was eighteen, the family lost all, or almost all, of their fortune. Rome had become the national capital in 1870 and was being transformed from a sleepy decrepit town, inefficiently dominated by elderly priests, into an almost modern city. The price of real estate rose daily, until the crash came. The Borgheses had been speculating heavily, and when the bottom fell out of the market and the banks asked for their money, they had to sell almost everything they owned to meet their obligations. This included the gardens on the Pincio hill (which the state bought and made into a public park, the Villa Borghese) and the villa itself, with its priceless collections of paintings, sculptures, tapestries, and Canova's naked Paolina (Don Scipione's great-aunt) in Carrara marble. To be sure, the family was far from destitute. The remnants from such stupendous wrecks are usually enough to maintain a decorous standard. They let the state apartments in the palazzo (in Piazza Fontanella di Borghese), and restricted themselves for the time being to the smaller rooms where once bachelor uncles and priestly tutors had lived.

To make a gentleman-like living, Don Scipione entered the army and was sent to artillery school. Like so many young men, he was at the time in revolt against his ancestors and his class. He began to see himself as something of a socialist. He hated the provincial overbearing ignorance of the Roman princes, their hostility to the new bourgeois ways of life, their indifference to the business and technical world, their flabby contempt for any kind of vigorous or dangerous adventure. Don Scipione was clearly transformed in this military period. He came in contact for the first time with young men from all classes and regions. He learned to concentrate, to command, to plan, to love and care for machinery. He was attracted to arduous mathematical calculations, read maps at a glance, remembered the terrain he explored as if it were a snapshot in his mind, organized meticulously the smallest as well as the most important expeditions. He also became an excellent rider and mountain climber.

A few years later the family shipped him to Paris, recommending him to all his French relatives and relatives of relatives, with strict orders to come back with a rich wife. Don Marcantonio, his father, had died; and Don Scipione was now the prince. It was hoped that, with the help of a spouse of means, the Borgheses could once more take on their leading position in Roman society. He was an intelligent man, tall, handsome, somewhat severe, impatient and intimidating, but, when necessary, a '*charmeur*' (as one old French lady put it) with impeccable manners, and '*très homme du monde*'. He soon fell in love with and easily got engaged to one of the richest and most handsome young ladies in Paris at the time, Anna-Maria de Ferrari (the de Ferraris were one of the ruling families in the ancient republic of Genoa), whose Russian mother, an Annenkov, owned vast estates and tens of thousands of souls. Don Scipione and Anna-Maria were married in Genoa and were a very

devoted couple until her mysterious death.* The Borgheses had two
daughters, no sons.

His passions (now that he had left the army, was the head of the
family, and could afford expensive hobbies) were politics of the lay left.
It was an unusual posture for a Roman prince, the descendant of Pope
Paul V 'Borghesius' whose name is written in large letters on the
pediment of Saint Peter's. He also had a penchant for adventurous expeditions to wild countries. As his daughter Santa (Princess Hercolani)
remembers him: 'His habits were extremely frugal. He did not cultivate
personal luxuries. He was the kind of man to whom one never knew
what to give. He did not drink, gamble, or smoke. He had to spend a lot,
to be sure, to live as a prince in Rome, prepare for his expeditions to
climb high mountains or explore little-known countries, as well as to
purchase automobiles, but always with a clear sense of moderation and
with a precise purpose in mind . . . He was not a religious man, but he
died reconciled with the Church . . .'

He was fascinated by economics, the 'social problem', and by politics
in an abstract way; he never had to apply his ideas since he never
managed his own business affairs. When the troubles of 1919–21 came
(farmhands' strikes, violence, riots, and occupation of lands) he left his
wife to face them alone. She did it bravely but with a vigorous conserva-
tive spirit, diametrically different from the moderate socialism Don
Scipione had been expounding and defending. He knew Sidney and
Beatrice Webb well, visited them whenever he was in England, and
adopted many of their ideas. He ran for Parliament and was a Radical
deputy for several terms. (He was still a deputy in 1907, at the time of the
Peking to Paris race.) His family remembers Don Scipione, speaking to
astonished peasants and working men, at open air meetings not far from
one of his estates. To show the extent of his democratic convictions he
would even go so far as to loosen his tie and open his stiffly starched
collar a few symbolic millimetres. Some of his relatives thought this to be
an indecorous gesture, a concession to demagogy unworthy of a gentleman.

His elaborately prepared expeditions had taken him to Syria and
Mesopotamia (1900); to Persia and Turkestan; to the great rivers of
Siberia, which he had navigated as far as the Pacific. He had earlier
taken on the Pamir mountains in central Asia, with the help of a group of

---

* When staying on an island she owned on Lake Garda, one day in 1924, she went,
followed by her dog, to plant a few oak saplings, and disappeared. Her body was never found.
Her dog sat waiting for her at the water's edge. The last person who had seen her was the
family chauffeur, Ettore Guizzardi.

guides from the Val d'Aosta. Apparently he never shot game to bring back to the fine taxidermists in Rome; he was only after scientific data and the pride of having conquered hitherto insurmountable obstacles.

In 1914, when the war broke out, Prince Borghese volunteered to return to the army as an artillery officer, and he saw action as soon as Italy entered the war in May 1915. In 1917 Sidney Sonnino, the foreign minister (an Italian Presbyterian with an English mother and a Jewish father) who was a friend of the family, sent him to St Petersburg as part of an international military mission which was supposed to convince Kerensky – and later Lenin – to intensify the war against the German Empire. Don Scipione had a Russian grandmother, Don Scipione's wife was half-Russian. He had hundreds of noble relatives and spoke Russian almost like one of them. He sent for his 18-year-old daughter Santa, who was then studying at Oxford, to work as his secretary. She remembers (as she recently told me) the confusion, the wild rumours, the riots, the demonstrations, the mutinies, the relentless sound of rifle fire, the *coups-de-scène*, growing from week to week until the Bolsheviks took over. Don Scipione began at first to make his official visits to various Ministries dressed in his Italian uniform, as if nothing had happened, and he ended by going to the Smolny (the old boarding school where Queen Elena of Italy had studied) in civilian clothes trying to make his way through crowds of vociferous revolutionaries, sailors, soldiers, and workers to the office of any impatient official who would take a moment to listen to him.

In the summer of 1917 Don Scipione and his daughter went to Stockholm as unofficial observers to an aborted international meeting of socialist parties. In the late autumn he was back in the army, at the Italian front; in 1920 he was once again in Russia, in Murmansk, with the Italian contingent of the Allied expedition. Back in civilian clothes, after the war, he busied himself with agrarian cooperatives and became the first president of the *Confederazione dei Consorzi Agrari*, which he had helped found. After Mussolini's 'March on Rome' he lost interest in public affairs. Italy was no longer the country he had known, for which he had fought. He used to call fascism '*sfascismo*', meaning a régime bent on dismantling ('*sfasciare*') everything. He died in 1927.

Luigi Barzini was born on 7 February 1874, four days earlier and three years later than Don Scipione, under the same sign of the zodiac. The Barzini family was far from distinguished. From humble farming origins in Tuscany, they had emigrated to Orvieto in the eighteenth century. They had been tailors for generations. My grandfather Ettore had enlarged the family business by manufacturing hats and uniforms for the Army, but he had died young, leaving several young sons and very little money. My father (who had no head for figures and business) went to Rome on his bicycle to find a job, any job. He was employed by a newspaper, *Il Fanfulla*, as a cartoonist. He attended trials, meetings, ceremonies, social events, to sketch the scenes and the protagonists, and wrote short witty notes to go with his drawings.

His break came one day in 1899 when he interviewed the famous operatic star, Adelina Patti. Nobody had managed to get her to talk for a newspaper for years. His story impressed a young journalist who had become editor of Milan's *Corriere della Sera*, Luigi Albertini. Albertini lunched with Barzini in Rome and asked him casually whether he spoke English. My father lied. He said that, of course, his English was good, a little rusty but in working condition. Albertini hired him on the spot as his London correspondent, and gave him 100 lire as an advance. With the cash my father bought a boater, a new suit, shirts, ties, gloves, a ticket to Milan, and an English–Italian dictionary. In London he wrote, among other stories, a few striking articles on Chinatown, the secret societies, and the opium smoking dens. When the Boxer rebellion broke out Albertini had no doubts about the man to send to Peking with the international expeditionary force. It had to be Barzini who could write, could speak English, and evidently knew the Chinese inside out. His articles, dispatches, sketches, and essays from Peking made him famous overnight. From then on he had never stopped travelling. He was in Argentina in 1900 (a *reportage* on Italian immigrants); in Russia in 1903 (the political unrest); in Japan in 1904 and 1905 (the Russo-Japanese conflict). He was the only European journalist with the Japanese Army at Mukden, the battle that ended the war. It was the biggest battle ever fought until then; it lasted thirty days, along a front of about a hundred miles, at a temperature of 30° C below zero. Barzini rarely took his uniform off, was mostly on horseback from dawn to dusk, slept and ate with the soldiers wherever he happened to be at the end of the day. The book he later wrote on the battle was used in the Japanese military schools as a textbook, and it is also considered an exemplary piece of literary reportage. He was later sent to the United States (the Harry K. Thaw trial, the San Francisco earthquake). His name had by then become a household word. When he was introduced to my mother she looked with surprise at the slight, tall, youthful man and said: 'So young and already . . .' He continued: '. . . and already so Barzini.' Who else could accompany Prince Scipione Borghese on his voyage?

After the Peking-Paris race he was sent to cover the first airplane flights wherever they took place. He interviewed the Wright brothers, and described the first air-crossing of the Alps by the Peruvian Geo Chavez (1910). Chavez crashed on his arrival at Domodossola and died a few days later; Barzini had been a good friend of his. He sat in the hospital room and coolly recorded the young man's agony, writing down everything he saw and heard until the end. His account is considered a classic chapter in Italian journalism, a sober Hemingwayesque tale of youth, daring, fate, love, death.

He was asked by the *Daily Telegraph* in 1910 to cover Edward VII's funeral for its readers. It was a rare and flattering invitation, for a foreigner from beyond Calais, to describe the last farewell rites for a dead British sovereign for his own subjects. Barzini was also supposed to be present at George V's coronation, in October 1911; but he had to rush to Tripoli where the Italian army was preparing a landing. He covered that war, the Balkan wars, World War I (from the British and French as well as the Italian fronts), the Versailles Conference, the Washington disarmament conference.

In Washington he conceived the idea of founding and editing an Italian newspaper in New York. He ran it for a few years, long enough for his oldest son and namesake to obtain an American education. Back in Italy he became editor of *Il Mattino* in Naples, a senator (equivalent to a life peer at the time), and covered the Spanish civil war. Towards the end of his life, he followed the Italian Army to southern Russia and was at Leningrad with the German Army in the depth of winter. He died in 1947.

Barzini was as tall as Prince Borghese, as slim, as elegant, as physically fit when the two men met in Peking, in 1907, for the first time. Their characters, too, had something in common. They were both reserved and taciturn, devoured by a sense of mission, of duty to be accomplished at any cost. They spoke little to each other but they silently admired each other's qualities. There also was, at the time, a small but practically impassable social barrier between the nominally Radical prince and the poor, if famous, journalist. Journalists still occupied a position similar to that of the *couriers*. The day before the Itala's arrival in Paris, many of Don Scipione's (and Donna Ina's) friends and relatives met him at Mons and gave him a big dinner at the hotel where they were staying. My father was not invited and ate alone in his room. He did not resent the slight. He thought it natural, and he never liked social gatherings anyway. Nevertheless he dedicated his book *Da Pechino a Parigi* to Don Scipione and asked him to write a preface. In it the prince acknowledged with gratitude Barzini's contribution to their common success and his admiration for his companion. He wrote: 'The telegraph and the press were the immediate instruments of the popular sympathy which our endeavour has enjoyed. They have spread everywhere your evocative prose, which gave interest and life to what were to us the monotonous and wearisome incidents of the trip. Scrupulously faithful to the truth, you have illuminated events with the light of their environment, brought out their precise value within the general perspective and the public responded to the poetry of your narration of our modern Odyssey. Nobody, however, will suspect, reading your book, what an exercise of will power and moral strength it cost you. I, who had the honour and pleasure of being your companion, and witnessed the efforts lasting two months, intense intellectual efforts in the midst of material discomforts, only know how much all this cost you. From these two months spent together I will preserve a lively admiration for you and a deep feeling of friendship which will resist time . . .'

The two men never met again in their lives.

The cast, as I said, was as well chosen as if by a good playwright. The three men all represented '*la nuova Italia*', in revolt against the provincial, resigned, mediocre, prudent life of their ancestors. One was the man of the people, still loyally attached to his feudal master by the ancient bonds, and yet an expert in the new mechanical arts. The leader belonged to a prestigious old papal family, had all the aplomb which came from his position and his money, but, at the same time, was a Radical deputy, a daring sportsman, an impeccable organizer of difficult expeditions. The Homer of their Odyssey was the most famous, widely read, and much imitated young writer for the Italian press. They somehow gave young Italians the idea that the country was not condemned to be a dusty museum of past greatness, an itinerary of crumbling ruins for foreigners to gape at, but could compete in the modern world with other countries, no longer over-burdened by the past. This is perhaps the reason why so many Italians of a certain age smile when they hear my name. It reminds them of their youth and forgotten hopes.

Rome,
September 1972.

THE HORSELESS CARRIAGE
OF 1907

For those interested in the technical details of the automobile in question we repeat some of the details given in an appendix to the original edition.

The car was constructed by the Italian firm Itala for Prince Borghese. It was a normal 35–40-hp 1907 model, with some detail modifications for the transcontinental journey. The engine had its cylinders (130 mm bore by 140 mm stroke) cast in two pairs. It had symmetrical interchangeable valves, low-tension magneto ignition, specially designed spark plugs (of an Itala patent), and an automatic carburettor which was almost impervious to changes of pressure or temperature (it was connected to the engine by very short pipes to prevent any condensation of gases). As a consequence the Peking to Paris vehicle was able to use low-grade fuel. Once when the supply of petrol failed to reach an agreed refuelling point, they purchased from a local grocer 'a mixture of hydrocarbons, more like ordinary paraffin than motor petrol'; and surprisingly enough the car seemed not to suffer at all, except for increased consumption and a thick exhaust. The average consumption of fuel was one third of a litre per kilometre.

The clutch was of the disc type (it was removed and replaced in Moscow); the gearbox had four forward speeds and a reverse; the fourth speed was obtained by a direct drive from the gearbox (without engaging the secondary shaft). It was made of tough nickel steel, never suffered any damage, and at the end of the journey seemed on inspection to be 'as new'. The same was found to be the case with all the joints of the differential axle, which showed 'not the slightest trace of wear'. The chassis was made of somewhat thicker girder steel than in the usual models of the day, and it held up admirably except for the inevitable traces of wear in the spring-hangers. During the journey the springs were damaged by the breaking of several of the leaves (replaced in Moscow). The radiator was of the usual honeycomb type. The manufacturers had no time to build a radiator of bigger capacity; and a supplementary fan was added for the ventilation of the flywheel (it proved quite useless and was removed before the crossing of the Gobi desert).

The seating accommodation consisted of two front seats and of one back seat placed between two fuel tanks (large enough to hold 150 litres each), behind which was a large chest for spare parts. (As Prince Borghese later reported, these were never needed and were in fact, luckily as it turned out, disposed of at the outset of the race in order to lighten the car.) There was in the back also a tank for oil and another for water, each with a capacity of 150 litres.

As for the tyres, they were made by the Pirelli firm in Milan, were 935 by 135 with a flat profile, and were used on the average about 2500 miles or some 4000 kilometres. The four tyres on which the Itala reached Paris were still in such good condition that they remained unchanged all the way back to Milan. The front right wheel proved serviceable on the whole journey from Peking to Paris, with a change of tyre only in Omsk. The choice of oversize tyres proved fortunate.

The technical summing-up made in 1907 has a piquant ring some sixty-five years – and several hundreds of millions of horseless carriages – later:

> On the whole the Peking to Paris race has proved conclusively that the motor car is a much stronger and more resistant machine than has so far been thought, and that the usual inconveniences of automobilism, and the frequent breakdowns from which tourists suffer, the breakages and repeated disasters to the machines, are due rather to carelessness or want of skill in chauffeurs than to any congenital weakness of the car itself. It may therefore be said that this industry has arrived near its perfection, and that varied and novel practical uses of the motor car are possible, for regular communications, for service in distant places, and for transport by road. But we must improve our drivers! . . .

Replying to a question 'If a similar journey were to be undertaken again, what would be advisable modifications?', the Peking to Paris team's recommendations included: a model higher off the ground, with stronger wheels and a better-protected petrol tank, more efficient springs, a more solid radiator.

A half-century later Luigi Barzini Jr contemplated undertaking 'a similar journey', and Fiat engineers in Turin began to plan a design for a fiftieth-anniversary model with all the most modern 'modifications' of a 'near-perfect industry'. The same route from the Great Wall to the Seine, once taken by the Prince, the Journalist, and the Chauffeur, was to be followed. But it was not to be. The Chinese authorities withheld visas and refused permission; they were not (or perhaps not yet) prepared to allow for another European adventure across their mountains, rivers, and deserts.

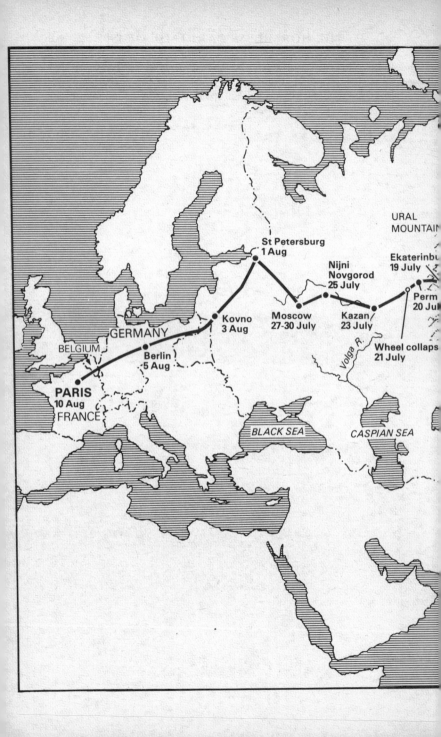

St Petersburg
1 Aug

Nijni
Novgorod
25 July

URAL
MOUNTAIN

Ekaterinbu
19 July

Kovno
3 Aug

Moscow
27-30 July

Kazan
23 July

Perm
20 Jul

GERMANY

BELGIUM

Berlin
5 Aug

Wheel collaps
21 July

Volga R.

PARIS
10 Aug
FRANCE

BLACK SEA

CASPIAN SEA

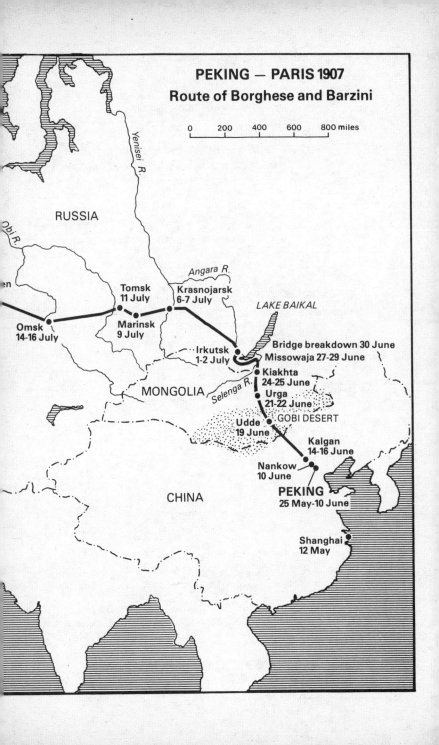

PEKING — PARIS 1907
Route of Borghese and Barzini

0   200   400   600   800 miles

Yenisei R.

RUSSIA

Ob R.

Angara R.

Tomsk
11 July

Krasnojarsk
6-7 July

LAKE BAIKAL

en

Omsk
14-16 July

Marinsk
9 July

Irkutsk
1-2 July

Bridge breakdown 30 June
Missowaja 27-29 June

Kiakhta
24-25 June

MONGOLIA

Selenga R.

Urga
21-22 June

Udde
19 June

GOBI DESERT

Kalgan
14-16 June

Nankow
10 June

PEKING
25 May-10 June

CHINA

Shanghai
12 May

I

FROM PARIS TO PEKING

~~~~~~~~~~

*Events of 18 March – Paris – 'Be at Peking' – Occupations
and Preoccupations of the Wai-wu-pu – Our Cars – Ettore*

At noon on 18 March 1907 – a date ever memorable for me – I was seated
at my desk, completely absorbed in studying the network of North
American railways. I was at the time passionately interested in railway
problems of all kinds. I wrote about them and talked about them, and
found food for my soul in the intricacies of railway regulations at home
and abroad. Suddenly a loud ring of my telephone bell, not a yard away
from my head, freed me violently from the meshes of American
railways.

'Who is it?'

'Good morning.' (I knew the speaker at once. It was Signor Luigi
Albertini, editor of the *Corriere della Sera*.) 'I want to speak to you. Can
you come and see me?'

'At once?'

'This minute.'

'All right.'

'Thanks.'

With a leap I was out of doors and in the first cab within hail. On the
way I passed rapidly in review the events of the last twenty-four hours,
trying to guess at the cause of that urgent summons. Was the paper in
need of its 'special correspondent'? An outbreak of war? No, even
Venezuela had been perfectly peaceful for a week or so. A revolution?
Scarcely. It was too cold, revolutions begin with the summer breezes;
they bloom with the flowers; it is only towards the end of April that
editorial offices hear of those first signs of the people's periodical
awakening to the breath of freedom, symbolized by the famous telegram: 'A Bulgarian (or Greek?) band has massacred all the inhabitants
of a Greek (or Bulgarian?) village.' Some unforeseen catastrophe,
then? Catastrophes have no closed season.

Nothing of the sort. Professional ardour had misled me in my forebodings of disaster. No grave matter had occurred in either hemisphere. When, burning with well-justified curiosity, I entered the editorial office – where the brain of our newspaper dwells – I found the editor perfectly calm and collected. He held out to me a copy of *Le Matin*, pointed at a few words printed on the first page under a huge black heading, and asked, 'What do you think of it?'

I looked, and read this amazing proposal:

WILL ANY ONE AGREE TO GO, THIS SUMMER, FROM PEKING TO PARIS BY MOTOR CAR?

I read it again, and felt a glow of admiration for the unknown inventor of such a plan. He must be a man of magnificent conceptions.

'What do you think of it?' repeated Signor Albertini.

'Magnificent!'

'Is it feasible?'

'Oh, that's a different matter. But even if it were to fail, the attempt would be sufficiently interesting to be worth making.'

'And would you undertake it?'

'Yes, with great pleasure.'

We spent the next few minutes looking through *Le Matin* of the following days, in search of other news of this strange journey. Replies to the challenge filled many columns; letters full of enthusiasm, for the most part too impulsive to last. One among them, however, arrested our attention, being from an Italian and also couched in a style cold and concise like that of a formal receipt. It ran thus:

I hereby enter my name for the Peking to Paris race in an Itala motor-car. I shall be much obliged for details as soon as possible, in order that I may make the necessary arrangements.

Prince Scipione Borghese

The name and the style made me think at once, *This* is a man who means what he says.

Don Scipione Borghese was already well known to me by his fame as a motorist, and a traveller. In 1900, after crossing Persia with a caravan (and partly through almost unexplored provinces), he had penetrated into Turkestan, travelled northward through the vast steppes of Baraba as far as Barnaul, thence by boat over the Obi and the Tom, reaching Tomsk and the Trans-Siberian railway, and so the shores of the Pacific. On the subject of these travels he had written a book – a scholarly book, full of the rigid exactitude of a navigation manual: minute, technical, calm – a book whose author could not but be possessed of a mind clear and balanced, and never unduly affected by the impulses of admiration, emotion, or sentiment. The author of that book was felt to be a man of science rather than a poet; in his work stood revealed the predominance of head over heart, of will over impulse. Prince Borghese appeared to me as a man of the sort that wills, judges, and acts. He would not have entered himself for the Peking to Paris race had he not been certain of starting; and once started, he would do all that is humanly possible to win. I felt immediate confidence in him.

All at once, interrupting his perusal of *Le Matin*, the editor said to me in a tone of sudden resolve:

'You ought to leave for China.'

'Quite.'

'The Peking to Paris race begins on 10 June. You can travel first across the States and the Pacific, and see some interesting things on your way – the close of the Harry K. Thaw trial in New York.'

'Yes.'

'The rebuilding of San Francisco; how matters stand in the Hawaii Islands; how Japan is recovering from the war; and the trip across Asia would complete your tour round the world.'

'Yes, and about the race?'

'I will communicate with you on your way. We shall ask Prince Borghese to allow us a share in his undertaking. I hope he will consent. In any case you shall find all in readiness at Peking, even if we have to provide you with a car ourselves. The first boat for the States leaves – let me see, here's a steamship company book – leaves the day after tomorrow, from France. "*Kaiser Wilhelm der Grosse*, of the Norddeutscher-Lloyd, from Cherbourg, 20 March, for New York." Can you start for Paris today?'

I looked at my watch, and called back to memory my recently acquired railway information, under heading 'time-tables'.

'Yes, I can.'

'Goodbye, then – and good luck.'

Yielding to the promptings of our Latin temperaments, and of a very real mutual liking and understanding, we embraced one another.

As I walked quickly down the office stairs, I met a colleague dully proceeding to his usual work.

'Where are you off to, in such a hurry?' he asked.

'On a tour round the world,' said I, quite seriously, stopping for a moment on the landing.

He burst into a laugh. 'You incorrigible joker! *I* know where you are going to really!'

'Where's that?'

'To lunch, of course: and it's late, and you are hungry. Goodbye!'

My friend's common-sense disbelief suddenly revealed to me the strange, unlikely aspects of my situation. I stood for a moment hesitating and disconcerted before I could answer 'Goodbye', and continue on my way. The old tales of adventure, whose characters, from beginning to end, travelled over all the continents and sailed over all the seas, are now written no longer, because even children would nowadays think them too unlike life; and yet one man still lives them through and through: the journalist.

That very day the Simplon express sped me towards Paris.

In Paris, at the office of *Le Matin*, great meetings had been held to discuss this race. They had been attended not only by people anxious to compete, but also by travellers and diplomats who had been to China, and by learned pundits who could give you information about no matter what part of the world, without having been there. The gatherings had been well attended and full of animation; reporters had accurately registered strange conversations in which more questions were asked than answers given. The matter under discussion turned out to be fuller of unknown quantities than a paper on higher mathematics.

On the whole, however, these meetings had undeniably served a good purpose. By dint of elimination they had succeeded in tracing out the best route to be followed. Telegrams had been sent to Peking, to St Petersburg, to Irkutsk, asking for different items of information. The wise and wily Wai-wu-pu, the State Council of the Celestial Empire, had sent, by way of reply, a question transmitted through the French Legation: 'How many motor cars are to leave Peking for Paris?' In what way their number could affect the State Council of the Celestial Empire is not indeed clear. Perhaps the Wai-wu-pu already stood in fear of an invasion.

The Russo-Chinese Bank in Peking had replied: 'The Nankow and the Ku-pei-ku Passes are broad enough for motor cars, but steep and stony.'

Broad enough! Paris thought this information extremely favourable, compared with the reports received about the other routes. The route of Turkestan via Samarkand, that of Manchuria via Mukden, and that of the Altai Mountains had all been pronounced equally impracticable. The only possible route was then that of Mongolia via Kalgan and Kiakhta, and via those passes which were 'broad enough'.

The unbiased judgements of the candidates for the race were not very encouraging. At a last meeting they issued the following rather pessimistic declaration:

The difficulties of this extraordinary competition appear to us as great upon careful consideration, and after several weeks of study, as they did at first sight. Peking to Paris may be an impossible project. This is the moment for some pioneer of the motor car to obtain from mechanical propulsion the means of crossing deserts, mountains, and steppes – of compassing half the earth.

Le Matin compared this voyage with one of polar discovery. The mass of the public said, more uncompromisingly than the competitors themselves: 'Peking to Paris *is* an impossible project.'

I must confess that when, on the morning of 20 March, I left Paris for Cherbourg, whence I sailed that evening, I thought with some considerable scepticism of my chances of returning to that town on a motor car straight from the capital of China; and in my inmost heart I thanked heaven – and Nicholas II – for the existence of a blessed Trans-Siberian railway, which, if need be, could carry me home again within a reasonable length of time.

Later on my journey I almost ended by forgetting the motor race altogether. It seemed no longer the real purpose of that flight of mine across the world, but only the last and doubtful episode in it – as it were, the nebulous finale in my 'looping the loop' of this planet of ours. The papers, too, no longer spoke of it. The whole matter seemed to have fallen into the silent abyss of oblivion, where utopias and impossibilities unfailingly disappear.

But not so. *Someone* still thought of it, worked for it, made and organized the preparations for it. I realized this on receiving a brief wire – a command, which I found awaiting me one evening at my hotel in New York, and which was given to me with the key of my room. I opened it on the way up to my room. I read and reread it, and stood so absorbed in thought that I arrived without knowing it at floor No. 14, where the porter inquired of me whether I wished to go up to the hotel roof. That mysterious and laconic document ran: '*Be in Peking by 1 June.*' Not a word more.

As punctual as an eclipse, on 1 June at six p.m. I alighted on the platform of the station of Peking – that commonplace station huddled at the foot of the ancient Tartar fortifications, below the imposing bastions of the Chien-men, as if to hide its meanness and profanation in the shadow of so much greatness. And that same evening an Italian gendarme brought to me at the Hotel des Wagons-lits a letter which had arrived for me at the Italian Legation, and a card.

The letter was from the office of the *Corriere della Sera*. It explained – after nearly two months – the telegram I had received in New York. It announced that I was to take part in the race, in Prince Scipione Borghese's Itala car. It also gave me another welcome piece of news. I had been appointed special correspondent for the London *Daily Telegraph*, in addition to my representing the *Corriere della Sera*.

Now, my journalistic career opened in London long ago, and I have kept a tender memory for the city which saw my maiden efforts; above all, I have preserved intact since that first visit upon English soil, a glowing enthusiasm for that centre of world activity, and a deep respect and sincere admiration for the English press. I was flattered by the appointment, and accepted it with pleasure.

The card delivered by the Italian official was that of Prince Borghese. He had arrived a week before. He bid me welcome, and appointed a meeting for the 6th. We had never seen one another, and, destined as we were to share for weeks bread and work, in the close proximity of á long and somewhat fantastic journey, we were both animated by a lively desire to meet. I should have gone to call on him at once, had not his card contained a warning that he was at that moment some hundreds of miles away, engaged in studying and testing the Kalgan route, whereby I was reduced to patient waiting.

That night I remained till late upon the veranda of my hotel, musing. I scarcely recognized the old Peking around me, the proud stronghold of changelessness which I had last seen seven years before at the time of the Boxer rebellion, damaged here and there by the siege of the legations, and by the retaliations of the civilized world, but still untouched in spirit and in main outline, true to itself, uncouth, unique, girt with the sacred line of its portentous walls. What I guessed to be the European quarter rose now in outline against the crimson sunset sky, with a crowd of European roofs of villas and palaces, a crowd of Christian steeples, of belfries, and clock towers: a modern western town, which partly hid the graceful pagodas of the Imperial grounds in the distance. Electric street lamps were being lighted, and one by one they showed up uniforms of European soldiers as they passed. Engines whistled shrilly on their way to the Ha-ta-men. Every now and then I could hear within the hotel the buzzing of a telephone bell, drowning for a minute the sound of an orchestra. And the orchestra – from Europe – was playing for a banquet of Chinese dignitaries, who ate without Chinese chopsticks. 'And we are now going to add even the motor car to all these lamentable innovations,' I said to myself, with a certain regret, 'China is disappearing.'

But not so; next day I perceived that China is by no means disappearing. All the innovations which had struck me so forcibly on my first arrival were in the fortified legation quarter; those innovations were prisoners, confined within a sort of European ghetto. Outside of this area and all around it lay the great unchanging city, the Peking of bygone ages. And in that true Peking, in an ancient palace with its courtyard screened with matting, sat a council wise and venerable: the Wai-wu-pu, or State Council of the Celestial Empire, watchful against the profanations of the west.

The Wai-wu-pu was presided over by the notorious Na-Tung, formerly a Boxer leader, and condemned to death by the powers; Na-Tung, whose execution had indeed been promised in the peace convention of 1900, but who, far from even losing the imperial favour, had now risen to the high estate of something like a foreign minister, saving his neck, and with that neck his head and his unaltered principles. At the special moment in question, the state council was gravely concerned in saving the empire from a new and terrible foe. This foe was called *chi-cho*, which means fuel-chariot, a graceful term invented on the spot to indicate the motor car. The talk centred entirely upon this *chi-cho*, just as in former times it had centred upon the *Huo-cho*, or fire-chariot, in Europe called the railway. Why are the *chi-chos* coming? What do they want? were the anxious and fearful questionings which filled the Wai-wu-pu's long hours of meditations.

It was inconceivable for a Chinese mandarin that the *chi-chos*' only desire could be a journey from Peking to Paris, without any further compensation for their pains. The journey to Paris could be accomplished by swifter, safer, surer means. There must, no doubt, be hidden and dark reasons for such unaccountable eccentricity. The Wai-wu-pu had not the slightest doubt that Europe was trying some new experiment at their expense: what *could* the nature of that experiment be?

Prince Ching, a man of broad views, was inclined to believe that Europe wished to find the best way of establishing swift communications with China by means of a regular motor service, and with no further need of railway concessions. The so-called motorists were, of course, picked engineers, under the orders of an Italian prince. Their plan would entail the absolute collapse of the Chinese railway company which was then laying the Kalgan line, and which had already reached Nankow; Prince Ching was a large shareholder in that company. Na-Tung saw matters in a more lurid light. According to *his* opinion, the *chi-chos* were bent on the discovery of suitable routes of invasion. Had not Mongolia always been the gate of danger? Was not the Great Wall purposely built to protect the empire on that side? And what wall could henceforth stop the progress of an army of motorists, ready to invade Chinese territory on the first pretext of a Boxer rising, and able to arrive in time, this once, to take the lives of those under the ban of the diplomatic corps? The Peking to Paris motorists were, of course, no less than officers under the command of an Italian prince.

The significance of the incident was heightened by the great interest which the French, Dutch, Italian and Russian ministers residing in Peking displayed in the success of this motor expedition. The first three countries, especially, subjected the august Chinese assembly to a heavy fire of official – and officious – notes requesting the immediate endorsement of passports for Mongolia in favour of their respective subjects (to officers or engineers). What was to be done?

The good of their Fatherland required the Wai-wu-pu to fight, and fight it did. It began by refusing all passports. European secretaries and interpreters paid numerous visits to the Centre of Government. The Wai-wu-pu gave them afternoon tea, but heroically withstood all arguments. After all, saying 'no' to Europeans is the very purpose for which the Wai-wu-pu was created. Europe wanted ports, mines, railways, universities, indemnities for the massacre of Christian missionaries – and China felt the need for some defensive organization. China established the Tsung-li-yamen, now laid at rest, whose chief duty it was to bring European demands under discussion, and to keep them there, referring the required answers to the distant future. After the Boxer rebellion, the powers would have none of the Tsung-li-yamen, and the Chinese government satisfied their requests by creating the Wai-wu-pu, which has this merit at least, that it no longer keeps European demands under discussion. It answers promptly 'no'.

But, under existing treaties, China had not the power to deny passports to foreigners simply wishing to cross a province in her jurisdiction. Besides, at this point a serious complication arose, a complication whose importance had not been fathomed or foreseen by the sagacious mandarin mind. *The cars had reached Peking.* Further, they were parading the streets of that capital, in defiance of orders by which their free transit was forbidden unless they would consent to be drawn by a mule – *two* mules at most. Now, if the passports were still denied, these infernal machines would obviously remain in Peking. They would continue to disturb the sacred peace of the capital, they would cause an upheaval in the popular mind, they would spread everywhere the fatal germs of western corruption, call forth the resentment of ghostly powers, the vengeance of ancestors, the wrath of the gods. To leave them in Peking was like leaving an enemy in his stronghold; better by far to help their speedy departure. So the Wai-wu-pu offered passports, but for Manchuria!

The diplomatic contests were renewed. The notes, the visits, the amiable afternoon parties began all over again. And the Chinese were slowly losing ground. They finally consented to send passports for Mongolia – with no mention, however, of motor cars. The Italian legation returned those passports. The Wai-wu-pu then sent others that read like so many indictments. 'The *chi-cho* is a new thing in China' – so ran those remarkable documents – 'wherefore the Chinese government will undertake no responsibility with regard to it. On the contrary, the said government will hold motor travellers responsible for any hurt or injury caused by themselves or their cars, and it hereby enables local authorities to seize moneys or goods as surety for any indemnity owed by the said travellers.' This was regular incitement to spoliation! The Italian legation also returned these documents and announced to the Wai-wu-pu that Prince Borghese and his travelling companions would start on the day previously arranged, with or without passports – and that the Chinese government was answerable for their safety. After vainly putting forward fresh pretexts against yielding to European pressure (among them was the fear that it was not prudent, for mysterious political reasons, to disturb the Mongolian princes) the Wai-wu-pu at last decided to grant the desired passports for Mongolia, content with obtaining one last satisfaction, by stipulating that no Mongolian translation should be made of those passports. The Mongolian princes would have been too much disturbed by such documents. Besides, something must be found that could be denied to these European invaders, on principle and to avoid creating a dangerous precedent.

For the small diplomatic society in Peking these negotiations had provided a diverting subject of witty conversation. But in point of fact the subject was a serious one. The attitude of the Chinese government remained unchanged by the foreign eruption seven years earlier; it regarded strangers with the same hostility, ignored the principles of their life with the same completeness, harboured in its breast the same arrogance and the same mistrust. Invasions, massacres, the war in Manchuria, all these in no way affected the Chinese mind or character.

The suspense about passports in no way delayed our preparations for departure. Supplies of oil and petrol, destined to be waiting for us at intervals on the route through Mongolia, had arrived via Shanghai and the Hankow Railway. A convoy of fourteen mules had left Peking with this cargo, and on 4 June a wire from the Kalgan Russo-Chinese Bank announced the departure for Mongolia of nineteen camels, under the command of a caravan guide, for the transport of oil and petrol to the depots of Pong-kiong, and of Udde and the town of Urga. The first refill awaited us at Kalgan.

Out of the twenty-five cars entered for the race, only five finally presented themselves. These were: a 6-hp Contal tricycle, two 10-hp de Dion-Boutons, one 15-hp Spyker, and our own 40-hp Itala. The first three were machines of French make and the fourth Dutch; our car was powerful but heavy, the others less powerful but light. The Itala car was 600 kg heavier than the next in weight, the Spyker, which, in full travelling kit, weighed 1400 kg.

In France everyone had agreed, since the first discussions, that a small car would have the best chances. A light machine would cover the ground less quickly on good roads, but it would, on the other hand, overcome any difficulty much more easily, and the route from Peking to Paris would probably be made up of difficulties. Prince Borghese, on the other hand, from his own long experience of motor travelling, thought it certain that a powerful and strongly-built car would best be able to stand the strain of an adventurous journey, and that the diminution in weight obtainable was not worth the corresponding sacrifice of power. A car of 2000 kg can surely go where one of 1400 kg can, and it has the advantage of an extra 20 or 30 horsepower.

In this trial between two tendencies, in this practical testing of two theories, lay one of the most important aspects of the race. And as early as the month of March, on the occasion of Prince Borghese's entering his name for the race with an Itala car, *Le Matin* called attention to the interesting struggle between the large car and the small one: 'the one able to go fast, the other able to go anywhere'.

The Spyker, the two de Dion-Boutons, and the Contal cars reached Peking via Ta-ku. On 4 June their respective drivers and my good colleague Du Taillis of *Le Matin*, went to see them through the custom-house at Tien-Tsin, had them loaded on two reserved trucks, and returned by the same train to Peking. Here an unpleasant surprise awaited them. During the journey one of the two reserved railway trucks had disappeared. Who could refrain from attributing this disappearance to the mysterious hand of the Wai-wu-pu? Yet it was soon proved – to the honour of the Wai-wu-pu let it be recorded – that its hand was perfectly innocent. The truck in question had been unaccountably mislaid, and was quietly reposing on a siding at some intermediate station, by one of those strange phenomena which will occur from time to time on the best managed railway. On their arrival in Peking those cars made up for the lateness of their arrival by crossing the city in every conceivable direction on the first and every successive day.

The Itala, which had already reached Peking via Hankow the week before, maintained a much greater dignity. It had made some trial trips outside the eastern gate, on the road to the Summer Palace, and then, satisfied with its own performance, it had withdrawn to the courtyard of the Italian legation, and given itself up to the tender care of Ettore, its chauffeur. The latter polished, greased, tested his machine, prowling around her to examine her from all points of view, as a sculptor examines his own creation.

Ettore Guizzardi, Prince Borghese's and my pleasant travelling companion, is a chauffeur not by training but by nature. He is the son of a railway mechanic, and has been familiar with machines from his earliest childhood. He understands all kinds of them at once, and judges them at a glance, as a horse-dealer judges horses. His history is a singular one. One day, ten years ago, there was a railway accident near a villa of Prince Borghese, at Albano, near Rome: an engine left the rails and overturned, rolling down a bank. The prince, who was in his villa at the time, hastened with his servants to render assistance. They found the engine driver dead. The stoker, a lad of fifteen, was wounded about the head and lay unconscious on the roadside. They picked him up and carried him to the villa, where he was nursed back to life. That lad was Ettore, and the dead man his father. When the boy had sufficiently recovered, Prince Borghese proposed to him that he should remain in the house which had given him shelter and become a chauffeur.

Don Scipione's motor car at that time was one of the early models, a 6-hp of the quaint pattern that has now disappeared, with the engine in the rear and the transmission effected by means of a belt, which when a hill was encountered had to be dressed with tar before it would do its work. Ettore mastered the intricacies of that machine at once, forced it into service, and was able, under the prince's guidance, to travel with it from Rome to a castle in south Hungary, owned by some relations of the Borghese family. After this feat of skill, Ettore was sent to study mechanics. He was first a simple workman in the Fiat works at Turin, studied naval mechanics in the Ansaldo factory at Genoa, then worked under other firms; finally, he obtained a mechanic's certificate, and returned to the prince's motor cars.

Since then, eleven cars have been subject to his domination, and he is now responsible for all the machinery in the Borghese household: lighting, heating, laundry apparatus, water-pumps. He has his own workshop for repairs and inventions. Yes, inventions; for Ettore creates, adapts, and applies new modifications to motor engines, and could, if occasion offered, give excellent advice on design and manufacture. He is full of resource; he can remedy immediately any accident to his machine; his resourcefulness is unlimited. He moves silently, with something of a soldier's manner. To a call he replies '*Comandi!*' (At your orders, sir!) In face and build he is like a *bersagliere*.

The first time that I saw him he was lying on his back under the Itala – motionless, with folded arms. I thought for a moment that he was working. But no, he was off duty, and later I found that that is one of his favourite pastimes, a way he has of taking recreation. When he has nothing special on hand he stretches himself out under his motor car, and contemplates it piece by piece, bolt by bolt, screw by screw, in long, strange colloquy with his machine.

II
THE DEPARTURE

Prince Borghese – The Car – Preparations – The Eve of Battle – Departure

In six days Prince Borghese covered 300 miles on horseback, exploring all the roads between Peking and Kalgan, and measuring their narrowest points with a rod as long as the motor car was broad. Princess Anna-Maria, his wife, and a young lady friend accompanied him on his rough ride; and the two ladies, also armed with measuring rods, shared his task of surveying the land. Every branch of every crossroad was scanned and searched, and the best path was noted. Prince Borghese returned to Peking with a whole topographic map in his brain.

The powers of that brain are prodigious. It registers with the faithfulness of a photographic machine all that the prince's eyes perceive or his ears gather. Names, dates, snatches of oriental speech, the most difficult things to remember, remain engraved upon that iron memory. Don Scipione never takes notes; he does not need them. His mind seizes and holds everything. He can tell you the landmarks of roads seen years ago. When he travels over new countries on horseback or in his car, he consults his map before starting for the day, and he seldom needs to look at it again. He remembers the branching of the ways, the lie of the roads, the distances; he can tell you the names of the villages, and does, too, pointing them out to you like an experienced guide.

If a man could remember all that he has ever seen, heard, or read in his life, that man would be possessed of a culture marvellously vast, deep, and varied. Prince Borghese is, in fact, an exceptionally cultured man, and he has a keen, clear intellect, which automatically sifts and classifies his knowledge. The office of librarian in this abode of learning (to use a bold metaphor) is filled by a magnificent imperturbability. Calmness, judgement, the power of logic invest his habits of thought with the exactitude of a mathematical instrument. He eliminates from his consideration of facts all those emotional elements in them which could dim his perception or distort his judgement. He might have been a general, or a Lord Chief Justice. An instinctive liking for people is rare with him, but he substitutes for it a regard, a respect which has all the more value in that it corresponds to some real quality. And he recognizes merit; he can gauge with wonderful accuracy the power of a mind or of a hand, the strength and resistance of a machine. His whole plan and organization of the Peking to Paris race is a proof of this precise judgement of his.

And no less than the talent of judging, he possesses the power of will, by which he imposes hard tasks always first upon himself. When he exacts a sacrifice from his companions, he is always the first to accomplish his part of it. In the pursuance of his object he can endure hunger, thirst, exhaustion, and say to himself: I am *not* hungry, I am *not* thirsty, I am *not* tired. His sufferings and those of others are as nothing to him in achieving the aim he has in view; sensitivity is a mere squandering of energy. He gives complete priority to achieving his object. It is as if he had given himself his word of honour that he would accomplish his aim, and must not at any cost fail in loyalty to himself. Herein lies the secret of all his successes. He will reach his goal by bending to his purpose every faculty of his being and every instrument within his reach. The matter becomes for him one in which his self-respect, or his ambition, is at stake. And ambition, although a fault in small men, is a virtue in great ones. It serves as a determining factor in the finest and boldest achievements.

I saw Prince Borghese for the first time on the day after his return from Kalgan. He wore his khaki suit, in which he was to accomplish the motor journey, and which gave him somewhat the appearance of an English officer. He is clean shaven, and the sun and wind had already bronzed those clean cut features which he inherits from the long line of his diplomatic ancestry.

Prince Borghese is thirty-five years old. By his face you would think he was forty; by his lithe, strong, slim body, twenty-five; for in the open air muscles grow supple and the skin grows tanned, and Don Scipione has always had a passion for the most difficult forms of sport. As an Alpinist he has conquered the most rugged Alpine peaks – and without a guide, and even in the depth of winter – just for the love of overcoming. He loves obstacles, because he loves victory. And to his mind, sport is nothing so much as an exercise of a man's fighting faculties. Mountain climbing, motor driving, horse breaking, are all training for the leadership of men.

And he has gained his spurs in these fights against odds which he so ardently seeks. Once, as he attempted to stop a runaway horse, he was thrown violently to the ground, and the carriage wheel passed over his head: he bears the mark of it to this day; another time, as he was breaking in a horse, he had a bad fall, and he was picked up unconscious, with his nose almost severed from his face. An excellent surgeon stitched up the wound; but an excellent surgeon is not necessarily also an excellent sculptor, and as a trace of that day's fall there remains a certain want of symmetry in the line of Prince Borghese's nose. The prince makes humorous and disparaging remarks upon that nose of his; he accuses it of changing colour according to atmospheric conditions, for all the world like a scientific barometer . . . But he exaggerates, and that slight facial anomaly of his is barely visible.

We greeted one another with the freedom of old friends: a handshake, and immediate talk of the race. What had given him the idea of taking part in it? It was perfectly simple.

For some considerable time the prince had gone on a long voyage every three or four years, and this year he had decided to visit Peking, which he had never yet seen, and where his brother, Don Livio, is chargé d'affaires at the Italian legation. Suddenly one morning, in Rome, in looking through the papers at the breakfast table, he saw the strange challenge published by *Le Matin*. The idea seemed to have been launched on purpose for him. He immediately sent a wire to the Itala firm of motor builders, inquiring whether they could undertake to supply him with a car for the race, and taking upon himself the whole responsibility for management and expense. Of course they replied in the affirmative, and then it was that he telegraphed to *Le Matin* entering his name for the race. He began making preparations at once.

He did not go to the Paris meetings, but sent a man (Fournier, the winner of the Paris-Bordeaux motor race) to represent him, and to keep him informed of any regulations which might be drawn up for the candidates. The only formality required was, however, a deposit of 2000 francs, to be sent to the racing committee of the French Automobile Club, which would refund the amount at Peking to those really starting the race. As regards other possible conditions, *Le Matin* had already issued an explicit declaration:

There will be no formalities or regulations. All that is required of candidates is that they shall leave Peking for Paris in a motor car, and shall arrive at their destination.

The car selected by the prince was one of the ordinary Itala 24 to 40-hp type. No alterations were made in the engine or the chassis. The angles of the frame alone and the springs were made more powerful than is usual, and the body of the car was placed on higher and stronger wheels. In order that the disparities of the road should be felt less, the biggest possible tyres were chosen among those made by Pirelli of Milan. The prince was particularly anxious that every part of the car should be of Italian make. The body of the car consisted of two front seats, for Prince Borghese and the chauffeur, and a back seat for myself. On either side of my seat was fastened, by means of iron hoops, a long cylindrical tank for petrol, holding 150 litres. Behind, a box, like those used in the artillery service, held our tools and spare parts; and over this box was another cylindrical tank holding water. Our luggage was to be roped on, over the box and water tank; and owing to want of space and to the importance of not overloading the rear of the machine, we had to bring our luggage down to the indispensable minimum; we allowed about 15 kg per head. A 100-litre oil-tank, furnished with a long pipe and a tap, was fixed under my seat. Under the front seats was placed our store cupboard, containing mostly canned meat. The chief peculiarity of the car was in the mudguards, which were made out of four long, solid iron planks attached to the running board by a system of hinges, easy to unfasten, and meant to serve as a track over small ditches, or sandy or marshy ground. Our car, so dissimilar in outline from any yet launched upon the world, had a singular and formidable general appearance. It looked like some strange ironclad machine, like some engine of war. To a flippant man, its great tanks might recall a less terrifying implement, and even some variety of the modest watering-cart . . .

The supply arrangements for the journey had been entrusted by Prince Borghese to the Russian firm, Nobel, with directions to establish depots every 250 kilometres or so along the way from Kiakhta to Moscow.

We could carry on our car supplies of fuel sufficient for 1000 kilometres, so that we were at liberty to vary our route a little, if we so wished. The Nobel firm owns nearly all the Siberian oil wells, and has great depots and distilleries in every Siberian town, private trucks always travelling on the lines, and transport caravans over all the roads. It had at heart the success of an automobile journey through Siberia, which might show the way to other motorists and lead finally to a great development of the petroleum industry. No one was in a better position than the Nobel firm to organize our garage service. And the preparations had to be commenced as early as the month of March.

The Russo-Chinese Bank, which also had a personal interest in promoting commerce between Europe and the Far East, did great service to Prince Borghese by providing him with most valuable information about roads, tribes, and the price of needful articles. It went still further, assuming the responsibility for the transport of oil and petrol across Mongolia, and it sent word to its representatives in Kalgan, Urga, Kiakhta, Verkhne-Udinsk, and Irkutsk, to render us every possible assistance. Indeed, to the Russo-Chinese Bank we were indebted on the first tract of our journey for the most cordial hospitality.

To complete our preparations, purchase had been made of the best geographical maps of the countries we were to cross. German maps of *Ost-China*; Russian military maps on a scale of 1 in 250,000, edited by the St Petersburg Chart Institute; the Russian official map of the routes and communications of the Empire.

By the beginning of April, the prince, Ettore, and the Itala were ready to leave Italy. They were to sail from Naples upon one of the fortnightly Norddeutscher-Lloyd boats chartered for the Far East. On the eve of his departure the prince was making his last arrangements and bidding his last farewells in Rome – having already sent the car and chauffeur off to Naples – when a wire came from Paris which gave him a shock of surprise.

In Paris, the 2000 francs deposit had already considerably diminished the number of prospective candidates. In several cases, their original registration was only due to a desire to appear in print: to be numbered for a while among the candidates for a Peking to Paris race was quite sufficient; to go further would be an unreasonable excess. This dampened the spirits of the faithful remnant. Every discussion at the Paris meetings brought to light new problems and fresh difficulties. Only discuss a plan long enough, and you will end by thinking it absurd; objections are the necessary food for discussions. Enthusiasm grows stronger by action, but weaker through words. Speech is too reasoning a thing; it foresees all obstacles and mishaps: it is pessimistic. If every hero were made to discuss for a moment the brave act he is about to perform, heroism would perish. In great or original undertakings, many points must be left to chance; there must always be some facing of the unknown; the adventure must always be entered upon with a certain amount of unreason. This unreason is called audacity, and audacity is too incompatible with logic and common sense to survive a long scrutiny. This is perhaps the reason why in Paris the original candidates for the race decided to give it up – left the plan at its embryonic stage of development, and renounced their desire to fulfil it. The wire received by Prince Borghese announced their resolve. The Peking to Paris plan was dead.

The prince replied: 'I sail tomorrow from Naples.' His decision made the others reconsider theirs, and a sense of pride prevented them from allowing an Italian prince to be alone in attempting an enterprise arising out of French initiative. Thus on 14 April the rest of the competing motorists sailed from Marseilles with their face towards the east, on a Messagerie Maritime liner bound for Shanghai.

They were capable men of some reputation as drivers, and picked by their respective friends from among hundreds of other chauffeurs and mechanics who had eagerly sought to join in the race. Cormier, one of the drivers of the de Dion-Bouton cars, had travelled over Spain and Hungary with machines of inconsiderable horsepower, and he was a convinced apostle of the small car for rough journeys. 'An 8-hp,' he had said, 'An 8-hp is all I require.' And he was given a 10-hp vehicle. Colignon, the other de Dion-Bouton driver, was also a tried competitor of difficult long-distance races. An interesting and daring type of character was represented by Pons, the driver of the Contal tricycle, who was preparing resolutely for his difficult task. He would be daunted by nothing but total impossibilities. He was a conscientious, good man, and ready to sacrifice himself. If his own life-blood had been needed to serve as fuel, I almost believe he would have given it freely.

This little French group was kept in constantly high spirits by the unfailing and naïve good nature of Bizac, the mechanic attached to the de Dion-Bouton cars, who was formerly in the service of the French navy. His life on ships and among giant engines had left in him an instinctive love for order and discipline, and a sublime indifference to fatigue and climatic variations. He was the living timepiece of his party, whom he would rouse at cockcrow, inexorable as fate and perfectly unaffected by those lively expressions and personal epithets which are apt to escape the lips of one suddenly roused from sweet slumber. With the expedition were also two journalists: Du Taillis from France, Longoni from Italy. I had met Du Taillis at the Algeçiras Conference, where he was correspondent for *Le Figaro*; and often the tedium of that useless and interminable convention had been sensibly alleviated for me by a quarter of an hour's conversation with him. He always had a good story to tell about current events, and he always told it with irresistible humour. He was an inexhaustible mine of information; full of minute details, of political *potins*, of diplomatic episodes, whose tales fell from his lips with an amiable scepticism; even the meetings of the convention in that famous 'Red Hall' became interesting as related by him, and every laughable, odd, or humorous incident occurring at that convention, such as occur at all international gatherings, was brought into brilliant relief by his pen. After a while, I left Algeçiras for Fez, and with

Algeçiras I left the conference and Du Taillis. And lo, one fine morning we meet again in China!

We were in the courtyard of a hotel amid a constant coming and going of Chinese servants, itinerant merchants, and customers arriving for lunch. Du Taillis's smiling countenance, broadened in outline by a short fair beard, was turned upon me with a certain intense scrutiny under his gold-rimmed spectacles. He was somewhat altered at one end of his person by the presence of an enormous tropical hat, and at the other by a pair of superb new leggings. But there was no doubt as to his identity. We started forward, and greeted one another most cordially. Then each explained his presence upon the sacred soil of the Celestial Empire, with amiable side thrusts at the Wai-wu-pu.

Longoni, that pleasant young fellow, had joined the expedition rather out of a love of sport than from journalistic obligation. He was to take his journey on a de Dion-Bouton.

Meanwhile the date for departure was drawing near. The European inhabitants of Tien-Tsin and Peking spoke of nothing else. But among them were still many sceptics. These were divided into two classes: the uncompromising sceptics, who did not even believe that we could start, and the others, who were content with foretelling an immediate return to Peking, after a vain attempt on our part to climb the Nankow range. That range formed, indeed, so difficult an obstacle to our progress that even Prince Borghese did not feel sure of overcoming it. The possibility of going by motor car over the whole of the Kalgan road had to be abandoned. First, because there is no road: for thousands of years the convoys of camels and mules, the carts and the palanquins, have travelled between Peking and Kalgan slowly marking out paths of their own and altering the line of their progress whenever a landslip blocked an opening or a flood made impracticable the tracks over the plain. Our motor cars would have to be towed by mules and men. Mules alone would not do, because you cannot demand from unreasoning animals the alternately cautious, or vigorous and concerted, action required upon a journey such as this; and it would have been highly risky to rely upon the mules' instinct in this matter. The men were to serve as regulators. But even thus towed could the cars pass everywhere? At several points in the road the prince's bamboo rod had found only the barest minimum of space required, and at those points the slightest mistake on the part of the men would do perhaps irretrievable damage.

There is in Peking an old-established carriers' business, a kind of private postal service, to which one habitually has recourse for the dispatch of goods to all parts of the Chinese Empire. It enjoys privileges;

it owns vehicles and horses; it has under its orders coolies and caravan guides. Prince Borghese asked the management of this transport service to assume the responsibility of getting his car to Kalgan. The manager, a Chinese as tall and lanky as a flagstaff, presented himself at the Legation to look at the *chi-cho*. A band of coolies followed him, armed with planks, crowbars, and the rest of the mighty paraphernalia used in China for the transport of the heavy sarcophagi. At a sign from their lean commander, all the men threw themselves upon the motor – to Ettore's great distress – laid the funereal implements upon it, and lifted it to test its weight. But they had not advanced more than two steps, staggering under its heavy mass, before the car took vengeance upon its assailants, knocking several to the ground. The thin man pronounced judgement: the *chi-cho* was heavier than a mountain. To carry it would be impossible. But if the noble and venerable lord Po (this meant Borghese) could lighten it by some thousands of pounds its transport could be effected by twenty-five men and four mules.

The 'noble and venerable lord Po' complied. We made the machine lighter by dismounting the body of the car, and substituting for it a modest seat ingeniously made out of a packing-case. The toolboxes were strapped on to the running board. To the mudguards were fastened the pickaxes and shovels. Strong ropes, both thick and thin, found a place inside the newly improvised seat, and over the latter, to make it better suited for its new and dignified office, was now spread and securely tied a sailor's mattress. Indeed, our machine underwent a complete transformation. And now, striking in its appearance, simple and slim, it conveyed an immediate impression of purpose and energy. It had lost all trace of luxury, or even of comfort – all sign of its origin as a means of enjoyment. It seemed framed for attack, meant to be hurled against some powerful enemy with the full impetus of its own blind might. And thus divested of all superfluous decking, it had become possessed of a new kind of beauty: the beauty of naked form. Even those pickaxes and shovels and ropes added to its look of fearlessness. It was indeed a pioneer. You could tell that it was about to go where none before it had yet dared to lead. Without exactly knowing why, we admired it more now than ever, and kept repeating as we looked at it, 'How beautiful!'

It was settled that coolies and mules should meet us in the neighbourhood of Nankow.

For the French cars and the Spyker the same means of transport had been engaged. And the whole of the operations were to be superintended by a detachment of French soldiers acquainted with the country and by five Italian marines. The commander of the Italian legation presented the Itala with her flag, a small flag made of bunting, and we hoisted it immediately. It was our standard for the fray.

If there were sceptics in China, these were still more abounding in Europe. I was made aware of their existence by the telegrams which reached me making conditional provision 'in the probable event of the race being abandoned'. To these telegrams I would reply by describing briefly the progress of our preparations. But over the wires there would return to me the faithful echoes of unalterable European disbelief. I began to feel disturbed by it. I feared that Europe might really be better informed than I was about the true state of affairs. Several times I ran to the prince, asking:

'Is there any fresh news, prince?'

'None.'

'No delay?'

'No.'

'We really start on the 10th?'

'At eight a.m.'

At last we ceased from calling it the 10th, and began to call it 'tomorrow'. It was the eve of battle. The trains from Tien-Tsin brought crowds of officers, European residents, ladies, tourists, and they even conveyed the military band of the French garrison, which immediately poured floods of harmony into the legation quarter. I spent weary hours in devising a choice of articles that should not make my luggage weigh more than 15 kg, and yet should include all necessaries; and all the hotel 'boys' were employed in assisting my heroic efforts. Meanwhile, the last orders were issued and communicated to legations and hotels: '7.30 a.m., meet in the yard of the French Voyron barracks; 8 a.m., start. Leave Peking via the Dosh-men Fort to the north of the city.'

I obtained and enjoyed important interviews with the high dignitaries of the Imperial Telegraphs, in order to make sure that the telegraph service was organized beyond any fear of mishap; and thus I conversed with good Chinese youths full of a phlegmatic desire to please, and always willing, in the intervals between cups of tea, to come to a perfect understanding upon every point. The telegraph offices of Mongolia, they assured me, would one and all be ready to receive and transmit my messages.

In the evening there were farewell dinners and toasts. A gravely courteous mandarin, the head of the Peking police, by order of the court presented himself before Prince Borghese to inquire what route we intended to follow through the town, as he desired to make suitable arrangements for the clearing and watering of the roads. Shortly after his visit we received the correct passports from the Wai-wu-pu. What miraculous change had taken place in the mind of that august assembly? None can tell.

Late that evening, in the solemn silence of the Peking night – a silence scarcely ruffled now and then by the sound of a tam-tam approaching and receding with the steps of the police watch – in the deep stillness of the eastern town made living and strange to me by the occasional mysterious booming of a distant gong, I, lying sleepless and troubled, felt a strange sensation of unreality and void. I was affected by the atmosphere of Peking, and the approaching competition seemed as unreal as a dream. All present events suddenly acquired for my mind the distorted proportions of things impossible. The very presence of a motor car in that ancient town seemed more absurd than would the sight of a palanquin going over London Bridge. To *feel* Peking around you is like feeling yourself launched backwards through time to some remote, immutable form of life fixed long ages ago. The civilization of the Chinese race achieved once a certain kind of perfection and, fearful of losing that, it refused to move further. One thing alone moves now in China, and that is Time. The very air wafts about you a dim languor which in time envelops and wins you, and no European who has lived long among the Chinese people has ever yet proved wholly impervious to that subtle breath of the Chinese 'soul'. It mingles, perchance, with the dust of so many old things, and is breathed in through the nostrils with a soothing forgetfulness of space and time. I *could* not see the Itala in my own mind racing over the roads of Chinese town and countryside. '8 *a.m.*, start.' But surely these must be empty words! At 8 a.m. the motor surely must stand still, and future generations must find it on the selfsame spot, transformed into a Chinese monument, like those enormous tortoises of stone that now adorn the inner courts of temples, an ornament and a symbol . . .

The day broke grey and cloudy: a menacing day it was. Until the night before the weather had been perfect, but during that night the Chinese deities seemed to have decreed the immediate inauguration of the much feared season of the rains.

'Is it going to rain?' I asked the 'boy' who called me in the morning.

He gazed up at the clouds; then replied unhesitatingly, 'Yes, sir, it will rain before noon.'

'And after?'

'It will rain afterwards, too.'

I reported the prophecy to Prince Borghese.

The Itala lay in readiness before the minister's little villa. Ettore was tying one more knot, pulling one more rope, and walking with long steps around his machine, himself shod with a resplendent pair of topboots. At seven o'clock that morning the marine escort had taken the train for Nankow, and the night before two carts, bearing our luggage and the dismounted body of the car, had left Peking under the command of Pietro, the *ma-fu* of our legation.

Nothing remained to be done but await the hour of starting: a most dismal occupation. The hands of the clock seemed to take hours in marking five minutes' advance. We began to exchange farewell greetings. Our friends stood around us, expressing their good feeling and wishes, and patting our car, as if to encourage it as one would a horse.

Suddenly a Capuchin monk, with an open, pleasing, soldierly countenance, arrives in haste, alive with enthusiasm, to give us his blessing. He is chaplain of the legation and of the Italian garrison.

Seven-thirty! An Italian *carabiniere* comes running in from the street, and announces that the French cars are at the barracks.

'Take your seats!' calls the prince, taking over by this short order the command of our little expedition.

Five of us mount upon the Itala: the Princess Anna-Maria (who has such a passion for travel and such indomitable courage that she accompanied Don Scipione upon his journey through Persia, and that the latter says of her, 'provided she can travel, she will even put up with going in a train'); Don Livio Borghese, Italian chargé d'affaires, a man as attractive and lovable in private life as he is able and accomplished a diplomat; Prince Scipione, myself, and Ettore. Don Livio and the princess are to leave us at the first stop – at Nankow.

I know not by what feat of balance and willpower all four of us find room upon that packing-case promoted to the dignity of a carriage seat. We take a tight hold of the ropes or the mudguards and, like unsteady riders, we measure with our eye the distance which parts us from kind mother earth.

Ettore, after turning the handle to set the engine in motion, has reduced himself to the smallest possible proportions, and is seated on the fuel tank, in the middle of an extra tyre, where he looks like a wrecked mariner suspended on a lifebelt. The engine snorts. The prince, holding the wheel, asks:

'Ready?'

'Yes, we are ready.' The car runs noiselessly along the sandy avenue.

'Good luck!' friends cry to us.

'Goodbye!'

At the gate of the legation the whole guard is drawn up and salutes us. The sentinel presents arms.

We are on the road. What unusual animation in this diplomatic quarter, where the rising hour usually comes so late! All the rickshaws in Peking are out, and arrive at high speed from all sides, anxious to please their exalted customers and patrons. Before the Voyron barracks is a crowd of Chinese among soldiery of every nationality. Trophies of flags adorn the walls, and festoons of evergreens surround the trophies. A motto is hung across the street: *'Bon voyage!'* It is the parting wish expressed on all sides. A naïve well-wisher cries out, *'Au revoir!'* and everyone laughs.

The barrack yard is packed. You might be in the *pesage* on a *Grand Prix* day. All the white population has chosen this for their meeting place. The few sons of Europe and America who dwell in the extreme Chi-li are gathered together on this spot. The very soul of civilized mankind seems to breathe among these walls. Whatever his nationality, everyone feels a sense of pride in the event which has called him here; there is felt to be among those present a solidarity of culture, of education, of instincts. A triumph of the west is being solemnized in the heart of Peking.

Among bank clerks and businessmen and European company agents there stand about in this yard, friendly and unaffected, ladies, members of the legations, officers, plenipotentiaries. The ministers of France, of Holland, of Austria and of Russia exchange greetings in many tongues. A dignified old gentleman of short stature, with a striking Chinese-looking little white beard and a penetrating, lively, energetic eye, passes, everywhere followed by friendly regard, among the people, who whisper, 'Sir Robert here too?' It is Sir Robert Hart, the famous political economist.

A little later a palanquin stops before the door of the barracks, and a young Chinese dignitary, the Mandarin Kwo, a secretary of the Wai-wu-pu, alights gracefully. He was nominated by the Paris committee of the race to be a member of a contemplated Chinese committee, and now he suddenly remembers the fact. He has come to represent the Imperial Chinese Government, and he does represent it, busily fanning himself and repeating 'Goodbye, goodbye' to us who are starting, and to every-one else as well.

The Itala has been left waiting outside. In the yard, pressed by the besieging mass of the curious, stand the two de Dion-Boutons, the Contal, and the Spyker, in complete readiness for the journey. The French machines are grey. The Dutch one, striped with white, red, and black, is also covered with great placards announcing the route it is to follow, the distances it will cover, and many other things. A large old Chinese cannon (taken by the French at the time of the siege of the Legations, and now adorning the enemy's barrack yard) stands close by in strange contrast to the motor cars. But for the present great event the old gun has decked itself out with flags and garlands and seems to take part in the rejoicings. It has followed the example of the Wai-wu-pu, and has grown reconciled.

The band plays military marches, whiling away the time during which the starters are fulfilling the agreeable formality of receiving back from a representative of the Russo-Chinese Bank the 2000 francs deposited in Paris.

Du Taillis wanders alone among the crowd, bearing upon his face the traces of a vague emotion.

The great moment has arrived.

Drivers join their cars. The engines fire, and the exhausts give out thick clouds of smoke. The voices of the crowd are pitched a tone higher. Several officers, who have ridden to see us, mount their horses. A hundred cameras are raised for a moment above our heads and waver, trying to find the focus; we run to hoist ourselves again on to the Itala, which is heaving and throbbing, anxious to start her flight.

The other motors issue from the yard.

There is no special order of departure. Chance places us in the following order of advance: de Dion-Bouton, driver Cormier; Spyker, driver Godard; Itala; de Dion-Bouton, driver Colignon; Contal, driver Pons. All cars stand firm waiting for the signal. The military band comes out of the barracks and heads the procession. The crowd surrounds us, bursting into shouts of enthusiasm. An elegant lady, Madame Boissonnes, the wife of the first secretary of the French legation, graciously consents to be our starter.

She raises the flag.

A moment of deep silence in the crowd. The cars alone are heard. The smoke envelops and isolates us.

The flag descends.

A great bursting of petards and squibs; and amid these war sounds we move. We are off!

The band, marching before us, rouses the echoes to a martial song. We advance at a foot pace. Cavalry officers ride on either side of us. The crowd follows us shouting, waving hats and handkerchiefs. Friendly voices call out our names.

We take the road which passes before the Austrian legation – a narrow street running between high walls as of some convent building. Isolated salutes come to us from the men stationed there; the sentries, unable to salute, smile amicably. We turn the corner of the Italian legation, and issue out of the diplomatic quarter on to the broad avenue which separates the latter from the native town.

As soon as our car comes into view, a sudden formidable shout is heard. The ramparts of the Italian legation are covered with our marines and, standing as if they were at sea upon one of their own great cruisers, the men send out to us their threefold salute: 'Hurrah! Hurrah! Hurrah!'

And within us rises a strange impulse, a sense as though we too could respond, and with a louder cry than theirs could fill this immense city with the volume of our heart-wrung voices. But we do nothing more than uncover our heads in silence. And our eyes run with a kind of tender awe along that line of strong, brave men, who one day may be called upon to defend the very walls where they now stand acclaiming us.

And now the band ceases from playing, and draws to one side. The farewell voices fade in the distance. Nothing more holds us back.

'Forward?' – 'Forward!' cry the drivers one to another, and the motors gradually increase their speed. The buzzing of the engines rises to a shriller note. Behind us the officers urge their horses to a gallop, but the distance grows between us and they are left out of sight.

And over the road lined by the Chinese soldiery, between two hedges of silent people, our five motor cars alone remain, pursuing each other through the capital of the Chinese empire at a speed which it has never known before, and which it may perchance never behold again.

III

ON THE WAY TO THE GREAT WALL

~~~~~~~~~~~~

The Wisdom of the Ignorant – Over the Bridges of
Cambaluc – Our Coolies – Nankow – The Sacred
Valley – Our First Glimpse of the Great Wall

By an order of the police all traffic was suspended upon our route for a matter of about five miles. The primitive two-wheeled little carriages which are used as public conveyances in Peking stood waiting in crowds at the crossing of narrow streets and broad highways. The crowd, disciplined and obedient, also waited in rows by the endless chain of low buildings and shanties which line the broader arteries of Peking, pressing against the black, smoky taverns which smell sharply of garlic, or arrayed along shops with sculptured wooden fronts, coloured or gilt, hung with shop signs bearing dragons and red silk fringes or lacquered plates covered with gold-lettered inscriptions, exhibiting that characteristic medley of forms and colours which adorns Chinese streets as if for a daily festival, and which moves, waves, vibrates, and seems to sway with the sound of life.

It was the usual population of the market-place, careless and picturesque, the everyday crowd, not one gathered together for this particular event. The spectacle of an automobile race left the good inhabitants of Peking in utter indifference. They looked at us without curiosity or aversion. Many deigned scarcely to throw a glance our way. You would have thought they had seen nothing else in all their days than racing motor cars. We felt almost humbled. We had expected evidences of the greatest amazement – and behold, we only met with a sublime indifference. The fact is, that nothing which a European can do has now the power to surprise a Son of Heaven. The miracles of our civilization cannot even attract the attention of a Chinese boy. It has long been admitted out there in China that we are possessed of magic powers, endowed with a mysterious force by which we can give life to things of steel, and make them capable of doing any kind of work; the thing is natural for us, and calls no longer for any wonder.

There are in this world two classes of people incapable of feeling real surprise. There is the man of great learning, who is prepared for all; and there are the profoundly ignorant, for whom everything is a mystery. These are accustomed to inexplicable things; everything transcends the limit of their knowledge, and nothing *does* surprise them, because everything *should*. The ordinary Chinese is among these: his philosophy is that of the unknowable; he has achieved the blissful serenity of the uninquiring, and therewith has found the true secret of happiness.

Advancing rapidly through a labyrinth of narrow streets, we reached the north side of the imperial enclosure. Chinese policemen wearing coats covered with white lettered inscriptions and straw hats elegantly poised upon a little chignon into the semblance of which they had twisted their long pigtails, showed us our way by pointing with long sticks. For a moment we saw from afar, above the yellow wall of the imperial city, the graceful pagodas of the Meishan (or 'Coal Mountain'), erected by the whim of an emperor in a part of his garden whence he could overlook the whole town. A little later we were at the foot of massive ancient walls, among the bastions of the Dosh-men Fort, a huge, grim fort crowned by one of the high castles which protect the gates of Peking. This construction, half fortress and half temple, menaces the plain with three rows of shutter-trimmed gun windows, like the portholes of some ancient frigate. Near to the gate the road is like the streets of Pompeii, so worn by time and so deeply rutted by the passing of a thousand wheels, that we are obliged to slacken our speed on reaching it. All around, the dull, noisy, heedless life of the suburbs flows on.

Now we are on the open road, among fertile orchards whose bounty is proffered to the wayfarer by a thousand laden boughs crossing his path. The first two cars, one of the de Dion-Boutons and the Spyker, stop. We do the same. They invite Prince Borghese to lead the way, and the Itala resumes her journey. Soon old Peking is out of sight, behind a thick plantation and a rise in the road. For the first time it occurs to us to look at our watch. We are late in starting – it is now 9.25.

The road went northwards, winding over sandy irregular ground, crossing a stream now and then; here broad like the bed of a river, there overrun by the life of the field; shaded at intervals by thick clumps of trees, whose cool silence gathered under its shelter tombs and sacred inscriptions standing amid the tall grass. We could not travel at a high speed. The car bounded and swayed, the roughness of the road and the undulations of the ground made it lurch and skid. Over the sand it had the elastic bounding of a feline animal. And Don Livio would say: 'I like the springing of this panther.' But the panther from time to time seemed to be trying to shake us off, and we had to hold on with all our might. We could see the transmission shaft, unprotected under our feet; we felt in immediate contact with the machine; and under our feet the road flew by confusedly, like the giddy play of some endless ribbon. The flywheel, with a revolution so swift that it made a musical hum, blew up from the road a thick dust which surrounded and enveloped us, coming up in thick clouds through the unenclosed machinery.

We could not go very fast, and the engine was getting heated. An engine is like a strong, well-bred horse, which pants, chafes, and foams when held in by the bit, and seems to find it restful when you give him the rein for a full gallop. The friction against the sand seemed to tire it too. Steam came puffing out of the radiator like the breath of a living being. Then we had to stop and pour cold water over it. We would ask the peasants for some, and they would fetch it from one of those many wells which nestle close to the poor mud huts of the Chinese countryside, in the shadow of tall trees as if in search of peace, and wearing such an enviable aspect of contented restfulness, amid the signs of village labour and the activity of the fields. Suspending their pails from a bar across their shoulders, as if they were platters or a pair of scales, the peasants would come and serve us. And they paid no more attention to our motor car than they would have paid to a mule.

We crossed quaint villages, noisy and sordid, and crowded with a half-naked population; the summer costume of the indigent Chinese being often limited to a pair of short breeches and a fan. Then we would ask the name of the village, just to make sure that we were not going off our track.

'Is this Örr-li-tien?'

And the villagers would nod approvingly, and show a naïve appreciation of our cleverness by beating their closed fans on the palm of their hands. A little further, we would ask:

'How far is it to Tsing-ho-pu?'

But this sort of question cannot fail in China to elicit a number of differing answers. 'Five *li*,' would cry an old man, spreading out his hands.

But a neighbour, with the same gesture, would open out three fingers, and another would say unhesitatingly:

'Eight *li!*'

'Is it three, five, or eight?' we would ask with a certain irritation, stopping our machine. Our informers would then draw prudently one step back, and with an ingratiating smile, would wish us a happy journey.

At the Tsing-ho we have to face the first obstacle. The ancient bridge which crosses it is almost inaccessible to a motor car; so we look for a ford, and scour the bank in all directions, hoping to find traces of some frequented path. But no, there is only one way, that of the bridge.

It is a most imposing bridge, one of the wonderful constructions attributed by European tradition to Marco Polo, but perhaps not more ancient than the time of the Ming dynasty. It is a magnificent piece of work, all built in marble. Its balustrades, sculptured with an elegance which has something European, and which might almost justify our tradition concerning the origin of the bridge itself, gracefully join the two banks with a line of singular richness, a superb white arch. It is the last remnant of past glories amid the primitive rudeness of a land which has forgotten all its former love for greatness and for beauty. Enormous slabs of marble once paved the bridge; but the traffic of centuries and the stress of time have broken and disjointed them. You would almost think that a slow heaving of the earth has tried to raise those slabs during the course of centuries, as if they were the lids of so many half-opened tombs. The bridge cannot have been touched by a builder's hand since the time when Peking was called Khan-bahlig (the city of the Khan) and Marco Polo reported her name as Cambaluc. How we should have admired this beautiful and historic relic, if only we had not been confronted by the task of conveying across it a 40-hp car, weighing 1200 kilogrammes!

The slopes leading up to each end of the bridge have disappeared. They have been carried off in fragments by the floods, worn away slowly by the heavy rains, eaten up inch by inch by the passing of millions of human feet – the passing of that torrent of humanity which for six hundred years has surged over those marbles. And now the only approaches to the bridge are rugged paths, at the summit of which crumbling stones form high ledges. Perhaps the level of the land around it has sunk with the glory of the Chinese empire, and even now the bridge shows the proud height to which the Chinese soil could rise when it sustained the steps of Kublai Khan.

Should we go for our coolies, and get them to drag our car over the tomb-like slabs of the old bridge? Prince Borghese does not wish to surrender himself so readily; he examines the area, and he finds places where the wheels can pass. The ingenious mudguards of the car are unhitched and placed over the stones to serve as rails. Ettore, awaiting the prince's orders, seizes the wheel, backs fifty yards or so, and waits. The rain begins to fall, and the wet stones shine under it.

'Go!' orders the prince, and he adds, 'The right wheel here. Look sharp!'

The Itala leaps forward, ascends with difficulty the steep incline, and reaches the improvised rails with its front wheels. But the rain has made both rails and stones very slippery. The machine skids. The heavy iron planks are thrown violently aside by the pressure of the tyres, and return like the napkin ring in the familiar trick.

The machine falls back motionless. Another try. The Itala backs. We hasten to put down the iron planks again, but Ettore says:

'Let's try it without a track!'

And he works up speed; he reaches the stones with a bound. After a moment's hesitation the front wheels touch the low end of the bridge. But the car has stopped. The back wheels revolve madly on the shapeless incline without succeeding in getting any hold of it. They revolve at a frightful speed, shooting off sparkling bits of stone with the nails of the tyre-covers. Ettore races the engine, and it roars like some strong thing in travail, emitting quick panting clouds of dense, white, acrid gas. We leap into the heart of that cloud to push the car with all our might; the scalding breath of the exhaust pipe assails us. We fail, and draw aside discouraged.

The car, which surely has a pride of its own, seems bent on conquering unaided. Suddenly the wheels begin to 'bite'. They stop an instant, as though to gather strength for the effort, and slowly, slowly they ascend. They mount over the first step, which is the highest, then the others. At last the car is all on the first marble slabs, and here it stops and rests for a few minutes. Then it commences, at a snail's pace, the difficult journey among the ill-connected flagstones. The car halts from time to time to plan an advance of one hand's breadth, to see how it can best avoid having more than one wheel at a time sunk in the ruts or caught between the stones. The car oscillates. It slowly, awkwardly goes down, goes up, sometimes draws back a step or two in order to change its path: it looks like an enormous tortoise, whose low shell almost grazes the ground, and whose four paws are spread out, strong and wary.

The descent on the other side of the bridge is easy, but full of interest. This is the first time that I see a motor car engaged in such work. This powerful machine, built for mad coursing at unheard-of speed, descends the uncouth stairway now with the caution of a child. The monster's whole strength is taxed by its effort to hold back. It seems to *see* the dangers, and to calculate the heights. It puts out its wheels like feelers, with infinite precaution, lays them down gently on the first step below without a shock or a start, and then comes down upon them like an intelligent giant, putting his strength to the service of his mind. It takes whole moments to advance one yard, until it sees the open road before it. *Then*, with one great bound like a leap of joy, it lets itself go freely, and seems unable ever to stop again, till we have to run after it crying:

'Enough! Halt! Hey, halt!'

We resumed our way over the open road, under a fine, continuous downpour which did for us what a well-intentioned bungler will often do for his friend: softened the road, but to excess, and so made mud and bogland all dotted over with pools of water.

We had to cross little rustic bridges, like those with which the wealthy Chinese ornament their gardens. We ran through narrow lanes between high, grassy banks crowned with willows, which gathered the raindrops and made them patter more heavily over our heads. And so through more varied landscape, which heralded the approach of the hills, and brought us the sense of being on the outskirts of that great plain of Peking which stretches like a sea of verdure, with islets of tree-clumps and nestling villages. Through the mist we could already catch a glimpse of a few dim, scattered heights, crowned by the characteristic outlines of Chinese pagodas.

Suddenly there gleamed white before us the marble balustrade of another ancient bridge, larger than the first, thrown over the Shi-keao-ho. We jumped down from our seats, muttering vague words of anger against the splendour of old Cambaluc. And our manoeuvre for the assault and conquest of the bridge recommenced. Fortunately the car had acquired a certain practice in dealing with tumbledown ruins, and in twenty minutes it had finished its archaeological excursion to the left bank of the river.

Here we found ourselves surrounded by a crowd of Chinese wearing little caps of a peculiar shape, and who came to greet us in a most friendly way. We begged for some fresh water – and the water came, in pails, in pans, in kettles. A fine old man of the Tartar type came forward and invited us to take tea in his house. He was quite grieved by our refusal, and confided to us that he was our friend. All those people were our friends too – how come? We discovered the reason for this good feeling when they pointed out their mosque to us, as they soon did, and with a certain pride. These were Mahometan Chinese; and the old man was their head, and the priest of their tribe. The Mahometan Chinese feel, by reason of their religion, more akin to ourselves than to their own compatriots. They know that our faith is founded upon the Old Testament, which they also claim among their sacred literature, having received it through Turkestan, somewhat altered on the way, somewhat coloured on its arrival, but still in substance the same.

We bid farewell to the venerable elder, speaking Arabic, his own sacred tongue. Then we got quickly again into our motor car, and sped out of his sight, leaving him and his people full of the same amazement they would have felt at a visitation from some character out of the book of our common heritage.

It was not long now before we perceived upon the horizon, dim and distant, the strange outline of the Kalgan range. Around us spread undulating lines of bare hills, which rose and sank before us, and seemed to close or scatter as we passed on among them. On our right rose that magnificent and imposing mountain amphitheatre, where sleep the ancient imperial dynasty of the Mings. The whole world holds not for any king a grander resting place than this. And its grandeur is not due to the temples, the arches, the giant images placed in it by man; the very nature of the place, solitary and sterile, has the indescribable majesty of a tomb. A tomb of demigods, it seems, with the eternal hills to encompass it. Some superhuman Will seems to have thus disposed them, to gather shade and silence over the sacred sleep of that great dynasty.

We *felt* the nearness of the sacred place. As in the approaches of a temple, there were numerous commemorative tablets, covered with ancient characters, fixed upon enormous marble tortoises or dragons, or upon pedestals with lotus flowers like those of the statues of Buddha.

The road became increasingly rough, stony, and mountainous. Presently we met our coolies. They had invaded a small village, and, on seeing us, they ran in disorder along the road.

They were commanded by an old headman, who, as a token of his dignity, carried a standard with a motto, *Obey your father's voice*, meaning to convey, no doubt, that obedience was due to himself. Further, the 'father's voice' was reinforced by a little whistle which he carried on a string round his neck. We called out to them to meet us at a further point on the road, and went past them ourselves. We wanted to use the car as far as possible.

We could now clearly see the Nankow gorge, like a narrow slit between two rocky mountains, and upon the summits of these rose high the towers of ancient forts. Other mountains spread ruggedly around this spot, showing fantastic outlines against the sky, and in the pale gloom of that rainy day, the landscape was stern; under the radiance of the sun it might perhaps have simply appeared wild. But the heights looked inaccessible, and the slopes of the mountains seemed like walls of bastions, armed for resistance.

Nankow means 'Gate of the South'. There are stretches of this earth of ours that might have been created purposely as fighting-grounds of our poor human race: fields for battle, places where Nature itself incites to attack and urges to defence: dread regions which surround man with a sense of lurking enmity, and seem to hide passes for ambuscades, and traps that lure one to destruction. Nankow has this character. The times of invasion are long passed, the fortifications which crown the valley are falling into slow decay, around that valley live probably the most peaceful tribes on this earth, and yet by its nature alone that cavernous deep conjures up thoughts of death and destruction, as though the walls which gird it were but the huge remains of some titanic structure.

At six miles from the town, at the entrance to the valley, we are obliged to stop. From now onwards the public road and the bed of the torrent which descends from the Nankow pass are one and the same thing. There are nothing but broken pieces of stone, boulders, sand, and pools. We have had to stop and wait for our men. They arrive, running, excited, to take possession of this *chi-cho*. There has lurked in their hearts a secret fear, perhaps, that it might escape them, and carry on its wing their hopes of gain. So now they arrive, shouting, like a band of highwaymen.

What a strange medley of costumes and get-up! Thick woollen bags in the shape of ponchos (which the Chinese caravan guides use as protection from the rain), blue, white, grey shirts, all equally old and torn, rags worn as turbans, lampshade-looking straw hats, tatters of all shapes and of all kinds; greasy clothes which must have swathed successive generations; a mixture such as olden days must have witnessed in the *Cour des Miracles* of old Paris. There were old men, young men, and boys; Chinese and Tartars; types of beggars and types of Mandarins – a mixture of poverty, old and new, of men in want out of every class, gathered heaven knows how, from amid the human crowds that swarm in lowest Peking – come to drag a motor car, and earn four days' wage to live on for a month, unconcerned, content, and talkative.

The old headman waved his flag and blew his whistle with swelling cheeks. That first whistle meant: Ready! Ettore fastened the thick ropes securely round the forepart of the frame, to the two brackets which serve in every motor car to support the springs, and a moment later, two lines of men bent low upon the ropes slowly towing on the great machine, while others helped by pushing it.

The rain was still falling steadily. Sometimes the car, as if it could *see* the great stones in its path, would stop quite suddenly with a rebellious jerk. That pulled the coolies brusquely back for a moment, and left them with their knees raised, uncertain of their balance, but they resumed their interrupted efforts together with what seamen call a 'chanty'. The old man would begin some old singsong, with a voice like the buzzing of a prayer-machine; and at the place for the chorus all the others would cry out together: '*Laè, laè, la!*' (Forward, forward, go!) and give a concerted, simultaneous tug. The headman's song was improvised. He just said whatever passed through his mind, for it is the sound and the tune which count, and not the words. But amusing things would come out sometimes, which kept the men in good spirits, and in the '*laè, laè, la!*' you could then trace a blending of real merriment with their fatigue. When the car had been pulled over some obstacle, the impetus of its own weight carried it sometimes suddenly for some way; it looked as if it would rebel, and would pursue those strange people for a little on its own account. Then the ropes grew slack, and the Chinese, all pleased, ran joyously, leaping and laughing, enjoying themselves like children at play, and covering thus tumultuously some distance on the road, until they were pulled back, and the ropes stood taut and motionless again. That band of men was interesting to watch. They were not porters, and represented no distinct class of men; they were simply the poor, and represented the people. The Chinese people stood before us here with its miseries and its virtues at work. Want, lightheartedness, indifference, simplicity, patience, activity, all the good and the bad qualities of a race, hidden under a comprehensive cloak, both sordid and sinister, were stooping there harnessed to our machine. The old man solemnly led the caravan, bearing his standard.

The precipitous mountain range of Nankow overhung the road and us, as we stood at the entrance to the gorge. The village nestles at the foot of the Nanshan Mountain, the 'Mountain of the South', which looks sheer down over the houses and, seen from below, seems to bend over the traveller. Great, ancient, crenellated walls, offshoots of the 'Great Wall', climb stragglingly up to the crests, themselves intact because almost inaccessible. Their destruction is left for time alone to accomplish; and time is infinitely kinder than man to the relics of greatness.

The village of Nankow looks like a casually heaped pile of stones. Its low, primitive dwelling places are built of stubble and mud; in front of these are laid high pavements made out of great boulders, and the middle of the road is left for the floods. This little rough town is defended by the remnant of an old fort.

We enter the single road of the village by a low, deep, dark gate. The rain has ceased, and for a few minutes the sun peeps out of a bank of clouds, and in its light the wet stones shimmer. The people stand in their doorways to see.

They look like people of another breed. These are the Chinese mountain race, strong and powerfully built and bearing marked traces of their Tartar ancestry. This small population, isolated from the rest of mankind, amid inhospitable, rocky heights, recalls to the mind of the onlooker some ancient garrison sent here in former times to guard the pass, and here forgotten. Indeed, these men may really be the descendants of the Tartar soldiery put here after the Manchurian conquest; men unarmed now, but still at their post, unconsciously keeping guard over a trust of many centuries.

The first day's march is over. It is a quarter to three by the time we enter the little Chinese village which Pietro, the *ma-fu*, has chosen for our halting place. We have covered less than forty miles. Our marines surround us festively, and announce that the luggage has arrived without mishap, that a good fire is ready for us in the best room of the place, and that chickens are roasting for our dinner, all of which news we receive with gratitude.

The Itala finds a berth among carts, mules, horses, and caravan drivers in the outer yard of the inn, amid the characteristic and bewildering confusion which reigns in such places in China.

Several times during the afternoon we wander out from the village in the direction whence we came, hoping to meet the other motor cars. We even climb the crenellated walls, from whose summit a vast tract of the plain is visible, but as far as the eye can reach there is unbroken solitude. At four p.m. we espy a group of people approaching the village from the direction of the Nankow railway station, which lies two miles away. They are dragging something. It is the Contal tricycle. Pons and his chauffeur, panting and streaming, assist in the work.

Pons's countenance is shadowed by preoccupation and regret. He has been obliged to retrace his steps into Peking, for as soon as he came upon the broken ground outside the town, his tricycle, excellent no doubt upon passably good roads, proved perfectly useless. That tricycle has two wheels for steering and only one for propulsion; the full weight of the vehicle is taken on the former, and therefore there is no weight on the drive wheel; any slight unevenness of the road presents an enormous resistance and the drive wheel merely revolves uselessly on the same spot. Pons has been obliged to go back, and to come with his machine by rail. He is resolved to reach Mongolia at any price, hoping to find an easier road across that province.

Shortly after sunset, Nankow is already asleep. Wrapped in a sailor's rug, lying on my *kang* and wide awake, I continued my journey in imagination the whole sleepless night through, exploring the country in my fancy. The torrent roared in the distance, marking the road which we were to follow on the morrow. Later, its voice was drowned by the rain which fell in a violent downpour, and a few great drops driven across by the wind came against my paper shutters, with a sound like the drumming of angry fingers.

It was still raining when Pietro, holding a little paper lantern, came to call us. It was raining at dawn; it was raining when we finally decided to start, after waiting in vain for a change in the weather. The coolies had been ready ever since three a.m. At 7.25 we left Nankow, leaving the princess at the inn, as she was to return to Peking by rail. Don Livio came with us as far as the Great Wall.

Our means of traction for the car were a Chinese crew and three willing beasts. The Peking Transport Company, after promising to provide us with four mules at Nankow, had sent us only *one* mule, an old horse, and a small white donkey. Prince Borghese remonstrated, but a representative of the firm replied to his protests by calling upon all the gods to witness to his solemn oath that these three animals, unassisted, could drag the *chi-cho* to the end of the world; so we, who only desired them to drag it to Kalgan, had to remain content.

At the moment of our departure, the good people of Nankow gave us the honour of a salute – with squibs. It is a custom with the Chinese to celebrate with great and noisy fireworks, and when he wishes to do especial honour to his guest, he places a couple of squibs at his own doorpost, and at a given moment, *pum! pa!* he fires them. This is for him the height of obsequiousness.

A few minutes later Nankow was out of sight behind a bend in the road. The path begins to ascend immediately, with long, low steps at intervals, and when we came to each of these steps the coolies would sing their chorus refrain, and urge the beasts to a special effort by flicking the whip in the air. The old man with his banner headed our advancing column. Our marines walked on either side of the car, giving it from time to time a good thrust with their shoulders, as if they were bringing a gun into position at the top of a mountain. Ettore, alone upon his machine, swallowed up in the folds of a limitless mackintosh cloak, somewhat similar to that of a Breton fisherman, held the wheel with the concentrated attention of the helmsman at his post, and gave his orders by hooting the horn of the car. One hoot, forward; two hoots, halt. But the coolies often needed the double hoot, and the strain which was put upon the horn now was the beginning of a progressive hoarseness of our Itala, which was destined to reduce her to absolute silence. Pietro, in solitary state on horseback, brought up the rear, under the shelter of a huge straw hat, which, by a fantastic arrangement of ribbons, had acquired the coquettish look of a lady's hat, *Directoire* style, and the worthy *ma-fu* wore this elegant headgear with a singular dignity. Surely no odder cortège than this can have ever filed through the narrow passes of the Chinese Great Wall. And when I add that Don Livio, Don Scipione and I rested from time to time by riding a pair of diminutive donkeys, so tiny that our feet touched the ground on either side, and that our raincloaks hid them with the grand lines of classical drapery, I shall have completed the description of this historical event with considerable accuracy.

The scenery around us changed at every moment. Above us there was a continual unfolding of mountain crests, rugged, bare, of increasing strangeness. Dark clouds swept over them, and a pale mist made them seem larger and more distant than they were in reality, adding to their sinister impressiveness. Below us was a torrent, also constantly changing, looking now calm and innocent like the merest streamlet, winding in and out by the side of the path, among green bushes and small clumps of willows; and later, violent and eddying, deep down in narrow chasms, at which we barely dared throw cautious glances from the edge of the road. Lines of old battlements descend from time to time, from the peaks of the mountains to the bottom of the valleys below, then reascend, and lose themselves in the distance towards some other height. They are crenellated battlements, protecting the 'beat' of outlying patrols; they are secondary defensive fortifications of the Great Wall – gigantic barricades.

Between two of these great fortifications lies a large village, Ku-yung-kuan. We entered its high, sombre walls, and found ourselves facing a wonderful arch of marble, which from a distance might have been thought to be of Latin origin, with a delicate reliefwork of friezes and figures; and it rose with giant majesty above the poverty-stricken dwellings of this village, the last relic of who knows what greatness and what splendour. Ku-yung-kuan was a seat of government in the golden age of the Chinese empire, when the great military mandarins, like the Roman consuls, whiled away their time of idleness by surrounding themselves with permanent tokens of magnificence.

While we accomplished the next ascent we were caught up and

outstripped by a sedan chair borne by quick eager bearers. In the chair, under an open sunshade, reposed a European, whom the natives saluted with deference. As he passed by he bid us good morning in English. He was a celebrity, and called by the Chinese 'The old gentleman who pierces mountains'. Pietro inquired why, and afterwards explained the matter to us, but before telling more of his tale, which bears upon Chinese civilization, it must be remarked that Chinese men of trade are by now convinced that, although the railway may disturb their sleeping ancestry, yet on the whole it is an excellent thing. Thus, many Chinese merchants and bankers in Peking decided some time ago to build a railway much needed by trade, and resolved to do so without allowing foreigners to take any part whatever in their enterprise. Capital, labour, company directors, all must be Chinese. Thus was formed the Chinese company of the Peking to Kalgan railway, which is already working as far as Nankow. The engineers too, of course, were Sons of Heaven, if with an American degree.

All went well so long as the line was laid on the plain. But when the mountains were reached, the engineering Sons of Heaven found themselves in serious straits. Their tunnels fell in. After each fall there were attempts at reconstruction, following all the rules of tunnel building, but the tunnels fell in again: a truly admirable Chinese constancy contending in vain against the obstinacy of China's mountains. There were many who saw in all this the avenging hand of their Dragon, whose great body itself, perhaps, was wounded by these perforations. Indeed, the obvious proof of his anger was that the mountains entombed and killed men: the punishment was undeniable. But the Dragon nowadays is losing credit in all except official spheres; and the merchants bethought them of western engineers, whose demon tricks might possibly overcome the invincible resistance of the Nankow range; especially as the works of the Simplon tunnel (as they heard), were coming to a successful conclusion just then. So the company resigned themselves to the necessary profanation, and begged the Peking-Hankow Company to let them have the gracious loan of a good engineer, to whom they might entrust the direction of their works. As an outcome of this transaction the 'Old gentleman who pierces mountains' put in an appearance upon his 'portable throne' among the mountain gorges of the Chinese Great Wall.

The ascent was difficult, and at frequent intervals we granted our men a well-earned rest. At the signal for breaking the lines, they let go their ropes and scattered themselves cheerily around, ready to reappear at the first call of their headman's whistle. The donkey, the mule, and the horse, in perfect amity, went quietly to graze together, dragging after them their long traces caked with mud. And the car was left alone on the road, with stone wedges behind each wheel, a wet sad object, humbled and with drooping banner. Our marines were gay, as sailors always are on an excursion, even under the rain.

They were five in number, picked for their strength and for some special talent: five talented athletes. One was a photographer and mechanic; he helped Ettore to watch over the advance of the machine at the difficult places on the way, and on a halt, he would turn up armed with a tripod, a large black cloth, and an enormous camera, found heaven knows where, and from that time until we resumed our march, we were under the observation of his lens, which followed us with severe scrutiny, like the uncanny single eye of a Cyclops. Another one was sicknurse and cook, and proved himself valuable to the sick and still more valuable to the sound; always ready to bandage a scratch scientifically, and to serve up a hot omelette with scientifically apportioned ingredients. The third was an electrician. The fourth a joiner. The last of all spoke Chinese with a beautiful Sicilian drawl, had been to Kalgan with the International Forces of 1900, and knew the way like a pilot. All were possessed of the enviable gift of a cheery temper; everything seemed done on purpose to make them happy. The very rain – that penetrating and insistent rain, against which not even our mackintoshes were a sufficient protection, and which filtering through them brought upon us a chilly sense of sadness – seemed to add to the cheeriness of our marines. Water is their own element; and with their linen uniforms soaked through and sticking to their shoulders they cheerfully went on among the puddles, defying the storm. Dear travelling companions, proud escort to our little flag; ready to laugh, and ready, if need be, to die.

A hoarse hoot of the horn, a whistle, the running together of our men, a song, a crack of the whip, and the march started again. Up, up we went, following the valley of Ku-yu-kwan, endless and increasingly rough.

Suddenly the valley grew narrow, and seemed to close before us. It looked as if there was no opening, as if the mountains had suddenly ranged themselves like sentinels barring the way. Presently we noticed a narrow gorge opening to the right, a kind of crack about forty yards broad, between overhanging rocks, a regular corridor between natural walls. The way so far had led through a gloomy country; that surrounding us now inspired aversion and horror.

Man must have begun long ages ago to feel the terror of that place, for he made it sacred soil; sacred, perhaps, because people never passed that way without a prayer upon their lips. That pass invites a prayer for heavenly assistance.

A mountain is in itself a mysterious thing to the natural mind of man. It is a reaching out of the earth towards heaven, and mountain summits seem in contact with the Godhead. At that special point a gateway opens, and all the races who have ever crossed its threshold must have seen it as the token of an almighty Will, as a divine work created for an unfathomable and hence terrifying purpose. Those immense jambs of basalt must have conveyed to man's imagination a warning against further advance. Beyond them must be something which claimed one's worship, and what we found there was deep, solemn shade. Our people crossed it reverently, as they would a temple, and so the narrow valley became, as it were, a temple indeed, surrounded by the desolate majesty of solitude.

That valley was, and is, the refuge of hermits. Every niche in the rock is a sanctuary, and there are sacred sayings engraved there in ancient Chinese characters, and others, more ancient still, in Tibetan, in Mongolian, in Manchurian: all of them the language of long-past generations. In a part of the rock, straight and sheer like a wall, there is fitted in, high up, a strange little construction, a little sanctuary, suspended in mid-air – the sacred home of a deity, placed in an eagle's nest. It is reached by a long flight of steps, hewn out of the stone and hidden here and there by bushes. Further from the entrance of the gorge is another of these hanging temples, another ancient shelter of man's faith, now falling to ruins. All round upon the mountains, at almost inaccessible heights, there are traces of similar constructions, all but destroyed by the storms which sweep down from the north and vent their fury in this narrow gorge which fetters and constrains them. Out of the boulders which have fallen from the tops of the mountains, and which lie on the bed of the valley, the pious hands of primitive artists have carved the image of Buddha, moulding the stone into the likeness of the human form, and impressing upon it the sweet and severe countenance of a divinity. A few huge images of the Buddha are carved with wondrous strokes upon the mountain itself. There are remains of great temples, now perished, a few broken columns and pilasters; no traces of the work of man in that place but they bear evidence of having been an affirmation of faith. Every soul facing that great reality has cried out: 'I believe!'

The religious significance of that road can also be traced in history: the religion of the lamas came into China through it. From the heart of Asia, where religions take their rise, waves of devotion have swept down that valley to win the Chinese soul to newer cults. Often strange pilgrims are met journeying there. When Prince Borghese was inspecting the road to Kalgan, a few days before our passing, he came across a penitent pilgrim, with shaven head and wearing a long, grey tunic, who went upon his way in continuous prayer, kneeling down by a vow at every three steps to kiss the earth. The prince made inquiries. That pilgrim was on his way to Urga, the Holy City. He would proceed in the same strange manner through all Mongolia and the Gobi desert. He would cover close upon a thousand miles, kissing the ground at every three steps!

The people are friendly and hospitable to these eccentric pilgrims, and the latter interrupt their task always at nightfall, leaving a great stone on the road to mark the point which they have reached in their progress, and whence they will on the morrow resume their way, and they go to the nearest village, to rest a while from their holiness.

It suddenly flashed upon our minds that we too, after all, were bent on a strange pilgrimage. We, too, had vowed a strange vow, and were faithfully keeping it. If the genuflecting pilgrim had in his turn inquired of the reason of Prince Borghese's journey, he would no doubt in his wisdom have greatly wondered on hearing it.

Shortly past a village called Pa-ta-ling, we perceived a tremulous line bordering the crests of the mountains before and around us, far in the distance. The line appeared and disappeared, faintly jagged, like a thing with teeth, and gradually showing to our sight, as it curved towards us, innumerable towers placed in a chain, like a row of giants at their watchposts.

It was the Great Wall.

IV

ON THE MOUNTAINS

We Pass the Great Wall – The Italian Marines Leave us –
At High Speed over the Chinese Country – Under the
Shadow of the Lian-ya-miao – An Anxious Moment –
Mongolia comes in Sight

Seen from the distance, the Great Wall, blending and fusing with the outlines of mountains like a prodigious architectural moulding on their crests and sides, does not look like the work of man. It is too vast; and yet what can be seen of it from any given point represents only about one-thousandth part of its extent. The thing seems a fantastic freak of the earth, thrown up by some great unknown natural force; the outcome of a cataclysm, not destructive, but creative.

As we approached, the Great Wall became more and more completely hidden by a crowd of peaks; and we only saw it again at the last turning of the road, when we were about to enter under its heavy double gateways, covered by still available bastions. The road near to the top is now no more than a channel in the living rock, and it is increasingly steep and difficult. We had been walking for eight hours under an unbroken sheet of rain. We advanced slowly, painfully, and had to stop every minute to remove stones to make a path for the wheels or to protect the motor car's flywheel from the projecting upward points on the roadway. All around us was gloomy and barren.

We were skirting a deep ravine. Suddenly, rising from its depth a line of telegraph poles came in sight, two telegraph wires resting on their insulators, crossing our road and the Great Wall. It was like the sight of familiar faces; *these* were friends to us, and would carry our news to the world outside. Poor ancient wall, the labour and pride of three royal dynasties and of some millions of men – it is not by the cannon alone that thou art rendered useless; a thread of wire suffices. The most distant peoples can quietly commune with one another above thy head, ignoring thy very existence!

The Great Wall is less imposing when seen at a smaller distance. It resembles the ordinary walls of a town, and for one whose memory of the Peking belt of forts is still fresh, it loses still more in comparison. But when we had passed it and we turned back to gaze at it from the road to Cha-tau-chung, we gave a sudden gasp. There ran the white line of the wall as far as the eye could reach. It rose, it fell, it followed the contours of the ground, plunged into deep dells, then sprang up again into view as with a leap. It showed now sideways, now frontwise, marshalling its towers in a hundred different ways; unfolding its battlements spread out before us one moment, only to group them the next in a sudden foreshortening. It looked like a wayward thing dallying and fleeing alternately over all its way to the opposite limits of the horizon, to the most distant heights whence it showed only like a scarce-perceptible threat. And so on still beyond them, so for 500 miles – all round the province of Chi-li – a portentous frontier-line. And this is only the *little* Great Wall. There is besides the great one, the *Wan-li-chang-cheng*, the 'Wall of the Ten Thousand Li', which we were to find on the north of Kalgan, and which runs for 1500 miles along the frontiers of China proper. And the walls are more than two; beyond Cha-tau-chung, on a stretch of flat country, we saw more towers, more bastions, like those we had seen in the Nankow valley.

The Chinese people spent more than a thousand years of their existence in building walls against the west. Their labours were only interrupted three centuries ago, when the Chinese throne was occupied precisely by the very Tartars against whose advent were raised those structures of bricks and mortar.

To our modern mind the Great Wall appears an amazing monument of Chinese fear, huge and senseless, both magnificent and ridiculous. We admire and we deride it. But we fail to remember that the Romans also defended the British frontiers by raising a double line of walls against indomitable Caledonia; and that there have been epochs in history during which the conditions of life caused men to think it reasonable, natural, or necessary to raise great barriers between neighbouring countries and races, between civilization and barbarism – even as today we deem it reasonable and necessary to do the great work (which may one day seem more imposing, more ridiculous, more Chinese than the building of the Great Wall itself) of laying upon the earth hundreds of thousands of miles of steel bars, of felling the forest of our lands to support them, and boring through the heart of our mountains a way for them to cover.

We did not enter the village of Cha-tau-chung, enclosed within a square wall with turrets at each corner. All Chinese towns and villages are so enclosed, in a perfect square, which, perhaps, still preserves the earliest form of entrenchment. We walked round the village, over a road which was partly flooded, but certainly in a better condition than that which crosses the enclosed and inhabited space; and we took a lodging, outside the North Gate, in a small Chinese inn, or rather wretched halting place for caravans. That day we had covered about twenty miles.

In the dingy courtyard surrounded by half-crumbling buildings we tested our engine at once. We feared lest the shocks and sudden leaps of the ascent had damaged it. But it sprang to life, and the crowd of on-lookers also sprang to life, fleeing for safety. Shortly afterwards, three Chinese soldiers arrived from the village mandarin. It is not clear whether to protect us or to watch us: we might consider them as our guard of honour, or of dishonour, as we felt inclined.

Don Livio left us immediately on our arrival, in order to reach Nankow in time for the evening train. We bade him farewell effusively, and continued our cries until he was lost to sight.

The damp air came in gusts through the rifts of our paper shutters, into our humble resting places. 'Pietro, we'll have a fire!' 'Pietro, hot water, please!' 'Pietro, some food,' and here comes Pietro, eager and smiling, busy with the charcoal-burner, with the teapot, and with eggs, answering our orders and our questions in an entirely original Italian dialect. Pietro is an invaluable servant. The son of an old *ma-fu* of the Italian legation, descendant of a line of *ma-fus*, which reigned over the stables of the Italian minister in Peking, he is often honoured with charges requiring ability and faithfulness. Thus he was accompanying us to Kalgan as our major-domo and interpreter – a kind of aide-de-camp. 'Pietro,' asked Prince Borghese, 'are you a Christian?'

'I am not a Christian – I am a Buddhist,' answered Pietro in that curious lisping pidgin-Italian peculiar to himself.

'Then why are you called Pietro?'

'My name is not Pietro – it is *Wu-tin*.'

'But when people call Pietro you answer.'

'Yes, everybody calls me Pietro, so I answer.'

One last order. 'Pietro, tomorrow morning call us at three, and let the coolies be ready by then.' And, wrapped up in things plentifully sprinkled with insect powder, we courted sweet sleep. Through the thin partition came the voices of our marines in the neighbouring room, telling of their native villages and of far-distant lands.

At half-past four on 12 June, we left Cha-tau-chung under a dull, cold sky, which prolonged the darkness of the night and made us shiver in our still damp raincoats. The marines had to turn back; they had orders to leave us on the second day of the march unless their services proved necessary. They accompanied us for a few hundred yards as far as an ancient tower, and there saluted us with a salvo of *evvivas* by way of farewell. The echo of their voices rang over the plain of Cha-tau-chung. For a long way we saw their white uniforms glancing in the faint light of the early dawn, and we heard the cry of fresh *vivas* growing continually fainter and less distinct, until men and voices were lost in the distance.

The coolies had drawn a fresh fund of cheerfulness out of their sleep. They ran on and leaped over the road, still muddy here and there, with laughter and with song. It amused them to drag a motor car. O blessed poverty . . .

With the breaking of day the sky showed large tracts of blue. A westerly wind scattered the clouds, pushing them back towards the sea in a confused riot, and suddenly a ray of sunshine lighted up some high mountains before us. A few minutes more and the whole chain of the Yean Jan which we were to cross appeared before us in a triumphant outburst of light, furrowed by crevices and ravines, and outlined in sharp peaks against the sky. It seemed to have advanced suddenly against us, a huge and imposing barrier, and behind it rose more peaks, more mountains of diverse heights, in lines, the one behind the other, until they blended with the blue of the sky. These were the outlying buttresses of that great mountain system, the Khinghan.

The sky was gradually clearing. We turned round and saw the shadow of the last little clouds abandoning one by one the heights of the Great Wall, and the mountains which we had passed the day before ranged themselves behind us, jagged and bare, marked by the indefatigable serpent-like wall, so marvellous that our eyes could not take in their fill of it. As far as the remote mountains of the Shan-si to the south, dim and scarcely visible, we could perceive the regular semicircle of towers; and we pointed it out to one another with a wonder ever increasing as before an impossible thing.

The ground rose slightly, the country was deserted. Sometimes after whole hours of solitary progress we would overtake some caravan with camels led by Mongolians in long-haired goatskins, and surmounted by octagonal hats similar in shape to the roof of a pagoda. These caravans were taking the last journey of that year. The Mongolian camels do not work in the summer. They enjoy the advantages of holidays and of country rest. In the hot months they are removed to the pastures of their native prairies, where they take rest and food sufficient for all the other months of the year, during which they fast and labour. This rest is needed by them also for the sake of their hoofs, which sometimes wear out during their mountain travelling to a point which causes the camel's death. The animal of the desert cannot with impunity be changed into an Alpine beast of burden.

At other times we were overtaken, in our turn, by palanquins drawn by mules, rapid private conveyances. These were carrying merchants to Kalgan, or imperial officials to distant seats of government. They were preceded by a vanguard of servants and mounted soldiers, and followed by a rearguard of muleteers leading remounts. The officials, as a sign of their dignity, carried suspended outside their palanquins the red cases containing their conical official hats. As they passed, the little curtains of their singular carriages were drawn aside, and their dignified Chinese heads would emerge, nodding with the swaying of the mules, and looking at us inquiringly.

We now came to the sandy stretch. We passed villages which once were rich cities, but now were very poor, surrounded by great falling bastions: Paoshan, now a group of mud huts surrounding a tiny temple which we could just see through the breaches made by time in the square enclosure of great walls, too spacious for the present village; and then Shi-yu-lè in the shadow of willow trees, Hu-li-pa surrounded with mud fortifications, Sha-chao which reminds one of Manchurian villages, and Pien-kia-pu which reminds one of nothing. The vertical rays of the sun beat strongly upon us and confused our thoughts. The hours passed with deep monotony, alike and oppressive. In our mechanical tramping (the animals had returned to Nankow) we thought with dim longing of some inhabited place to which we must be drawing near. We placed a vague trust in the next village which we were to find. We sought for it with our eyes, we hastened towards it as though with the sight of it were to cease our fatigue, the heat, the sadness, and the great dazzling light in which we seemed to be sinking and melting. We advanced, vaguely hoping to find some novelty in every coming village. The coolies' cheerfulness had disappeared. Nothing was heard but the shuffling and trampling of feet, the panting of the men, the creaking of the sand under the heavy wheels of the car. From time to time the silence would be broken by Ettore's commands, and a sudden hooting of the horn. Halt! now comes a difficult pass.

We almost wished for these difficult passes, to bring us to a sense of our present surroundings. They necessitated a noisy activity, the use of hands and mind. 'Here, pass the spade! the hoe! . . . Dig a way for the right wheel . . . Pull! we'll move this boulder . . . Hey, fetch the crowbars! . . . Attention! one, two, three!' So our little band stirred feverishly for a little while in the squalid waste of that deserted country, then the coolies shouldered their ropes again, and on they went with a *laè, laè, la!*

Over the door of a lonely hut we saw the words '*Deutscher Feldtelegraph*', the last remaining sign of the famous international military expedition against the Boxers. The words are reverenced here by the people, who believe them perhaps to be a sacred motto of the west.

We have reached the walls of a city, Huai-lai, facing, to the south, a high isolated hill crowned by a temple which was once used for a few weeks by the Europeans as their barracks.

Here we stopped to give an hour's rest to our men, who went to spend it in the town, thus spreading the news of our arrival. And all Huai-lai turned out in a body to see us. The sound of an advancing multitude was heard approaching the city gate. First came the children, ever in the vanguard of a crowd, then a few minutes later we were surrounded by hundreds of people, who pressed up to the motor car, smiling and respectful. They inspected it, they touched it timidly. Then growing bolder they questioned us, welcomed us, admired us. Many raised the palms of their hands, on which rested cages with singing birds; for on fine days every good Chinese of moderate position takes out his cage on a daily walk – and this is his chief occupation: an elegant traditional pastime.

We were meanwhile lunching on cheese and corned beef. Seeing us eat greatly entertained the people of Huai-lai. They discussed the nature of our food. An old man told us by signs that he wished to taste some. He would not swallow the cheese, but seemed to approve of the meat, and expressed his opinion to the people. The people passed along their comments. The old man desired to extend his investigations to our drinks, and we handed him our wine bottle, which he brought to his lips after some hesitation, having first waved aside the proffered glass with contumely. He sipped, tasted, sipped again. Finally he drank with such a will that the bottle emptied itself down his venerable throat with a loud gurgling. After this he was a sworn friend of Europe. He smiled upon us with gleaming little eyes, spoke to us volubly, got on to the automobile and enthroned himself there, amidst the applause of his fellow-citizens. He learnt to toot the car's horn; he tooted it and was happy. We experienced no slight difficulty in dislodging him from his throne when the coolies returned and it was time to resume our way.

We passed near other mud villages, other small ruinous temples, lonely huts, small houses that seemed to have been dropped by some big town on a journey over that road. A red rag hanging from a stick over the door marked those huts as halting-places for tired travellers, or as tiny inns for mule drivers, and our men would stop to swallow hastily a cup of tea, and buy with a few *sapecas* sweetmeats rescued from the flies.

Many small villages seemed uninhabited; not a soul to be seen, not a sound heard there. They seemed to be in hiding, or to convey the message to us: 'Keep at a safe distance!' Ta-tu-mu, a town with high, crumbling walls, looked like a ruin deserted centuries ago.

The road grew narrower; we often found ourselves in deeply sunk paths carved by the waters into the sand or the stone. We were walking up the bed of a torrent. Around us rose like giants the mountains which we had seen at dawn – of a burning yellow tint and without a blade of grass. We were ascending the second mountain step which divides the plain of Peking from that of Mongolia: the second step of three. The centre of Asia is reached as one would reach the threshold of a temple: by three ledges and three terraces. Below, on our left, opened the great valleys of the Shan-si, saturated with light and with blue.

At certain points there was scarcely room for the car, and infinite caution was needed. Here and there it was necessary to use the pickaxe, to measure with the swiftest and most accurate glance the width of the road immediately before us. Often the advance was known to be a risk, and was undertaken only with an eye on the axles of the car, and with hand prepared to stop the machine instantly, if need arose, with the grip of the brake.

At the village of Tu-mu-go, about thirty miles from Cha-tau-chung, we emerged quite suddenly from the mountainous ground. A green plain lay before us, invitingly. Our fatigue disappeared, as if by magic. 'Stop!' we cried to the coolies. In a moment they were drawn aside under Pietro's orders, and we had unharnessed the three beasts. We coiled the ropes eagerly round the lamp-springs, we unfurled our little flag. A turn to the handle, and the motor begins to snort. We leap on the car, and are off. Off, over the winding and uneven path, without a thought for the bounds, the jerks, the shocks on our progress. The machine is only in second gear, but we seem to be flying. Large rainpools stand in our way, but on we go over them, throwing up great jets of mud and water; spouts come up through the frame of the car and splash us. We laugh. We are seized by a strange intoxication; it is the reaction against the long silences and the depressing slowness of our recent mode of journeying. And we are conscious also of a new joy: the intense and inexpressible satisfaction of doing a thing that has never been done before. We experience the inebriation of conquest, the exaltation of triumph, and with it all a kind of astonishment, a sense of unreality, because of the strange thing this is – the running of such a race in such a country! We see pagoda roofs among the trees. We feel as if we were breaking the stillness of a thousand years, as if we were the first to give with one rapid flight the signal of an awakening out of some great sleep. We feel the pride of a civilization and a race, and are conscious of representing something more than ourselves. The civilization of Europe overshadows us; it is symbolized by the speed of our flight. The great longings of the western soul, its strength, the true secret of all its progress, is embodied in the short word – *faster!* Our life is pursued by this violent desire, this painful insatiability, this sublime obsession – *faster!* Here in the midst of Chinese immobility we truly carry with us the essence of our feverish advance.

We cross big villages and small ones. Barely-clad children flee. Men and women look at us with calm surprise, with a quiet and friendly curiosity. We see strange costumes, more picturesque than those of Peking, perhaps more ancient. There are green, red, white, yellow, blue garments always coloured in the brightest tints. All the world over, the inhabitants of the countryside love lively colours, and perhaps this is because they have the flowers always about them. On the threshold of the houses, where little crowds gather, there is a many-coloured kaleidoscope flashing in the sun; above, project the typical Chinese roofs with their charming curves. We could not have a stronger sense of the Farthest East surrounding us. We pass on swiftly.

At the sound of our car the labourers look up from their work amid the verdant fields; they look at us, shading their eyes with their hands. Someone cries: '*Huò-cho lae!*' (Here is the railway!) Someone else repeats the exclamation. After a glance all return to their work without raising their eyes again, and quite convinced that that railway of which they have heard so much has arrived at last. But the thing matters little to them. It matters little to most, down here. We pass by a woman washing some clothes in a ditch; she deigns us with just one glance and goes on washing her clothes as if hundreds of motor cars passed her way daily. Elsewhere, on the contrary, people call to one another, they run to see us, follow us running in the dust, with a great look of wonder on their yellow faces. The soul of this people is an impenetrable mystery. Who knows but what the different effect produced by the arrival of the motor car in the several villages may be the result of some real difference of origin among their inhabitants – curiosity being Tartar and indifference Chinese?

We reach a city, Tum-ba-li, whose gates are so narrow that our car cannot enter them; so we go round by way of the fields quite slowly. At a village we stop for water. The car is thirsty, and so are we. A good-natured crowd surrounds us, gives us clear, cool water, and starts upon a minute examination of the lower part of the automobile. They discuss, they draw nearer; some bolder youths bend down to the ground to look better at the flywheel. Then all bend down. That flywheel evidently puzzles them. We also look, vainly trying to discover what it is that so attracts their attention. The scene is decidedly ludicrous. At last one picks up courage, and, more by signs than by words, asks us for an explanation. Ah! at last we understand. They are asking: 'Where is the *beast*?' The horse, which is not in front, must surely be inside. 'Indeed,' says one, pointing at the radiator with an expressive piece of mimicry, 'indeed, it drinks water through a hole!' But it is difficult to see how and where the unhappy animal is confined. Ettore tries to enlist their enthusiasm by a demonstration lesson, and opens the engine cover to show the cylinders. But the people continue to look underneath with the greatest persistence; and we depart leaving them still perplexed.

We have caught up the palanquins which passed us this morning. The muleteers dismount quickly at our passing to hold their shying beasts, rearing a little. The palanquins stop, lying half across the road, as the mules attached to them show a great difference of opinion concerning the route to be followed. From behind the agitated and raised little curtains we catch another fleeting sight of the dignified travellers gazing upon us with an expression of deep amazement, not entirely free from misgivings, and flying past them, we cry a joyous farewell. This is our revenge.

It is evening, and we duly halt at a charming village, Shin-pao-wan, of patriarchal antiquity. Within its walls is an alluring stillness: the only sound is the singing of birds. Hanging from the lintel of every door are two or three cages with larks from the desert. The larks are singing and their melodious notes fill the air with a strange, penetrating, full, and strong music, which the people like to listen to as they sit on the threshold of their houses. The Mongols carry these singing prisoners, so beloved by the Chinese, by thousands down from the plains; and the Chinese give to the voice of the lark a preference over every other sound, as if they almost felt in it the presence of something divine.

The road through the village is flooded and changed into a lake in which are mirrored houses and blue sky. And it must have long been so, for that little incursion of water seems to be respected, and willows have had time to grow along its banks, drinking in the quiet waves. The people walk all round over the high pavements. No cars enter the village.

And now comes a little cortège, advancing like a vision of bygone
years. On a white mule with red silk trappings a great lady passes in rich
satin dresses, with her face painted white and pink, her lips covered with
incarnadine, her hair adorned with flowers: a little figure that might have
walked down from a Chien-long vase. Peking fashion does not reach this
distant spot; here survive the customs of centuries ago. The lady is
preceded and followed by attendants. She is perhaps on her way to
a feast. We halt to look at her while she is crossing a small arched
bridge; and at the sight of us she gracefully veils her face with her
sleeve.

We now wander about the village, leaving the car in a caravanserai
outside the walls. On our return we find the courtyard full of people and
camels, carts and horses. Some caravans have arrived. The servants are
all in a bustle, weighing out great heaps of fodder for the animals,
rushing about to take great dishes piled up with pancakes or steaming
rice to the guests. In one corner of the yard is an old wizard engaged in
making incantations for the recovery of an old sick mule, by means of a
lighted candle and of magical words, and the mule bears his incantations
resignedly amid a silent circle of lookers-on. In the vast smoky kitchens
all the fires are lit, and against the reddish light of the tallow candles
stand out the silhouettes of the busy cooks, with their bare shoulders
shining with perspiration, backs bent, labouring like the smithies of
some ancient forge. Round the automobile another crowd persists in
looking for 'the animal', and the conviction is forced upon us that the
idea of an animal really appears to the peasant as the most reasonable
explanation of this new phenomenon of swift traction. The most intelligent suspect that it is not here a question of a horse, but of some
unknown and fabulous animal made a prisoner by us, and when they
hear the hoarse cry of the horn they say they have heard his voice. Amid
the tumult of this motley crowd are two Russian soldiers, with bayonets
in readiness; they are soldiers of the Russian legation sent to escort the
Russian mail through Kalgan and Kiakhta. They come from Peking and
are able to give us news of the other motor cars, which we know reached
Pa-ta-ling last night. The soldiers have met our colleagues this side of the
Great Wall; they say that they are to pass the night at Huai-lai. Since
dawn we have travelled less than a hundred kilometres; the others will
overtake us at Kalgan.

A voice by our side: 'Dinner is ready!' and here comes Pietro,
triumphantly carrying dishes of his own concoction, smiling behind the
steam which rises from them. Pietro can even cook.

Later, between dinner and sleep, as we sit outside our rooms enjoying cigarettes, we face the great black shadow of high mountains outlined against the starry sky.

'Those are the mountains of Ki-mi-ni,' remarks Prince Borghese.

'More climbing?'

'Yes, and difficult. Kalgan is beyond.'

'Shall we get there?'

'Who knows? Tomorrow will be a field-day.'

And so indeed it was.

It was still dark when we left. There was scarcely enough light to pale the stars in the east. It was difficult to see the path, and the old headman of the coolies, familiar with these places, went before us exploring. We could not take the risk of advancing by motor, and besides, we had only a few miles of plain to traverse before entering the mountain passes of Ki-mi-ni. Our Chinese boys pulled easily, following the rapid step of the mule, the donkey, and the horse. At sunrise we were at the foot of a grand and singular mountain, the Lian-ya-miao.

The Lian-ya-miao is isolated among the other mountains and is higher than any; it looks like a chief among them. It is washed on the south by the River Hun, and overlooks its course for a tract with huge rocks descending sheer down upon its waters. The Kalgan road passes over the Hun-ho, now along the banks of the river, now on the slopes of the mountain, now on sand, and again on rocks, climbing or descending until, having turned round the mountain, it abandons the river and advances between low hills towards the Hsien-wa-fu table-land on whose threshold, at the foot of more mountains, Kalgan is situated.

Under the mountain of Lian-ya-miao the city of Ki-mi-ni is built in the plain. At the corners of the city walls rise graceful little pagodas. A few temples, with gabled roofs surmounted by decorative dragons and adorned with bells, peep out above the bastions. Of Ki-mi-ni nothing else can be seen. It is entirely enclosed by its high, square walls, like so many other Chinese cities: strange cities, by which we passed without so much as catching a glimpse of their interior; mysterious cities defending themselves from the stranger's curiosity as they would from an enemy. As one walks outside their bastions in silence and solitude it seems almost impossible that beyond those great even walls there can be people, roads, houses, market-places, joys and griefs. In China everything is surrounded by walls: the empire, the cities, the temples, the houses. The Chinese ideal of life is that of a tranquil captivity.

Having passed this city we came to the bank of the Hun-ho in the shadow of Lian-ya-miao, whose rocky sides towered above us.

Over the summit of the mountain we saw a temple. How was it built? we ask one another in amazement. Pietro hastened to tell us. That temple was not made by man; no man could have made it. The truth is that it was made by Buddha himself. He descended from his heaven under the semblance of an old woman, many centuries ago, and in one single night he erected the sacred building. In that same night, having changed into an old man, he built a bridge over the Hun-ho, the remains of which are still visible. Pietro pointed out to us the two ends of a stone bridge now in ruins and overgrown by brambles.

It is curious to note how common among the peoples of the Far East is the legend of a god coming to do great works upon this earth in the shape of an old man or an old woman. The temple and the bridge reminded me that in Japan in one night the goddess Kwannon, also in the twofold shape of old man and old woman, is said to have carved her own twofold image on gigantic tree trunks, and one of these self-portraits is still worshipped at Kamakura, where I myself have seen it. Divinity and old age are often fused in Asiatic legends, perhaps because divinity and old age are there equally the objects of veneration.

The river was somewhat swollen by the rains, its broad and turbid waters wound capriciously in and out in its vast sandy bed. At one point the mountain suddenly pushed out her rocky flank as far as the waters. When the river is shallow the caravans can ford the Hun-ho and continue their path upon the other bank. But we would not risk a crossing through the surging waves. We decided to take a mountain path which rose boldly before us with a sudden leap and disappeared immediately among the rocks. We began our climb.

The path was cut out of the rock. It followed all the twists of the mountain. It took such sudden narrow turns that at certain moments we could not see ten steps before us, and at others we came suddenly to an abyss. It never let us guess its direction. We were met with continuous surprises. To our right rose the rocky wall, on our left we skirted the precipice ever deeper as we ascended. In the depths was the river. As we ascended there came gradually in view beyond the river an interminable horizon – the valley of the Sang-kan-ho, the pale mountains of the Hwang-hwa-shan, dim, ghostly, like spectres of themselves. Our glance penetrated far into the Shan-si. At intervals the path grew narrower. Sometimes there was scarcely room enough for the wheels of our car, and those were moments of anxiety. On the side of the track in old times little walls had been built, now falling or fallen, and as we looked over them we had the sensation of being suspended in mid-air. We saw camel convoys advancing along the Hun-ho like lines of insects. Sometimes great boulders hung over our heads, and then almost instinctively we hastened our steps till we had passed them.

The management of the motor car became fatiguing and difficult. We worked with the Chinese, now at the wheels, pushing the spokes with our shoulders, now helping at the rope and directing the men's efforts. The coolies were admirable; something of our eagerness and our enthusiasm had entered into them. Attentive and willing, they gave us their whole strength and intelligence. They put pride into their work. They had learned the way of overcoming certain obstacles and they applied their knowledge without waiting for the word of command. They watched our gestures, tried to guess our thoughts. They had perfectly well understood the steering movements, and when they saw the front wheels so caught among the crevices and the stones as to make steering impossible from the car, they ran to free them, pushing them towards the best side to help Ettore as he held the wheel. The meaning of some words of our language was no longer a mystery to them. *Forza*, *avanti*, *fermi*, *piano*, *attenti*, had all become words full of meaning to their ears. Added to this they had an inexhaustible fund of good humour, a desire to be happy at any price. When a difficult pass was successfully overcome there would be loud rejoicing. After the intense excitement of a special effort, they found a will to sing with still panting breath. They fêted their little victories. They found a thousand subjects of conversation and laughter, until the cry *attenti!* made them bend silently again over the taut ropes. They felt urged to greater effort also by seeing us always ready to pull the rope, with our shirtsleeves rolled up, uniting our energy with theirs. They felt prouder because of this. If they were sensible of any humiliation in the nature of their work that work was dignified in their sight by the part we strangers took in it.

We never knew what time of the day it was, because we did not wish to know it. On certain journeys it is best to leave one's watch at home; it is a bad companion, discouraging one by its proof of how slowly time passes. It is better to remain with one's illusions; and in times of labour one always has the illusion of having worked many hours, of having traversed great distances, and of being near the place and time of rest. One's watch is apt at such times to say to one: 'Poor friend, what thou hast done is nothing. The evening is far away. In one hour thou hast advanced two miles.' An hour, then, seems an eternity, and if one is tired one feels weary, if one is weary one feels undone.

We lived outside of time. We had the sensation of having been for an indefinite number of hours on a march among the mountains. And this sensation of endlessness accustoms the heart and makes one reconciled.

The day was reddening above us, the blazing sun warmed the rocks, setting them aflame. If we touched the stones we drew back our hands with a sense of being burnt. The air was motionless and hot, as in a furnace. The mountain seemed to be breathing upon us its breath of a giant asleep. Some of the coolies had stripped themselves down to the waist, and the rope pressing upon their bronzed shoulders sank deep into the muscles, wrinkling the skin. But these were all porters by profession, and their shoulders were hardened by the shafts of the palanquins they had carried and by the yoke for the water pails. They seemed unconscious of the friction, and they seldom shifted the rope from one shoulder to another with their rapid characteristic movement.

Suddenly the climb was ended. The descent which opened before us cut into the mountain, even steeper and still precipitous. We unharnessed the animals and transferred the ropes to the pivots of the back springs. All our efforts were now directed towards keeping back the car on this rapid declivity. All the men got ready in two lines, as they would for a tug-of-war. Ettore engaged first gear so that if the ropes should snap, and the brakes give way, the car would not hurl itself forward with headlong speed, but would be kept back by its low gear. And in this way it would still be possible to direct, if not to stop, the machine.

When all was ready the signal was given: 'Forward!' and the grey monster began its downward plunge. It seemed to be avenging the insult it had received in being dragged. It was the motor car, now, that wanted to flee, taking advantage of every moment of diminished tension on the part of the men, ready for flight, sensitive to the least slackening of the ropes. You might have thought it was watching the moment for rebellion, unwilling to suffer any control of its strength. An instant alone sufficed, our concerted effort was broken for one moment, the tension of our muscles slightly relaxed, and the great machine sprang forward, dragging every one after it, and for a while seemed not to feel even the bite of the brakes. With our bodies thrown back, our chins over our chests, our feet planted firmly on the ground, with stiff arms and knees, and clenched teeth, holding our breath, all of us, the Chinese and ourselves, took part in the struggle. But it was only a moment, brief though poignant: the new, well-lubricated brakes bit slowly, but *did* bite. Ettore understood his beast, and was confident; he knew how to tame it in time. When we wanted to stop, we ran to put great stones under the wheels with the eagerness of people building a barricade to keep out the enemy. And then we rested awhile, leaving the motor car alone, bent forward in an obstinate attitude, with the ropes trailing in a winding line like two long tails behind it. Very soon we reached the plain, and cheerily started again upon our road between the mountains and the Hun-ho.

The path led us towards a village, Shao-huai-huen, half-hidden among thick willow trees, and surrounded by rice fields. The road now became muddy; the ground, greasy and black and saturated with rain, gave way under the car. Half the spokes of the wheels disappeared in it, and the mud adhered to the body and the tyres of the car, massing itself there and giving fantastic shapes and dimensions to the wheels. The car seemed to be moving over rolls of earth. Our shoes, too, were uncomfortably burdened: the mud clung to them, obliging us to shake our feet violently from time to time. We slid, our step grew heavy. The coolies had to stop every few moments to rest. We met a mule caravan loaded with Mongolian furs. Two of the mules, frightened by our car, left the path and immediately sank knee-deep into the mud.

Near the village the road was covered with water. To the right and to the left spread rice fields surrounded by high banks, and flooded too. There was no choice, we had to go on. Our men bared their legs and went in. The long fording of this stretch of water seemed to be progressing favourably. We were hopefully measuring with our eye the distance which separated us from dry land: two minutes more and we should be safe. But the water bubbled under our feet, and suddenly the car stopped.

'Forward, forward!' cried Ettore.

'Fools!' we exclaimed. 'They go and choose *this* moment as the proper time to rest!'

'Pull – it's dangerous to stop now – we're sinking.'

But the poor Chinese had not stopped on purpose. They were perfectly well aware of the danger, and they were pulling excitedly as hard as they could. The three animals stiffened their legs under a shower of blows, and stretched out their thin necks. The ropes were taut, the chassis groaned. In vain – the machine seemed nailed to its place. Several times they renewed the attempt to move it, now slowly, now with sudden jerks, trying every means in their power. Some other way must be devised. We were preparing to fasten chains to the trees and work by pulleys, but the Chinese, feeling under the water with their naked feet, found that the wheels had struck against something. Pietro reported:

'Big stone.'

'A big stone? Here is the iron lever to work with.'

We were ready to demolish a whole mountain if need be, when, feeling with their hands in search of a place for leverage, the coolies realized that the obstacle was not a stone, and Pietro explained:

'Big roots.'

The obstacle in our way consisted of the roots of a gigantic willow which stood not far away, itself joyously decked with green, and as indifferent to our plight as if it had had nothing whatever to do with it. There was little choice but to cut through those roots with a hatchet – a new and singular experience in motor driving. Anyone seeing us there would have thought us to be engaged upon the fabulous enterprise of cutting water. The blows came down evenly, following the direction of a stick driven into the bottom to mark the place where the offending object should be struck. The severed roots were tied up, pulled apart, torn out, broken and twisted until the wheels were completely free, and then we made our way swiftly out of the bog and did not stop for some miles, happy to have found a way which, however bad, had no hidden pitfalls. This brought us again to the river-bed, and then again among fields and through woods and villages. At every well we stopped to bathe our hands and faces voluptuously in the fresh water.

'Where are you going?'

This question, spoken in English and sounding in our ears just as we passed a solitary and deserted temple, made us turn round in astonishment. We only saw a Chinese sitting in the shade of a tree, watching us. Was it he who had addressed us? It was.

'Where are you going?' he repeated.

'To Kalgan. And you, who are you?'

'I am an engineer of the Kalgan railway.'

'And what are you doing?'

'I am studying.'

'What are you studying?'

'The Kalgan railway.'

'I hope you find it pleasant.'

'Wait.'

'Why?'

'I want to say "How do you do".' And the good engineer interrupted his railway study, which looked so much like sweet repose, and came gravely to show us that he knew European customs. He shook hands with each of us and repeated, 'Goodbye, goodbye,' and then returned to the shade of his tree.

We stopped to eat some impossible pancakes in a village inn at Shan-shui-pu. While we were there the courtyard of the inn suddenly resounded with the clattering of two galloping horses' hoofs. Two

Chinese soldiers dismounted. They were ragged and dirty; they wore a cartridge-belt, rifles slung across their shoulders, and broad poignards at their belts: the whole surmounted by two brigand faces. Pietro ran to us.

'Soldiers of the mandarin of Hsin-wa-fu!' he cried to us.

'What do they want?'

'Come to see us by order mandarin.'

The brigands looked at us, mounted again, and disappeared.

We soon resumed our way, and shortly afterwards the mountain had us again in its grip. Two rocky buttresses stood before us in a storm of reddish peaks. Two more passes and here we were again, stumbling among the boulders.

But the road was worse than any so far traversed. We had to fight, not so much against the difficulties of long, steep climbs, like those on the Lian-ya-miao Mountain, as against the obstacles opposed to us by the naked granite. We were advancing over rocks full of holes and bumps, of crevices and sharp points. The flowing of the water, the hoofs of the mules, and the large feet of the camels had barely softened in so many centuries the worst jaggedness of the narrow path. The car, however cautiously and slowly we proceeded, swayed on the unevenness of the ground. It had now one wheel, now another, caught between the stones; it slipped down with hard jolts from the jutting points of the road; it got the rims of its wheels gripped in deep depressions. And we listened anxiously to the metallic creaking of the chassis strained by the continuous pulling, to the slight wheezing of the wood, or the wheels, to countless scarcely perceptible sounds coming from we knew not what part of the machine, faint moans of the steel that seemed to come from the work of destructive insects. All the joints of the motor car were undergoing a strain for which they were not meant, and those sounds bore witness to infinitesimally small displacements, tiny deviations which might, however, prove the beginning of some disastrous damage. It was the skeleton of the machine suffering and expressing its fatigue; and the fatigue of a machine is not to be cured by rest. There were moments when every step presented a new problem. Ettore steered standing, in order better to see the road near the wheels. His hands were hurt by the strong vibrations of the wheel, which would not answer to the action of his arm.

Suddenly, two of our coolies let go of the rope with a yell and began pummelling one another. All the others leave their work and with infernal yells mix in the fight. The old headman blows with all his might into the little Whistle of Obedience. Pietro from his driver's seat shouts too. We do not know what to think. Is this a mutiny? A revolt? We throw ourselves upon the disorderly men like policemen dealing with a subversive demonstration and make way for ourselves until we succeed in laying hands upon the first two Chinese, who, in the meantime, have caught one another by their pigtails and are busily scratching each other's faces. It looks like a women's fight.

'What is it now?' we thunder. 'To work!'

'Pietro, what is the matter?'

The incomparable Pietro explains the matter to us and sends us into shouts of laughter. The two coolies have been quarrelling upon a point of honour. One has said to the other: 'You are not working – why did you come?' The insult is a grave one, and the other coolie, a lad with a girlish face which has won him the nickname of 'the Young Lady' (from ourselves at least), throws himself upon the offender to pull his pigtail. This insult, however, is more than any good Chinese will stand. The whole party have to throw themselves between the combatants to stop their fighting.

'Pietro, how will this matter end?'

'It is already ended,' he replied, with a surprised look. 'Pigtail pulled, everything finished.'

And indeed we see our heroes pulling the same rope and working still together without a shadow of resentment. Of their fight no other trace remains but a few scratches, which they wipe from time to time on their sleeves.

The difficulties of the road engaged our attention again immediately.

The path was set between walls of rock so near to one another that we could touch both by spreading out our arms. With what anxiety we crossed those long winding passages! We felt as if the car *must* remain fixed there. To go back would have been impossible. Near the ground the sides of the road sloped in such a manner that one of the wheels was always a little way up the side of the rock, and the machine advanced on a slant. A wonderful eye and marvellous judgement were needed to steer it; it was a question of inches – of an inch, rather. Sometimes Ettore would put down all the brakes, and thus stopping the machine he would turn, exclaiming despondently, 'We can't go on!'

Then we had to set our hands to the pickaxe, pull down some jutting stone, measure, try again, putting the men alone to the ropes with a cry of '*Ma-man-ti!*' (Gently!) Our voices were echoed back to us all round; the mountains seemed to say of their own accord '*Ma-man-ti!*'

The greatest danger was for the back wheels. They were sometimes forced together so strongly that they inclined inwards in the shape of a V. We feared that the spokes of the wheels and the differential axle might break. But once relieved from the pressure they always, to our great joy, resumed their normal position. There were moments when I could scarcely refrain from thinking that perhaps the partisans of small motor cars were in the right after all. Three inches less in width and we could have gone forward with our eyes shut. At one turning, we heard a crash, followed by a sinister creaking. 'There!' we cried, full of anguish. The side of the car had knocked violently against something. Fortunately, the damage was limited to the mudguard, which had splintered, and to the running board, which had been twisted and bent back. Ettore was quivering with rage: he would have given half his life to be already out of those endless gorges.

The narrow passes soon began to alternate with stretches of sand. The rocks grew smaller and the sand more extensive. On the sides of the mountains towards the north the strong winds blowing from Mongolia have heaped up dunes and buried the rocks under their own debris. In the ravines the sand forms broad, smooth depressions that look like great yellow rivers. Little by little we found ourselves upon the rounded dunes, following roads traced over the sand by the long-continued passing of the caravans; and from up there we saw spreading before us like an ocean, blue and dim against the limpid horizon, the Mongolian tableland.

There, great prairies and the desert awaited us. There lay flight, freedom, a way to the west.

We waved our hats aloft and threw out into the blue sky an enthusiastic shout: *'Evviva!'*

V

ON THE THRESHOLD OF MONGOLIA

~~~~~~~~~~

The Curiosity of a Mandarin's Son – The Telegraph and Opium – Fighting the Bog – Kalgan – Between the Ta Tsum-ba and the Tu Tung – All Ready

The Mongolian plain with its vast sea-like surface in a peculiar way appears higher than the highest mountain. It seemed to heave as with a prodigious tide. It is over 6000 feet high. It has been said that China is the land of paradox, and this is a curious instance of the fact: its mountains stand below its plains; at a lower level than its endless prairies stand outlined the mountains of Kalgan, with the towers of the Great Wall scattered upon their heights.

The sight of that free horizon opening towards our goal filled us with a new courage. We had been walking for twelve hours, but now our fatigue disappeared. Forward, forward! we said to ourselves, and we hastened our steps and descended the steep slopes of the dunes towards the sandy plain of Hsien-wa-fu. Behind us, faint in the distance, the mountain Lian-ya-miao, which we had passed that morning, was slowly disappearing from our sight.

The plain is spread with old tombs, crumbling arches, memorial stones, small ruined pagodas. We were drawing near a great city, and in China the approaches of great cities are sacred to the records of the dead; death sanctifies all the people who are buried there, whose spirits have so great an importance in the life of the living and exercise so great an influence upon it.

Hsien-wa-fu is the capital of the district. It is the seat of the government, which is defended by a garrison and even by a small fort, built since the foreign invasion and prudently hidden in a clump of alder trees outside the walls. We could already see the city walls lifting their battlements over the burning plain, in a line that quivered in the haze. Suddenly our attention was attracted by a great cloud of dust coming from the direction of Hsien-wa-fu, and soon we saw that it arose from a group of galloping horsemen. The little party advanced swiftly towards us. It comprised Chinese of all conditions, or so they seemed from their garments. The cavalcade was headed by the two sinister-looking soldiers who had come to see us while we ate our pancakes at Shan-shui-pu: those people must then be coming for some purpose concerning ourselves. When they had drawn near, all stopped, without even taking the trouble to greet us. They observed us attentively for a few minutes, with evident displeasure, then turned back their horses' heads and went away at a gallop.

We, who for a moment had flattered ourselves that they were coming to greet us and perhaps to offer us hospitality, and had prepared for the occasion our repertoire of Chinese salutations and compliments, could not understand the reason for that strange manoeuvre. But Pietro had had time to speak with one of the two soldiers. He informed us:

'See young man dressed blue silk on horseback? He the first and all others after?'

'Yes. Well?'

'Young man is son of the mandarin. See fat man with spectacles and straw hat like my hat? Fat man is great wise man, teacher of son of mandarin. Others are friends, officers, servants . . .'

'But what did they want?'

'To see the motor car run. Motor car not running, every one much disappointed and go away.'

And, after all, one could scarcely blame them. The son of the mandarin of Hsien-wa-fu, who, no doubt, is a Progressive, does not have the opportunity every day of seeing these famous western machines that run like the wind. One day he receives an official telegram from the Wai-wu-pu announcing that a *chi-cho* is to pass through the province; he afterwards learns that a *chi-cho* has passed at reckless speed through villages and cities, spending the night at Shin-pao-wan; he sends soldiers to explore and they return full gallop, bearing the news of its arrival. To see the *chi-cho* run, it is evidently necessary to go far, and a regular expedition is formed in hot haste; then, as the expedition advances on its way, the foreign wonder appears on the horizon, draws near. It seems slow in coming, perhaps because of one's impatience . . . A little longer, and the son of the mandarin with his tutor and with his companions find themselves before a slow massive car drawn by a little donkey, a mule, and a horse, assisted by a willing band of the Sons of Heaven . . . No, indeed, they cannot be blamed for showing themselves thoroughly disgusted!

At the entrance of the town, which spreads outside the walls like the untidy overflow of a city too greatly compressed, a great crowd awaited us, whose curiosity had been enlivened by the movements of the mandarin's horsemen. They surrounded us, raising the most abominable dust, and they accompanied us to a caravanserai.

Ours was not exactly a triumphant entry. We were given the kind of popular greeting which is usually reserved for a circus. There stood around us the same happy-go-lucky, curious, ragged crowd, thirsting for a show and ready to disperse as soon as the hat comes round.

We entered the yard of the inn and the people entered after us. The car stopped in the middle and the people stood in a circle around it. There was no means of dispersing that crowd. What could one do? Down there, they so seldom see Europeans, they have so little contact with us, that they have had no means of learning to know us, and therefore they do not hate us. We had a patient and benign public. It took an interest in our clothes, admired us from hat to shoes, smiled at the sound of our words, and – waited. It waited for some marvellous event worthy of beings that are accounted marvellous. And, adding fuel to the fire of its expectations, our coolies enlightened the crowd about the wonders of our *chi-cho*.

Ettore's pride was suffering. Since the moment we had met the son of the mandarin he had been itching to do away with the towing ropes and to enter Hsien-wa-fu at top speed. At last he felt a sudden irresistible need for an outlet to his feelings. He gave a turn to the handle of the car, took hold of the wheel, moving the starting lever, and the car bounded forward and began a furious race round the courtyard amidst indescribable confusion, tumultuous scattering and flight. The onlookers did not know where to run for safety. They ran here and there as if they had been shut up with a mad bull. But they soon perceived that the bull was tamed, that it was running steadily round and round the well, that it passed exactly on the same points and had not the slightest desire to destroy! Then they stopped. However, another danger much more serious for them appeared at that moment. It came through the door in the shape of a squadron of Chinese soldiers armed with clubs, commanded by an officer who looked like a coolie except for his gold braidings. The clubs went up over the crowd and fell on many shoulders, but not for long, for in a few seconds not a shoulder was to be seen to receive them: the courtyard was deserted.

After so complete a victory, these representatives of the Mongolian army occupied strategical positions. Two soldiers by the door, two by the sides of the car, two as sentinels on the road, and the officer in the kitchen of the hotel. We might rest without uneasiness: the Mandarin of Hsien-wa-fu was giving us ample protection and means of defence. Later, he sent a representative to ask us when we were going. Could he have shown us greater regard?

There is one thing in Hsien-wa-fu that I shall never be able to forget, and that is its telegraph office. I shall never forget that wonderful place for several reasons; first of all, because I had to walk three miles to reach it, and three miles, of course, to return, and that day we had walked over thirty. On a solitary road within the walls, the telegraph wires fall from their posts upon a house as silent as a temple. In this temple I found two clerks entirely absorbed in an important and delicate operation which the Chinese laws have recently prohibited. The clerks were smoking opium, lying flat upon their *kang* with pipes in their hands and wrapped in a cloud of the fragrant, thick, slow smoke of the narcotic.

'May I send a telegram?' I asked politely, after the usual exchange of greetings.

Perfect silence. I sat down. A few moments later I began again:

'I wish to send a telegram . . .'

One of the smokers came nearer, attended to I know not what business about the room, looked out through a door, and called for some tea.

'Will you please send a telegram for me?' I called out again.

Some vague notion of something happening began to dawn on the mind of the imperial functionary. He looked at me and said in a more or less English jargon:

'We are in direct communication with Kalgan and with Peking. Three hours a day with Kalgan and three hours with Peking. From seven to eleven with Kalgan and –'

'Excellent! My telegram is going to Europe. Do you take telegrams for Europe?'

Silence. The tea arrived. I sipped a cup while preparing to write my telegram. Then I repeated:

'Do you accept telegrams for Europe? – Do you, or do you not?'

The attendant quietly examined me as if he saw me at that moment for the first time.

'Europe. We are in direct communication with Kalgan and with –'

'And with Peking – I know, but –'

'Three hours a day with Kalgan and three –'

'And three hours with Peking, I know.'

'From seven to eleven with –'

'With Kalgan, I know. That will do. Thank you. Goodbye.' And I fled, fuming, murmuring words which although rich in energy and expression do not merit the glory of diffusion through the Press.

We intended to go the whole way from Hsien-wa-fu to Kalgan (more than twenty-five miles) by motor, excepting the overpass of Yu-pao-tung, an extremely steep, but short, hill declivity, situated about half-way. Some of our men had already been sent to Yu-pao-tung and had left the hotel at midnight; but we found the road so bad, with mud or stones or sand alternately, that we were obliged to have recourse to our coolies again for the first nine miles. At 5 a.m. on 14 June we slowly resumed our way, amid the monotonous tramping of the Chinese towing the car. We were crossing vast sandy plains at the foot of the dunes.

The masses of sand which the winds of Mongolia sweep to the Chinese frontier from the desert seem incredibly great. The sand accumulates from the north upon every rock, upon every obstacle, like snow on the wings of a cyclone. Over the walls of Hsien-wa-fu there is so much that it has almost buried them. The crenellations alone stand out.

In half an hour we had got over the pass of Yu-pao-tung. A regular, narrow passage threatening in appearance but hospitable enough in reality, and one which affords no further obstacle than an incline of forty per cent and the presence of some large boulders which submitted unresistingly to be rolled out of the way. In that narrow passage there remained, isolated, raised, and therefore disused, a track of road paved with large stones which do not come from the locality itself, and which must have been dragged there from Mount Shi-shan, the other side of Kalgan. This track is a surprising relic of ancient Chinese civilization. There must once have been real roads then, and beautiful ones. What was China like in those remote times? What traffic, what stream of riches spread over valleys and plains and flowed over great wonderful roadways and superb bridges towards Peking? How many centuries ago was it?

Before a small and graceful temple surrounded with trees we stopped to get the motor car ready and to prepare everything for the journey to Kalgan, which we were now to accomplish alone. Mule drivers, peasants, and boys gathered around us, the news of our departure given out by the coolies penetrating even within the temple. A young monk appeared on the top step of the stairway which leads to the sacred enclosure, looked out, and disappeared, only to return shortly after guiding a bent and tremulous old priest. We could see that the old man was blind. The young one told him all that happened, and the blind man witnessed thus, without seeing it, the wonderful flight of this magic chariot over those places, which he knew so well through the light and memory of his youth.

This blind man seemed to us a symbol. Were there not indeed all around us a people living on in the past alone, witnessing without realizing it the powerful eruption of a civilization and a life unknown to them? What impression could we leave behind us among those people, except the impression of a mysterious violence?

We drove on, winding over the beds of torrents, over paths carved out by the waters. As we advanced along the bottom of a broad river-bed, the slimy soil impeded our progress. The wheels revolved in vain, splashing mud, ploughing it up, sinking into it.

'Full speed backwards!' cried Prince Borghese.

The wheels revolved in a contrary direction, but the car did not move an inch.

The engine was getting heated, and we had to wait for it to cool. Some Chinese returning from the market of Kalgan just then passed above, parallel with us, along the bank of the river. We called to them for assistance, but they paled and fled, swaying under the weight of the baskets they carried. That great panting, blowing, and smoking object terrified them. We resigned ourselves to wait for the coolies, but after half an hour or so we noticed that the burning sun had somewhat dried the mud moved by the wheels, and had hardened it. We renewed our efforts, and a few minutes later the machine began to move, though still scarcely perceptibly. The wheels revolved at a speed of sixty miles an hour, and the car advanced at that of sixty inches. We succeeded in backing one yard, then two, then five, and from that point drove it on again at full speed. It went again into its own ruts roaring and emitting jets of smoke, with short explosions. Then it slowly rose vibrating, reached dry ground, and then suddenly, with a panther-like bound, threw itself forward, free.

Kalgan is hidden among the trees at the opening of a valley. This singular Chinese city suddenly came into sight at the turning of a road. It looked like the cities one sees pictured upon Fu-kien tapestries: varied and picturesque, spreading over the bank of a wide, snowy river, the Ta-ho, or 'Great River'. Outlined against the mountainous background of the dark and rugged Mount Shi-shan, it lifted towards the sky its old pagodas, its *pae-lôs*, or votive arches, and the elegant roofs of its temples: an irregular mass, consisting of untidy little groups of houses, palaces and trees, a confusion of buildings and plants that seemed to crowd at one end of the great stone bridge over the Ta-ho, as if waiting to cross it.

We did not cross it. The ancient and grandiose Chinese bridges inspired us with too much reverence; we preferred fording. We went down into the bed of the river, where a whole population of tanners were busy washing the skins of Mongolian goats, great heaps of fleecy skins.

The air was full of the smell of hides and tanning, which came from the city itself, whose lanes we were now entering. We passed between mud huts surrounded by palisades, between suburban dwellings of primitive character, which told us how near we were to wild lands and to primitive people. We came out into the market-place, which swarmed with Mongolians in their fur caps; a market-place covered with booths, carts, horses, full of cries and bustle. People made way for us with a look of astonishment, and we were conscious of creating silence everywhere in our wake. Some soldiers in red tunics ran in front of a palanquin, surrounded by mounted officers, one of whom solemnly carried a red umbrella, the badge of command. This was in honour of the great mandarin within the palanquin, the President of Justice in Kalgan, a beautiful, round, fat Chinese, resembling those porcelain mandarins with unsteady heads that are always nodding 'Yes'.

We entered into the 'Upper City', which slopes down to the valley. In the middle of the road a European awaited us. It was Monsieur Dorliac, the director of the local branch of the Russo-Chinese Bank, and he came to offer us hospitality.

We accepted gratefully the kind invitation of that hermit of civilization, who lives far from his kind in a sort of Chinese or, let us say, Russo-Chinese house, initiating the natives into the mysteries of bills of exchange. The yard of the bank became Ettore's workshop, and we encamped in the bank's offices. With a few hours' work the Itala recovered its normal aspect, discarding the packing-case and acquiring its proper body and its own tanks again. We found our first deposit of fuel and oil awaiting us, and stored it in those same tanks. As we knew we should have to travel in a very hot climate, we fitted an open exhaust, resembling those used for racing machines, in order to diminish as far as possible the heat of the engine. This was attached to the case of the engine, like two small phonograph trumpets, and the exhaust fumes could thus escape freely as soon as they were formed.

Ettore's work was watched by a huge public. The authorities had sent six soldiers to guard the entrance to the bank, with orders not to let any one in. This was a grave mistake, for a Chinese soldier naturally has a certain number of friends, relatives, and creditors, to whom he owes a debt of good nature and kindness, and whom he allows to pass whenever he mounts guard. But the number of creditors, relations, and friends of *six* Chinese soldiers is equivalent to the average population of a town; for which reason, through a door bolted and barred and guarded by six men, there flowed in upon us a stream of people like water from a jet at continuous pressure. If the guard had consisted of twelve soldiers, the bank could have been looted with perfect ease.

A considerable number of people had climbed on to the nearby roofs, and a whole procession was climbing the mountain of Shi-shan, perching upon the vantage points of its rocks, absolutely disregarding the danger of landslides, which on the Shi-shan continually cause loss of life; and all these people were prying from afar into the secrets of Europe.

Missionaries came to call upon us, dressed as Chinese, but with their heads covered by beautiful European hats. They described to us with great realism the horrors of the Boxer rebellion in Kalgan, a rebellion which would have certainly made victims and martyrs of all missionaries if they had not fled in time by way of Mongolia. One of them gave us valuable information concerning those Mongolian provinces, with which he was well acquainted. For many years he had been there regularly, distributing Bibles, buying horses, doing excellent trading.

The whole Russian colony too, consisting of three members, came to call upon us, and we, gathering with them round their samovar, listened to their three grave voices speaking softly of Siberia with a melancholy suggestion of nostalgia. At that moment, among Europeans, tasting Russian tea and enjoying the excellent products of Slav cookery, we almost cherished the illusion of having travelled several thousand miles from the capital of China. But we had only, alas, covered about 150 miles, and of those only about sixty actually by motor car.

That was indeed a day given up to the exigencies of social intercourse. The Chinese authorities, besides providing us with a bodyguard, had also posted about the town a proclamation concerning ourselves. The Kalgan people were warned of our arrival; they were to consider us as friends, as we came with no hostile intention, and therefore they were to respect us. The people of Kalgan were to make way for our machine, not to approach it, and much less to touch it, as such conduct might bring about some grave mishap. Transgressors would be taken in charge and condemned to penalties to be decided hereafter. Enormous square red official seals were appended to these proclamations. The people of Kalgan crowded to read them. We owed some thanks to the authorities, and therefore we went to call upon the Ta Tsum-ba, that is, the representative of the Wai-wu-pu, a very high dignitary, whose authority extends over the whole of Mongolia; a kind of master of the frontier, whose own name is Tai-Tsui.

Over the Ta Tsum-ba's house was unfurled the Yellow Flag with the Dragon. He himself was awaiting us, and both he and his suite had decked themselves out to receive us, wearing embroidered vestments, gala hats surmounted by buttons of all colours, peacock feathers waving from those buttons and falling upon the nape of those venerable necks, many-coloured belts, satin shoes. When he saw us he heartily shook hands with himself, according to the Chinese etiquette. Everyone shook hands with himself, and then came bows, compliments, expressions of goodwill, prayers for a long life, and so on. All this was seasoned by enormous cups of tea with rose or jasmine flavour, and by varied sweetmeats of a mysterious nature, which the Ta Tsum-ba offered us in person with his own long-nailed fingers bearing jet rings. This was to do us the greatest honour.

Tai-Tsui's preoccupations were the same as those of the Wai-wu-pu. He inquired whether upon our journey we took notes, whether we were gathering observations on the road.

'Notes? Observations? Never!' said the prince.

'And at Irkutsk,' asked the Ta Tsum-ba, 'at Irkutsk, of course, you intend to take the train?'

'No.'

'And yet all those who go through Mongolia to Europe take the train at Irkutsk,' observed the astonished dignitary. 'It is very convenient. In ten years' time there will be a train here too.'

After the visit to the Ta Tsum-ba came the visit to the Tu Tung, namely, the Tartar general put by the Tartar Court of Peking by the side of every Chinese governor as a controller to command the Governmental forces – a dignitary therefore almost all-powerful, the true tutor of all subordinate mandarins. The Tu Tung of Kalgan is called Chen Sung. He dwells in a palace which looks like a temple, surrounded by a belt of red walls, and from its high flag-posts bearing strange inscriptions of the *fus*, or Government offices, fly both the military standard and also the national one with the image of the Dragon.

More embroidered garments. More gala hats with long red fringes, buttons, jade ornaments, peacock feathers. More variegated belts and satin shoes. Hearty handshakes, bows, and compliments, aromatic tea, champagne, and sweetmeats.

The Tu Tung is also in favour of the railway, when the railway is entirely Chinese, but he is averse to tunnels. He once travelled by rail on the Hankow line. He is therefore not merely an amateur judge of the matter – he is well-informed, and judges from experience. So long as you travel in the open, all is satisfactory, but when you enter a 'gallery' you experience a most disagreeable impression.

'But there is no danger,' observed Prince Borghese.

The Tartar general knew perfectly well that there was no danger. The disagreeable impression was due to the darkness.

'You pretend it is night,' suggested Prince Borghese with a smile.

'Ah, it is not the same thing.' And the Tu Tung Chen Sung, through his interpreter, proceeded to explain his meaning. The distinction he drew lifted just a tiny corner of the veil which shrouds the Chinese soul from our eyes; it revealed a little of the exquisite sensitiveness of the oriental.

'The darkness of night and that of the tunnel are entirely different; they have not the slightest resemblance. That of the night is sweet, that of the tunnel is harsh . . . There is as much difference as between joy and grief . . . The darkness of the night opens, that of the tunnel closes . . .'

After this lesson upon the various darknesses we returned to the bank, barely in time to receive the visit of the Ta Tsum-ba. Conveyances were arriving with the officers of the suite, and the neighbourhood was packed with people whose shouts warned us of the approach of the mandarin. The palanquin of the latter, escorted by soldiers and borne by a large number of men, entered into the courtyard; and immediately the Ta Tsum-ba alighted clad in very gorgeous garments with coloured embroideries, wearing an amethyst necklace and carrying a fan. The Russo-Chinese Bank was full of a rustling of satin clothes.

On his way out the Ta Tsum-ba desired to see the *chi-cho*. He greatly admired the ingenious system by which you could blow a horn without putting your mouth to it. He watched attentively the motor's movements backwards and forwards, and finally re-entered his palanquin after having shaken hands with us after European custom – a concession to ourselves made in special consideration of our persons and of our (the European) house. *'Shu-ba!'* (Make way!) cried the soldiers, raising their clubs; and the cortège departed.

Next came the Tu Tung with a still larger suite. We were inflated with pride and tea, especially with tea. The number of cupfuls which etiquette had obliged us to swallow was incalculable. Night had fallen, and still we received complimentary calls. Monsieur Dorliac's samovar was at continuous pressure like a locomotive. About dinner time came also E-Le-Ho-Tai. He is a mandarin who serves as official interpreter to the Wai-wu-pu, who speaks and writes English, and yet had had no opportunity to express his sympathy sufficiently to us in the presence of the Ta Tsum-ba. He therefore came to express it now, dressed in a red silk robe. He looked like a Chinese Cardinal. He brought with him valuable objects which he insisted upon presenting to us as a souvenir. To the prince he gave a large embroidered bag, to me a little packet of scented herbs full of camphorous resin (such as the Chinese chew in order to perfume their breath – it smells like a wardrobe), to Ettore a tobacco pouch. E-Le-Ho-Tai begged a favour of us: he desired to have a ride on the car, and this was granted to him. Our orthodox Chinese friend seemed to me to represent the most pleasant liberality of thought, but in Mongolia it is dangerous to be a liberal thinker: very real and effectual 'excommunications' strike down the offender, root and branch.

Even some priests of a neighbouring temple, which was perched in a picturesque manner on the side of the Shi-shan, came to look at the motor car. Their temple has a gong which sounds one note every minute during the whole night. At last we remained alone with that solemn, sweet, indescribably impressive sound. It had the insistence of a warning voice. Our imagination carried us afar, and that note called us back sternly like a voice uplifted for ourselves alone. It was a voice that filled space, that shed its sound with the regularity of a great breath, and little by little it changed, became deeper, stranger, vibrating like a far-off choir, like a blending of a thousand sounds and a thousand lamentations. We seemed to hear in it the fabled voices of the Chinese night.

The following morning, 15 June, was spent by us on horseback in reconnoitring the road towards Mongolia. It was found possible to travel over parts of it without assistance, but the last heights would be scaled with the aid of coolies and mules. Afterwards the prairies would begin. After our journey of the previous days everything seemed easy now, but one danger threatened us: the rain. The valley of the Shi-shan-ho in times of rain is subject to sudden and violent floods, and as the road consists literally of the bed of the river, caravans overtaken by the fury of the waters have no hope of escape. Disasters are frequent there, and every flood bears human bodies to Kalgan, amid uprooted trees and carcasses of mules and sheep. That day it rained for several hours, and the sky threatened a worse downpour. We were, therefore, waiting impatiently the arrival of the other motor cars, which we knew had reached Hsien-wa-fu.

There were two roads from Kalgan to Urga. The principal and better known is a road called the Mandarin road, which swerves a little north-west for about five hundred miles as far as the village of Sair-ussu, where it divides into two branches – one directing itself straight northward, and finally reaching Urga, the other one curving to the west through the mountainous region of the Altai range, and by way of Kobdo traversing the land of the Kalmuks and ending at Semipalatinsk. The second road, at about twenty-five miles from Kalgan, points straight northwards and goes direct to Urga. The first one is more frequented, although the longer by some one hundred miles. It has post relays and markets, and is used by Chinese carts, being therefore generally preferred. The second is a camel path, and crosses almost entirely deserted regions from beginning to end. The Chinese distinguish them precisely by the names of Cart road and Camel road. We chose the camel path. The choice is reasonable, although it may seem strange. Traffic in general, and the passing of carts in particular, breaks up the ground and makes it bad for a motor car. In Mongolia, and in the desert of Gobi, we were to find ourselves able to get up speed only in crossing virgin land. There are plains over which the best road for the automobile is where no road is marked!

A few years ago we could not have risked ourselves without a guide over the endless Mongolian prairies and over the desert. Now there is an invaluable guide along the camel road: it is the telegraph. You blindly follow the lines of the telegraph poles for about eight hundred miles, and you reach Urga. In those distant regions, over the endless solitude of central Asia, the nearness of the telegraph meant for us nearness to our own world, and this was a further reason for the choice we made.

On the morning of the 16th, at eight a.m., we heard a great sound of voices. We ran up the road. A cry had rung across the city like a flash of lightning, from the bridge over the Ta-ho to the Russo-Chinese Bank, 'They are coming!' It heralded the arrival of our French friends, who were entering at that moment into the city. We went to meet them in a festive spirit. We shook hands; we greeted one another; we told one another our difficulties. They had spent the night encamped at thirty *li* from Kalgan. Their journey too had been difficult, but it had also been pleasantly interrupted by the various occupations of camp life: the improvised cooking of meals in the open air, the fighting against the rain, the awakening in the coolness of the dawn. Under the Lian-ya-miao they had found the Hun-ho not too swollen to be forded, and they had been able to avoid the picturesque and detestable ascent which we had had to make. But they had had no means of avoiding the other climbs, which were still harder and more difficult.

In a moment the courtyard of the bank seemed transformed into a workshop. Everywhere lay cans of oil and of fuel: screw-wrenches, hammers, tyres, spare parts thrown about in confusion. The cars exposed their shining mechanism to the eye through their open sides, and they gave themselves up meekly to the performance of their toilette. The chauffeurs, their hands covered with grease, disappeared between the wheels, and spread themselves at full length under the cars. They turned levers, unscrewed nuts, hammered away, cleaned everything. All unnecessary parts were discarded and thrown away in order to lighten the machine. Pons was sawing his mudguards, Bizac was removing the silencers (those heavy cylinders which divert the gas in order that it may escape noiselessly). Then the engines were tested, listened to, tested again, and the courtyard was filled with noise, smoke and fumes. By the evening all the cars were ready. To the luggage had been added some goatskin wraps which Pietro had bought for us in the market-place.

The farewell banquet hospitably given to us by our kind host, Monsieur Dorliac, was a melancholy affair. We were tired, and had nothing to say to one another, because our minds were all filled with the same thought, and our hearts harboured the same impatience. We were about to leave Kalgan, and with it all contact with civilization. Until now we had been within reach of ready help from Peking if it was wanted. We had crossed populated and prosperous regions; we had been constantly surrounded by a crowd of people. If we had had any need to turn back, it would have been easy for us to do so; the sea had not been distant – and the sea carries one home. On the morrow we were to launch alone into the unknown. This was a decisive moment. It was the *lâchez tout* of the aeronaut. We too at a given moment would say to our men *lâchez tout*, and would disappear in an immense solitude. Our departure from Peking had not seemed to us so full of import as did now this other departure, which we awaited with a feverish desire and yet with anxiety. At Peking we had before us Kalgan, but at Kalgan there stood before us the centre of Asia – a fascinating mystery. Urga, the nearest city, was at a distance of seven degrees on the map.

At the end of dinner the French, the Italians, and our Russian host all clinked glasses fraternally, and after exchanging sincere good wishes we parted, with one last reminder of the hour fixed for our departure.

'Four o'clock, then?'

'Four. Good night.'

'*Au revoir.*'

VI

OVER THE MONGOLIAN PRAIRIES

~~~~~~~~

In the Bed of the River – Among the Towers of the
Wan-li-chang-cheng – We Launch out upon the 'Green
Sea' – Mongolian Hospitality – Towards the Desert –
Pong-kiong

'We left Kalgan this morning. We are now, at eight a.m., crossing the Mongolian frontier. Excellent roads. We have travelled by motor alone for over eighteen miles in the bed of the Shi-shan. We have been on heights of between six and seven thousand feet. Beautiful scenery.'

This telegram, hastily scribbled on the flyleaf of a notebook, was delivered by me on the morning of 17 June to a young and obliging attaché of the French Legation, who accompanied us on horseback as far as the limit of the prairies. I implored him to dispatch it before nightfall from the telegraph office of Kalgan. If I had entrusted him with a document upon which hung the safety of an army, I could not have been more solemn in my exhortations or more effusive in my thanks.

A newspaper correspondent is always inclined to consider the loss of his communications as a serious misfortune. He has something of the passion of the historian, and a mislaid dispatch represents an irreparable blank in the immediate history which he is recording; and besides, there is in him a certain paternal affection for his hastily written records of events. His mind accompanies them on their way. He estimates the length of time which they will take to reach their destination. He calculates the difference between the times of the different countries; he pictures to himself his dispatches arriving at the editor's office by night at the hour of going to press, and being deposited among other papers on a great table under the glare of the electric light . . . Their loss would be an act of treason! Journeys, expenses, difficulties, all these can be rendered useless by some futile contingency by which a dispatch is left in the bottom of somebody's pocket or by the side of a path. The punctuality of the press service can be affected by many varied circumstances, such as the power of a horse, the honesty of a Chinaman, the state of the weather. This uncertainty concerning the fate of his own work is one of the most painful trials of a special correspondent in a distant land. For there he is obliged to have recourse to the first means at hand to forward his dispatches to the nearest telegraph office, and it is impossible for him to receive communications directly. He is isolated from his fellows and in the dark concerning everything, lost in doubt. I had keenly at heart the delivery of that short telegram, also because of this special reason, that at that moment it seemed to me to state the most important event in the world:'*We are now crossing the Mongolian frontier!*' I repeated these words to everyone with a kind of enthusiastic amazement.

We were in a little green valley among the last undulations of the ground, and among soft, round hills which were, no doubt, the last outlying heights of that rugged chain of mountains which we had crossed, and which stood out in the east, still high on our horizon. At the opening of the valley we saw the prairie, level and monotonous, losing itself in the distance.

We had stopped for the last preparations. The morning journey had been glorious. We had been obliged to wait for our departure until the gates of Kalgan were opened, for by a custom which no doubt dates from times of war and sudden attacks, the cities of China close their gates every evening and have them guarded by soldiers. Through the deserted street we arrived at a closed door and came up to a sentinel sleeping at his post. The sentinel awoke, the gate was opened, and in the first light of the dawn we ran down the narrow valley of the Shi-shan-ho, zigzagging over the pebbles of the river in order to avoid boulders and stones.

The valley, enclosed between steep hills, was still full of shadow when the rocky summits of the mountains began to catch the flame of the early sunbeams. Daylight was triumphing above, and the night was fleeing before its face. Yet the darkness seemed to wish rather to hide than to flee: it did not want to be routed. It delayed its scattering, and veiled with purple shadows the winding gorge up which we made our way at a speed of twenty miles an hour.

In this swift flight the open exhaust-pipes gave out deafening explosions as violent as rifleshots, and coming in such close succession that we felt as if we had with us a machine-gun in full action. The echo of this sound filled the valley. We had to shout before we could hear one another. Pietro seemed terrified. For we were taking Pietro with us, on top of the luggage. He was hanging on to the rope in order to resist the swaying and leaping of the motor car, and he remained silent and still, wishing perhaps in his heart that he could be at that moment on the back of the wildest horse in China rather than where he was.

'Is it all right, Pietro?' Prince Borghese, who was driving, would ask him from time to time in perfect good faith.

And Pietro, with eloquent hesitation: 'Y – y – y –yes . . .'

Over a height by the side of the road rises a great rock strangely like the ruin of some medieval castle, with sharp peaks which seem the remnants of old towers. Down from the valley you can see the sky through an opening in this strange building of nature like the arch of some massive bridge. In the light of dawn that singular natural edifice, still dark, but clearly outlined against the blue sky, has a singular impressiveness. The Mongolians who pass along that valley look at it with an almost religious veneration. There is a legend concerning that rock. One day Genghis Khan, the Conqueror, who is a god now in Mongolian records, as he passed at the head of an army over the same road which we were now following in our motor car, stopped under this strange castle built by chance, and, as if he found in it something hostile and warlike, he took an arrow from his quiver, fitted it to the string, and shot at the rock. The arrow struck hard upon it. And the effect of this imperial archery is that hole. That bridgelike opening is nothing but the wound received by the mountain and made by Genghis Khan. It is true that the wound is so great that a mounted man, and perhaps even a motor car, could pass through it. But who can tell how large were the arrows of Genghis Khan, or how powerful were his arms?

Towards the end the valley grows narrow and the river rumbles deep down in its depth. We began our last ascent. The other cars, behind, followed us slowly. At the foot of the steepest part we waited for the coolies, who had left Kalgan on the night before but had not yet arrived. We were observing an old temple half-way up when we saw a curious figure appear on the stony path before us. It was a very tall and very thin Chinese, a kind of great dried-up mummy, carrying very carefully a dish full of eggs, a teapot, and some cups, and when he saw that we were watching him he began to bow deeply as he approached. His yellow, bony face had a smile like the grin of a skull. He put down his dish, poured out the tea into the cups and offered it to us; then he offered us the eggs and bid us welcome. We owed the honour of his acquaintance to the Ta Tsum-ba. Our good friend had sent word that the authorities of all the places which we were to cross should do us homage. But in those half-deserted regions there was only one authority, and it was precisely that good, smiling mummy, the head of a scarce and poor population nestling on the side of the mountain; so he had come down at dawn as far as the little temple, and there had set himself to boil our water and cook our eggs and await us. When he had seen us from afar he had started off to meet us, swinging out on his long, thin legs. We were friendly in our greeting, and the 'authority' hastened to lay a little notebook before us, making signs that we were to write in it.

'What!' we exclaimed, 'a collector of autographs?'

'He want writing,' Pietro explained, 'to show the Ta Tsum-ba he have obeyed orders.'

'Ah! a testimonial, then.'

And the prince and I wrote all the possible and imaginable good about the thin man, who in the meantime had subsided, and was restoring his strength on eggs and tea.

The coolies arrived with five mules, and a few minutes later the valley of the Shi-shan-ho was disappearing from our sight in the distance below.

We were climbing the last buttresses of the 'Big' Great Wall.

Of the immense Wan-li-chang-cheng, the towers alone remain. Between them stretches a long heap of stones, all that is left of the fallen walls. The skeleton of the walls was of mud, but that of the towers of stone, and this is why, after twenty-one centuries of existence, those towers are still at their posts on the watch. They were built in the third century BC. Since then cities have disappeared, nations have been dispersed, civilizations have crumbled away, and powers have fallen – but they still remain. They remain chiefly perhaps because they are useless: in this world, all things useless and superfluous endure marvellously, for no one touches them.

Those towers thus isolated on the bare back of the mountain look from afar of a prodigious size. They rise at equal intervals within calling distance of one another. They were purposely so built in order that the cry of the sentinel's voice might be passed along the chain. One tower called to another in the night.

The motor car, dragged by the coolies, went over a winding path, but the prince and I climbed the rocks in a straight line until we reached the first towers. There we stopped, full of admiration for the sublime sight which opened before us in the luminous clearness of the morning air. We could see the endless Mongolian tableland far enough to appear almost like an ocean, broken up on the west and suddenly coming to an end with an overhanging brow over the plains of the Hwan-ho, falling down upon it like an immense blue cataract. Below, near to us, was a strange landscape like the landscape of a dream. A huge pile of reddish hills, cut, tortured, furrowed in every direction by a thousand crevices; sterile, varied and yet similar, like the waves of the sea, and so dimmed by the distance that they took on a fantastic shade as of the living flesh; a rosy chaos, a motionless storm. To the east rose the gigantic mountains of the Great Khinghan chain, an imposing array of peaks, shading off, as it were, dissolving, in the excess of light. And beyond these, we knew, lay the vast plains of Manchuria. Shortly afterwards we began to descend. We were entering Mongolia. It was eight o'clock. In the valley at our feet we could see the roofs of miserable villages huddling together in the folds of the mountains to shelter themselves from the winds of the desert.

You go down for a little, northwards, and almost immediately you find yourself on the prairie. The region of the rocks comes to an end with those towers. You are in a different land. If China has no longer any frontier lines on those peaks, Nature jealously preserves hers. We passed a caravan station: about fifty ox-carts laden with furs and coming from Sair-ussu stood in a line close by a poor hut. The oxen, freed from their yoke, grazed freely all around: small black oxen they were, with long horns, and of a special breed strong enough to endure the fatigue and privations of long journeys. From the hut a Chinese came out, another dignitary, but without eggs or tea, who in deference to the orders of the Ta Tsum-ba was here to offer his services. Prince Borghese only asked for one favour – that he would show us the way to the Camel road, as we were still on the road to Sair-ussu. The Chinese told us to continue to the first post station, which we should recognize easily 'because it has a flag and some soldiers, but especially because there is not another building within a radius of many miles'. We therefore ran no risk of a mistake. From the post station onwards we were simply to follow the telegraph lines. The telegraph, our official guide, was now entering upon its service.

An hour later we stopped in a meadow near the post station. We were about thirty miles from Kalgan. About eleven o'clock the other cars joined us there, and now the last feverish preparations began. The definite arrangement of our luggage was a very long and difficult operation. We built it up into a pile, and had to pull the pile down again constantly; there was always something too much in it, or else something was left behind. On the grass were scattered furs, biscuit boxes, bags, and ropes. All things not strictly necessary were given to the coolies: camp-beds, mattresses, empty cans. The engines were overhauled, tested again, examined afresh. The Itala was covered by a large square hood, supported at the corners by four iron staves, and at night that same hood taken down from the car and opened in a different manner was to serve as our shelter.

Around us had now gathered a new public. There were Chinese soldiers armed with rifles who had come from a southern mud fortress; caravan drivers who had abandoned their convoys for the moment in order to come and see what these extraordinary doings in the prairie might mean; Mongolian inhabitants of the neighbouring *yurtas* who had gathered together, bringing with them their moon-faced wives with their wild-looking hair covered with ornaments. All these people crowded around us, watching the car with cautious curiosity, and following our movements with profound and open-mouthed attention, as if they were attributing to every movement of us, incomprehensible foreigners, a great and mysterious significance. They had the expression with which one watches the incantations of a wizard. In order to keep the crowd at a convenient distance Ettore described a large circle round the Itala, tracing it with the end of an iron bar, and nobody dared to pass that terrible sign.

It was in vain that we sought to pack our baggage in the space destined to it. Beside the load of the tanks, we carried with us a supplementary provision of fuel and oil, bundles of tyres, and food for ten days, and we thought it too risky to leave behind any of these things. The luggage had to be spread over the back seat as well. We agreed to travel all three of us on the front of the car, two on the seat and the third man at their feet, sitting on the left of the floor of the car with his legs on the running board. The position of this third man was not very comfortable, but we were to take it in turns. Ettore was the first victim. It was two p.m. when we started on our way, after a hasty lunch chiefly consisting of corned beef. The prince was at the wheel. The other cars came immediately after us.

Pietro had already left, in order that he might be at Kalgan before the closing of the gates. He had said goodbye to us, thanking us effusively in his very best and most elegant speech, as though, indeed, we had done him the greatest favour by bringing him about 200 miles' distance from Peking, and had then disappeared in the direction of the Great Wall, followed by his coolies.

We ran down the valley and broke out upon the plain. The hills closed behind us as the distance between them and ourselves grew greater. They huddled into the appearance of a receding shore. We were launched.

After the first few yards we made a painful discovery. The excessive weight of the things we were carrying pressed so greatly upon the back spring that at the slightest leap of the car the chassis came down heavily upon the differential casing. We had to go slowly, but the ground was uneven, and the blows still fell frequently.

'We will break either the springs or the differential!' exclaimed Ettore, who looked as if the thuds fell upon his own heart.

'There is no immediate danger,' replied the prince, still quite cool. 'But the car cannot stand this for long. We shall have to lighten it.'

'Immediately?'

'No, at the first stop. We shall not go very far.'

'What shall we take from the load?'

'Everything we can possibly spare. We'll see.'

In the meantime there was some improvement in the surface of the road. For a few hundred yards we found it even possible to go quickly. From time to time we came upon tiny Chinese villages, surrounded by fields of barley and of *kao-liang*, scattered like oases over the desert plain. These represent Chinese colonization; for China is invading slowly but surely all the so-called lands of conquest in Turkestan, as in Mongolia. With small garrisons and a very few officials she rules immense regions inhabited by a warlike but scattered people. The Chinese emigrants overflow into these regions, and their agrarian instincts attach them to the land. They represent agriculture, invading little by little the land of nomadic tribes. This is a greater force than that of armies, because the nomad does not love the earth and does not defend it. He withdraws towards the free spaces; he yields without knowing it. The Chinese people are spreading now towards the west as they have not done for centuries. It is a recent phenomenon which is taking place quietly and unobserved in the heart of Asia. The expansion of China, baulked on the coastline by the interests of the whole civilized world, finds an outlet landward. It gains in certain provinces as much as fifty or sixty miles in ten years, and this manner of colonization has a wonderful power. It transforms the inhabitants; it turns them all into Chinese. There are in western Mongolia ancient centres of life where no Mongolian, but only Chinese, is spoken.

It was near one of these villages that we encamped that night. At the strange sight of our coming, the women fled, springing painfully on their deformed feet, to hide in the plantations on the other side of their dwelling places. They were afraid of us. The men, on the contrary, came to look at us while we were changing the hood of the automobile into our camp tent – a great tent held up in the centre by the car itself, and so arranged as to shelter the machine as well as our own persons. A short distance away, the de Dion-Boutons, the Spyker and the Contal, arranged themselves in the ingenious manner used for military convoys, that is, with the cars in a circle and the tents at the centre.

Prince Borghese had decided to lighten the Itala by sacrificing the mudguards, the poles destined to support the hood, some iron bars which we carried with us as levers, a pickaxe, and half our provisions. All these things were given away to the Chinese who helped us in our work. One brought us a pail of water and he would get a mudguard; another one supplied us with eggs and he would receive a pickaxe. Those good people thought us quite mad, but they went home gaily, dragging iron bars after them, or nursing tins of jam in a fold of their dress. And now we lighted our bivouac fires.

Truth to tell, the bivouac fires are more picturesque in descriptions than in reality. In Mongolia there is an entire absence of any vegetable fuel, and the inhabitants have to burn duly dried and prepared camel's dung. Our companions were provided with beautiful pressure-stoves, but we had not foreseen the difficulty and had with us no apparatus of the kind, so that we had to have recourse as cheerfully as we could to our soldering-lamp. Such were the 'bivouac fires' around which in our shirtsleeves we busied ourselves. Du Taillis superintended the cooking of a most wonderful soup which you buy in cakes, like chocolate, and which contains all the principles of nutrition. I, with my soldering-lamp, tried to coax a kettle to boiling-point. It will be seen that the cooking was left to journalism, but – I am sorry to own it, for the sake of the journalistic profession – the results in the Italian field were deplorable: our dinner smelt of petrol, oil, and grease.

Three mounted Mongols suddenly appeared upon the scene. We had met them and passed them two hours previously. One of them, an athletic-looking youth, was dressed in purple silk with a yellow pointed hat, embroidered, and also of silk. He looked like a chief. They dismounted and tethered their horses, spread out some carpets near us, lit a fire of camel's dung (of which the Mongolians always carry a little bagful on their travels), and they squatted. The silk-clad youth approached us with great bows, smiling and showing Chinese curiosity concerning everything he beheld. He started an active but mysterious conversation with us, during which each side made heroic efforts towards understanding the other. Fortunately, Prince Borghese possessed a precious manuscript which contained a few hundred Mongolian words and their translation. So we succeeded in understanding that our interlocutor really was a chief, and that we were due to pass near his village, and that he wished to invite us to stop in his house. All this was certainly worth a few tins of corned beef, and we delivered them with due ceremony into the hands of this illustrious personage, whose joy and gratitude knew no bounds.

Suddenly we heard the sound of a galloping horse advancing towards us. It was now dark, and we only recognized the newcomer to be a Chinese soldier, when he stopped a few feet away, asking:

'Po-lu-ghe-se?'

The prince recognized in those curious sounds the Chinese rendering of his name, and went up to the soldier. The latter dismounted and delivered some papers to him. It was the post – the last post from Peking – which had reached Kalgan at nine o'clock that morning. That man had covered more than sixty miles in about eleven hours. He had been ordered by the Tu Tung to overtake us, and so he had overtaken us. As soon as his mission was done, and before it had occurred to us to stop him, he had mounted again and galloped off. What wonderful soldiers these Chinese would make, if they only had just a *little* courage!

That unexpected arrival of news in the middle of the prairie, at the solemn hour of night when solitude seems sadder and deeper, gave us a strange thrill. Our letters were greetings, good wishes, friendly voices reaching us at the gate of the desert, and they seemed to us in that place more significant and more precious. When we had run through our correspondence in the evening twilight we remained together conversing, seated on the luggage, smoking, while things around us grew dimmer and were gradually lost in the darkness, and the very outline of our faces disappeared little by little in the deepening shadow. Darkness seems to isolate and separate one; it ends by making one silent because it gives the sensation of being alone. And when in the darkness nothing else could be seen distinctly but the tiny red speck of our lighted cigarettes and a faint white colour of the papers on the ground, we became entirely silent. The blue sky was dotted with a thousand stars.

Our Mongolian companions had fallen asleep round the dead fire. Another Mongolian had joined them on a camel, and the humps of the animal as it lay there motionless showed up against the dying light in the west, assuming a grandeur like that of a monument, and reminding me of those gigantic stone camels we had seen adorning the tombs of the Mings. We could hear the horses grazing a little way off. The Chinese had disappeared.

'Well, now let us lie down,' exclaimed Prince Borghese; 'tomorrow we shall have to get up at three.'

We made ready our sleeping places under the tent, and then began to get together our things, which were lying about on the ground. I noticed at once that a number of small things were missing: a knife, a silver mug, a hunting case. And yet they were there quite a short while ago – I had used them myself. Were there robbers about? The discovery of these thefts was not reassuring. At that moment the prince asked me:

'Did you take the cartridges?'

'What cartridges?'

'The revolver cartridges that were just here.'

'No.'

'They have been stolen, then. They are all gone. Our only useful weapon now is a Mauser pistol. Unless they have stolen also . . .'

'The cartridges for that?' I asked, with a certain uneasiness.

'Just so. No, those are here. They were among the luggage. We will load the Mauser anyway.'

'Let's keep on the alert. A theft of cartridges is a serious matter.'

'Ettore, keep the pistol within reach.'

I went to our French friends to tell them about this matter, and they too lay down with their weapons within reach.

But we never had in our whole life a more tranquil night than that. The robbers, who probably were only the inhabitants of the neighbouring village, were content with the possession of the cartridges, the mug, the knife, and the other small objects which they had already taken, and they kept prudently at a distance. On our side, we learnt how to be more on guard against admirers.

That night the piercing cold pursued us even under our furs, and it awakened us some time before dawn, while we could still see, through the slits of our tent, the firmament glimmering over our heads.

When we got up, we found that the Mongolians had gone away before us.

The first of us to leave camp was the Contal tricycle. The night before it had reached our camp considerably later than any of us. It had been stopped several times by the irregularities of the road. On certain points it had had to be pushed by its two willing and dauntless drivers, and the engine had at times been greatly heated by its efforts to overcome the obstacles of the road. The tricycle, then, had been the first to leave, in order that it might have a handicap in its favour over the 130 miles or so which we had agreed to do that day. This had been decreed by unanimous voting.

About an hour after the tricycle had left, the two de Dion-Boutons and the Spyker also left close upon one another. We were kept back by our luggage; we *could* not find a suitable way of arranging it. Our luggage, indeed, was a thorn in our side until nearly the end of the journey. It was a torment to us, a nightmare. In the building and preparing of the car, everything had been foreseen, considered, and ingeniously provided for – except room for the luggage. No way was provided of disposing of it or of adequately securing it. We were obliged to tie it with ropes fastened to the different parts of the car. But the ropes, which shrank in the damp of the night, stretched out again in the sunshine, and got loose, so that the load changed place, swayed, gave way: and this meant long hours of work before we could fasten it up again.

The sun was rising when we started. It was nearly five o'clock. We followed the traces of the other vehicles over the wet grass. After passing near some small Chinese colonies we found a path, and an hour later we caught up with the Contal, which had stopped. Pons and his companion had alighted and seemed occupied in working at something in the engine. The prince, who was driving, slowed down in order to give help if needed. But after an exchange of greetings Pons told us to go on, saying he did not require anything. We thought that he was waiting until the engine, perhaps over-heated, should have cooled down a little; and so we got up speed again. Half an hour later we overtook the other cars, which were advancing singly. We greeted them and went on. The next meeting place was the telegraph station of Pong-kiong.

Our efforts to lighten the load of the car had produced the desired effect. The springs were elastic again, and the chassis remained at a reasonable distance from the differential. The Itala was going at twenty miles an hour.

Suddenly we noticed that the telegraph poles were almost disappearing on the horizon to our left. We probably had taken the road which leads to the River Kerulen, to the east of Urga. We retraced our steps.

No more Chinese fields now, nor mud huts. There lay before us only the wild plain, green and even. From time to time some low group of slate rocks broke the monotony of the slightly undulated horizon. The solitude was so deep that the sight of a man was an event to which we called one another's attention.

'A man riding . . . down there!'

'He's seen us. He's galloping.'

It was like being on board during a long sea voyage when the passengers call one another up to the bridge, saying, 'Look, there's a boat . . . down there!'

We came to a small herd of those little squat, strong Mongolian ponies, which have such wonderful endurance, and which gave proof of it by providing the only means of transport during the Tartar conquest of China.

An inexplicable curiosity drew those horses towards us. As soon as the strange noise of our engine, never heard by them before, reached them echoing in the great stillness of the plain, they all raised their heads from the ground and turned towards us, and the sight of this fleeing monster seemed to give them no fear, although they usually are timid animals. Perhaps they felt some curious affinity with that swift-running thing. And they would come, arriving all together, with one great onrush. They seemed to want to annihilate us with one furious charge. They ran with a peculiar mad stampede, which in the pampas is called a *desperada* and which passes like a hurricane destroying everything. But at ten yards' distance from us they would suddenly stop with stiffened knees, with the promptness and cleverness of Arabian horses in a *fantasia*. Then they would start again, running by the side of the car, and would accompany us at a gallop until we had outrun them. Then, suddenly, they would change direction and scatter and return to their wild pastures. It was a magnificent sight, especially when the strange escort was galloping by our side, and we had under our eyes all the beauty, the spring, the energy of the horse in a free, wild gallop.

The same manoeuvre would be repeated almost unaltered by each herd – could it have been suggested to the horses by some common instinct? What was passing across their little brains? They seemed to be guided by the hand of an invisible rider, so disciplined were they. One would think that the present horse has inherited the warlike spirit of its ancestors in the invading Tartar armies.

Scattered shepherds stood about near their cattle: long, fine-coated cattle, which are sold in large numbers every winter in the great market-places of Peking. A few of the men tried to approach us, urging their horses to the greatest possible speed, but to their very great surprise they were not able to overtake us. Then they would stop to look at us, without moving, until we disappeared below the line of their horizon.

There were moments when we were running at a speed of thirty or thirty-five miles an hour. Never had Mongolia been traversed so swiftly. We would have outdone even the famous coursers of Genghis Khan, which rode so swiftly from one end of the immense empire to the other, bringing the emperor's orders and the news of his victories.

That speed inebriated and dazed us. Not so much for the physical sensation of its swiftness, not so much for the mad joy of flight which is the essence of the passion of the motor car, but rather through a deep, full, and inexpressible intellectual satisfaction, that came from being *there*. At times we were caught by a sense of surprise, the lucidity of our thought was veiled as in a dream, unreasonable doubts clouded the clearness of our perception, we forgot ourselves and then remembered suddenly, and interrupted the long silence, saying to one another:

'We are in Mongolia!'

'Yes!'

Once Prince Borghese suddenly turned to me, saying:

'I try to realize that we are soon to cross the Gobi desert – I can't believe it!'

I had been thinking the same thing that moment. There was in us an inexplicable mixture of confidence, resoluteness, determination, and vague incredulity. It was something like the feeling of one who, determined upon victory, throws himself armed to meet his enemy in a mist. When we thought of the nature of the ground, the stability of the weather, the powers of our machine and our own powers, we felt confident. But when we tried to visualize the distant places on the globe of the world, and when we called those strange lands by their names, then our certainty failed us. The problem seemed then to go beyond pure technicalities; it seemed to comprise many incalculable elements. We were a prey to the mysterious and awful fascination of Asia. The desert became personified in our mind; that terrible adversary of man, that destroyer of caravans, that feared divinity of death would defend it. We thought of it as of an undaunted mighty power. The very word *desert* inspired us with awe.

From time to time we saw a *yurta*, low and round, like a beehive. That small grey cupola covered with felt is the habitation of the Asiatic nomad tribes, of the Kirghese and the Turkomans, exactly alike on the banks of the Aral and of the Irtysch and of the Tola; and it alone would suffice to prove the common origin of all the races of the centre of Asia, their common descent from the Great Mongolian trunk. I had seen the same *yurtas* in Russia at Mukden.

The roaring of our car reached as far as those huts, and the men would come out precipitately, looking and making broad gestures of surprise; sometimes they would leap on to the backs of horses grazing close by them, and would follow us obstinately, shouting and waving their long shepherds' crooks as if they were lances.

It must have been about eight in the morning when we arrived in the neighbourhood of a small group of *yurtas*, a regular little encampment. There were some men on the look-out upon a sort of scaffolding, and they gave the alarm. Then followed a confused crowd running towards the road, and making signs to us. When they arrived within a moderate distance, we recognized among them our good Mongolian chief of the day before, clad in his gorgeous purple robe, making violent signs to us that we should stop. This was his village, and he wished to honour us with his hospitality. He was so effusive and whole-hearted that we could not disappoint him and continue on our road, as we should have wished, and the Itala, with a beautiful sweeping curve, came to a stop within the enclosure of the Mongolian camp.

A moment later we were sitting in a circle in a most beautiful *yurta*, that of the chief.

In the centre was a lighted fire, and its acrid smoke, slightly perfumed with musk, went up through the central opening of the cupola. A fine old man, the father of our friend, entertained us ceremoniously with a pontifical stateliness of movement, and an old woman, his mother, placed respectfully before us dishes of cheese, bowls of sour milk and cream, cups of smoking tea, and glasses full of a sweet, clear liquor made with fermented milk. The glasses, of a European make, had been taken out with the most jealous care from a little Chinese cupboard of which the old man kept the key: that was a treasure-cupboard, the family safe. We saw reposing in it the tins of corned beef presented by us the day before. While we were conscientiously imbibing a quantity of milk, we heard some words which gave us a shock of surprise.

'*Sprechen Sie Deutsch?*'

A young Mongolian, just arrived, had uttered that simple and so entirely astounding question. He spoke with an excellent German accent.

'*Ja,*' replied the prince, at the height of astonishment. '*Ich spreche Deutsch.*'

And the young Mongolian began to converse in Goethe's native tongue. He asked what was the speed of our machine, and found the answer satisfactory.

'But where did you learn to speak German?' asked Prince Borghese.

'In Berlin. A distant place is Berlin!'

'In Berlin?'

'Yes, I was there two years.'

'Oh! And what did you do there?'

'I did the Mongolian,' he replied gravely.

We thought he was joking, or that perhaps he had not understood our question.

'What were you doing in Berlin?'

'I was a Mongolian! I was a Mongolian!' he repeated deliberately. Then he added: 'I was at an exhibition, you see. There were people of all races. There was an encampment of Mongolian *yurtas* with its horses, its dogs, and its women. And a great crowd came to see us every day and spoke to us, so I learnt German.'

'Do you like Europe?'

'Yes. And you, do you like Mongolia?'

'Very much.'

He seemed satisfied with us and with this answer, which showed him how enlightened our judgement was.

When we came out again we found a group of horsemen cantering round the motor car, and Ettore, seated upon the latter, serenely drinking his portion of milk. All the male inhabitants of the encampment were preparing to escort us, and had got to their horses.

We started at high speed, surrounded by this picturesque cavalcade, with the clatter of fast-falling hoofs upon the hard earth and the sound of the men's long, wild cry. Around us many-coloured garments and long ribbons, which the Mongolians wear hanging from their pointed hats, fluttered in the wind; and manes and pigtails flew behind. But our guests were mistaken about their chances of accompanying us. In vain they urged on their horses by voice and whip, in vain the poor animals hurled themselves on, *ventre à terre*. A moment later our car outstripped its escort, the sound of which was lost in the distance, and we were alone again in the grassy wilds.

Many of those men were lamas. You could tell them by their shaven heads; they had no other signs of their priesthood. There are so many lamas in Mongolia that they comprise the greater part of the male population. If the father of a family has five sons, he gives up three to be lamas. There are shepherd lamas, caravan lamas, lamas who deal in horses: they must needs follow the trades of the people when they comprise a whole people themselves. The whole of Mongolia is an immense convent, but lamaism has quenched the ancient valour of the race: a people of warriors has become a people of philosophers.

We travelled on for several hours. The landscape around us changed at intervals, when the stretch of the prairie was broken by vast tracts of land, quite sterile except for a little short, thick grass. The nature of the soil changed too. We passed from pebbly tracts to sand and then again to the irregularity of short, stony passes. Then came prairies again; but we saw no more droves or herds, no more smoking *yurtas*. The sun was scorching. We met a convoy of camels drawing curious little two-wheeled carts. Another caravan was encamped near a well. Few and far between, figures of riders would appear on the line of the horizon.

A little later we found no sign of life except around the wells, and these we could detect from an enormous distance by the confused groups of camels and of blue tents which always gathered round them.

If you look at a good map of Mongolia, you will find names and dots along the lines of the caravan roads, and you will receive the impression that these mark villages and towns. They only mark wells. Every well has its name. It is only a small hole in the earth, in whose depths the water quivers and sparkles, and yet it has the importance of a city: it means life, it *is* the life of the traveller. It is the life of commerce, the life of cities, placed a thousand miles apart, which prosper through that commerce; the life of far-off populations, which that commerce and those cities feed. The riches of Kalgan, the riches of Kiakhta, have drawn their sustenance from the wells lost among the solitudes of the Mongolian plain.

The wells mark the halting places of the caravans. They are at a distance of twenty to fifty miles from one another. In the winter you camp round them by night; in the summer by day. You put the harness and loads of the camels apart in a line. At each end of this line you fix a lance in the earth, more through the following of a tradition than as a present threat; then the men encamp and the animals are left free to pasture, if there is any pasture around.

We too stopped at the wells to draw water for our machine, and to slake our thirst and refresh our hands and our face, and we would then spend a few minutes with the caravan drivers, who gazed at us with a respect only equalled by their surprise. Those good people gave us no sign of hostility. They called to heel their big, fierce, long-coated watchdogs, and sometimes they helped us to draw the water with certain implements of theirs made with a skin and a stick. But they always avoided touching us.

By midday we might have thought we were in the heart of the desert. Our car fled over almost entirely barren soil. The earth was of a reddish colour and had undulations, sometimes gradual but at other times sudden, which obliged the prince to keep his attention always fixed on the road, in order that the car should not come down with too much force on the inequalities of the ground: for the springs might have broken. Any slackening of the speed made us feel the heat more intensely. We were tired, dazed by the sun and the light. We were beginning to regret our abandoned hood and its shade.

Halfway up a short but steep climb, the car suddenly stopped. The fuel in the tank was exhausted. This tank held 83 litres, sufficient for about 130 miles; and we had not yet reached the telegraph station of Pong-kiong, which we had thought was little more than 110 miles from our last stopping-place. Could it be that we had passed it? We had not always followed the lines very scrupulously; we had occasionally slackened our attention, and Pong-kiong might possibly be at some distance from the main line of the telegraph poles, connected with it by some branch wires . . .

We asked ourselves all these questions, feeling by no means cheerful, whilst Ettore put into operation an ingenious system to syphon the petrol from the supply tanks into the engine. The day was so hot that we saw the vapours of the fuel rising in wide transparent spirals, through which the outline of the objects beyond it looked tremulous.

As we busied ourselves round the automobile on this halt, we discovered another serious mishap. A portion of the load was missing. It had fallen off, through a slackening of the ropes. We had lost the entire personal luggage of the prince!

What were we to do? Go back to look for the luggage and for Pong-kiong?

We decided to continue on our way.

We persuaded ourselves that the luggage of two people might be made to do for three; also that if Pong-kiong was left behind, we could do without that halting place and could afford to plunge immediately into the desert, seeing that our store of water was intact, and that we had victuals for five days and fuel for 500 miles. We mounted again and were off.

The ground was easier. For stretches of ten miles at a time it would offer an excellent track, which allowed us to go at the highest speed. A little thin, grey grass would show up here and there, and by the marks on it we could trace the quaint zigzag paths followed by the camels. Caravans do not always follow a single road. They simply walk in the same direction, but form hundreds of parallel paths, which make one think of furrows made by some ancient gigantic plough.

At a certain point we saw far away in the distance a dark dot, which might have been a hut. As we approached it, the dot became rectangular. It spread, it appeared what it was, namely, a mud-coloured little wall. We were going at a speed of about twenty miles an hour, and it was not long before we could see a mud roof showing behind this little wall. A line of telegraph poles approached that wretched-looking little building, which was so much lower than themselves.

'Pong-kiong, Pong-kiong!' we called out, with the same ring in our voices that Columbus's sailors must have had in theirs when they called out their famous cry, 'Land! land!'

Obviously, we had miscalculated our distance by about twenty miles.

Pong-kiong was not on our map, and we had only been able to guess at the most probable site of it.

'Pong-kiong – that thing down there?' asked Ettore, full of contempt for it. 'I thought that Pong-kiong was a village!'

'Of course not. It's a well. A well and a telegraph station. That's all.'

But that 'all' entirely satisfied us.

Had we seen the most marvellous palace in the world rising before us at that moment, we should not have been happier.

VII

IN THE GOBI DESERT

~~~~~~~~~

The Telegraph in the Desert – The Contal still Missing –
On a dry Sea-basin – The Effects of the Sun – Udde

At the well of Pong-kiong we were expected. The little Chinese telegraph clerk who has charge of this station came to meet us outside his enclosure, and received us with great signs of joy.

It is a matter of great regret to me that I cannot remember the name of this hero, who lives in the desert in order that the East and the West may commune. The nearest town, Kalgan, is almost 200 miles away; Urga is 500 miles. No matter what may happen to that man, he cannot escape from his post. The very vastness of the space around him serves for him as a prison. Before he can reach the haunts of men he has to travel for a week from well to well. No one can give him assistance. The isolation of a prisoner in the cell of an ancient fort is not so absolute or so terrible as this. The prisoner feels the life of the world, its echoes reach him, and he can associate his thoughts to them . . . The most frightful thing in the desert is its silence.

True, the little Chinese at Pong-kiong is supported in his solitude by two joys: a little girl and the telegraph apparatus. His affection for these two objects fills his existence. The little girl is his daughter; the apparatus is his friend. For long hours he is wrapped in the tick-tack of keys and receivers, listening in them to the voices of the far-off world – voices from St Petersburg, from London, from Tokyo. He merely transmits the messages; the news passes him: orders, mysterious diplomatic communications, passionate words go by. When the great conversation of the continents is over, the telegraphist takes advantage of the clear line himself, and then a less important conversation commences. The operators in the desert greet one another, tell one another the small news of the day, their trials, their hopes. These conversations take the place of the daily paper for those hermits.

The telegraph station of Pong-kiong resembles the home of the

Chinese peasant: three small buildings, low, made of mud, lighted within by large *grilles* covered with paper, which occupy the whole of one wall of the room. These buildings form three sides of a square, and are surrounded by a wall with a single entrance on the south side, crowned by a number of telegraph insulators, curious ornaments, which resemble a gruesome row of white teeth over a dead jaw. Against the wall on the north side the wind has collected a heap of sand. On windy days the sand penetrates everywhere. It comes through the shutters, it enters every room, and the sky grows dark and the air grows dim. Outside you cannot see more than two steps before you. The telegraph wires shriek and howl; the darkness is such that lamps have to be lit. The last storm had been raging four days before our arrival.

Three other men live with the telegraph clerk in that enclosure: two Chinese and one Mongolian, charged with keeping the line in good repair. They have to repair the wires broken by the storms, and to erect the fallen poles. To help them in their labours they have three camels at their service. The camels are left to graze in the neighbouring fields, and we had seen them on our arrival. They had stretched out towards us their funny, peaceful, wrinkled, and satisfied faces of antediluvian animals.

The best room was ready for us. Upon the *kang* were flaming red rugs and cushions, and on a table was a superb Singapore pineapple, just taken out of its box, all fresh and fragrant – a delicious sight. We threw ourselves first upon the pineapple, and then upon the rugs; and there, stretched out on that *triclinium*, I summed up the impressions of the day, in writing, on the imperial telegraph forms.

When our host took over my dispatch I sat down by his side in front of the apparatus. He seemed embarrassed. He consulted the Chinese regulations, looked at regulation tariffs, counted again and again the words of the telegram, and then carefully wrote on the top of the form '*No. 1.*'

'Is it the first telegram of the day?' I asked.

'No, sir,' he replied. 'It is the first from this office.'

'I beg your pardon?'

'Your telegram is the first to start from the office of Pong-kiong.'

'This year, do you mean?'

'No, sir, from the time the office was started, six years ago.'

'In six years you have not sent one telegram?'

'Not one.'

'Then why ever is there an office?' I asked, after a pause, still full of astonishment.

'Because the distances are too great and we have need of relay stations.'

Our conversation was interrupted. Kalgan was answering. My telegram had now started on its journey.

Kalgan was to receive it, and would pass it to Peking. Peking would transmit it to Shanghai, Shanghai to Hong Kong, Hong Kong to Singapore, Singapore to Aden, Aden to Malta; Malta would forward it to Gibraltar, and Gibraltar to London. It would take eight to ten hours to reach its destination, but Pong-kiong is eight hours in advance of central Europe, and the dispatch would, by the clock, arrive only two hours after its departure. It was now 4.15; between six and seven p.m. my telegram would be in the editorial offices of the *Daily Telegraph* and the *Corriere della Sera*, and the following morning English and Italian readers would know what our motor cars had been doing today in the desert of Mongolia! There is something so great in these human victories over time and space by means of wires and sparks that there are moments when the soul even of a journalist, most accustomed of all to the marvels of speed, is overcome by a sense of wonder and of pride.

About six o'clock the other cars arrived. We spied them from a distance, when they still were but the tiniest specks over the endless even ground, so distant that they seemed motionless like ships on the horizon. The Spyker was the first to enter the enclosure, where Ettore was overhauling our car, and where I was obstinately trying to induce a piece of lamb, harder than any tyre, to consent to be cooked. Du Taillis jumped down from his seat, holding up a grey bag and crying:

'Who does this belong to?'

It was Prince Borghese's baggage. To find the lost luggage, as well as finding Pong-kiong, seemed the height of good fortune. And yet there are people who manage to get lost in the desert.

'Did you pick it up long ago?' I said.

'Oh, yes, a good many hours ago. We were still on the grassy stretch.'

'Was it left on the road?'

'No. As we passed, some Mongolians made great signs to us. We stopped, and then they gave us that piece of luggage, making us understand by signs that it must have been lost by you.'

'Mongolians? Honest barbarians? Miserable people of the wild who give themselves the luxury of returning picked-up goods?'

'Yes, and without even asking for a tip!'

'But my dear friend, where ever have they gone to, the brigands of the prairies? Those men whose actual duty it was to be to assault us.'

'They are probably gone to Europe.'

'But this is the downfall of all the romance of travel! It was scarcely worth while coming to this remote desert to receive gifts of milk and the restitution of our baggage.'

'It's just *too* sad!'

We waited in vain for the tricycle to arrive. Our companions expressed their settled conviction that Pons had turned back. I telegraphed immediately to this effect. We had no sort of anxiety as to the fate of Pons and of his companion; they were still in the inhabited zone, and could, no doubt, easily find hospitality and help.

Several hours later, the piece of lamb proved as rebellious against mastication as it had been against cooking. The telegraph clerk who had got it for us was greatly distressed. We comforted him by showing him that a hungry European is not daunted even by a dish of parchment, and after this we lay down on the *kangs*.

During the night, the purple light of the moon invaded my room, and I was awakened by it. I raised myself on to my elbow and then for the first time I realized what absolute silence is like. What we usually call silence is only the absence of certain noises and certain voices; it is only the rest from human sounds. But as we listen to it, if we are in the country we hear the rustling of the trees, the waving of the corn, the murmur of waters, the shrill note of insects, the distant howling of dogs; and if we are on the sea we hear the beating of the quiet wave against the side of our boat, like a gentle clapping of hands, or the breaking of high breakers against the rocks. There, I heard *nothing*. There was no vibration, no life. There was the sensation of I know not what fabled emptiness, of an unearthly void. I felt full of anguish: it was as if I had been suspended between the abysses of space. I felt the impression of an infinite isolation.

When I lay my head upon my pillow, I heard the regular, rapid, loud, metallic sound of footsteps. I sat up again with a start, listening. The sound ceased suddenly.

'Bah!' I said to myself. 'It must be the effect of that lamb – it was an indigestible dish!'

I lay down again and the tramping recommenced, distinctly audible in the deep fearful stillness.

Then, completely awakened by the effort of listening, I understood suddenly what that sound was, and I could scarcely withhold a smile. Intending to get up early, I had put my watch under my pillow.

On 19 June by sunrise we were already on our way. We overtook and passed the Spyker, which had left shortly before, and we sped on towards the north. Our next appointment was that evening at Udde, the nearest telegraph station, near another bridge – as far as we could judge, about 170 miles from Pong-kiong.

The morning air was chill, and the first rays of the sun seemed to carry no heat with them. They were almost horizontal, and the car projected a long fantastic shadow which jumped over the tufts of grass and trembled over the sand, passing swiftly like the shadow of a great bird on the wing.

The road was good, and the motor car, in fourth gear at times, flew with quick panting over the stillness of the plain. A few miles from Pong-kiong we found some more green. We were now re-entering a zone of prairies, softly stretching over slight undulations.

'What is that running away down there? – there!' suddenly cried Ettore, pointing to our right.

It was an antelope, about a hundred yards from us. It was making for shelter, with that rapid and elegant bound, typical of antelopes, which is swifter than any gallop.

'Shall we chase it?' I said.

The thought of chasing an antelope with a motor car at sixty miles an hour was extremely seductive, but the prince remarked that a chase might lead us very far out of our way, and that we had a good distance to cover. And there was a further argument in favour of leaving our game alone – we had no rifle.

A moment later, we arrived near a small herd of gazelles, so graceful in all their movements, with their grey backs and their white feet – as lively as young colts. They stopped at some distance from us, and turned their long, flexible necks round our way to look at this new strange being which dared to break into the stillness of their pastures. What they saw seemed not to reassure them, for they took up their flight again in a long line, till they disappeared from our gaze.

Sometimes, though seldom, we also met men. Once five or six Mongolians on horseback tried to race us. They were at half a mile's distance, to the side of us, and they galloped for a long while making wild gestures.

Suddenly we saw appearing, all white, over the deserted prairie, a thing that looked like a palace with small white buildings round it. We turned towards that strange colony. As we drew nearer, it seemed like a vision of ancient times.

After all the learned reconstructions by archaeologists of the architectural styles of ancient Asia, no one can fail to have *some* idea, however imperfect, of the general aspect of the most famous ancient capitals. In thinking of Babylon or Nineveh, for instance, who has not pictured to himself square, massive buildings with walls slightly inclined back like the sides of a pyramid, giving the illusion of majestic fore-shortening? Windows and doors broader at the base, like the windows and doors of mausoleums: the whole ending with terrace-roofs, simple and grand as tombs. Some ruins of ancient Egypt give an instance of that pyramidal slant, which endows walls with a stability capable of enduring for thousands of years, and which has a marvellous effect in perspective, giving to the eye the illusion of an immensity, as if the decreasing upwards was due to some prodigious height. When through photography Lhasa was revealed to us, and we found that type of building repeated there, we were surprised by the extraordinary biblical severity of the Forbidden City, which preserved for us living architectural forms of ancient civilizations. These forms had not reached it from India with its religion, nor from China with its political sovereigns, but must have been transmitted to it by the west of Asia twenty or thirty centuries ago. The seclusion, the stillness, the quietude of Buddhism, which have turned Tibet into a temple, have here kept up at least the tradition, if not the sense, of this art.

We were now before buildings belonging to this same style of architecture; but they were far, of course, from possessing the impress-iveness of the Lhasa temples. The desert yields no materials for con-struction, and who knows whence the stones of this place had come, all carried hither by camel caravans? It was the shape and not the size of them that gave them their wonderful severity of outline. It may even be that much impressiveness was added to them, in our case at least, by the associations which that outline had in our minds, by the analogies which it suggested to us, by the thoughts which it evoked.

The chief building was a temple, all white with lime, adorned at the top by a red frieze with terracotta ornamentations, possessing a simple grace and something of a Greek flavour. Similar ornamentations went round the door and the trapeze-shaped windows, each of them pro-tected by a small roof. Long brass tubes stood out beyond the line of the roof, like the oars of a galley, to gather and pour down the rainwater. The other constructions round this one, though much smaller, re-sembled it exactly; we thought that they must be the dwellings of monks. We left our car and wandered about on foot among those sacred places. No one was about, the place seemed abandoned. We heard not a voice, not a sound.

We were about to return 'on board', when from a little door an old man came out, advancing with small steps. He saw us and stopped. He was tall, dressed in a bizarre costume which left his arms free and bare;

he was thin, with the wrinkled face of an old woman. We approached him, did him reverence, photographed him, spoke to him. He neither moved nor answered. He showed no surprise and no fear. He seemed simply absorbed in a deep meditation upon the mystery of our being and of our presence in these places. He looked at us without being able to understand. In his eyes was the effort of concentration. It would be impossible to guess at his age; he seemed strong, and yet decrepit; on his face were marked the lines of incalculable years.

We got back to our machine, and we turned round to look at him as we were speeding away. He was still there motionless, still gazing upon us, poor, lonely, mystified old man!

The road we followed sloped perceptibly downwards. About eight o'clock we came to a kind of ledge. The meadows had again disappeared. The thick, grey, sparse blades of grass came back, timidly gathering in larger patches, between which were vast zones, sterile and bare. We were now upon the threshold of the real desert.

Gobi, in Mongolian, means a cavity. The desert is an immense depression in the centre of Mongolia – it is the cavity, the *gobi*, which once held a sea. We now stood upon the bank of that departed sea. It was a regular shore, steep, with a sudden falling made by the breaking of the waves. We were now to enter on a lower plane: the bottom of the ancient sea. It had its inlets, its promontories, its little peninsulas clearly visible. Before us the sterile plain stretched to the uttermost distance, undulating, seeming to rise again on the horizon, because of the same optical delusion by which a sea horizon always looks higher than the shore.

A steep descent of about twenty or thirty yards launched us on these hard, flat sands which had once known sea storms. We began a fantastic race across the strangest and most desolate landscape, a race which was both an assault and a flight.

Gradually, as we advanced, the earth became more barren, more squalid, more sad; now flat and even, now irregular on the surface, broken up by sudden uprisings; now made up of crystalline sand that sparkled in the sun; now viscous, the colour of trodden mud. There was no form of life on it, except certain little lizards of a colour so like that of the earth that they became invisible the moment they stopped. You could almost have taken them for tiny bits of the ground, suddenly grown alive and splashing away here and there from under the wheels of the motor car.

The hours succeeded one another with a deadly monotony. The heat with the advancing day became more burning. The air seemed motionless, and we took in with great joy the freshening breath which the speed of the car brought against our faces. We were passing from the coolness of the morning to a tropical temperature, without intermediate zones. We noticed a curious phenomenon: the sun was absolutely burning, yet the shade was still cold; and we had the sensation of one who warms himself before a big fire in the heart of the winter, when he feels himself tingling with heat on the side of the flame, and numb with cold on the other. The sky was of an inexorable limpidity. So limpid was it, that our eye could not measure the distances. We saw everything quite close to us. The horizon seemed always a few miles away, yet we had to run for hours before we could reach any landmark seen clearly at great distances on the brow of some hillock.

This terrible transparency was due to the entire absence of moisture in the atmosphere. The dryness of the air began to cause us a suffering which increased every moment. Our skin was parched as with fever, and the sun beat so hotly on our hands and faces that it was as if there was centred upon us the most powerful light of an immeasurable lens. We had been conscious of the same feeling the day before; indeed, it was upon the road to Pong-kiong that there first came to our minds the simile of a lens, by which to express our sensations; but we had not then guessed that in the real desert the power of the lens would increase by so many degrees. We now understood why caravans never travelled during the day. But as for ourselves, by this time we neither would nor could stop. The only relief we could get we got by speed.

We only found one well. About ten o'clock we went down a further step, on to a lower sea-level. This second 'shore' probably represents some halt in that long retreat of the sea which was to end in its annihilation, and which lasted perhaps thousands of centuries. The ground was white with saltness. In certain places it reminded me of the area round the Dead Sea near Jericho, but here there were no green banks of Jordan. We were running over a dead land, over a part of the earth which lived too soon for the human race. Who knows but what the sight around us was an exact prophetic vision of what our own world will be in some millions of years? – dried up, dead, lying under an unalterable blue which will give it a moonlike aspect in the infinite spaces of the firmament.

The most cruel part of the desert is about forty miles long. Caravans always try to cross it on a single march. They fill their barrels and skins with water at the last wells, and they start by the light of the stars. The road they follow is now marked by whitening bones. Bones of camels, of mules, of oxen and horses are scattered here and there over the whole of the caravan road we were following. But in the desert those traces of slaughter are almost continuous. Often a storm will overtake convoys, isolate them in the denseness of its whirling sand, oblige them to stop, and then destroy them. All old or tired or footsore animals fall there. It is a place of agonies. There is breathing about it an indescribable spirit of death, and I don't know where it comes from – perhaps from the lugubrious aspect of the landscape, from the oppressive strangeness of its bare outline, from its changeless absence of colour, or from its heavy stillness full of anguish. It emanates from all things around, and impresses with a sense of some unknown and imminent danger, of a continual threat, of an ambush; of some inconceivable sorrow, for which you prepare with passive resignation. One thought alone survives in your heart, one desire rather, a shapeless, vague, unheeded but still persistent desire: that of escaping, of treading no longer over that dead body of a world – of being freed. You look to the horizon as to a place of salvation and rest. Beyond every gap you expect to find the object of some vague aspiration of your soul. However slight a hill may be, you imagine it must hide something unexpected and good waiting for you beyond it. But you pass hills and gaps, the horizon which was before you becomes the horizon which you leave behind, and the desolation seems endless. Your mind becomes inert, your soul is drowned and lost in an unconquerable sadness. The time of your departure from the last halt lies dim in your memory among the mists of the past; to your stunned intelligence all grows dark, all seems immeasurably far and dim. Your departure and your arrival seem equally distant. You know this only, that you *must* arrive, that you *will* arrive, and from this idea comes the only strength remaining with you: the great power called Patience. You gather your patience, and so, *On!* All the resisting faculties of your mind and body are disciplined in the service of patience . . .

We had ended by becoming silent, almost as though by an instinct desiring to hoard all our energies. Besides, a word means a thought; and there are moments when thought itself costs too much labour.

About ten o'clock we were in the heart of the worst zone of the Gobi. The two caravan halting places at either end of this zone are marked by an enormous quantity of *obos*, that is, of the peculiar altars of the nomadic Mongolian. The *obo* is perhaps the first kind of altar that humanity ever erected. It consists of a heap of stones. In order to implore the protection of the gods before crossing the desert, and to thank the same gods for granted safety after the desert is crossed, the pious caravan driver takes a stone, lays it upon an *obo*, kneels down and prays. From our first entrance into Mongolia, while the Great Wall was still within sight, we found *obos* upon the summit of hills; those were not like the *obos* of the desert. Perhaps they had been abandoned; they were damaged by the storms and reduced to shapeless little masses.

The *obos* which we found here upon the threshold of the most desolate region of the desert often bore a terrible likeness to the figure of a man. These too were erected upon little heights like the first ones we had seen. But these were shaped, cunningly, and were crowned by the skull of an ox or a horse. They truly seemed altars erected in honour of Death. More than once from a distance those little piles outlined against the limpid sky really seemed to our saddened eyes like the figures of men, and in the whitened skulls which crowned them we thought we saw men's faces. There were so many that they made a crowd, and the presence of human beings, no matter of what kind, would have been for us a source of joy – it would have broken the monotony and the long solitude of our journey. In the desert, all men become dear to a man, not so much perhaps because of a sense of human brotherhood, or through a solidarity against the common dangers, as because they offer the comforting spectacle of *life*. We would look at all those upright 'men' scrutinizingly, then wonder at their stillness, but think that perhaps they had seen us and had stopped out of wonder . . . and then suddenly the unbroken solitude would stand again all round us, more heavy and more painful than before, as the imagined crowd turned into stone, and its faces were changed into skulls as though by some dismal power of magic.

At the foot of every *obo* were little strips of paper with prayers written in Tibetan characters, or little flags discoloured by time also bearing traces of sacred writings. The Mongolian people have a poetical superstition, by which they believe that the wind in waving that paper and those flags shakes the written prayer out of them and bears it up to Buddha. In passing over this place the air would therefore be filled with prayers as it is filled with perfume when it passes over flowers. Does not the use of incense in our own religious ceremonies bear some analogy to this thought?

We owed also a practical kind of gratitude to those *obos*, for by the process of building them the road had been freed from all stones. And who knows whether the origin of this strange religious usage may not lie in the need to improve the stony road? So the charitable act of clearing a way for other men may gradually have turned into a religious rite amid a people for whom every action and every event immediately acquire a mystical significance.

Suddenly we noticed that the radiator, the lung of the motor car, was not breathing freely. In the great heat of the desert the current of air produced by our speed alone was no longer sufficient to refresh the water of the engine's cooling-jacket; and this water was evaporating with a violent and continuous rush from the vent of the radiator. For a long time (or at least for what seemed to us a long time) we had been looking for a well, to change the water in the engine. We did not want to use that of our reservoir unless we were obliged to do so by extreme need. The reservoir held scarcely fifteen litres, and it would be wiser to keep them for a last emergency. Any accident to the motor car might leave us suddenly stranded, and that water would then be our only hope of salvation.

From time to time one of us would exclaim, looking intently towards the horizon, 'A well! Down there I see some vegetation – there is a dark patch.'

'Yes, yes,' would reply the others eagerly.

Illusions are easily communicated. But the dark patches either did not exist or turned out to have been shadows. We were at last obliged to have recourse to the water in our tank, and we stopped in order to transfer it to the radiator. The earth seemed to burn under our feet. There came up from it a heavy sultriness and a blinding reverberation of light. We were tormented by almost unbearable thirst. When we saw the water gushing out of the reservoir and sparkling in the sunshine, we could not resist the temptation, and drank it greedily, with our eyes half shut to enjoy it better, our mouth sealed on to the syphon – the same syphon, by the way, which was used for transferring the petrol. The water was hot and smelt of petrol and of varnish – at any other time it would have seemed nauseating, but all is relative in this world. The prince was the most moderate of us three; he scarcely moistened his lips, and soon he begged us not to exhaust that precious store. Our monotonous flight over the desert recommenced.

At midday we began to see a few blades of grass in some slight depressions where a little moisture had evidently collected. Soon after we were surprised by the flight of some wild birds, and it was not long before we saw a little stagnant pool in a large cavity. Along its banks were solemnly stalking some cranes and other birds of the same order. We stopped to take water, and Ettore went to fetch it with the cooking pan. The water was absolutely undrinkable – fetid, yellowish, slightly salted. We gave it to the motor, which has no palate. Still, that water signified by its presence that we were already out of the sinister range of absolute aridity, and now it was not long before we found wells surrounded by some encamped caravans.

*

Near one of these wells were lying two sleeping Chinese. They were, perhaps, two poor wretches returning to their native land by short journeys on foot. They had not even a tent to protect them from the sun; their only baggage consisted of a few rags and a bag. Half naked, stretched out on the sand, which seemed made of molten metal, and with their heads uncovered, they were fast asleep. Near them were the smouldering remains of a fire, and on this fire was a teapot still steaming – the teapot never absent from the baggage of the poorest Chinese any more than the samovar is from that of the poorest Russian. We could not understand how men could have the power of resistance necessary to stand the deadly torment of that heat. When they heard the sound of our car these men awoke, and raised themselves a little to look at us with sleep-dimmed eyes; then they lay down again. They must have been broken and stunned by their sufferings. What was the pain of our journey compared to theirs! We thought again of that pilgrim whom the prince had met near Nankow, that man who was to cross the desert kissing the earth at every three steps, and we thought that the two Chinese on meeting him would perhaps feel for him the same pity that we felt for them now . . .

The water of the wells along our track now was clear and cold. After having slaked our thirst, we always filled a reserve pail of it, and now and then on the way afterwards we would pass one another full glasses of it. Among the effects of the heat there was one at least which proved useful: the very slight consumption of fuel. In the mixture of gases which, ignited by the electricity of the sparking-plug, produces the power, there was now a minimum of petrol vapour. We could see this by the working of the automatic inlet valve. It had to be completely loosened, and it became evident that the air entered in the carburettor in extraordinarily large proportions. Prince Borghese remarked that we were going more by air than by gas.

As the day advanced, the heat grew more and more. The sun, which had risen on our right, now began to beat down upon us from the south, on our left. I had despised, at the time of our departure from Peking, the cork helmets with which Prince Borghese and Ettore had provided themselves, and I now found myself obliged to defy the burning heat of the Gobi under the modest shelter of a panama hat, whose brim was constantly lifted from off my forehead by the effect of the speed at which we travelled, so that my face remained completely unprotected. In a few hours the sun changed our faces into grotesque masks, and I, alas, was the most grotesque of the three! We became entirely scarlet. Our faces swelled and cracked. We could not bear upon them even the light touch of a handkerchief. Cool water, which on the preceding days had given us such delicious relief, produced now a disagreeable burning. Here and there over the more sunburnt places our skin was blistering. We had the sensation of being slowly baked. Our reddened eyes burned; our lips were swollen, arid, cracked. Ettore especially suffered greatly with his mouth, the corners of which were bleeding, and horribly in his hands, which had for some time been roughened by his work with the machinery, and which the sun now broke till the live flesh showed in the wounds; his swollen fingers trembled with the pain of it. The wonderful amount of courage and dignified pride and self-abnegation which Ettore showed in these trying circumstances, forgetting all pain at the moment of need, can never be sufficiently recorded or praised. The man forced his wounded hands to do the hardest labour, whenever for any reason it became necessary for the work to be done, and the marks of his blood would sometimes remain on the tools and parts of the engine. When he had scrupulously finished his work, he would look at his wounds, and murmur, with that smile of his, like the smile of an overgrown boy, 'I'm afraid we're not doing very well.'

If we had still had above our heads the excellent protection of our hood, we might have laughed at the sun. However, we comforted one another by saying, 'This, too, will come to an end.'

We raced after the endless line of telegraph poles in a kind of dream. That line had peculiar attractions. In this great monotonous landscape, it often assumed varieties of aspect which interested us. Now it ran straight like a fantastic, thin, black line, traced from one end of the horizon to the other. Then it would show its line of followers, turning in an orderly manner like soldiers on a manoeuvre. This idea of the soldiers came more especially when we saw the poles climbing up the slopes of the height, looking as if they were there for an assault. Over the ridges that pattern of lines, one close upon the other, often formed a strange, nebulous moulding, now similar to the tracing of a Gothic spire, now like a rugged mountain at an immense distance. We noticed all these things with a childish delight in minute observation. Our thoughts were just then of the most extraordinary puerility. I would sometimes surprise myself by counting the poles mechanically, starting at random and always ending by losing count. The oppressive aspect of a journey like this for those who are not driving is inaction. You first observe, then you think, then you let your fancy roam at will, and at last your tired mind loses itself in vague wandering: no vision wakens it any longer. You remain in a state of tacit insensibility. Your brain is drowsy and filled with the sweet wanderings of sleep.

'A *yurta!*' exclaimed the prince.

It was two in the afternoon. Those words gave us a shock as if they had announced some great marvel.

'Where? Where is it?'

'Down there to the left, under those rocks.'

'We're coming back to the world!'

'They must be nomads on a journey. There are no pastures – who *could* live here?'

We looked for a long time at the *yurta*, outside which stood a tethered horse. Soon after, we saw a laden camel led by a Mongolian, who stopped to make wild gestures to us. We waited for him, and the Mongolian ran up, drew from his tunic a great roll of linen, and began slowly to undo it. Within the first roll was another, within this other a third . . . Finally, from the last roll came out a telegram, which the man laid before us with great solemnity.

The telegram was addressed to Du Taillis, so we gave it back to the caravan driver, telling him to continue his way towards the south. He carefully made up his roll again – an excellent expedient against losing a precious document, but one certainly not advisable for men of business. We saw that the camel was carrying two cans of petrol, and then we understood. The Spyker, probably short of fuel, had telegraphed from Pong-kiong to Udde to have two cans sent from that depot, and the cans were on their way. At Pong-kiong we had ourselves given the Spyker a few litres of our fuel, and I think the two de Dion-Boutons had also given some of theirs.

At four o'clock we were in a region strewn with low rocks, which stood here and there on the plain like reefs upon the sea. The day before, we had had difficulty in seeing the station of Pong-kiong, which we thought lost; now the opposite thing seemed to occur, and we saw Udde in every distant rock. At every step we suffered some delusion. In order not to lose sight of the telegraph wires, we tried to follow them everywhere, over hills, amongst stones and boulders. Our progress became difficult. Towards five o'clock we saw a high mound of rocks. At its foot, and lying among the boulders, was a little Chinese house: Udde. A few minutes later we were entering that little place, so similar in all ways to the one we had left that morning. We felt as if it was the Garden of Delights.

We were received not by one, but by two telegraph employees. This happened to be a moment of change. The old operator of Udde was about to leave his post, and was preparing for a caravan journey of seventeen days, which was to take him to Kalgan. In the meantime he had to initiate his new colleague, who had arrived a few days previously, to the duties of his office.

That man, about to leave the desert, was completely happy, and his happiness made him communicative. He followed us everywhere, smiling. If we turned, we were sure to see the thin little Chinese, armed with a great rope and with a great pair of spectacles supported in the middle, ready to confide in us the fullness of his joy. While I wrote my telegrams he kept speaking to me:

'I am going to Shanghai.'

'Oh!'

'Yes; because I come from Shanghai, and I am a widower,' – here came a shy smile. 'I am a Christian.'

'I am glad to hear it.'

'My father wants me to marry again. So, as soon as I arrive at Shanghai, I am going to marry –' (A laugh.)

'And are you in love?'

'I? No. I do not know my betrothed. My father has chosen her for me.'

'What if you don't like her?'

He looked at me with surprise and smiled condescendingly, saying again:

'My father has chosen her for me. That is our custom. I leave the day after tomorrow. Ha, ha!'

That evening we waited in vain for the arrival of the other motor cars.

We devoured a little rice and some of our unending corned beef in silence, and we lay down upon the ground wrapped in our furs. We had forgotten to eat any lunch for two days, so violent had been our thirst in the burning desert.

VIII

THE CITY IN THE DESERT

~~~~~~~~~

*The Distant Mountain – A Panorama of Devastation –
The City in the Desert – A Mysterious Motor Car –
Chasing Antelopes – Urga*

Udde was our second base of supply, and there we found fuel, oil, and grease, sent to us by caravan from Peking – a mass of packages and cans, which took up a whole corner of the courtyard. A little of the fuel had leaked out on the way from some defective cans. Nevertheless, we had enough to fill our tanks, and we even left a few canfuls behind us, with word to the telegraph clerks to give this to our colleagues if they had any need of it.

Shortly before dawn on 20 June, a Mongolian who came from the well of Udde, more than one *li* from the telegraph station, brought us news. At the well he had found caravan drivers just arrived from the south after a long night's march, and these men reported that the 'stranger-chariots' had encamped the night before at 180 *li* from Udde (about sixty-five miles). We thought that the report must have exaggerated the distance. Their caravan could not have covered more than 100 or 110 *li* in the night, and our companions' cars could only be about forty miles, or less, away. Prince Borghese decided to wait two days for them at Urga, the capital of Mongolia, where we expected to arrive next day – just as we had waited for them before at Kalgan.

The stars were still shining in the west when we left for Tuerin, the next telegraph station, at roughly 200 miles' distance, after taking some good hot tea and bidding a grateful farewell to our hosts.

The morning air was cold, and we wrapped ourselves up in our furs, which seemed scarcely sufficient to protect us; but three hours later we had already thrown them off on to the back of our seats, and by nine o'clock we were suffering again the torment of the same scorching heat as the day before.

We could have sworn that the heat grew more burning from day to day, although in fact it was we who felt it more because of the excessive sensitiveness of our burnt skin. As the day advanced, not even the breeze produced by the speed at which we travelled could give us any relief. We felt at times invested, as it were, by the breath of a furnace at white heat, something like what one feels in coming too near to some unseen devouring fire. Thirst assailed us again, continuous and tormenting. The extreme dryness of the air parched our throats and, as it seemed, also the whole of ourselves. The sight of a well was a great occasion of rejoicing. I recall the act of putting my lips to the rim of the pail to drink the cool, clear water as one of the most exquisite pleasures I have experienced in all my life. We took deep, long, strong draughts, standing with our feet in the mud of the well, with our heads thrown back, and the water pouring over our faces, and running down our necks and streaming over our clothes – so great was our eagerness to drink of it deeply, to enjoy its sweet freshness with all our senses at last!

When the torment of thirst and fire began again after these intervals, we tried to make our longing bearable by the power of our imaginations. We pictured to ourselves, and quaffed in fancy, the coolest drinks we could think of. Ettore usually imagined a great glass of chilled beer, troubled at first by the froth, but growing clearer from the bottom little by little, and making his throat tingle with its bubbling, whilst the 'dew' outside the glass trickled down through his fingers. Now and then he would offer me his glass of beer, and receive from me, as a generous return, cups of iced coffee. I don't know why iced coffee should have become my favourite spiritual refreshment in the desert, but it did. And we each of us gravely determined to indulge in a regular surfeit of our chosen drinks as soon as we returned to the civilized world, looking forward to the real enjoyment of these things as if our present thirst must pursue us to the doors of our own homes. We longed regretfully for all the glasses of beer and all the cups of iced coffee we had absorbed in the past without appreciating their enormous attractions, and without valuing the true happiness that they could give . . .

Udde and the rocks disappeared together out of sight. For long hours our journey continued through an endless series of valleys enclosed between low, reddish sand-hills. Over the hills we found a few brief stony passes, a few heavy sand drives that tried the motor, but for the most part the ground could not have been more favourable for motor driving. Our machine often flew at the swiftest possible speed over virgin plains. We left every trace of road or camel path, and imprinted the mark of our wheels upon soil never trodden before.

This was probably the first occasion when a motor car could run at the very height of its speed outside the tyrannical limitations of any road, free to turn its impetus whither it would, and to follow its own caprice like a wild horse. We were delighted with these long swift flights towards freedom, but the subtle anguish of solitude and silence penetrated deeper and deeper into our hearts. For hundreds of miles we were the only living beings over the whole vast space of our horizon, and we felt at times a vague secret and persistent horror of that isolation. We had a dim instinctive sense of some hostile power present before us, of some strong wild enmity of the very earth against us.

I wonder why it is that we always personify the earth and think her mighty? We call her Mother Earth; we find her now smiling, now severe; we attribute expressions and feelings to her. She has characteristics that call out in ourselves various responses; there is something resembling a soul, and a great soul, in her. In the desert we felt this more than ever instinctively. When you are alone in the country, you have the sense of joys and sadnesses deriving only from the mysterious life surrounding you; in the desert, this unseen power breathed out aversion and evoked mistrust. You might think that the desert loves its silences and protects them; it is like an immense cemetery which will not brook profanation.

We wished we could at least see a tree: a tree is sometimes a companion, a giant friend, offering hospitality and refreshment in the shelter of his open arms. From Kalgan onward, we had seen no trees. The day before, not far from Udde, we thought we had found some: on the bank of a dried up and stony torrent we saw seven plants in a line – seven miracles! We approached them, and found that they were shrubs smaller than ourselves, like tamarisk. The bareness of the ground had made us misjudge their size. Nevertheless, we looked at them as at a great rarity, taking pleasure in their shape and in the fact of their existence.

It must have been about ten a.m. when we came again upon the prairies.

The grass began here to cover timidly with green the bottom of the little valleys; then it spread to the hills, growing more even and thicker. From the green came the chirping of birds, first uncertain, scarce, distant, then louder, continuous and joyful. There were thousands of larks in the desert, and also a strange kind of white-breasted partridge, and herons with tufted heads. These happy dwellers of the air rose up in clouds round the car. There were moments when they entirely surrounded us. We felt that there must be some water close by, and we were not mistaken, for a little later we came to a little muddy pond covered with yellow rushes and crowded with white flamingos standing motionless on their long, red legs, and, with other water-birds, black-headed ducks and geese. At intervals a few antelopes, disturbed by our arrival, would raise their pointed faces from the grass and shoot away like darts.

The swiftness of the motor car gave us landscape effects unknown to caravans. In one hour we passed from sands to prairies. The slow step of the camel would have taken a day to cover the same ground, and the abrupt transition would scarcely have been noticed.

We traversed an even and perfectly flat plain, with one unbroken flight of forty miles, which we hoped would continue till our next halting place, but the plain and the prairies ended, the song of the larks was still, and we had to advance cautiously in a bare, stony, and deserted zone. We were again in the grip of the desert. We stopped at a well in the camp of a Chinese caravan; the half-naked caravan drivers, coming out of their blue tents, drew near.

'How far is Tuerin?' we asked.

They pointed northwards with an expressive gesture that meant, Very, very far.

'How many *li*?'

They did not know. One of them said, 'Two days.'

Another one spoke at great length about Tuerin and about a mountain, and showed us a point where the road led over a small range. We just succeeded in understanding that Tuerin was to be found at the foot of a mountain, and that the mountain might be seen from the high point of the road to which the man was pointing.

This was all perfectly accurate. When the car reached the first little range to which the man had directed us, we saw outlined on the horizon before us an enormous rock, like Gibraltar, in the desert. It must have been no less than fifty miles distant, and we could only see it by reason of the extreme transparency of the air. It was pale blue, and so dim that we kept losing sight of it, as happens on the sea when you sight a very distant shore. It seemed to vanish by moments, the vision of it dissolving in the luminous distance. We then had to follow patiently with our eye the line of the horizon, and the slight, tremulous apparition would show up again.

Our road went down, and the mountain of Tuerin set like a star. Now began another endless series of dry and sterile valleys and heights. At every hillock we expected to see our 'Gibraltar' nearer, but we could no longer see anything. The hours passed, and seemed endless. We felt tired, broken, almost as if our strength were being worn out by the powerful labour of the engine. We seemed at times to be almost pushing the car ourselves with our assiduous longing; we accompanied it so intensely with our will that its work caused in us true physical exhaustion. The road was not always easy, and we followed every movement of the machine with a vigilance that kept all our nerves at a tension.

The great rock did not reappear. We kept repeating to one another, 'From up there, in a few minutes, we shall see it.'

But it did not come back. Each disappointment seemed to throw us back hundreds of miles. After four hours' journey we ended by not believing in it any longer.

'That mountain was simply a group of telegraph poles!' I exclaimed, pointing to the strange dim shapes which the long line of poles traced upon the horizon by the effects of foreshortening.

'If it had been a mountain it would not have disappeared,' remarked Ettore wisely.

'And yet it could only be a mountain,' decided Prince Borghese, whom in my heart of hearts I could not help calling obstinate.

We became convinced that we were still very far from our goal, and we fell into a resigned despondency.

That day the uncomfortable seat on the floor of the car had fallen to my lot. That corner provided ever-varying experiences, not always of an agreeable nature. One was obliged to sit askew, with one's feet to the left on the step of the car and one's head facing the road – a graceful position for a Naiad on a fountain, but somewhat uncomfortable for a long journey! One's face, at the level of the engine-case, received all the warm breath of the machine; and to this was added a certain difficulty in keeping one's balance at the turnings and at every big jerk of the car, so that one had to hang on to some object in order not to be suddenly thrown off by the effects of centrifugal force. All this is insignificant, and may be even amusing on a short journey taken for one's own diversion. It becomes serious, however, on a run of many hours, when the fatigue and ennui deaden little by little both muscles and brain, and when a forced immobility, the silence and monotony of the road, the heat and the long watchfulness, end by producing a relaxation of every faculty: a torpor which is not that of sleep, but rather is a forgetfulness of self, of place, of time, an irresistible abandonment and dimming of consciousness. One falls into a quiet and inert delirium. One's eye gazes out without comprehension; all things lose their meaning and their value. I remember I watched for an indefinite length of time the revolving of one wheel whose large tyre seemed to me a great precipitous cataract, even and endless, which exercised upon me the attraction of water in the deep. The ground under my feet fled past like those strange and fearful rivers which cross our dreams in a fever. At a certain moment everything appeared to me veiled, confused, fleeting. One thing alone I understood: that I was in danger of falling. There was a small fraction of my mind still watching. In the dimmed consciousness, the instinct of self-preservation still kept guard like a sentinel, but I could not pay any heed to its alarms. I felt myself falling; I let myself go; gave way gently . . . More than once a hand caught me vigorously by the shoulder, and I heard the voice of Prince Borghese say:

'Take care – I thought you were falling.'

Then I would reply, with the shamefacedness of one caught asleep:

'No, no, there is no danger of that.'

The mountain reappeared before us suddenly, about ten miles away. It seemed made up of one gigantic block of stone with precipitous walls, rising sheer up from a hill formed perhaps from the debris of the rock itself. Evidently, the great series of plains and heights which we had just crossed formed collectively one vast dip, an immense cavity, a '*gobi*'; and this had prevented us from seeing the Tuerin mountain again after our first distant glimpses of it.

Gradually, as it approached, its outline became stranger. It was not one single block of stone; it was a group of rocks, a mass of reefs piled one over another, a conglomeration of jagged edges, similar in some way to an immense *obo* erected by the religious fervour of a people of Titans.

Three-quarters of an hour later we penetrated among the masses of its boulders in a fantastic-looking region. We found ourselves climbing the sides of the hill which we had dimly seen at the foot of the bizarre and weird masses of rock. We felt as though we were in the midst of one huge ruin, among the remains of a crumbled world. Those strange enormous stones seemed fallen from some height, overturned, pushed, broken by the fury of an immense cataclysm. Here devastation was added to desolation. The desert slept no longer in the quiet stretch of its plains. Here it rose up impetuously, assuming a violent mood; it prepared no longer to repel, but to crush.

The machine climbed up the caravan road, panting; and the sound of its effort was echoed all round. Our eyes sought the telegraph station among the rocks. Without noticing it, we had lost the guidance of the wires, and were now, as it were, abandoned in those sinister solitudes. We could not find our longed-for refuge.

From a bush close by, there suddenly came out a fox, and, instead of fleeing in fear, it followed us for a while, docilely, like a dog, stretching out towards us a sharp, thin, striped muzzle, and dragging a thick flaky brush behind it; it soon disappeared. We reached the summit of the height on the west. The rocks on that side were rounded off and had a strange look, like the backs of gigantic animals diminishing in height towards the plain.

Suddenly, over that prodigious crowd of boulders, we saw shining in the sun four golden globes. They were alike, all of the same height, symmetrically disposed. We looked at them with intense and silent curiosity. They seemed to be balancing themselves over the crests of stormy waves turned into rocks, down to the left of the road, a few hundred yards before us. Presently, we perceived a broad, empty space among the boulders, and our curiosity turned to wonder, and our wonder to astonishment, as the confused images in that vast sunny shelter took upon them the consistency of reality. A few moments later we stopped our car and began looking eagerly at the incredible spectacle of a city: a singular, a fabulous city. We dominated it from a height. The rocks guard it all round and serve as its walls. The golden globes crown four grand temples which stretch in a line to the south. These sacred edifices had nothing in common with the temple seen by us near Pong-kiong, the temple with the old motionless priest. These were erected over four great wooden platforms like the Buddhist buildings of Japan. They seemed entirely made of wood: coloured, sculptured, gilt. Their roofs were raised at the corners like Chinese roofs, but without terminating in that characteristic line which reminds one of the corners of a tent, from which it probably is derived. These roofs finished upwards in a pinnacle, upon the extreme point of which was the golden ball. They were isolated and exactly alike. Their look of grandeur came from that isolation. Round them was not a plant, not a vestige of green: just sand and a few rocks. The city stood a little apart; it reverently left an empty space between its temples and itself.

It would be impossible to imagine a stranger city than this. It consisted of a number of small, square-roofed, white houses, built of lime and wood, and standing in lines on either side of straight, broad streets. The city and the sacred edifices seemed new and deserted. The streets were empty; in the great light which bathed them we saw not one human figure. This place, which had suddenly appeared before us as if by enchantment, seemed uninhabited, except for a few dogs, which we saw crossing the streets from time to time, trotting among the houses and lying down in groups in the shade. The city was silent, like the desert which surrounded it.

Who could be living in those places? They could only be monks: we must be passing some wild nest of the ancient Buddhist faith. We left the car and approached this monastery, climbing up an enormous rock.

Only people who make prayer and meditation the aim of their life could preserve such immobility and so great a silence. From every great centre of population, at every moment, one clear, strong, happy sound is heard: the voice of childhood. Its absence sufficed to tell us that only monks lived down here. We did not descend among the houses, for fear of causing some dangerous outburst of fanaticism, and besides, we were too eager to reach our resting place. We went back 'on board' and continued our hunt for the telegraph station. The mysterious city disappeared from our sight.

We saw a shepherd tending his small flock, which grazed in the shadow of the mountain, but he was too far off for us to address him. We began to descend the north side of the mountain. No telegraph station came in sight. We turned back and decided to question the lamas of the sanctuary.

We turned back again, and then went on foot towards the monastery buildings. Someone had seen us. Men came out from the streets and, followed by the dogs, began climbing towards us. Heading them all was a venerable old man. The prince turned to him with a gesture of greeting – the old man turned and fled. The greeting was repeated to a young man, who received it undaunted and with a courage worthy of the occasion.

What is the way to ask a Mongolian lama how to reach a telegraph station? We exhausted all our repertoire of Chinese words likely to serve our purpose, and made all the signs which in our judgement would indicate wires, poles, little house, sending off telegrams (here we copied the sound of the telegraph keys, as we thought, with wonderful fidelity: *tick – tick, tick – tick, tick*). But we succeeded in obtaining only one practical result: we sent the whole lama convent of Tuerin into a shout of laughter. That was something, however: their mistrust at least was dissipated. A sense of humour overcame their reluctance, and the monks crowded round us and became our good friends. But we did not find the road.

Prince Borghese then had a happy idea. He took his notebook, drew upon it some lines which might represent telegraph posts, adorned them with insulators and stretched lines across them. The lamas followed his work with the keenest interest, pressing upon one another, craning their necks to see over his shoulder. They were of all ages, clean shaven and with close-cropped heads, wearing yellow or red mantles and robes. Many wore their mantles twisted round their waists and thrown over the left shoulder like a toga, and covering their heads with one corner of it. Robes, mantles, and men were equally soiled: for, alas, water is scarce in the desert! Who knows what a memorable event our arrival was for those hermits, isolated there from the world in order that they may study and meditate upon the sacred texts of Buddhism? Mongolians carry their sacred books, which have come to them from far-off Tibet, into the most desolate places. They hide them as you would hide a treasure. They seem to think that the sweet teachings of Buddha cannot be followed or understood except amid solitude and silence.

After having drawn the wires, the prince tried to represent the telegraph station into which the wires disappeared. Then tapping upon it with his finger, he made the lamas understand that *that* was the subject of our inquiries, the final purpose of that long work of art. The lamas grasped the meaning of this hieroglyphic, and started off to show us the way, shouting and gesticulating. When they reached the road they were surprised by the sight of the car. They surrounded it, and examined it with mistrust. A number of dogs had followed the monks and were closely inspecting the car all round, with a decided want of good breeding. Ettore thought the moment to start the engine had come, and he gave two vigorous turns to the handle. The engine was started noisily; lamas and dogs fled precipitately towards the sacred city . . .

Fortunately we had made out from their talk that the way to the telegraph lay eastwards through narrow passes winding amongst the rocks. The car managed somehow to climb the steep slopes leading to a high ridge of the hill, and crossed a kind of corridor among the boulders, descending on the other side. Then we came to a meadow already covered by the evening shadows, and in the midst of this meadow we found the third telegraph station of Mongolia, as small as its sisters, also built of mud and equally seductive to our imagination.

'Do you know,' said the Chinese telegraph clerk, with great eagerness, 'another car has passed? It is on the way to Urga.'

'Impossible!'

'Yes, and it did not stop. It flew as fast as the wind.'

'What can it have been!'

'I saw it quite clearly. It came from the direction of Udde.'

'But when?'

'A few hours ago.'

Who could have outstripped us? We had noticed nothing. Perhaps while we were trying to find our way . . . Or else one of the de Dion-Boutons had travelled all night and was preceding us.

'Are you quite sure?' we asked. 'Was it a motor car?'

'Perfectly sure. It came from Udde. It was going to Urga, and I telegraphed about it at once.'

'Was it like ours?'

'Much smaller – oh, much!'

'Would you ask Udde for details about all the cars, immediately?'

And the obliging Chinese set himself before the apparatus. A moment later he looked up, exclaiming gravely: 'Udde is dining. He demands five minutes to finish his dinner.'

When Udde had dined, we got the required information, which our telegraph clerk transmitted eagerly to us as he read it on the tape.

'The Itala left Udde this morning at four.'

'Quite right. Next?'

'The Spyker stopped yesterday at 100 *li* north of Pong-kiong for want of fuel, which was sent to it by camel . . . The de Dion-Boutons have arrived together at Udde to-day at one p.m. They left at two . . .'

'Nothing more?'

'The tricycle Contal has so far not been signalled either at Pong-kiong or at Kalgan . . . The Tu Tung of Kalgan has sent some cavalry to its assistance. That is all.'

It was obvious that the Spyker was at least 300 miles from us, and the two de Dion-Boutons about 150. The mystery of that motor car which had passed a few hours previously without stopping was solved; how *could* we have failed to understand it at once?

'The car you saw was *ours*,' we said to the astonished clerk. 'It was *we* who passed down there. We did not stop because we had not seen the telegraph office, and we have been looking for it ever since in all directions except the right one.'

'The car that passed seemed so much smaller,' he observed, doubtingly.

'That was because of the distance.'

'Ah! it is true. The distance does make things seem smaller.'

And with this profound truth, the telegraph clerk was apparently satisfied.

On reckoning up the distance we had covered, we found that that day we had travelled the first 1000 kilometres from Peking. In order to celebrate the event, we decided to have a sumptuous banquet. A shepherd lama, who chanced to be in that neighbourhood, sold us a lamb, which we paid for with silver parings (for no coin has currency among Mongolians) duly weighed in a little pair of scales made for the purpose, with which we had provided ourselves at Kalgan. The lamb, entrusted to the able care of the telegraph clerk, reappeared a few hours later transformed into a gigantic dish of steaming boiled meat, which seemed to us the most delectable sustenance in the world. We were soon smoking our cigarettes before the mangled remains of this dish and, seated round a candle fixed in the neck of a bottle, we talked over our adventures of the day and the strange city of the desert, whose streets had never been trod by the foot of woman; we discussed our future journey, and settled upon the place of our next halt. We had completely forgotten fatigue and thirst, all the suffering of that long day, twelve interminable hours borne under the scorching sun in a continuous overwhelming tension of our nerves, amid a thousand doubts and a thousand anxieties.

How small and negligible past difficulties seem! The future urges us on, so that we never waste time in looking behind us, and this tendency to forget pain is man's greatest good fortune. Every morning at the time of starting we felt strong and ready for our journey, because we had lost the exact remembrance of our experiences of the day before. A beneficent mist spread over past suffering, and at our departure we always imagined every difficulty to be over. Oblivion and hopefulness were our strength.

Our race had much in common with life.

Tuerin is on the edge of the desert. South of Tuerin is a sterile squalor, north of it the green splendour of the prairie. That high rock seems put there as a signal, as a lighthouse, to mark for travellers the limits between the dead earth and the living earth; to say to these, 'Make ready,' and to the others, 'Courage!'

The road from Tuerin to Urga seemed most beautiful to us, perhaps because we came from the Gobi. We found everything delightful: the view, the road, the sky. For even the sky was changed. There were clouds on it now, and we admired them, especially when their great flying shadows ran over us like the touch of a light caress. We went at a speed of thirty, sometimes forty miles an hour. The ground was slightly undulating, and we let ourselves slide into the slow depressions with the full impetus of both speed and weight. We were happy, we talked, we found a thousand things to speak about; we called one another's attention to all we saw. We thought aloud.

Ettore asked us what time we were to arrive at *Kalgan!* – yes, Kalgan, because Ettore, out of a certain love of simplicity, had eliminated from his mind the names of most places on our route, leaving only a few as a convenience of speech. Those few he applied without petty consideration of detail to every locality he wished to mention. It was a kind of jargon peculiarly his own. *Kalgan* meant to say 'the city which . . . etc.'

Ettore's memory rebelled against geography. Names passed over it without stopping, like birds on the wing; and this is why, when he did succeed in grasping one, he would not let it go again, but made it do for all the others which had escaped him. His good-humoured indifference to the route we were to traverse had some enviable points, and we smiled at his geographical errors, not because they were errors, but because of a certain fresh naïveté and a primitive simplicity of mind which they revealed. We experienced near Ettore that pure kind of pleasure which one always derives from contact with the unspoilt soul of a big intelligent child. For him the matter of our journey was embodied in two clear truths. First, that we had to run from morning to night, or nearly, every day for two or three months. Secondly, that, in order to arrive, the car must be driven carefully, watched over, listened to, examined, cared for, cleaned, lubricated – continually, unremittingly – with all possible intelligence and energy. And this was *his* business. At night, when we arrived at our halting places, he never ate nor slept until he had finished seeing to the machine; and he would sometimes spend long hours lying in absurd positions under the hot body of the car, with burning oil dropping about him. At times, he would get up from his bed at the most incredible hours, seized by a sudden fear, and then we could hear him undoing nuts, taking apart bits and pieces in order to observe the most delicate organs of the engine, putting everything back. By dawn he was invariably ready to start . . . for 'Kalgan'!

That morning we came again upon great droves of horses, which repeated their spirited manoeuvres round us. We met some shepherds and cattle drivers; we saw some *yurtas*; black and long-haired shepherd dogs pursued us; flocks of sheep were slaking their thirst at the wells; and here the caravans were able to travel in the middle of the day. We were re-entering the zone of life. Everything cheered us; when we were not speaking we sang. The prince, at the wheel, whistled his favourite air, '*La Petite Tonkinoise*', to which I improvised an elaborate accompaniment.

Groups of antelopes were grazing afar and, surprised by the motor car, they would take flight, crossing the road before us. We had not yet noticed this curious method of flight peculiar to antelopes, and which often brought the poor terrified animals, outdone by our speed, within a few yards of us. Hunters know these strange tactics perfectly and never gallop directly towards their game (whose running is swifter than that of the Mongolian horse), but deviate almost as though to leave it aside, knowing that the antelope will be sure to come their way of its own accord, and thus pass within shooting range. It is a primitive piece of cunning that makes the hunted animal cross the enemy's path at a right angle, in the hope that that enemy's very impetus may take him off in the wrong direction and oblige him to lose time in turning round to repeat his pursuit.

Suddenly I saw in the prairie, at a few miles on our left, a long red streak moving swiftly. It moved to the right, tremulous, raising a slight cloud of dust.

'Look, look!' I cried, pointing to it. At first I did not know what it might be.

'It is running like a train.'

'They are animals.'

'Are they antelopes?'

'Yes, yes; you can see them perfectly well now.'

'Here is one alone before the others.'

'Look at their legs – and that gallop!'

'A wonderful sight!'

'Superb.'

'How many do you think there are?'

'Who knows? Five hundred perhaps.'

'A whole population of antelopes.'

We had arrived within five hundred yards of them. We could distinguish the large, compact herd perfectly well in its flight. It was about to reach our road and cross it, according to the usual tactics.

'Let us pursue them.'

The prince changed gear and pressed down the accelerator. The engine roared more loudly and more shrilly, and we leaped forward and flew over the hard sand of the path. In a few seconds we saw that the herd would not all have time to pass before us, and we felt a cruel satisfaction in the confusion we would create among the animals.

'What speed are we doing?'

'Fifty to sixty,' answered Ettore.

We felt a wind like a hurricane blow in our faces. I had the idea of taking the Mauser to shoot at one of the animals and bring it triumphantly to Urga tied over our baggage, but I could not translate my idea into action. We had caught up the herd with amazing swiftness. The antelopes had changed their direction, and raced by our side divided into two groups. For a few moments we were amid this strange flock, enveloped in the dust which the close scampering of those thin, nervous, swift feet beat up. From time to time one of the timid animals, mad with fear, fell, rolled over, was trodden upon or leaped over by the others, shook itself, and in a flash was in flight again. We were shouting in the excitement of the chase – shouting because at certain moments one becomes wild, and all the savage instincts latent in us seemed to awake, and we possessed no other weapon than our voices. Unable to kill, we seemed to want to frighten, and our cries increased the fear of our victims to the point of paroxysm. Soon the tumultuous confusion of their stag-like lithe and tawny backs turned abruptly sideways, and dispersed far away in the prairies.

At ten that morning we entered a mountainous but easy region. We were leaving the Mongolian plains for good; the mountains of oriental Siberia and of Trans-Baikalia reached out towards us their uttermost counter-forts, their last ridges. We soon penetrated into a valley which hid us finally from the endless vastness of those plains, from which we were issuing somewhat stunned and dazed, like people landing after a long sea journey.

The *yurtas* and the flocks grew more frequent. We met a Mongolian sumptuously dressed in red silk, accompanied by another one, ragged enough to be recognized as his servant. The two were resting, seated upon the grass, with their horses' bridles on their arms. On seeing us arrive, they got up precipitately, frightened, and made as if to escape, but it was too late, and a moment after we passed swiftly by them. When they saw that we came with no hostile intention, they were brave enough to look up and burst into irrepressible laughter. That 'chariot', our car, running alone, evidently seemed to them a joke, an extremely funny thing, an amusing absurdity. It was to them as if we had forgotten to put the horses in the car, and as if the vehicle, more absent-minded than ourselves, had not noticed it and was running all the same. They laughed and laughed, doubled over, with their hands on their knees . . .

An enormous number of prairie dogs were playing about on the grass. They ran towards their burrows, and before hiding they never failed to look at us curiously, raised on their hind legs in an attitude which was comical, because it seemed so human. When their den was too far to be easily reached, the intelligent little animals would let themselves fall suddenly to the ground as if struck by lightning, feigning death, only to revive hastily as soon as we had passed. We welcomed the presence of those prairie dogs, because we knew that they dwell in large numbers in the province of Urga. They betokened the vicinity of the Mongolian capital.

It was eleven o'clock when we found ourselves at the foot of the sacred mountain of Bogda-ola, a word signifying precisely 'holy mountain'. On the other side of it we were to find the River Tola, and on its banks the Holy City.

The peaks of the Bogda-ola were covered by a thick, dark wood of small pine trees, which spread into the valleys in long streaks. These were the first trees we had seen for nearly 800 miles, and we looked at them with the keenest satisfaction. We had left willow trees, poplars, alders down there on the frontier of old China, and here we found pines; from the varied flora of temperate climates we had passed to that of the colder regions. The general look of the landscape told us the distance we had travelled. We felt already surrounded by a certain northern severity; we felt that we were nearing Siberia.

We came out upon the vast valley of the Tola, and towards the west we perceived Urga uncertainly, as in a mirage, dotted with white buildings that must have been sanctuaries. It was a long time before we reached it. The River Tola and a whole network of its tributaries crossed our road several times. You can traverse them by Russian bridges, but the Mongolians prefer to ford them, and we ended by doing the same, entering several times resolutely into the river, quickly, for fear that we might sink, following the marks of wheels and sandals. This passing of the large grey machine, surrounded by high 'banks' of water like a torpedo boat, was a singular spectacle.

There is not only one city at Urga – there are three. There is the Chinese town, the Mongolian, and the Russian one. Each is several miles distant from the others. Three great peoples, the Slav, the Mongolian, and the Chinese, meet here without blending or communing. There is between them the bulwark of an age-long hostility. The three cities seem almost inimical. They look like entrenched camps. Each is encircled by very high palisades, such as were used in ancient times in war to break the impetus of a cavalry assault, and high palisades also enclose separately their dwellings and their temples. The roads are nothing but monotonous corridors between wooden walls, sad and uniform.

There must be some danger menacing them still. These defences must have more than a traditional value. The Russian consulate, a little villa built in the Siberian style of architecture, isolated between the Chinese and the Mongolian cities, has fortifications all round: trenches, ditches, wire nettings, loopholes, all the most modern and efficacious aids to defence. It possesses guns, and has a garrison of Trans-Baikalian Cossacks. A little further west, near the Mongolian city, the Tartar general, the Tu Tung of Urga, who is commander of the Chinese garrison, has also entrenched himself in a square fort, defended by earthworks with strong wooden supports, and crowned with battlements and pierced by loopholes, guarded by sentinels at each corner. China and Russia have entrenched themselves here, as one would in a conquered land. Which of them is the true master?

The true master is certainly not that deified sovereign of the Mongolian people, the Grand Lama, the living Buddha, who lives secluded in a lama monastery close by. You can see the white buildings which belong to that monastery from afar as you approach the city. Buddha is said to delight in living upon this earth, dwelling in the body of three men: three men alone in the world. One of these is the Dalai Lama of Tibet; the second is that of Urga; the third is at Peking, chief of twelve hundred lamas in the Great Temple of Yung-ho-kung. Although all three possess the soul of Buddha, there exists between them a notable difference in value; that of Tibet is the most sacred, and that of Peking is the least sacred. The difference consists in a greater or lesser power of benediction, which greatly resembles the *baraka* of Arabians. The Dalai Lamas are venerated, not in proportion to their moral worth, but in proportion to their usefulness. When, four years ago, at the time of the English expedition under Captain Younghusband, the Dalai Lama of Tibet fled from Lhasa and took refuge at Urga, the good Mongolians left their own god for the Tibetan god, whose benedictions are considered to be much more efficacious, and then the rare spectacle was beheld of a fierce hostility between two Buddhas.

Round that unfortunate divinity of Urga are wound the many threads of political intrigue. An intelligent, energetic and daring man at the head of the Mongolian people might become dangerous to Chinese sovereignty. This is, perhaps, the reason why the living god never grows to be more than a child. To let yourself be worshipped is an easy task, which even a child can perform, and when the young lama comes to an age when he must shortly become a grown-up and independent man, he dies: dies, suddenly and mysteriously. But he has already named his successor, and another child mounts upon the tragic altar. This sudden death is one of the most constant miracles of the divinity. The soul of this god cannot dwell except in a child . . . It is whispered, however, that the child dies strangled.

The last Grand Lama has happily survived the critical moment, and the habitual miracle is undergoing a delay which some choose to explain by the vigilant protection exercised over the lama by the Russian consul. The Russian consul at Urga is a great diplomat, of the Buriat race, which is akin to the Mongolian. The consul is an intimate friend of the living Buddha, and has a free entrance to the sacred enclosures. The Chinese governor is far from possessing the same authority as of old over the Grand Lama; it is, in fact, said that the latter detests him heartily. But if

this divinity is still alive, he seemed to be reduced, by precocious vice
and by the abuse of liquors, to a state bordering upon complete idiocy. It
is as if they had wished to strangle his soul at least, when they proved
unable to strangle his body.

It is certain that those entrenched and fortified camps, the proliferat-
ing intrigues, the wild tales of murder, the visions of strangely clad
knights passing at a gallop through the streets along the high defensive
boarding – all these give one the impression of living down there in a
grim, medieval Asiatic world, and the sudden appearance of our motor
car in that place contrasted with all existing circumstances there to an
extent that made it seem non-real.

True, however, the Grand Lama himself possesses a motor car, a little
car given to him by the Russian governor as a compensation, perhaps,
for the rivalry of the Tibetan Buddha. That little carriage has never by
itself moved one yard. As soon as it arrived at Urga, the young Buddha
sent two men to push it round the yard, hoping that thus it would start its
race and could continue its wanderings alone. But the car did not fulfil
his expectations. Then the Dalai Lama decided to have an ox harnessed
to it, and sent it thus to his summer residence, where it lies now rusting,
and where it will remain until some other European power sends the
lama the further present of a chauffeur.

IX

URGA

~~~~~~~~~~

At the Rusky-Kitensky Bank – A Strange Pilgrimage – A Chinese Governor on our Motor Car – Departure from Urga – We Sink into a Bog – A Disastrous Descent

Of the three cities of Urga, the first one to which we came on arriving was the Chinese one. We entered there because the telegraph did. We had grown so accustomed to following the two wires everywhere, with the completest confidence, that we should have let them lead us no matter where without demurring. They were Chinese wires and they chose for their halting place the Chinese city, before leaving again straight for the north over some rugged mountains. Their task as a guide was about to end. They took us through the narrow, dirty streets of the Chinese city, and suddenly leaped over a palisade and left us plunged in perplexity.

Our arrival made the people gather at the gate of their enclosures. We caught rapid glimpses of courtyards encumbered with packing-cases, with camels, with children; of Chinese buildings with railings of a complicated geometric design, and of little showy, many-coloured temples. Behind the primitive defence of these hoardings we saw the signs of prosperity and labour. The inhabitants here are all given to trading on a large scale. They are enriched by the commerce of tea, wool, fur and horses. They are regular organizers of caravans, owners of hundreds of camels and oxen. They certainly knew that we were coming, for they looked at us curiously, but with no great amazement. The telegraph had spread the news of the *chi-cho*, and these pigtailed emigrants had gained through contact with the Russians, and through their constant relations with the western world, a practical sense which enabled them to look at the motor car from an absolutely calm and sensible standpoint. Some asked us whether we came directly from Tuerin and, on our replying affirmatively, turned to the others, warmly discussing the event.

It was in the streets of the Chinese city of Urga that we first saw the

women of northern Mongolia, whose headgear is so extravagant and
was so new to us that we could not refrain from looking at them with
decidedly indiscreet insistence. Certainly the married women of northern Mongolia succeed in making of their headdress the most original
masterpiece of fancy-work that could be imagined by the collective
minds of a hundred generations of women. Their hair comes down by
the side of their face in two flat bands, very wide, and each one firmly
plastered. These bands in no way have the appearance of hair. They
seem two enormous black, solid spatulas framing the women's faces,
standing out so far that they are almost as wide as the shoulders beneath
them, and terminating in a point over the chest. They are kept open by a
quantity of ribbons, disposed like the ribs of a fan, which form a singular
kind of halo; and they are laden with silver rings and twinkling little
coins, among which we were delighted to recognize many Russian coins
of ten and twenty copecks – this was a further sign that we were near the
Muscovite Empire. Naturally a headdress of so complicated a nature can
be indulged in only once in a lifetime. At the time of her wedding, the
Mongolian maiden leaves the dressing of her hair to the skilled mani-
pulations of a professional artist, and ever after she limits herself to its
upkeep. She dusts her spatulas from time to time and sticks them up
again when necessary. There is no danger that the use of a bath may ever
threaten the perfection of that wonderful work of art.

At the very moment when we knew no longer which direction to take,
and had begun asking everyone where the 'Rusky-Kitensky' Bank might
be (we were awaited at the Russo-Chinese Bank), a Chinese soldier
arrived at a gallop. He had come to show us the way. We passed near a
line of little white pagodas built in the Tibetan style, dimly resembling a
gigantic game of ninepins, and coming out into the open we saw a
European palace rising upon the summit of the hill. I cannot tell the
sudden joy that overwhelmed us at that glimpse of Europe in the heart of
Mongolia. It was as if we had been shown our own homes. We did not
yet know what the building might be, at that distance of three or four
miles and surrounded as it was by constructions which looked like sheds
or stables; but we knew it must be a friendly household; it *looked*
friendly, even from here; it was a comfort to us to see it merely because
of its familiar outline. Soon we saw the words 'Russo-Chinese Bank'
written in large letters and in four languages over its façade. We came up
triumphantly, tooting our horn with enthusiastic persistence.

At the entrance-gate stood a *tarantass*. Two Cossacks were passing
along the road and stopped to look at us; we bid good-day to them
effusively. From a little door there looked out the bearded face of a

moujik; but it disappeared almost at once, perhaps to announce our arrival.

'We seem to be already in Siberia!' we exclaimed, congratulating one another as if the journey were over.

And now the door of the bank opened, and a pleasant gentleman, M. Stepanoff, the director, came forward to meet us hospitably, not without manifesting a certain surprise at our early arrival.

'Why, it is the *Italian* flag!' he exclaimed, looking at our flag, which fluttered happily on the rear of the car. 'Welcome indeed, Prince Borghese! Ah, honestly, I did not expect you here. I know the desert, and your car seemed too heavy. I thought you would get left behind. I was convinced that the chance of the lighter machines was – Well, welcome anyway! This way! – all is ready.'

All indeed was most delightfully ready. The whole house was prepared for our reception. Russian, French, and Italian flags adorned the stairway. In a great hall sparkled a long table spread with twenty or thirty covers, laden with sweetmeats, with spotless serviettes artistically folded, and superb crystal and porcelain that made one utter exclamations of pleasure and surprise.

'I will notify the committee at once,' said our host to us, after having shown us our rooms.

'The committee?'

'Yes, the Russian committee for the reception of the Peking to Paris competitors. I will tell them of your arrival. They were all to be here to receive you – but we had no idea that you could arrive before night. We heard from Tuerin that a car had left this morning at 6.30. It is over 150 miles. You must forgive us if our reception has not been all that it should.'

So there was a committee! This was western civilization. We thought with gratitude of all those good people who had joined forces to fête us, to comfort us after our travels, suffering for our sakes meetings, discussions, inter-office memoranda . . .

M. Stepanoff was the president and the soul of this committee. At Urga began for us the memorable series of sincere and generous greetings on a large or a small scale, which gave us, along the whole course of our long journey, the continuous support of friendly sympathy; which opened before us the gates of palaces and the doors of huts; which made us feel everywhere surrounded by the sweet atmosphere of true hospitality, of that hospitality which says, 'Come, this is thy home.'

From the windows of our rooms we overlooked all the valley of the Tola and its scattered cities. The Bogda-ola was before us, vast and high,

with its imposing crest covered with pine trees. A legendary account tells
that on that peak is the tomb of Genghis Khan, and this would be a
magnificent tomb indeed for a conqueror.

Perhaps it is this legend that makes the mountain a holy place. To fell
trees or to hunt up there would be considered a sacrilege. Nobody even
climbs the mountain, for fear of disturbing the sleep of the great
demigod. The Mongolians, if you inquire of them the reason why they
never go upon the Bogda-ola mountain, reply that the mountain was
made by their god for his own pleasure-ground, and that he alone
frequents it, enjoying there the pleasures of walks and of the chase. In
their imagination the mountain is like a private garden of Divinity. Like
all primitive inhabitants of vast plains, they have a religious veneration
for mountains. It is always the summit of some height that they choose
for their *obos*. They climb in order to pray. Every elevation of the
ground was made, they think, to bring together the earth and the sky:
and the Bogda-ola is the highest mountain they know, therefore it must
be the most sacred. It is, moreover, covered by a wood, an impressive
mystery for a man of the prairie. In Mongolia there is a kind of cult for
the tree, because it is rare. Who knows what dim reverence that strange
shape issuing from the ground wakens in the simple mind of the nomad?
Often it is worshipped like a fetish, and we ourselves passed, even in
southern Siberia, many a deified tree along whose branches there waved
in the wind innumerable strips of paper with their written petitions.

The Itala was the goal of an innocent and fantastic pilgrimage. The
news of its coming had spread over all this province, and the event had
created a commotion in the whole valley of the Tola. People came from
the three Urga cities and from their far-off *yurta* encampments. The
Chinese, a practical people, had organized a service of mule-drawn
vehicles to take the curious to see the *chi-cho* and to lead them back to
their home palisades. You could see those singular vehicles, resembling
somewhat already the Russian *telega*, arriving by fives and by sixes
crammed with people wearing their Sunday best for this solemn occasion. We called them the 'omnibuses'. Real *telegas* were not wanting
either. They came from the Russian city, bringing an air of holiday with
the lively colours of the Slav costumes; and a crowd of Mongolians came
from all sides on foot and on horseback. Lamas dressed in violet or
yellow silk, crowned by pagoda-like hats; caravan drivers; shepherds
and women by the shoal, wearing thick boots, and balancing their
headgear, which looked like a Medici collar put round their head –
smiling and chattering. From time to time a Cossack would push his way
through the crowd and make a wide tour of inspection round the car.

All the crowd stood round with respectful admiration, as before a sacred mystery. The Mongolian population of Urga had been warned several days before, by means of the native bank agents, of the approaching arrival of carts which could travel without a horse to draw them. The authorities had wished to prepare the people, in order to avoid any possible outburst of fanaticism or superstition on the sudden arrival of such strange engines in the holy city. For some time past the bank had received daily visits from Mongolians, who came to make inquiries concerning these chariots which could run alone. Their questions were of an amusing naïveté. These people thought that the wonderful vehicles could not run on the ground, but no doubt sped through the air. They wanted to know from what distance one might gaze upon them without danger. They asked: would it not be imprudent to stand in their way, even if the cars were standing still? The most widely diffused conviction was that these cars were dragged by an invisible winged horse.

'But how can the strangers guide the invisible horse?' the people asked of M. Stepanoff, after listening with imperturbable solemnity to the most ingenious explanations intended to convince them that there was no horse there.

Primitive people live constantly in a world of fables; they explain everything by the intervention of the invisible. Their ignorance sees a mystery in every event, and a hidden power in every mystery. A miraculous and constantly repeated intervention of the gods in human affairs represents to their minds the normal government of the world. It does not surprise them. They believe in the existence of a winged horse, but cannot believe in a complicated creation of the human intellect. In their mind the impossible becomes truth, and truth becomes the impossible.

We do not know how far the sight of our machine modified the previous opinions of the citizens of Urga concerning motor cars. It is certain that the crowd pressed admiringly round every side of the Itala, except in front of it. The road before it was free, and the Chinese agreed in considering this measure to be wise and prudent. The name given by Mongolians to the motor car was the 'Flying Engine'. It is probable that news of it, borne towards them at camel's pace, reached the far-off tribes in the form of a new legend. Even the Grand Lama had taken great interest in the approaching event of our arrival. A mounted courier was immediately sent to warn him that we had arrived.

In the afternoon the Chinese governor came to call upon us. An official courier arrived at a gallop to announce his approach, and shortly after the cortège of this high dignitary appeared over the stony roadway, wrapped in a cloud of dust. The palanquin was carried with marvellous dexterity by four Mongolians on horseback; the shafts of the vehicle were simply resting upon the men's saddle-bows, and those four bearers galloped, keeping their distances with a wonderful precision. If one of them had swerved a hand's breadth, that poor governor, with his whole palanquin, would have come to an ignominious end. A crowd of Mongolian and Chinese cavalry, of officers and of dignitaries, preceded and followed the eminent mandarin. There was something of a primitive nobility and fearlessness in that many-coloured group which came upon us rushing like a storm. No expression equals in fierceness that on the face of a Mongolian soldier with his long, drooping moustache.

The governor, however, notwithstanding the terrifying grandeur with which he surrounded himself, was the most benign and the most courteous of Chinese. He spoke without saying anything, after the best diplomatic traditions. He smiled at every one, laughed at everything, took tea, and returned on his way in his swinging palanquin with his galloping escort.

We also received a visit from the Tartar general. He was greatly impressed with the news that our car was a 40 hp. Dear me! we had almost more horses than he. A serious military problem presented itself at once to his mind. A thought tormented him: was there in Europe a regiment mounted on this kind of multiple horse? If there was, all the Tartar generals placed to guard the frontiers of the Celestial Empire were perfectly useless. Ten motor cars would take Mongolia in four days! . . . We assured him that this new cavalry regiment did not exist, and he was greatly relieved.

That evening a Mongolian official, wheeling a little handcart (Mongolian officials are unpretentious beings), stopped at the back door of the bank, holding out a piece of red paper upon which were traced some Chinese characters. The paper was the visiting card of the governor, and it came accompanied by presents. The presents stood in the little cart, obstinately refusing to leave: they were two superb rams, which the official ultimately reduced to obedience, some bottles of Russian wine and boxes of preserves. Having deposited all these goods upon the ground, the Mongolian official, whose hat was adorned with the button of a sixth-class mandarin, insisted that we should inspect the cart to see that it was empty, and also verify that he had stolen nothing. We testified to the truth of both statements.

At Urga we found our third depot of fuel and oil, the last consignment sent from Peking. The fourth depot, at Kiakhta, was to be supplied through Siberia. Should we find it at Kiakhta? Would there be no hitch in the organization of our supply? Would no delay, no mishap stop us halfway on our journey, through want of fuel or of lubrication? We turned these questions over in our minds with a certain anxiety, for we were absolutely without news on these points. The prince had received at Peking a telegram from St Petersburg announcing that he would find at Kiakhta a list of the refill stations chosen for him, and a statement of the amount of supplies which would await him at each station. We felt uneasy, and, as events proved, not without cause.

In any case, at Urga we filled all our tanks full, in spite of the increase thus caused in the weight of the car, and thus we had enough supplies for 1000 kilometres, or just over 600 miles.

In the afternoon Ettore came to announce that the machine was ready for us to start. He always used to convey this information by just one word – *Finito* (All is ready).

'Everything in good condition?' asked Prince Borghese.

'Perfect. I have inspected everything. The engine is like new.'

There was nothing left for us to do, but wait for our fellow-motorists. And the waiting was made very pleasant for us by the people of Urga. The committee entertained us most nobly. It consisted of some Cossack officers, a medical officer who had been through the war in Manchuria, heads of commercial firms, ladies who longed for the life of St Petersburg and Moscow, and one spotless and well-bred Englishman who looked like a diplomat. He was an able pioneer of the wool and leather trades.

The stables had been put at our disposal, and I from time to time, enthroned upon the lofty Cossack saddle, betook myself to the tele-graph office in the Chinese city to dispatch my telegrams and ask for news of my colleagues. That evening I learned that the two de Dion-Boutons had arrived at Tuerin at five in the afternoon. They were expected to reach Urga the next day. There was no news of the Spyker; neither Pong-kiong nor Udde could tell us anything of it. For three days and two nights then the Spyker had been helpless in the desert. The Mongolian rider, with his telegram wrapped up in linen, and his camel-load of fuel, had not yet reached her. On the Spyker were its driver Godard, and my colleague Du Taillis. Our experience of the desert was too recent for us not to think of them at every moment with deep commiseration. The terrible thought of a further torment was added to the picture of their sufferings which rose constantly before our minds. We knew that they were about to be freed, that help had left Udde for them on the morning of the 19th, and was drawing hourly nearer to them. But we asked ourselves, *Did they know it?* Had they the knowledge, the certainty of their approaching liberation? What anguish and what tortures could not their doubt add to their physical suffering in the desert? One is strong when one is sure – who could reassure them? What would I not have given to be able to send them just one word by those wires which passed so close above their heads, carrying thousands of words of mine to a newspaper! We were indeed relieved next day when I received a communication from Udde: 'Spyker arrived – all satisfactory.'

22 June was given up to returning the calls we had received. We entered into the fort where the Tartar general entrenches his authority, and we sipped a few cups of tea before the eminent warrior, dressed in his gala uniform and surrounded by his *état-major* of befeathered Mongolians. The governor received us in his official residence and asked a great favour of the prince. We were far from expecting such a request as he proffered, from so perfect a mandarin as the Governor-General of Mongolia. His request upset all our ideas about China, all our most cherished conceptions of mandarinship. It was a rehabilitation of the Wai-wu-pu – it opened out a new horizon before the Celestial Empire. His Excellency begged to be taken out for a ride in the motor car!

'Most willingly!' exclaimed Prince Borghese, enthusiastically. 'And where would you like to go?'

He had no special desire. The governor merely wanted to go in the motor car, and to be taken for a triumphant tour through the streets of Urga. Unless I am very much mistaken, his chief desire was to be seen on this magical chariot. It might greatly increase his prestige.

The car was at the door. The mandarin, most pompously clad, with enormous silk sleeves which covered his hands, topped by the coral button which is a sign of the highest degree of mandarinship, wearing a hat adorned by two peacock feathers, first walked right round the machine inspecting it with great care. Then he mounted, while the prince took the wheel and Ettore sat on the step. By now, the news had spread, and the crowd was fast gathering round us. All the moustachioed Mongolian officers and soldiers looked alternately at their chief with an anxious and even terrified expression, and then at us, with diffidence.

The Itala started. It took a wide curve before the *fu* to cross a little bridge, and then sped into the open. The Mongolian governor had grasped the armrests of his seat very firmly, but he seemed completely enraptured. His little pigtail fluttered in the wind, and the men of his suite thought perhaps for a moment that their lord was being kidnapped.

They threw themselves upon their horses tethered to the railings close by, leaped to their saddles and dashed off after the diabolical engine, shouting. Then every one who happened to be within reach of a horse threw himself in their wake, and – down there there are horses within reach almost anywhere – horsemen came out on all sides: lamas, soldiers, men of the prairie. They arrived late. The motor car was already out of sight, and they could only follow the other men on horseback, but they went all the same, urging on their beasts to a mad gallop. Only a few better-mounted officers succeeded in keeping near the car. Like a great hunt the wonderful cavalcade continued: a savage horde thundering on at a gallop. It disappeared in the dust. It plunged tumultuously into the roads. Festive cries echoed all round. Many of the horses carried two men. That race was but a game, yet the scene preserved all the appearance of an episode in a fight. Urga seemed to be invaded by a victorious barbarian army. It was a vision of other times, to which the defences of the enclosure provided a true warlike background. You would have thought that the whole ancient world was up in wild pursuit of that small modern thing which fled before it without horses.

The governor desired to be taken as far as the Russo-Chinese Bank, where his palanquin came to call for him. This promenade had an unexpected political consequence. That evening the living Buddha sent word to us that he would let us know in only a few days' time whether he could grant us the privilege of beholding his countenance.

'But how is that?' we exclaimed. 'He was so anxious to see us.'

'Oh, that's understandable!' somebody murmured. 'He is offended.'

'Who? – the living Buddha? – and why?'

'Because of the governor's ride.'

'Really?'

'Most certainly. He is punctilious about priority, and he dislikes the governor.'

'So that we are out of favour with him?'

'Irreparably.'

'What a pity! We would have been glad to give him a ride too.'

But we resigned ourselves to our misfortune without too much heart-burning.

In the afternoon of that day, the de Dion-Boutons reached the town of Urga. Their drivers also, Cormier, Colignon, Longoni and Bizac, had suffered in the desert that radical change of complexion which transformed our own faces, although they had been protected on their march by a commodious hood. Their machines were in perfect condition. The

Spyker, which had reached Udde that afternoon, was to remain two days behind. As for us, we were urged on by a fear which made our departure necessary. We feared that the crossing of the River Iro, about forty miles south of Kiakhta, might prove a serious obstacle to our progress if we waited here any longer. For the Iro is fordable only during the dry season; one downpour of rain suffices to change it into an insurmountable obstacle. There is a ferry across the Iro, but it is not on the road which we were to follow. A Russian merchant coming from Kiakhta told us that the height of the water of the river was at that moment about four feet, a considerable height for a motor car to attempt to cross. It was certainly not desirable that this height should be given time to increase; even as matters stood, our crossing seemed a somewhat serious problem, and now the weather gave signs of breaking up: the clouds which had so delighted us the day before were growing immeasurably. The prince decided to leave on the following morning, 23 June. The de Dion-Boutons were to remain in Urga one day longer. The Itala would wait for them a whole day at Kiakhta.

The private apartments of the Russo-Chinese Bank were all lit up that evening. The great table, laid in the hall and bathed by the light of the candelabra, was to enter upon its solemn service. The committee, to a man, came to be our hosts at the banquet they were giving in our honour. We could have sworn that we were seated at a European public dinner, very far indeed from the capital of Mongolia, had not the presence of the Chinese 'boys' serving as waiters called us back from time to time to the consciousness of our surroundings. The conversation, French, Russian, and German, rose up on all sides, creating that pleasant hubbub of a banquet, in which the people who speak are always in so great a majority over those who listen.

I myself was of the minority that evening. I listened to the wife of the medical officer, who was describing to me her journey from Kiakhta to Urga, and who concluded her description by saying:

'I don't know how you will manage to pass with your motor car.'

'Well . . . we have come across the Gobi!'

'I don't know the Gobi, thank heaven, but I can assure you that the way to Kiakhta is the most horrible thing I have ever seen in the way of roads. And I have been to Manchuria! Think of it – four hours, for four whole hours we were gripped by the mud, unable to free our sinking *tarantass*, and with the prospect of continuing our way on foot. I have already told you this episode. We must have been ten versts from Urga, and this was the fourth time that we were sinking.'

'Was the weather unfavourable?'

'Excellent – just like now. You will see for yourself what a terrible thing that journey is.'

'Let us hope that our experience may not be too painful, madame,' and I smiled condescendingly. The tale of the most terrible travelling adventures left me calm. Feminine sensitiveness carries its victims sometimes to the most natural and pardonable, but yet remarkable, exaggeration.

I could not have imagined at the time how entirely right my neighbour was. I would never have believed that the road between Urga and Kiakhta would have given us a nostalgia for even the desert, and that a few hours after this conversation we were to tremble for the safety of our machine.

We left the bank at dawn, taking the most elaborate precautions not to wake our new friends in the sweet hours of sleep. We must have looked like burglars escaping with their booty after plundering a safe. Like all Russian banks, that of Urga too must have stood in some fear of the revolutionary 'Communists'. All night long it had a Cossack guard sent by the Russian consulate, and the good youths looked at us from their posts, on our departure, with evident misgivings. They seemed not to know whether they were to salute us or to raise the alarm. They decided to salute, and we sped freely on toward the Mongolian Urga, from which the road to Kiakhta takes its start.

But it was not easy to find this road. We no longer had the telegraph line to guide us – that convenient Ariadne's thread which had led us for nearly 800 miles – and the early-rising Mongolians whom we met fled, as soon as we stopped the car to question them. Fortunately, at the bank we had provided ourselves with a little bag of Russian small change, and by showing a silver piece of twenty copecks between our thumb and first finger, we succeeded as if by magic in stopping their flight. Prince Borghese with his knowledge of Russian, and I with mine of Chinese, succeeded in conveying our meaning by dint of asking repeatedly the way to Kiakhta and that to Maimachen. We turned northwards, left Urga behind us, and penetrated into a broad green valley, following unknown paths which crossed one another capriciously among tufts of grass and disappeared completely from time to time.

We had not been travelling for more than a quarter of an hour before the car stopped suddenly, and almost turned over on its left side.

The engine kept going, throbbing tumultuously, crackling, giving out clouds of white, sharp, acrid smoke. It seemed to be sensible of a danger, and to be collecting all its mighty strength with resolute violence in the effort of escaping, but we were nailed to the ground. Looking out, we saw the left wheels deeply sunk into the mud. The back wheel continued revolving rapidly, as though trying to come out of its bed by the mere impulse of a desperate speed; there was exasperation in that furious collected effort of the great machine.

'Stop! stop!' cried Ettore, seeing that the revolving wheel dug into the mud. 'We are sinking deeper.'

The engine stopped, and we stood for a few moments silently observing the position of the car, thinking of the best way to save it. It was sunk so deeply on the left that the axle and the fuel tank on that side touched the ground. What was to be done? How could we three lift and transport a weight of 2000 kilogrammes? We tried the engine again, assisting its efforts by pushing the car ourselves with all our power. It was perfectly useless. Probably not even all the coolies we had left at Kalgan would have sufficed just there. The most urgent thing to do now was to raise the sunk part of the car, because, tipped as it was entirely to one side, the weight of the machine strained the back wheel and spring, threatening to break one or the other. Ettore set to work with levers, but the levers sank into the soft earth. To hold them up we should need some planks, so we took some from the floor of the carriage. The planks creaked, broke, sank. Then an idea came to us: we might dig out the ground round the wheels and under the car, so as to form a slanting plane which the machine could easily climb by its own strength. And so we began, digging deep with our spade, and passing the spade to one another when we were tired.

After a few moments of excited and silent work, we saw, however, with a kind of terror, that we were digging the grave of our machine. The more we broadened the space round the wheels the more they sank. It was the lateral pressure of the earth, and not a hard bottom to it, that kept the wheels up at all, and this lateral pressure we were destroying by our work. There was, strictly speaking, no bottom to the spot where the wheels were sinking. The bog became soft and watery; it was a whole lake of slush crusted over, and the two wheels had broken through the crust. Such was the situation.

In the meantime, the wheel of the car was so twisted by the strain placed upon it that it ended by touching the body of the car with its upper edge, and from time to time it cracked threateningly. I was mentally apologizing to the wife of the medical officer, whose tales I had heard with so much scepticism. We must now be near the places where her *tarantass* had sunk, and the weight of a *tarantass* is not one-tenth that of a motor car.

We told ourselves that Urga was near, at little more than an hour's walk, and that in three hours one of us could be back with a good relay of men, a load of planks and beams, and horses . . . but we could not make up our minds to go and ask for that help. It was a question of pride; a justifiable weakness. We pictured to ourselves one of us returning to the bank on foot, panting and muddy, the surprise of our hosts, the tale of our sinking and the confession of our impotence, the generous offer of help, the people coming to behold the vanquished motor car: that car which had paraded so ostentatiously over the roads of Urga. We pictured all this, and it seemed that it would bring us just a shade too much humiliation. No, no, we must get out of this difficulty without asking for help from Urga. A captain whose ship lies aground does all he can to disentangle it before he resigns himself to hoisting the signal of distress. We felt the same kind of pride.

'If only we had some wooden beams,' we exclaimed, looking around us, as if beams might sprout up from the ground.

'Oh, for our four iron mudguards!'

A caravan drawn by oxen, led by Mongolians, and advancing towards Urga, passed at a few hundred yards from us on the slope of a hill. It was advancing slowly, and we, all absorbed in our useless labour, had not noticed it. But, as soon as we saw it, without so much as exchanging a word, we understood one another at one glance, and ran precipitately towards that long line of carts. The carts were loaded with beams. They were thin pine trunks, destined, no doubt, to furnish the traditional palisades of the Holy City.

A few coins convinced the Mongolians of our good intentions. Besides, they had no doubt understood the reason of our coming, they must already have had some experience of similar accidents. We each took a beam on our shoulders, the Mongolians did the same, and down we ran towards the motor car. Then, by trying and trying again, using our pine trunks in all possible and imaginable ways, we succeeded in finding a system of levers which was to save us on that occasion and on all similar occasions in the future.

It was a perfectly simple contrivance. Imagine a double lever, whose point of resistance at one end serves as a fulcrum to another lever of the same size, acting immediately upon the nave of the sunk wheel. The strength of two men is sufficient, if the beams are long, to raise a motor car by this system of leverage, and when you have at your service the strength of four or five men, one lever alone is sufficient for the purpose. As we raised the machine gradually by this means, with the willing co-operation of those good caravan drivers, we took care to fill the depressions made by the wheels with some stones which we went to gather from a ditch close by. The car, at every halt in the work, pushed these stones down into the mud, but it pushed down so many that it ended by standing on a solid base of them, a regular substructure.

After two and a half hours' desperate work, we had all the four wheels at the level of the ground. The only thing remaining to be done was to drag the machine away backwards out of this unsafe place. We took out the ropes and attached them firmly to the chassis – we thought of the Great Wall – and we began to pull all together, the Mongolians and ourselves, with all our might. But we could not succeed in moving the heavy car by one inch. It was still embedded between the stones and the earth, and we dared not set the engine going for fear that its sudden impulse might cause the machine to sink again.

'Why, there are the oxen – those great oxen there!' exclaimed Prince Borghese.

Great ideas are always the simplest. Five minutes later three oxen were yoked to the car. In the meantime more people had gathered round. A few shepherds had come trotting down to see what was this extraordinary movement in their meadows; a few lamas from a sanctuary whose white walls we saw gleaming on a neighbouring height; some women from a far-off group of *yurtas*. The oxen, urged on by goad and whip, pulled willingly, but with no visible result. Then we all got to the ropes with the oxen, the caravan drivers and ourselves – and then everyone else, shepherds, lamas, women. Wherever was a bit of free rope, there came a hand, and the car finally decided to follow us to safety. It now at last stood on firm ground again, and all those hands appeared immediately before us, open, to receive well-earned compensation. One of the men spoke a little Russian.

'Where is the way to Kiakhta?' Prince Borghese asked him.

'There are two ways to Kiakhta. One goes over the mountains, the other goes over the plain. The one over the plain is the best.'

'Will you show us the best one?'

'It is this road, where we are standing.'

'Then show us the worst, please.'

He showed it to us, and having finished our preparations and put back ropes, planks and tools, we went off in that direction. Our departure caused a very reasonable astonishment in all those people who had helped us to extricate the car with so much difficulty. They had not seen us arrive, and they probably supposed that it was a case of some strange ammunition wagon, whose horses were, perhaps, at some distance away. The sound of the engine made them draw back with a movement of fear; the starting of the car made them laugh. They were all hilarious and satisfied, and could not help laughing, just as those other two Mongolians had laughed when we had met them on our way to Urga. Indeed, this exhilarating effect was always produced by the car, amid all the more simple and more naïve people: admiration is a sentiment exclusively appertaining to the man who *knows*.

The path went down among valleys, climbed over hills, wound on, somewhat stony and sometimes steep, and would have been very bad, if not impossible, for a cart drawn by horses. We were obliged to proceed very slowly, with every caution, but comparing it in our minds to the road we had left we found this quite pleasant.

'Here at least there is no sinking,' we exclaimed at every moment. And then, the blue sky had come: it was a glorious morning. We passed near meadows covered with flowers, and skirted little woods of birch trees – our first birch trees. We filled our lungs with the fragrant coolness of the Siberian spring, and were never sated with our enjoyment of all these new things. The hours passed, alike, but not monotonous. After that accident of the bog we found everything easy, everything simple. We had become patient. If we lost our way, if we had to steer by compass and the imperfect markings on the map, we resigned ourselves to do so with perfect complacency. 'Better this than sinking,' we said to ourselves by way of consolation. The danger we had escaped in the bog had endowed us with new virtues.

Our machine climbed easily over the most rugged ascents. At ten o'clock we found ourselves upon the summit of a high hill, and we stopped in order to admire a most wonderful landscape. Behind us was a slow, broken descent of green hills, ending in the great, blue, luminous valley of the Tola. Urga was out of sight, hidden in the folds of the more distant heights. But, almost as though to mark the place where it lay, to show a pious traveller where he was to turn his anxious eye to find the sacred residence of the living Buddha, a white pagoda looked out from a peak and seemed to sparkle in the sunshine. Some Mongolian riders, looking like soldiers, had got down from their saddles and were also looking towards Urga. We disturbed their contemplation by our advance, which made their horses restive. We now got up speed.

There is a reverse side to every medal. That hill, after having presented to us such a pleasing and picturesque side, now showed a disastrous reverse. The descending path was a precipitous incline all in a straight line from the top to the base of the hill. It was encumbered with stones, with bits of flint, and slanted just a little bit towards the left, where it was flanked by a deep ravine. Ettore, who was driving, suddenly applied the two most powerful brakes of the machine and disengaged the clutch. The car dragged on for a few yards with the driving wheels almost motionless, jerking over the stones until it reached two bigger stones and stopped. Then the brakes were slowly released, but the machine did not move.

'We shall have to take away these stones in front of the wheels,' remarked Ettore.

The prince and I got down to do this, but the stones were firmly embedded in the soil, and we did not succeed in moving them.

'It doesn't matter,' exclaimed Ettore. 'With a tiny shove of the car I can get over the stones and go on.'

No sooner said than done, he engaged the clutch again. But that manoeuvre very nearly led to a catastrophe. The slope of the road was so steep that the car, after surmounting the obstacle, leaped down the slope, unhindered by the footbrake, and in the short time which it took Ettore to put on the handbrake too, which is more powerful, the speed had already become excessive and could not be checked.

The machine had taken the upper hand. It bounded over the stones with such impetus that every shake raised it from the ground. It seemed to be descending by leaps and bounds. There were moments when it stood on the back wheels alone, as a shying horse stands on his hindquarters. Then it would fall again with a thud. It had a violent, swaying movement which made it bound over to one side and another. The luggage was coming undone. One could hear the sinister sound of the iron pieces – a metallic resonance.

Prince Borghese had remained hanging on to that furious monster, and was violently dragged and shaken by it. He had been by the side of the car when Ettore started the machine, and on seeing it run out of control, he had made a swift attempt at holding it back. For a few moments, urged by an unreflecting and desperate desire to save it, he made a determined though useless effort to halt its descent. He had seen the danger and was instinctively fighting against the inevitable, putting all his faculties and all his will into the fight.

'Put on the brake! put on the brake!' he cried.

Unable to hold the machine back, he at least would accompany it. He would not abandon his hold. Firmly gripping the body of the car, he was a prey to all its bounds and all its swiftness. Ettore sat silent, bent over the wheel. The whole man was gathered in the effort of attention. He was spying the moment when he could recover the mastery over his machine. His presence of mind won the battle. I have already said that the road sloped a little to the left. At a point where the slope was very pronounced, Ettore swerved suddenly to the right, and took the car over some heavy stones. The car rebounded, but slackened its speed. A few minutes later it was tamed, and ended its descent docilely, answering obediently to its driver.

The flight had not lasted more than twenty seconds, but to us it had seemed endless. I had followed it on foot, running and shouting, uselessly, 'Stop! stop!' as if everyone's greatest desire had not been to stop! I caught up with the motor car at the bottom of the road. The machine, standing still, gave out a smell of burnt oil, a crackling as of a frying-pan.

'This time we have had a narrow escape,' said Ettore, coming down from his post and wiping his brow. 'I don't know how we've got here. It is a miracle!' Then, turning to me with a smile, 'Did you see her leap?'

'I should think so! It looked as if everything must go to pieces.'

'So I thought it would. There was a moment when I thought all was lost. I thought – now we are done for.'

'Which moment was it?'

'Did you notice, halfway down, when I turned a little to the right?'

'Yes.'

'It was then. I said to myself, Now you are either saved or smashed.'

'Well, this time it was "saved". But were the brakes not working?'

'They were working all right, but to keep them in good condition they have to be heavily lubricated, and that prevents them from acting at once. They slip. Over the road they work excellently, but can these be called roads? We've done all the roads in the Alps, haven't we, your Excellency? And we have never had anything like this.'

The prince was smiling and looking up at the road he had covered in that unusual fashion. He seemed entirely absorbed in fixing it in his memory. One always has a sense of rejoicing after a danger. Presently he pulled himself up, exclaiming:

'Let's be off – it's late. I want to camp tonight on the banks of the Iro.'

The machine was carefully inspected. No damage done. We packed and tied up the luggage again, and each taking his seat, we went off at high speed.

'They say,' said Prince Borghese to me, jokingly, 'that when you have had two misfortunes in one day, a third one is sure to come.'

'Shall we prepare for the third?' I asked, with a laugh, and we seemed to be defying that third misfortune. Let it come, if it would! We felt strengthened by the experience gained. We knew now the dangers of the mountain and the plain – what could we fear? But we were mistaken, and we were to find it out only too soon.

The third misfortune came.

X

ON THE WAY TO KIAKHTA

*The Third Accident – Among Mongolians and Buriats –
A Race through the Night – Across the Iro – Our
First Wade – Kiakhta*

The road between Urga and Kiakhta – that is, the route followed by
caravans – crosses a chain of mountains enclosed between the rivers
Chara-gol and Iro, both flowing from east to west towards the Orkhon,
which is the largest tributary of the River Selenga. Those mountains,
called after the Chara-gol River (but also, according to the map, known
by the name of Argal Mountains) are rugged and steep. The road over
them had been described to us as presenting peculiar difficulties. And
for this reason we had decided to avoid it.

We intended to make a circuit round the ill-famed mountains
approaching the valley of the Orkhon. For hours and hours, with no
guide except our common sense, passing over a network of lines and
paths, leaving them from time to time if they seemed to be taking a
wrong direction for our purpose, and often running with no path at all,
we crossed hills, plains, and valleys. Often what seemed a road led us up
to some quite unconquerable obstacle, to paths only fit for goats, and
then we were compelled to turn back patiently as far as the last parting of
the ways. When we could, we asked shepherds and caravan drivers for
advice, but their replies were always very uncertain. Most of them
pointed to the north. Kiakhta lay on the north, and they knew no better
way of reaching it than to walk in that direction.

We mistrusted abandoned paths, and often got down from the car to
examine whether the traces of traffic on our path were recent or old. We
preferred untried ground to a path which had evidently been abandoned, because this abandonment was always justified by some serious
cause. Abandonment warned us of danger. In fact, when exploring an
abandoned path on foot, we would always discover that the ground was
swamped or flooded, or that the water had worked out some wide
crevice for itself. Sometimes we would find fresh marks of transit

suddenly interrupted before us, and then, with a little investigation, we would find a deviating track on the grass, and would follow it forward. Thus we profited by the experience of nomads and caravan drivers whom we had never seen. People who had passed over those regions days previously, and who were now a great distance from ourselves, served us as guides, just as much as if they had been there walking before us.

At two p.m. we came out upon a plain covered with green bushes and tall grass. We did not notice at first sight that the vegetation was entirely aquatic, but even according to our calculations the River Chara-gol could not be very far. Before us rose the first steps of the Argal Range. Suddenly we noticed that the road seemed to be abandoned, and we scarcely had time to exchange a swift word before the car sank and stopped. It had entered into a turbid slime, the crust of which, dried up by the sun, presented all the characteristics of solid earth. This time the machine leaned over to the right.

On jumping out we immediately noticed a strange phenomenon which severely taxed our courage. The soil under our feet was heaving. It was as if we had been walking over floating cork. This crust gave way without breaking; it sank under the pressure of one's foot, ready to spring up again as soon as the pressure was removed. At every step the ground felt like indiarubber. It was obvious that below that slender surface there were depths of water, and we thought for a moment that it all formed an abyss. We wanted to feel how deep it was, and tried to measure it with the handle of our spade; the long stick slipped down as it would have slipped into a sheath. It gave us a sensation of horror to see it thus sucked in. We understood that the mass of mud would swallow up our car if we did not succeed in saving it at once.

We looked all round us. We were alone. The hot and silent plain was quite deserted. We began to work but with the feverish anguish of men performing a useless task. We were fulfilling a duty; we would not give way without a fight, and we were ready to fight with all our powers for the survival of our machine, but we had no hope of victory. We were like men struggling in vain for the life of one beloved and doomed. We were working rather to deceive ourselves, to give ourselves the illusion of being useful. We knew that we could not do anything, we three alone. There were no cities near, where we might run to ask for help, whence we might fetch workmen or machinery.

'If we could find a horse!' said Prince Borghese. 'If we could find a horse, I would ride to Urga. I should arrive tonight, and by tomorrow evening I could be back with some men . . .'

It would be too late. By the evening of the next day the car must inevitably have been swallowed up.

'This time it's all up!' exclaimed Prince Borghese, even he, who never lost his courage at anything. 'It's all up. This morning when we sank the first time I felt sure that we should get out again – but now . . . ?'

And we were already thinking, each one to himself, of the long return journey on foot over the mountains of the Chara-gol, with a bag on our shoulders, on our way back to Kiakhta, silent, like prisoners of war, depressed with the vision of a lost battle.

The work of our levers produced no result except the immersion of the levers themselves into the ground and a further breaking of the slight, solid crust which still supported the motor car. It went on sinking, slowly, inexorably.

The hub of the right rear wheel was the first thing to disappear. The axles, the fuel tank, the differential box, were every moment embedded more deeply in the mud. The running boards which, on our first stopping, were a good twelve inches from the ground, a few minutes later were firmly planted in it. The car was slowly but surely disappearing. Our hearts seemed ready to break, like the heart of a wrecked man witnessing from the shore the death-throes of his boat. We started feverishly to try and lighten it. We unloaded the baggage, took down the toolchest, the provisions, the spare tyres, and threw everything in a heap upon the grass. There was nothing else to be done, and now we stood there looking, motionless, obstinately searching our minds for a remedy.

'Let us have a cup of tea,' said Prince Borghese, after a long silence.

Those few words were almost like a signal of desertion. To make tea now meant leaving our machine, ceasing from lavishing upon it our useless efforts.

A stream close by provided the water, which we boiled over the flame of our soldering-lamp, and we made tea in a saucepan from which we filled our cups.

Stretched full length upon the ground in our shirtsleeves, hot, be-grimed with mud, we sipped our tea slowly, absent-mindedly, gnawing at bits of biscuit. We had lost the habit of lunching. On our journeys we never could make up our minds to stop for food; we had only one desire, that of arriving at the next halting place; and our unsatisfied appetite was but one more incentive to waste no time. Now we had ample time to satisfy our hunger.

We decided what was to be done. One of us was to remain encamped near the car and the other two would make their way to Urga, find men, timber, and horses, and return as soon as possible. We had no hope that a caravan would arrive, for we were on an abandoned road.

But, lo, quite suddenly, there came in sight a caravan far away among the tall rushes! It was a line of carts drawn by horses, and over the horses we saw *dugas*, those typical wooden arches of the Russian harness. It was a line of *telegas*.

'Russians, there are the Russians!' I cried, and ran as fast as ever I could towards them, jumping over bushes, sinking now and then in the mud, calling out to them, waving my arms violently to attract their attention.

Russians seemed to us at that moment almost compatriots. We felt the affinity of our race with theirs, here in the heart of Mongolia. And their presence here meant salvation. When I got near, I perceived that the *telegas* were full of people dressed indeed in the Russian fashion, but of the Mongolian type. These were Buriats. I was now facing a Buriat tribe 'on the trek', with its women and children. Their chief rode on in front, dressed in a red vest, wearing a Tartar cap. The expression of his countenance was scarcely reassuring. I invited him to follow me and he, giving orders to his tribe to stop, came with me.

He spoke a little Russian. He looked at the car and asked:

'How heavy is it?'

'One hundred and twenty *pud*. I will give you a good recompense if you drag this car away from where it is. Will you undertake to do it?'

The Buriat chief remained wrapped in thought for a few moments, and then he replied:

'Yes, I will.'

'Very well. Bring your men and your horses.'

He went back to the *telegas* and made them approach us by another few hundred yards. Then, the women got down, got some fuel and made fires; but the horses were not unharnessed and no men came. Half an hour later the chief returned alone.

'Well,' said the prince, 'what are you about? When will you start working?'

The Buriat showed no anxiety. He asked:

'Will you give me fifty roubles?'

'You take this car out of here, and I will give you fifty roubles.'

The man returned to his people. The horses were left harnessed to the *telegas*; the men still remained near their conveyances. This behaviour began to look strange.

In the meantime, some Mongolians were arriving at a gallop on their horses. They came, heaven knows from where. Their vulture eye had seen from afar this strange object in difficulties on the plain, and they were coming to see it. We were soon surrounded by a crowd, who looked on and discussed the event. The Buriat, perhaps made curious by this movement, approached us for the third time, still alone. Prince Borghese asked him again:

'When are you setting to work? You have asked for fifty roubles. I will give you fifty roubles, but be quick. Bring your men here.'

The chief shook his head.

'Do you want more?' asked the Prince.

'No.'

'Then what are you doing?'

'It cannot be done. It is an impossible task.'

And the man went away.

Why would he not try? Or else why, once he had recognized that the undertaking was an impossible one, why would he not depart with his *telegas*, instead of remaining nearby – and why then did he leave his horses still unharnessed as though he wished to keep them ready for flight? There came to my mind a suspicion that these Buriats nourished some project unfavourable to ourselves. We were nailed to the ground, and they knew it. We could not get away. Might not the question about the fifty roubles have been put just in order to find out whether we had money or not, and to judge of our possessions from our open-handedness? The Buriats were many and we were three. The Mongolian steppes offer immunity and shelter; no laws govern there except those of tradition and the power of might.

The Mongolians who stood round us had understood one thing, namely that we offered money in exchange for help. The circulation of the *word* 'rouble' is much wider than that of the coin. They immediately set to work, trying to lift the car by the strength of their arms. We felt revived by this kindly disposition. Wooden beams were needed. I do not know what unconquerable eloquence we succeeded in giving to our gestures, but we actually succeeded in describing planks by some prodigious piece of mimicry, and we were understood. Three of our new friends got them to their horses and went off full speed, reappearing half an hour later with some long, thin planks dragging behind them from their saddle-bows. We could have embraced them.

And now we set to work. In order to lighten the machine still further, we dismounted the body of the car and, by the help of our Mongolian friends, placed it upon the grass. With the planks, we built our simple lifting apparatus. We had to proceed cautiously, because the ground threatened to give way under the levers, and our planks, too old, creaked and threatened to break. But the car, little by little, began to rise. Under its wheels we placed thick pieces of wood made out of one of the planks by means of a hatchet. It was a slow, patient piece of work. It took us three hours to heave our machine out of the deep ruts it had made. We now attached the ropes to the back part of the frame, and all together we tried to drag the car away. But all our efforts were in vain.

Could we not get some oxen? After having described planks by mimicry, we found it perfectly easy to describe an ox, and we soon had round us a whole herd, which must have been grazing a few miles off. The insufficient length of the ropes only allowed us to use four oxen together. The poor brutes pulled and pulled, but got no nearer than we had done to moving the motor car. We saw, however, that if the oxen could only make one simultaneous effort they would succeed. The excited beasts pulled at intervals, one after the other. How could we convince them of the advantages of perfect harmony. We had a stroke of genius: we must start the engine!

The success was complete. At the sudden noise, the four frightened oxen planted their feet with one accord firmly on the ground, put down their great horns, roaring, and advanced with a simultaneous and resolute impulse towards flight. The car swayed. Ettore, who had climbed on to the machine, put down the accelerator, and the sound became deafening. The four terrified beasts pulled desperately, and suddenly the car came out of its furrow with one bound. We had a moment of deep thankfulness.

We put the body of the car back in its place in a very few minutes. The luggage, the spare tyres, our provisions, and the tools were all loaded again hastily. Half an hour later we were ready to start. We generously distributed a large number of roubles among the Mongolians, and they received them with enthusiastic exclamations and the most effusive signs of friendship. At this point the Buriat chief approached and put out his hand too. Prince Borghese said to him smiling:

'No work, no money.'

The Buriat drew back his hand with a surly glance, and replied:

'I have no need of your money.'

And he added words which we did not understand. Then we saw him get to his horse and sign to his tribe that they were to continue their journey. The long line of *telegas* continued its advance, and was soon lost in the distance.

We asked the Mongolians for a guide. One of them offered himself, mounted his horse, and told us to follow. All the others escorted us. They were full of the most naïve joy. They galloped in high spirits around us, shouting and laughing. Some of the horses carried two riders, just as we had seen them do at Urga in the governor's escort. Our guide fulfilled his duty with the most dignified bearing.

We were traversing a true labyrinth, from time to time skirting stagnant pools, winding in and out among high rushes and tufts of iris plants in the vast and desolate swampy plain. The sun was setting, and from the earth rose a mist which gave an inexpressible air of sadness to the landscape.

On the outskirts of the plain our strange escort abandoned us and scattered. Our guide showed us the road we were to take if we wished to avoid the mountains and then left us to ourselves. His horse was trembling with fatigue. It was almost dark. After greeting us and thanking us for the reward we had given him, the man lay down upon the grass.

We continued our way. We were in need of water both for the engine and for ourselves, and could not stop until we found some. We expected to see the River Chara-gol come within sight at any moment. We looked anxiously before us, and at every dip of the road, at every thickening of the vegetation, we said, 'The river must be there . . .' But the river was not to be seen, and we continued seeking it, on and on, with ever-renewed and ever-disappointed hope.

The moon was up. We had no lights; at least, we had lamps, but they were not prepared for lighting. We were amid lofty heights, and our path followed narrow valleys, climbed, descended, was scarcely visible through the grass which covered it. We strained our eyes to see it for fear of missing our way, and to our tired eyes under the spectral light of the moon, all things appeared to take on terrifying, uncertain, fantastic outlines. The profiles of the hills, the deep shadows of the valley, the shrubs along the road made us start sometimes, because we did not recognize them. They took on mysterious and indescribable shapes. We thought we were witnessing a strange movement of the things around us, a silent gliding past of unknown forms. All those who have travelled by night over unknown and deserted regions must have seen these strange transformations, and on returning by day to the same places must have been surprised to find them so changed. It is almost as though the earth were in the habit of profiting by the darkness of night to live a freakish life of its own. In the night all that there is of the fabulous, impossible, and absurd in our fancy comes out and takes a place in the shadow. No two people ever see the same things in a landscape by night. Each person sees his own landscape.

And so each one of us in that memorable night perceived something which to the others was invisible; rivers, houses, motionless men – visions which vanished on our approach. The ground seemed good, but from time to time we heard the sound of scrunching under the wheels and felt these sinking a little, and the engine began to pant. Then we put the car at full speed, so as not to get caught in the sand. At one point we really saw some living beings move: they were camels. We passed near an encamped caravan. Two men were standing near the path. They turned round with a sudden movement and did not stir again. We wished we could have seen the expression of their faces on beholding the sudden apparition of this enormous black mass, which fled roaring over the solitudes of the Daturbada.

'What time is it?' said the prince, whose watch was broken.

I cautiously lit a match and looked at mine.

'Nine o'clock.'

We had been travelling since four o'clock in the morning; seventeen hours of unbroken work, under the most exhausting nervous tension. We were tired, and were not yet anywhere near the Chara-gol. We could not possibly miss it, for its course was to cross our way.

The moon was now descending towards the horizon. The night was peopled with stars. I could no longer see the path at all, and was filled with admiration for Ettore's unhesitating moves, driving as he was as though he had been on the best country road.

'A light, a light!' we exclaimed, suddenly seeing one in the distance.

'It must be the fire of an encampment pitched on the bank of the river,' said the prince.

Our courage revived, but a few minutes later the light had entirely disappeared. Yet we had had time to fix in our minds the point where we had first seen it, and we were anxiously scanning that bit of the darkness with our eyes. When we arrived there, a few minutes later, we found ourselves by a small group of *yurtas*. We stopped. A pack of barking dogs surrounded us. The silhouette of a man appeared on the threshold against the glare of a lighted room. We asked him for some water, and he offered us all he had, out of an earthenware jar. It was hot, greasy, muddy water, full of earth deposits. We asked him where the nearest spring was, and he pointed across the road with a movement that meant 'quite close'. We beckoned him to guide us, but he refused. He was afraid of us.

We continued as far as a meadow, where we decided to stop. While Ettore was pitching the tent, the prince and I started on a search for the spring. The prince carried the pail and I the spade (a pail for the water and a spade for the dogs). I represented the defence, and a defence was most necessary, for Mongolian dogs are noted for their ferocity.

By now the moon had disappeared, and the whole earth seemed asleep under the pale firmament. After much searching we succeeded in finding a little stream of muddy, stagnant water. It was so bad that we could not drink any, in spite of our thirst. When we returned to the tent we made some tea, which turned out the most abominable tea that can be imagined. We consumed in silence a large supply of jam; we sipped that detestable boiling stuff (mixed with much sugar), and we crawled on all fours under our tent. The night was divinely still.

We took the precaution not to leave anything outside our tent, and Ettore, loyal to his charge, kept the pistol within his reach. Stretched out upon the grass, and wrapped in the sweet warmth of our furs, it was not long before we fell into a deep sleep.

In the middle of the night I was awakened by Ettore's voice calling: 'Who's there?'

He had raised himself upon his elbow, and I could hear him feeling for the Mauser.

I listened in suspense.

Then I heard close to us outside a low, short patter, clearly audible in the silence of the night.

'Who's there?' cried Ettore again, with a sterner ring in his voice.

No one answered. A gust of wind came past, and the sound was repeated. It was a rapid, slight, and incomprehensible little patter, quite close to us. Gently, gently we lifted a corner of the tent and looked . . .

'I very nearly pulled the trigger!' exclaimed Ettore with a smile. 'Whoever would have thought she could make so much noise! She woke me up!'

It was the flag. Our little Italian flag, hoisted on the motor car, fluttering, moving lightly at every breath of wind. She seemed to be living and watching.

The place of our encampment was only a few miles from the river, which we forded swiftly, early on the morning of 24 June. We had left the mountains to our right, and we were drawing near, towards the west, to the source of the Orkhon, over a series of marshy plains. But we were well on our guard now against the snares of the ground; the lesson had been hard, but useful. We never advanced with the car here before carefuly exploring, studying, and discussing the way. Dangers surrounded us on all sides. Often we suddenly felt under our feet the heaving of the hidden slime, and we drew back shuddering, as if we had trodden upon a reptile. We called out to Ettore, who followed us slowly with the machine: 'Back! Back at once!' and tried to find firm ground.

Sometimes there was no firm ground there, and we had to go back and find another path. Gently, slowly, patiently, we succeeded in extricating ourselves from these muddy places and in reaching the hills which stretched bare and sandy between the Orkhon and the Iro.

Ever since the evening before, we had noticed here and there on our road some marks which interested us: the traces of a cart and of European footsteps. When for thousands of miles the only traces you see are those of Chinese shoes and Mongolian boots, the footprint of a European looks like a friend. These footmarks went in the same direction as ourselves, and they were recent. At times they disappeared. In the plain we had lost them, and then we found them again and felt a strange pleasure at the sight of them. We discussed them: were they old? were they recent? These must have been made only an hour ago – perhaps less than that. They marked the steady, long tread of two young men. The men could not have been cart drivers, because the Siberian cart driver always leads a number of *telegas* in a line, and here, on the contrary, two men formed the escort to one cart. The cart cannot have been very heavily laden, for the traces of its wheels were not deep. It must have carried some precious merchandise of little weight and requiring a strong escort . . . It is difficult to realize what small things suffice, in the monotony of a journey such as ours, to awaken one's curiosity and to provide an inexhaustible subject of conversation. The faintest trace or sound of life carries one's fancy away into the beautiful unexplored world of conjectures. It is one's only amusement.

Down a slope we overtook our European friends. They were two fair, well-built Russian youths, who looked like workmen. A woman, equally young, carrying a child in her arms, looked out at us from under the curtain of their little cart. We exchanged a greeting: '*Do svidania!*' This was our first Russian salute.

The Orkhon now appeared before us, surrounded by a thirsty crowd of strong trees, and winding in its immense green valley, over which some herds of cattle were grazing. We came upon it from above. For a moment we thought it was the Iro. Then the path turned northwards, descending the slopes, and led us over other plains, where we were obliged to return to our former system of exploration. We passed streamlets, tributaries of the Iro, crossing them first on foot so as to explore their bed and to find the fords most suited to the motor. Some heavy and difficult tracts of sand told of the neighbourhood of a great river. Finally, the Iro appeared, broad, clear, and swift.

We had reached it at last – but how were we to cross it? Would it be possible to ford it by motor power alone? Ettore waded into the water. He had not gone a hundred feet before we saw him in up to his waist. He came back, saying:

'We must find another means of crossing this. The bottom is good, but the water would cover the magneto. The ignition would fail, and we should be left in the middle of the current. The current is very strong, too – a moment ago it nearly bowled me over.'

We thought of making a raft, but a raft strong enough to carry our car would have had to be made with at least two layers of planks, and must also be very large. Where should we find so much timber? Looking round us, we discovered near a clump of trees an old hut, a forerunner of the *isba* by its shape, and surrounded by a small enclosure.

'Let us buy the hut,' I suggested, 'demolish it and make a raft.'

'It would take us ages,' said the prince. 'Let's first try to find something quicker.'

A few Mongolians came out of the hut and approached us. Among them were women with their faces surrounded by the usual strange headdress, which looked like the flaps of an elephant's ears. More people came up on horseback along the sunlit bank.

There was just a chance that we might get to the ferryboat which ferries the carts across. There must be some path leading to the landing-stage. We asked the Mongolians, some of whom understood a little Russian.

No, there were no paths. Further on, towards the mountain, the bank became all rocky. We should have to retrace our steps over all the road we had done today, and to pass over the mountain – if the mountain was possible to pass.

There was one other means of advancing: we might take out the magneto and then tow the car to the opposite bank from here. The engine, covered with a coat of grease, would not suffer from contact with the water unless it got into the cylinders. We decided to try this immediately. We told the Mongolians what we intended to do, and that we needed some oxen; adding that we would pay well for their services, but that the oxen must be brought at once. The men set off immediately, and a little later, turning round, we saw a group of oxen arriving on the scene, as if by magic, under the guidance of two horsemen armed with long goads. And we all three solemnly agreed that the Mongolian is the most civilized and most courteous race of the universe.

Ettore worked for a long time lying face upwards on the hot sand under his motor car. He took off the casing which protects the engine and the flywheel from below; he unscrewed the magneto most carefully; then covered the more delicate parts of the machine with rags dipped in oil, wrapped up his magneto safely in his own jacket, and finally pronounced himself ready. The ropes were tied to the car and the oxen put to the ropes. Then a most unusual kind of towing-navigation began, and we travelled by it across the water for 300 yards. All our Mongolians went into the river with the oxen and the motor car – some on foot, some on horseback, by twos and threes on each horse. Even the women got astride their horses to follow this nautical procession. The prince was mounted upon one horse, left to his own undisputed possession. I had got on to another horse and was about to start in all comfort on my fording journey – was, in fact, busily engaged at the moment in raising my camera beyond the height of probable splashes – when someone suddenly plumped himself down behind me on my saddle. The intruder was a Mongolian, to whom this seemed a most natural procedure. He hung with friendly confidence on to my shoulders, laughing, and thus we reached the other bank together, in fraternal amity.

In the middle of the river, the wheels of the motor car were completely under water, and the stream passed with a deep gurgle right over the floor of the car. The oxen wavered for a moment, pushed as they were by the tumultuous current which made them deviate, but by cries and goading they were made to renew their effort, and a minute later we saw the unusual spectacle of a motor car coming out from its bath, dewy and streaming, leaving a long track of water behind it. Between the moment when we left one bank, and the moment when we reached the other, two and a half hours elapsed – a long time for a journey of 300 yards!

An hour later we were ready to start for our journey over the last tract of Mongolian territory. We warned those kind people of the arrival of more cars like our own, and were off. Just as we left, there seemed to rise among our friends an apparently very serious dispute over the distribution of the money they had earned. We might have thought there was going to be bloodshed among them, had we not known that Mongolians have a horror of shedding blood; their religion forbids it, and they obey the letter of the law. When they want to avenge themselves on an enemy they strangle him.

We ran on swiftly. We were eager to pass the Russian frontier; I do not know why; we had the impression that on the other side of the Russian frontier the difficulties of our journey would be ended; we harboured, in fact, the glad illusion that our progress beyond that spot would be reduced to a long series of promenades. The reason for our mistake was, perhaps, that on the maps the roads beyond Kiakhta were marked by two lines instead of only one. Was not this the proof of some great change to come? Those two lines were refreshing to look upon. From time to time we spread out our map for no other purpose than to run along those lines with our eye, and gain a foretaste of the joys of uninterrupted racing at forty miles an hour.

About twenty-five miles from the Iro we entered into the shade of majestic pine woods. It was a sudden transition from the baked and naked earth to this woody landscape. In a few minutes we felt as if we had been at an infinite distance from the Chinese Empire, whose soil, as a matter of fact, we were still treading. We exchanged expressions of admiration and enthusiasm, as if we had never seen a wood in all our lives. At the foot of the great strong trunks stretched a soft mossy carpet. We breathed in the aroma of the resin. There were green stretches that gave one a desire to stop and enjoy the shade, seated upon the trunk of some old fallen tree.

'How beautiful!' we kept repeating.

'It feels like a park.'

On thinking it over again, the beauty of that country was not so very overwhelming, but the pleasure of it was great for us. The Bogda-ola had presented forests to our sight, but only from afar; here the forest surrounded us, and the difference is very great when you come from the desert. The road was somewhat sandy, and encumbered here and there with raised ridges, but it was relatively easy. A few hours later, however, a change occurred in the weather which made the forest almost intolerable: the sky clouded over. When the sun is hidden the company of trees becomes too sad; it adds shadow to shadow; the darkness becomes oppressive because it is unbroken, and it has all the sadness of the evening twilight.

When we came out of the pine wood a vast horizon opened before us; we saw towards the north the gathering clouds of a storm. Below the distant mass of the more purple and threatening ones there lay over the earth a streak as of a rising mist. It spread like the smoke of a fire, rapidly. The air was still. We came upon a sandy plain, where we found a caravan of cart drivers encamped. We stopped, because the fuel in our tank was finished and had to put some in from the reserve. Suddenly the solemn stillness of the air was broken and a violent gust of wind passed by us, howling. It was the forerunner of a hurricane which, a few minutes later, beat down with fury over the plain, making a blinding cloud of dust. The direction of the wind changed as in a cyclone; a sinister darkness surrounded us.

This was our farewell to Mongolia. We were now witnessing a

phenomenon frequent enough in these provinces – a sand-storm. We were in the centre of a vortex; our car was shaken by it. We all crouched down low on the machine. The sand travelled along the ground like some fluid matter, forming yellow streams, heaping itself here and there and rising in whirlpools. The greatest fury of the storm, however, lasted only a few minutes, and half an hour later the wind fell entirely just as suddenly as it had started. We saw it passing away to a distance, just as you see the shadow of clouds flying over the earth.

Kiakhta could not be very far. It was now 4.30 in the afternoon. We wanted to arrive in time to go through the formalities of the custom-house before nightfall, so as to be able to sleep on Russian soil. We tried to hurry on, but the road took us over sand dunes in which our wheels sank; and the sand was loose and lying in heaps and caused an increasingly heavy friction. Our driving wheels began to turn without making way, slipping; the engine panted and grew hot and the steam came out of the radiator hissing. We were in want of water, and for fear of damaging the machinery or causing some parts to seize up, we gave the engine long rests. The machine gave out considerable heat, and each time we waited till it was cool again. During these intervals we went on preparing the road before the car with a shovel, and clearing away the sand as far as possible until the hard ground was uncovered. Then on again. We assisted the efforts of the car by pushing it. We seemed to advance inch by inch: it took us an hour to cover half a mile. Finally, we arrived at the top of a steep slope. Halfway down it lay Kiakhta. It was less than two miles away, but hidden in a valley which sheltered it from the wind, and this is why we had not seen it before. It seemed to be proudly hiding from the profane.

Kiakhta gave us the impression of a superb grandeur. The images of things seemed larger to our starved senses. The first vision of that Siberian city had the fascination of a beautiful dream. We saw sharp spires, white houses with windows, roofs with chimney-pots, factories with tall chimneys: all of these most wonderful, most incredible things. Those lines surprised us: they were so entirely familiar. It seemed as though Europe had come to meet us at the gate of Mongolia. We had arrived, then! We felt elated and proud and gazed upon the city, white among the green of the trees, so grand looking, and felt a kind of pride as if we had conquered it. We had been anxiously watching for its appearance, and yet the sight of it there came to us as a surprise. Its presence was like a revelation.

From that moment on, the word Kiakhta was indelibly stamped upon the mind of Ettore, and shared with Kalgan the honour of designating all the cities of east Russia.

On this side of Kiakhta lies a low and confused mass of little houses – Maimachen, the last Chinese town. Urga is composed of three cities, Kiakhta is composed of two, and the little houses of Maimachen crowd up against the Slav buildings, on the frontiers of the two empires, there, almost as though to resist invasion. The Russian and the Chinese cities are not here at any distance from one another as they are at Urga. Here they touch one another. They look as if they were jostling one another, disputing the ground between them, foot by foot. The neutral zone is only a few feet wide, a small, greyish-looking 'green', on which rises, like a sentinel, the tall pillar marking the frontier; yet the proximity of these two cities has produced no intimacy between them. On one side you get the most typical Chinese life; on the other typical Russian. A city, such as might lie on the banks of the Volga, is here joined to a city which would be in its proper surroundings on the Yang-tse-Kiang.

What surprised us most at Maimachen was exactly this unexpected coming upon the most typical traits of Chinese cities. This place resembled less a town of the Chi-li than one of the Hu-pe: it was more a southern than a northern Chinese town. Indeed, its inhabitants all come from the neighbourhood of Hankow, from the very heart of China. They come from the tea plantations, and they come because of tea. Kiakhta and Maimachen owe their existence simply and solely to the tea trade, which flows (or rather, used to flow) with long lines of camels, across the desert. Kiakhta has come to fetch the tea, Maimachen is here to deliver it. That place has been for centuries one of the greatest trading centres of the world. The tea trade has created fabulous riches along the whole line from Hankow to Moscow; its passing has left a trail of prosperity over two continents; and it is still one of the most valuable sources of gain to two peoples. These two peoples have a standing appointment in those solitudes. Maimachen and Kiakhta are China and Russia doing business.

The inhabitants of Maimachen have carried here all their customs, all their tastes. The outer walls of their houses are rough, all alike, bare and grey, because the Chinese never displays his wealth to the passerby. But through every open door we could see the interior of spacious gay-looking courtyards, and over the screens which sheltered the family from the stranger's gaze, and up the columns of the buildings, were painted long spirals of brightly-coloured dragons and monsters, strange crowds of gesticulating people, long flights of phoenixes in elaborate traditional designs, amid large-lettered glittering Chinese inscriptions wishing their beholder 'Long life' and 'Good luck'; all the showy display of figures and words which in China have the duty of repelling ill-fortune and of welcoming good. This exuberance of ornamentation and symbols is characteristic of the most Chinese places of China, of those beyond the Yellow River, where the Tartar influence has not yet spread.

The people of Maimachen were greatly impressed by our arrival. They had seen us come down the sandy hills, and now they ran out upon the roads to meet us. There soon stood before us a crowd of Chinese people with their blue garments and their waving fans. There was not a single woman among them. For this is a peculiarity of Maimachen, the strangest you can think of in a city of thousands of inhabitants: there are no women. I do not know whether this is due to any clause in the treaties with Russia – for Russia fears the numbers of the yellow population on the whole line of its oriental frontier – or whether it is due to a resolution of the Chinese themselves, who have a great repugnance against settling far from their country, afraid, as they are, through traditional religious beliefs, of having to suffer after death a most grievous exile of the soul. Be that as it may, the fact remains that Maimachen is a city entirely composed of men. Exactly the opposite extreme is met in a village at three *li* from Maimachen, which is inhabited by women only.

A Chinese youth made a sign to us to stop, and addressed us in English. He begged the honour of giving us hospitality, even if only for a few minutes, as all his colleagues had done from Kalgan to Urga. He was the director of the telegraph office.

'I have sent word of your arrival to the Chief of the Police of Kiakhta,' he said to us, welcoming us into his own private house, 'and in the meantime, you can rest awhile, wash, take some refreshment . . .'

We had been reduced by our journey to an almost indescribable condition. Our faces were literally black with dust, and over our clothes was a thick crust of all the different kinds of mud with which we had come into intimate contact along our way: the black mud of the bogs, the yellow mud of the Chara-gol, the white mud of the Iro. We were given hot water, cold water, soap, combs, towels, brushes; and then cigarettes, wine, milk, biscuits, and jam. We used or tasted everything, and were transformed within and without. Then we went off, grateful and comforted, to the chief of the police, who, we were told, was waiting to see us.

A moment later we were out of the Celestial Empire.

Near the frontier-marking pillar, on the green, stood at attention the first *gorodovoi* we met, in his white tunic, wearing the flat uniform cap, his sword slung across his shoulder, his breast adorned with red braiding. He raised his hand, commanding:

'*Stoi!*' (Stop)

He gave us a stiff military salute, at the same time clapping his heels together. Then he got on to the car. Standing upon the step he pointed in the direction we were to follow, and commanded, 'Forward, to the right.'

The car moved, as obediently as a recruit.

We were entering the Russian Empire.

XI

TRANS-BAIKALIA

∿∿∿∿∿∿∿

We are Granted Official Protection – Siberian Hospitality –
The Motor Car and the Tea Trade – Towards
Novi-Selengisk – Crossing the Selenga –
A Rising Country – The Train

The Chief of the Police of Kiakhta, receiving us in his office, told us with a grave look upon his face that he had to speak to us about serious business, and had some important documents to communicate to us.

The prince and I looked at each other worriedly; our host's manner might almost have heralded a warrant for arrest or a decree of extradition. But we soon found that he always became thus gloomy and solemn when he spoke of business, no matter what kind, and that he was only gay and free in general conversation. There was a distinct difference between the chief as the official and the chief as the man; and he marked this difference by putting on a different expression and demeanour. He was a pleasing type of bureaucrat, however, and proved one of our best friends at Kiakhta. He was short, fat, old, talkative, effusive, cultured; and he spoke many languages. At the present moment he was wrapped in his professional air as in a livery.

He took our passports in order to sign them. He announced to us that the customs officials had received special orders for our free transit, and he delivered to us, against a formal receipt, some documents which had arrived from St Petersburg, and which were, indeed, certificates of the most benevolent official protection. On the mooting of the Peking to Paris plan the Russian government had declined, through its foreign minister, to assume any responsibility concerning the personal safety of the motorists, especially during their journey across Siberia. We were therefore most pleasantly surprised on receiving at Kiakhta an official letter from the minister of the interior – a *podorojné*, commanding all the authorities of the places we were to pass to give us their help in case of need; also a letter from the Governor-General of the Imperial Police, assuring us of the fatherly protection which the whole force would extend to us, and, further, three special permits authorizing each of us to carry two pistols. The official matters satisfactorily concluded, the Chief began to laugh, rubbed his hands, and took on the friendly manner of his private capacity.

Then he gave us the latest news and put us *au courant* of the events of the day. The Duma had been dissolved; order reigned in St Petersburg; there were riots in the south of France; near Naples there had been a motor accident . . . Then he offered us some champagne and drank to the success of our expedition. It was he who accompanied us to the customs-house, who introduced us to the many officials of the place and to M. Sinitzin, the manager of the Russo-Chinese Bank, and to the more notable persons of the town. He was in a word a most precious and friendly guide for us.

At the customs we had to sign a declaration binding ourselves, Prince Borghese and I, to take the car outside the frontiers of the empire. This was indeed the sealing and formalization of our most lively desire, now become the subject of a solemn official document. They put a brass plate with a Number 1 on to our machine, and the same number was painted on the glass of our lamps. This ended, we were left free. M. Sinitzin desired us to be his guests, and took us to his large house – all built of timber – which was also the office of the Russo-Chinese Bank.

We shall never forget the affectionate and patriarchal hospitality which was extended to us. The whole house was full of movement. It trembled and creaked under the hasty steps of barefooted servants dressed in the most characteristic traditional costumes of Siberia. The fires in the kitchens were kept constantly lighted, because food was always being served. Dishes came up, worthy of Homeric banquets: enormous roast joints, great boiled fishes, quarters of lamb, steaming soup in casseroles as large as fish ponds, heaps of caviare, of sturgeon, of salmon, of geese, of *pirowski*; and bottles of every kind of wine and liqueur; and fruit, which was precious, because it had come there all the way from Italy. In the centre of all this a gigantic samovar purred like a cat full of contentment. But what we appreciated most of all was the goodness, the kind and eager attention. We were surrounded by a friendly and home-like atmosphere, a constant desire to make us forget that we were in a foreign land, very far from those we loved. Our tastes were studied and our desires were often forestalled. Everybody round us was bright and cheerful. The good Madame Sinitzin, quite indefatigable, lavished attentions upon us in a most motherly way, forgetting sometimes her elegant modern toilette in order to abandon herself to the usual occupations of a housewife. She generously bestowed the treasures of her maternal instinct upon people entirely strange to her. She had no children, either young or grown-up, of her own; so she had adopted as her own daughter a Buriat child, Falia, and this untamed young thing softened the solitude of her life. Falia gave us flowers, and whenever she saw us serious or wrapped in thought she would come up to us and smile.

There was a continual changing of guests at the table. Friends arrived, sat down with just a word of greeting, and took their places in the family circle with a freedom which betokened a long intimacy. You could tell that among these people each one's home was open to the others. They spoke in grave and quiet tones, through which one felt that their hearts were as open as their hand. Many of the guests were tea-merchants. All those men, simple and homely in their ways, clad in the customary Siberian silk shirt, and wearing enormous boots – strong in body, bearded, and with the moujik's sweet expression in their eyes – all of them were merchants, and all had been enriched by the tea trade.

Kiakhta is a village of millionaires. In the little timber houses, painted with lively colours and standing in a line along the wooden pavements, separated from one another by little rustic courtyards full of *telegas* and sledges, there live in exile, families which might own a palace in Moscow or in St Petersburg if they so wished. Scarcely any tea passes now through Kiakhta; the source of their riches has been dried up for some time, but these families will not leave. They remain in the land which has made them prosper, and near their sumptuous cathedral, which holds more treasures than all the other churches in Siberia. They are kept there by their love for the place, by their ignorance of luxury, their habits and also their hope. They entertain a vague dream that the ancient way of the desert may again be peopled with caravans, and that the little city, now so silent, may awaken again to the sounds of a busy life.

'You have no idea,' a customs-house official said to me, 'what Kiakhta was seven or eight years ago. You see those broad deserted streets? They were not sufficient to contain the great moving crowd on days of arrival and departure. As many as 5000 cases of tea used to be unloaded here in a day; nearly fifty million pounds of tea passed this way every year. The great commerce began in October, and during November, December, and January, at Kiakhta, there was one long fair and one long feast. There was no rest, even by night. Often it snowed, and people were pleased, because the snow prepared a way for the sledges. Sinitzin and many others employed in summer as many as fifty camels each, so as to be the first to take the tea to Nijni Novgorod at the time of the fair.

'You see those great brick buildings down there behind the church? They used to be storage buildings – the *Gostiny Dvor*. Hundreds of workmen were employed there day and night unloading the goods from Mongolia, sorting the tea that had been damaged and packing up the cases for Siberia again, covered with camelskins. Those buildings were used for auctions, and hundreds of thousands of roubles changed hands there as if they had been copecks. Immense caravans of sledges left from there for the Baikal. All the yards were full of horses, and in the evening there would be great balls, great banquets. At Troizkossawsk, the nearest town, there was a theatre. You drank and laughed and spent money without a thought. Now, suddenly, after two centuries and a half of that life, Kiakhta is a dead city.'

'Has there been little tea this way lately?'

'None.'

'Does it all go to Vladivostock?'

'Yes. It all goes by the railway. Trade rallied a little two years ago during the war, when all the railways were commandeered by government for the transport of troops, but now the game is up. How can one fight against the railway? The roads are completely abandoned. No one passes there. You will see.'

'But what about communications with the Trans-Siberian railway? Kiakhta is surely not isolated?'

'No, but now we prefer the rivers as ways of transit. There are some boats running over the Selenga from Verkhne-Udinsk to Ust-Kiakhta, and from here to Ust-Kiakhta the road is still good for *telegas*.'

The information that we received everywhere about the roads could not have been more disheartening. 'They are horrible, impossible, execrable,' the chief of the police had said to us in his impetuous way. 'You found swamps in Mongolia? Here you will find worse! You will come upon such bogs as you have never seen in all your lives. You will have to go down slopes fit to break your necks – and up steep places almost needing a crane to lift you over. Do you want to know more about it? I will today get my agents to question the only men who frequent that road, namely, the telegraph employees, who go there to keep the telegraph things in order. You shall have all details from them. As for me, I firmly and sincerely believe that your car cannot pass.'

'Impossible!' we exclaimed, with the most grieved surprise, thinking of those beautiful double lines upon our maps. 'And yet we have got over the road between Urga and here.'

The misadventures we had experienced in crossing Mongolia presented an immense interest to all these tea merchants. The news of the Peking to Paris race had greatly stirred the public of Kiakhta. Men's hopes had risen again. The result of this test of automobilism across Mongolia was anxiously awaited. Would it not be possible to substitute the motor car for the camel, and thus become able to compete successfully in the transport of tea even against the railway? Our arrival caused great excitement. We had done the journey from Kalgan to Kiakhta in seven days, while the caravans took twenty days to do it. The old tea merchants of the place asked us a thousand questions – the price of fuel, the possibility of taking heavy loads, the cost of the machine. They took the matter very seriously, and discussed it among themselves. From what they said we understood that the principal reason why they remained in Kiakhta was that they were waiting for the Russian or the Chinese government to build the railway across Mongolia: a reasonable enterprise, and therefore bound to come. It might take a long time, but the thing must surely come about. Then Kiakhta, communicating with Hankow directly and freely by rail, would pump all China tea from the very fields where it was produced. And now the motor-race had come to throw a fermentation of ideas and plans over this quiet and patient expectation of a Mongolian railway line. But the car, excellent and rapid though it was as a means of communication even over the desert, could not be said to have proved itself a profitable means of transport on a large scale; the Itala could not have carried more than 400 pounds of tea to Kiakhta, and at a high cost of nearly a shilling a pound.

As announced by the telegram which the prince had received in Peking, a complete list of our refill stations was delivered to us at Kiakhta, giving also the amount of oil and petrol we should find at each station, and showing the distance in versts between the various depots. But not a single drop had yet reached Kiakhta. The fuel that we still had in our tanks would perhaps be sufficient to take us as far as Lake Baikal, but we could not be quite sure even of that. The difficulties of the road from Urga had often subjected our engine to great strain, thereby increasing the fuel consumption, and if the road before us was equally bad, all our resources would be exhausted before we could reach the next depot. The next depot – would we ever see it, except upon our map? Would we not be stranded, heaven knows where, and have to stop for weeks?

Fortune came to our assistance. Several years ago, one of the richer merchants of Kiakhta had the idea to get himself a little motor car, and with the motor car he also procured a large quantity of fuel. The little car had the good inspiration suddenly to refuse to work, and the blacksmith of the place had not known how to diagnose its complaint, so that the fuel was left at the bottom of the tank, just as if it was waiting for the incredible event of our passing and needing it. It was M. Sinitzin who first remembered his friend's car. As the agent of the Russo-Chinese Bank, he was to have been the depositary of our own supply. He remembered just after we had in vain bombarded half the Russian Empire with urgent telegrams, and as we were resigning ourselves to tempt fate and go. So now we completed our provisions.

On the evening of the 24th I learned from the telegraph office at Maimachen that the Spyker had reached Urga that day. On the 25th that same office informed me that the de Dion-Boutons and the Spyker had left Urga at dawn.

That afternoon it began to rain.

'Alas for those bogs which the chief of police described to us so vividly!' we said to one another.

And we thought of those dreadful stretches of slime, of those lakes of mud which threatened our advance, and over which the rain would soon destroy every trace of a path. A little rain is useful because it steadies the sand, but too much changes the sand into mud; and this bad weather looked as if it would settle down permanently. It settled down so far that it accompanied us for the next 3000 miles. That day one of the steady, even, monotonous downpours which make one think of the winter, even in the middle of the greatest heat, was falling. In the evening we were told that some Mongolians had seen lights over the Urga road from the height of some sand dunes, and that they thought they must be motor cars. The idea seemed to us absurd; the cars had left Urga that morning, and could not be the same night at Kiakhta. And so it proved, for, overtaken perhaps by the bad weather, they took three days to make the journey. We decided to leave next day. Madame Sinitzin was terrified by our recklessness.

'Poor things!' she kept saying, looking at us with great pity, and sighing. 'In this rain and with no shelter to your carriage! *I* will take care that you have something to sustain you.'

And the next morning, on getting up very early, we found that excellent lady bustling about, surrounded and helped by the servants. The kitchen was in full work.

'Here, the wine bottles!' cried Madame Sinitzin, bending over an enormous rush basket, and a servant would arrive with her arms full of bottles, which disappeared into the basket. 'Quickly, the roast chickens!' – and lo, six chickens followed the bottles down the dark abyss. 'Is the lamb cooked? Bring it here,' and a smoking quarter of lamb would go down with the rest; then oranges, new bread – everything wrapped up in beautiful paper parcels. 'Dear me!' exclaimed the lady when the load seemed surely complete, 'I have forgotten the beer and the brandy.' And more bottles were packed into the empty corners.

'For whom are all these wonderful provisions?' asked the prince, rather taken aback.

'For you, Kniatz Borghese.'

'Oh, but it is impossible, thank you. You have victuals here for a whole regiment. No, no; my car is already too heavily laden – and with the mud that awaits us we cannot add to the load, Madame.'

Grief, both comical and sincere, appeared upon the face of the poor lady when she heard this refusal. She looked at us in silence, and wrung her hands. Then, timidly, for fear of going too much against our wishes, she added, 'Will you not take anything . . . for such a long journey? Take *something* at least.'

Just to please her, we took two chickens and two bottles of wine, which Madame Sinitzin wrapped up in a little bag, shaking her head and looking as if she were saying to herself, 'They will die of hunger and thirst, poor things.'

It went on raining and raining. In the courtyard our car, all in readiness, stood waiting. We bade an effusive goodbye to our hosts, who stood with uncovered heads at the door of their house wishing us a good journey; and were off. The sound of their voices reached us over the road; we turned round and saw them still waving their signs of adieu. It was sad to think that very probably we should never see those good, generous friends again.

Kiakhta was still asleep in the quiet, still, livid dawn. A few moments later we were crossing the town of Troizkossawsk close by, with its little grassy cemetery scattered with crosses, and tombstones washed by the rain. Troizkossawsk has a park of birch trees in the middle of the city, great barracks at one end and grand schools – private schools which show the wealth of the land – standing in a line with the little white and blue wooden houses, along the unpaved and just now muddy principal street. A few shutters began to open, and a few dishevelled heads and sleepy faces leaned out to gaze upon us with astonishment. An early-rising shopkeeper was busy opening his shop; he interrupted his proceedings on seeing us arrive, and drew back into the opening of the door, almost as if to hide himself, quite frightened and surprised. The police-man on duty at the crossroads gave us a military salute. A few Cossacks were down by the river, giving their horses a drink. It was a little clear river, with steep grassy banks, which ran through the middle of the town and served in the winter as a delightful skating-rink for all the boys of Troizkossawsk and of Kiakhta. When we passed by, all the horses on its banks shied, terrified. We saw a handful of soldiers returning to their barracks, no doubt from picket duty, and the men, all wrapped in their heavy grey overcoats, and covered with mud as far as the knees, broke the ranks out of excitement, and to observe us better. There was an immediate glittering of bayonets over their heads.

The road changed into a mere path as soon as it was out of the town, and led us through silent dark woods of fir trees and birches, in which we heard nothing but the distant, ceaseless falling of the rain. We shivered with cold under our soaking mackintoshes, while the water ran down their folds. Could it be possible that Mongolia was still so near, that Maimachen with its crowd of blue-clad Chinamen from the Yangtse, was only a few miles away? The burning desert, the wild prairies, where the camels and antelopes live, seemed now things of a dream or a nightmare. The change had been violently sudden; all was altered – landscape, people, climate. We felt as if we had been transported out of Asia by some magic power. This was Russia indeed – Russia, the same on the banks of the Selenga and on those of the Dnieper, of the Volga, of the Neva. Russia, alike over the whole surface enclosed by her boundaries, not Asiatic and not European, as different from China as it is from France. This was Russia, enfolding us. Alexander II said, I think, that Russia was a sixth part of the world, and it is true. The marvellous uniformity of this empire makes of it a thing by itself.

The change enraptured us. We found ourselves suddenly in surroundings like those of our native land. On issuing from the woods we saw fields enclosed by rough palings made with the trunks of young pine trees; this was the first division of property, the first sign of ownership over the land that we had seen for thousands of miles. Here and there on the fields were the black *isbas*. The rain made the colours of the distant landscape seem fainter through the mist, and it brightened the colours of the things near us. The plants, refreshed by it, acquired a strange vivacity of tints. We liked even these effects of the rain, the vivid colourings, the veils of vapour; for our eye had lost the habit of gazing upon them, and now we found in them again the features of familiar scenes. We met *telegas*, driven by moujiks with red shirts and fur caps, often wearing trousers with a broad yellow band and military caps (these were Cossacks out of service), and a few *tarantass*, now and then, like little leather boats suspended between four wheels – one of the safest and most uncomfortable carriages in the world, when you travel lying

1b

1c

a   A contemporary caricature of Barzini

b   Prince Scipione Borghese

c   Luigi Barzini

2a The *Itala* and its chauffeur, Ettore Guizzardi, in Peking: 'The chief peculiarity of the car was in the mudguards, which were made out of four long solid iron planks attached to the running-board . . . to serve as a track over small ditches, or sandy or marshy ground.'

2b A view of the *Itala* before the race.

3b

a   The starting line-up: 'Drivers join their cars. The engines fire . . . the motors issue from
e yard.'

b   The departure from Peking: 'And over the road lined by the Chinese soldiery . . . our five
otor-cars alone remain, pursuing each other through the capital of the Chinese Empire . . .'

4a 'The possibility of our going by motor-car over the Kalgan road had to be abandoned . . . we would have to be towed by mules and men.'

4b On the Mongolian plain 'a few of the men tried to approach us, urging their horses to the greatest possible speed, but to their very great surprise they were not able to overtake us.'

5 'In China everything is surrounded by walls ... at the corners of the city walls rise graceful little pagodas. A few temples with gabled roofs peep over the bastions.'

6a   On the banks of the Hun-ho: 'Near the village the road was covered with water. To the right and to the left spread rice-fields surrounded by high banks and flooded too. There was no choice, we had to go on. Our men bared their legs and went in.'

6b   'The Kalgan road passed over the Hun-ho, now on sand, and again over rocks.'

7a A well in the Gobi desert: 'It is only a small hole in the earth and yet it has the importance of a city: it means life.'

7b 'We changed the hood of the automobile into our camp tent – a great tent held up by the centre of the car itself . . .'

8   At Urga, the Governor 'begged to be taken for a ride . . . the *Itala* started. The Mandarin Governor grasped the armrests of his seat very firmly, but he seemed completely enraptured.'

9   On the road to Kiakhta the car became stuck and sank 'so deeply that the axle and the
fuel-tank touched the ground . . . oxen were yoked to the car . . . and it now stood firm on the
ground again.'

10a Crossing the Iro: 'All our Mongolians went into the river with the oxen and the motor-car – some on foot, some on horseback . . .'

10b Travelling along the Railway Track: 'That superbly even, level, clear road was full of attraction after the ruts, the woods and the ditches of the other.'

11a

11a, 11b   The accident at the
bridge: the car 'plunged with its back
towards the abyss . . .'

11b

12a, 12b The accident at the bridge: 'Not many minutes passed before a good many people arrived . . . The rescue of the vehicle began.'

a   On the road to Kansk 'we found the so-called "black earth", which is certainly one of the most fertile soils in the world, but also the most hostile to motor-travelling.'

b   'That day was some Slav holiday . . . Men and women were gathered outside their houses . . . When we passed by they interrupted their singing and a great shout of surprise rose . . .'

14   Making a new wheel: 'It looked like a medieval wheel, but it was strong enough to resist any shock or strain.'

15a   Heading for Berlin, word of the car's arrival spread: "It's the Chinese!" they cry. "It's the Chinese!" Barzini is on the right (with cigarette), the Prince next to the car.

15b   'We make a kind of triumphal entry into Cologne, with a large cortège of motor-cars. We cross the swift, clear Rhine over a bridge of boats.'

16a

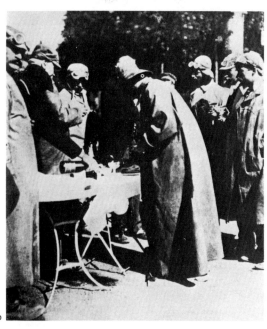

16b

16a, 16b   The French frontier: 'Our hospitable Parisian colleagues wish to celebrate . . . The still fields echo many *"Evvivas"* to France and Italy . . . and quickly on to our cars.'

upon some straw. They went by at a trot, their Buriat drivers whipping up their horses now and then with a peculiar sweep of their arm. From time to time we passed a rough group of little houses, and over the biggest of them would always be a shield with the double eagle, marking it as an imperial post station. And now came the postal diligence, as low as a sledge, drawn by *troikas*, galloping up an incline. It was coming from Ust-Kiakhta. The passengers, all wrapped up in furs and with their caps drawn down over their ears, looked out curiously at us.

The road had been disgracefully slandered by our friends of Kiakhta. They had spoken so much ill of it that we almost ended by thinking it excellent. They had all agreed in calling it worse than the road to Urga! But after all this was natural; for they did not know the road to Urga, while they did know that to Verkhne-Udinsk, and one is always ready to speak ill of one's acquaintance. The things one does not know about always seem better.

We crossed muddy plains, went up ascents that were not always easy, and came down declivities not always comfortable; but there were no bogs, none of those terrible abysses which had been so vividly described to us. We went on quietly at twelve miles an hour without interruptions. By seven o'clock we were at Ust-Kiakhta on the Selenga. There stood a few *isbas*, blackened by the storms, a little church, a broad, muddy road; and on this road a police officer, elegant, adorned with decorations, clad in a spotless white tunic, was waiting for us. We caught a glimpse, between the houses, of the river beyond.

'How may I serve you?' asked the officer, courteously saluting when the car came up near him.

'Is there any danger of missing the road to Verkhne-Udinsk?' said the prince.

'No,' he replied, 'not if you follow the telegraph line. But at Novi-Selengisk, at about seventy versts from here, leave the wires and take the path to the left across the River Selenga. The telegraph runs on to the right of the river.'

'Thank you – and there is a good ferryboat, I believe?'

'Yes, but I am afraid that it will be small for your car.'

'We shall see.'

'When do you expect to reach Udinsk?'

'This evening.'

'This evening?' asked the astonished officer. 'But it is 230 or 240 versts from Kiakhta! How wonderful!'

'If the road were good, we should get there by midday. Goodbye. Thank you.'

'Will you not take some tea?'

'No, thank you.'

'I hope you will have a good journey.'

A moment later he cried:

'Would you like a guide, a man on horseback?'

'No – no, thank you – no need.'

'Follow the telegraph.'

And so we followed the telegraph line, over a number of grassy paths, over a vast plain, and then up some hills. We passed among cultivated land covered with stubble, and often went by villages nestling at the foot of great wooded heights, little heaps of black, small houses, all alike, dominated by a white church with a tall, sharp spire and a green roof. Near the inhabited places, windmills slowly turned their great arms. The rain had stopped.

The first Siberian villages one passes through seem delightful. They have all the attraction of stillness, all the enchantment of country life. They look extremely picturesque, with their little houses all built of rough tree trunks, surrounded by wooden enclosures, joined to one another by plank paths, which are necessary for walking in the open when it is raining and the road is muddy. We dwellers of the West love all this roughly-worked wood, all those unpolished beams, cut out with great hatchet blows and turned into the walls of a home. We love them because they are trees, felled from some great forest, which speak to us vividly of its shadow and its life. There is wood everywhere in Siberia. It takes the place of iron, of masonry; it furnishes domestic utensils and often the tools of labour. You would almost think that as there was the age of stone and that of bronze, so there now exists a civilization of timber: the Slav civilization. We like all this because it is simple, and wakes in us far dim memories and desires for a free and primitive life. Those houses, with their hanging roofs, with their doors sheltered under a porch that spreads over the road almost inviting the passerby to enter, with those small windows whose white varnished shutters stand out gaily against the darkness of the wall – those houses look homely and cosy. They have flowers on their windowsills and curtains to their windows. They give the impression of a quiet wellbeing sheltering itself from the gaze of the world.

But soon you notice an oppressive thing, and that is, that the first village is like the second, the second like the third, the ninetieth like the hundredth, and so on for ever. The houses are all built on a single model; the churches are all identical. Everything is the same everywhere. One chief road, broad enough to avoid the spreading of a fire if one broke out on one side, and on either side of this road the people's dwelling places; behind these the stables; at the entrance of each village the village church rising up on the green. There is nothing to distinguish one village from another except its name.

At every spire that he sees from a distance, the traveller has the elusive hope of some change to come. The church seems larger than those seen before, the village looks more beautiful, and one longs to reach it soon, full of revived curiosity, urged by the need of seeing different things. But the village resembles its neighbours, near and far, as one soldier resembles another. Soon uniformity produces monotony, and monotony melancholy, and one longs for the white villages of one's own land, each with a fascination of its own, an expression, a personality that cries from afar, '*Sono io*' (It is I) . . .

For some hours the road took us away from the banks of the Selenga, as far as the bare valley of its tributary, the Tschiko, whose course we followed for some time, marked as it was by the green life along its banks. Not far from the mouth of the Tschiko we found the Selenga again, vast, with its white milky waters flanked by an exuberance of green bushes bending over the banks. On the bank a little group of *isbas* seemed to be preparing to ford the river and go to Novi-Selengisk, whose white church was even now showing us its steeple a few versts away. This was the ferry place. A little raft made of ill-connected planks was journeying over the river. We got down from the car. The boat was now on the other side of the river. It had taken a *telega* there, and we could just see the latter disappearing among the shrubs. Two old men with thick ruffled beards and eyebrows approached us, followed by some barefooted little girls, who had before looked at us with fear, and had fled when we got close to them. One of the old men asked:

'Do you wish to cross?'

'Yes. Will the boat carry us?'

'How heavy is your car?'

'A hundred and twenty *pud*.'

'That's a lot – but the boat will take you, provided your car can get on to it.'

And he began to call the boatmen. The boat came, propelled by two long oars, worked by two boatmen each. It crossed the river on a slant, and came to the side of the landing-stage. It was not a proper boat; it was a flat raft, a kind of floating platform. We measured the width of it in paces. It would only hold the car sideways. How could we get it on? by towing it or by using the engine? Would the planks bear the weight of the car? At the time those seemed to us very serious problems. This was only our first naval manoeuvre.

With a sure eye and an accurate knowledge of the machine it was just possible to embark by driving the motor. Ettore took the wheel, brought the motor back, and prepared to make the wheels pass over the exact points which the prince marked out for him on the planks – the points of greatest resistance.

'Ready! Forward!' said Prince Borghese.

The car started, got its forepart on to the raft, which shook under its weight; the planks gave way a little as the wheels passed over them, and then jumped again like springs. The front wheels were on. But at this moment the heavy weight of the machine was all pressing on one side alone of the ferryraft, so that the latter dropped down suddenly as far as the water, and the car found itself with its front wheels half a yard lower than the back ones, which were still on the landing-stage. Ettore put on the brake. The ropes which held the boat – they were quite thin little ropes – began to creak. If they had broken, the raft would have suddenly sprung away from the bank, and the car would have plunged into the river. These ropes were immediately strengthened, and the ferrymen took hold of them. The machine could not go back, so it went resolutely forward, veering to the right, so as to come sideways on to the floor of the raft. Then the back wheels took their place there too, and the raft regained its horizontal position, lying a little lower on the water, but in perfect balance. At the moment when the automobile was all aboard the Russians round us gave a cry of fear. They saw it advancing with a bound, and thought that it could not restrain its impetus in time, but must precipitate itself down the other side into the water. But the intelligent machine stopped suddenly, in exactly the right position, as if it had been put there by the slow and mathematically accurate working of a crane. During the rest of our journey incidents of this kind produced very little impression upon us. We got accustomed to unsteady bridges, to old, ill-built ferries, and to the always accurate 'recklessness' of our car.

The boatmen took up the oars, and began to row vigorously. Behind them the old man, holding a short pipe between his teeth, held the tiller.

At the bend in the river, we suddenly saw a steamboat before us. We gave an exclamation of surprise and joy, and fastened admiring and affectionate eyes upon that little old steamer, as it worked its way up the current towards Ust-Kiakhta, panting painfully through its high funnel, propelled by a large wheel with blades, which made it look like an itinerant water-mill. This was the first steamer we had seen since we started our journey. We greeted it as a modest pioneer of civilization, a far-off vanguard of that great power which conquers the world – a friend whom we could ask for help. It represented to us some indefinable bond between ourselves and the West towards which we were speeding. Its siren gave a hoot to warn us of its coming, and that sound so like the familiar calls of factories echoed strangely up the wild valley. The steamer passed laboriously by us, and we, still rocked by the waves in its wake, came to the land.

One of the boatmen showed us the way. Near the river there was some miry ground, but we came out of it quite easily. We reached Novi-Selengisk, a village slightly larger than the others, with a school, a chemist's, and a few little shops with dusty shop windows. We passed almost unnoticed through its great deserted road, overgrown by the grass, and the news of our arrival only spread from house to house just as we passed out of this quiet little village into the country again. We heard excited voices calling to one another and shutters opening violently, and we saw people come out running from their houses and stopping on the road as we sped out of sight. We traversed a chain of bare hills with mild undulations, still untouched by the hand of man, and went on, leaving the valley of the Selenga to the east of us. A vast stretch of quiet waters came in sight in the valley – the Hussin Lake. There was not a single village on its shores; no boat has ever sailed those waters. But the lake is sleeping now through the last few years of its solitude: Slav emigration is slowly coming upon it.

We now passed only a few post houses, hiding in the dips between one hill and the other, almost as if afraid of their great isolation. But it was not long before we came to a valley inhabited by what seems a new nation. For ninety versts, as far as Verkhne-Udinsk, we were in a new and rising country. The whole region of the lower Selenga is verdant with recent cultivation and pastures, covered with flocks and cattle, scattered over with villages, conquered by human labour. Seven years ago it was inhabited only by a few families of Buriats. The miracle is due to the railway. The exploitation of Siberia has begun.

Few regions, even in European Russia itself, have the fertile and prosperous look of that valley in Trans-Baikalia, which so recently was a year's journey from Moscow. Now the journey need not take more than a fortnight to accomplish, and in this fact lies the secret of the prodigious transformation. Distances are disappearing. The immense virgin lands of Slav Asia have come near to the people, and are offering themselves to cultivation and work. And the railway acts as a great disseminator of energy. It provides labour for the fertile soil. Masses of peasants go down there to adopt this as a new fatherland within their own native country. All Siberia is rising to life. Almost unknown territories, which were formerly scarcely more than geographical expressions, will become little by little empires within the Empire.

We passed through entirely new villages the colour of freshly-cut wood, which gave out a strong resinous aroma from trees recently felled in the forest. Many peasants, the last arrivals, were still engaged in building their houses, and were working with great alacrity so as to have them ready before the first cold days. Farther on our road, here and there, down the valley and scattered on the slopes of the hills, we saw other villages showing their white steeples among the green foliage. The work in the fields was in full progress. Droves of cattle and horses were grazing about these same villages, and, alas we caused a tumultuous stampede among these herds! Horses and oxen fled before the motor car. The children, whose games were filling the streets with joy and laughter, ran off into their homes terrified at the sight of us. Women with red neckerchiefs on their heads and with bare feet came out precipitately to put their chickens, geese, and pigs in a place of safety, more eager to save all these treasures than curious to know what the danger was that threatened them. There were cries, the fluttering of wings, neighing, barking, all the sounds of a village in alarm. The men alone remained motionless and silent, almost stunned by this strange fleeting apparition; they halted in their work and greeted us respectfully, uncovering their fair heads and bowing. They did not understand what this strong thing might be, and so became humble before its unknown power. The powerful may hurt – and to salute is to declare yourself an ally.

There were moments when the landscape around us became very picturesque. Small lakes crossed by little fishing-boats lay along our road, breaking into the wide stretch of the fields with their irregular outlines, and bringing into the flat expanse of the plain luminous patches, as it were, of blue sky. Little watercourses flowing among still pastures under the shade of the grey willow trees, went gently on to turn the wheels of the water-mills. On that road we still met with traces of Asiatic life, but we could tell that these were the last signs in its wake, as it fled before the invasion of the white races.

We came across *obos*, as in the desert. They were not Mongolian *obos*, but Buriat ones. The difference between them is very slight. The Buriat is simply a Mongolian become half Russian. He speaks Russian, wears the same clothes as the moujiks, and a Mongolian cap and boots. He dwells in an *isba*; he believes in Buddha; he owes fealty to the tsar; he smokes a Chinese pipe and drinks vodka – this is the Buriat. The chief difference between himself and his brother of the prairies is this: that he sometimes tills the earth and the Mongolian never does. The Buriat has taken the first step towards civilization by refusing to move! Nomad peoples will always be barbarians; civilization only begins when the tent is transformed into the house. Among many Slav villages, we also saw Buriat ones. Several little wooden huts flew small white flags, the same prayer-flags perhaps, which wave in the wind giving to it to bear away the written pleading with which they are covered. Sacred banners were fixed also on the *obos*. Often in the middle of an *obo* rose a tree with its branches trimmed with strips of paper which fluttered in the wind. At about fifty versts from Verkhne-Udinsk we saw, far to the right, a lama monastery; a group of buildings with Chinese roofs painted in green, like those of the oriental Orthodox church. Verkhne-Udinsk is the capital, as it were, of the scattered nation of the Buriats, just as Kazan is the centre of the scattered Tartar people. We became aware of being near the approaches of the town by meeting with numerous crowds of Buriats returning from the market on horseback, in groups for purposes of mutual defence. They took no notice of us.

At six o'clock that afternoon we arrived at the top of the hill, and the wide circle of the mountains on the horizon spread out before us, enclosing the vast valley of the Uda down which our eye could travel for miles. In its dim purple depths we could see the flowing of the river which comes from the east to mix with the Selenga, and dies together with it in the Lake Baikal. At the foot of the more distant heights, which were covered with dark, thick woods, we saw confused white piles of buildings, from which rose the slender points of church steeples and spires; it was Verkhne-Udinsk, lying at the meeting of the two rivers. We kept our eyes long fixed upon it before we came down to the plain, where we knew we should lose sight of it. It was a great landmark on our journey.

Verkhne-Udinsk was not merely a stopping place; it marked the end of a long phase of our travels. It was a turning point. From Peking till now we had followed a road leading distinctly north-west, although Europe lay to the west. We had approached Europe by only half the distance which we had in fact covered. Here at Verkhne-Udinsk we were finally and suddenly to turn our faces to the west. Our race began from here to reach clearly on towards those sunsets where we saw, in a glory of the evening sun, the way of our homecoming.

The road became difficult. We went jolting over deep holes and great dips in the road, and splashing through the mud. We ran over broad puddles, which we had to feel first with our feet to make sure that the bottom would hold us. We knew we should have to cross the Selenga on a boat, so we began looking out for a path to the ferry, amid a complicated entanglement of deep ruts. The plain was watery, uncultivated, overrun by dwarf willows and rushes – the exclusive vegetation of the swamp. Little streams flowed over it in winding lines, and we had to cross them by small wooden bridges, which looked as if they had been built temporarily many years before, and then forgotten. We were just tackling all these small difficulties when there reached our ears a long, shrill, penetrating whistle which we recognized at once, and which made us turn faces lit up with joy towards the direction whence the whistle had come.

'The train,' we exclaimed, 'the train!'

We could just see the rails of the Trans-Siberian line beyond the Selenga. We could distinguish the little red houses of the watchmen and the telegraph poles, all lying at the foot of pine-clad hills; among the trees a puff of white steam floated by, dispersing high up amid the pine woods, and pursued, as it were, by a loud, continuous droning. The train then came within sight, swift and panting: the invader, the triumphant conqueror of Asia was passing! It sped towards Irkutsk, towards Europe. I do not know how much of it was due to our hard mode of journeying, or to the sense of solitude and isolation from which we had now been suffering from some time, but the simple and commonplace sight of a running train seemed to us a new thing, full of deep and far-reaching significance. And with an impulse of enthusiasm we hailed it with a long shout: '*Evviva!*'

The ferryboat which took us shortly afterwards from the left to the right bank of the Selenga was different indeed from the other on which we had embarked that morning. This one consisted of a floor as vast as that of a dancing hall, lying on two supports like a floating bridge. It could carry ten *telegas* at a time with their horses, and could easily have transported a railway engine. It was carried across by the force of the current itself. When we came to it, it was engaged in ferrying across the carts returning from the market of Verkhne-Udinsk, which crowded upon the right bank of the river, patiently awaiting their turn. It was mere child's play to embark our machine upon it, to land on the other side, and to go swiftly up the steep incline on the other bank: arriving shortly afterwards in the city, which lies low between the Uda and the Selenga, all white, bright and picturesque, and with the oriental aspect shared by nearly all Russian cities, due to the number of cupolas of their churches, and to the pointed steeples which resembled minarets.

We went under the triumphal arch of the city, and, entering the principal road, we began to search for our fuel supplies. The triumphal arch is a constant feature of all the Siberian cities which used to be the main road to the Pacific. Of course it is always made of wood, just like the houses, the barracks, the churches of these towns; although in some cases it has naïvely tried to put on the appearance of marble or stone. All these arches were erected on the occasion when the present emperor, Nicholas II (then tsarevich), passed through these places on his return from Vladivostock, where he had opened the works for the Trans-Siberian Railway. He is probably the only Russian emperor who has ever traversed the whole of his vast empire. The event was indeed worthy of being commemorated with triumphal arches.

We found no trace of any deposit of fuel left for us, but the principal grocer of the town agreed to sell us his whole supply of benzine, about fifty litres, which probably represented the supply of the whole town and of the neighbouring district. Down there benzine is much used, but only in drops, because it has not yet come out of the first phase of its social existence, that of a drycleaner.

Verkhne-Udinsk is a city of soldiers; it is a great military centre of Trans-Baikalia. Down there we saw the new military uniforms of the Russian army, only planned, alas, after the war was ended, and when the conspicuousness of the old-fashioned uniforms had already caused a terrible number of casualties, contributing no doubt to some considerable extent to the Russian reverses in Manchuria! Now the Cossack guard is dressed in khaki, all along the frontier. The only pity is that this change marks the end of a long tradition.

In the evening silence, the bugle calls rang out from the white barracks of the high part of the city; patrols passed along the streets shouldering their rifles, and there was a clanking of swords and spurs over the wooden pavements. Numerous sentries came on duty at the doors of banks and public buildings. Even the telegraph-office was occupied by the military: there were soldiers at the door, soldiers armed with rifles and bayonets in the little public waiting-room, and in the office, and before the safe. I felt as if I was writing my telegrams in the ante-room of a prison.

We took up our lodging in the best *gostinitza*, an old wooden inn full of enormous stoves and of beds without sheets, and full of a heavy smell of pent-up humanity, as if there was still left in that air the breath of the countless travellers who had been there. We had not slept in an hotel since leaving Hsien-wa-fu. Indeed, it is inaccurate to say that we slept here, for a whole army of insects seemed to be perfectly accustomed to insect-killing powder, and followed their own bent perfectly regardless of the powder we had brought; these insects must have been as inured to poison as Mithridates himself. Our car lay in a small courtyard lined with dilapidated sheds and encumbered with empty barrels and carts, with packing-cases and with fowls.

By three a.m. the next morning we were up and silently sipping our tea. The day was already bright. We were now coming to the latitude where the night is never quite dark in the summer months.

It was raining.

XII

ON THE BANKS OF THE BAIKAL

~~~~~~~~~~

Along the Selenga – A Rebellious Ascent – In the Mud –
The Abandoned Road – The Bolshaia Rieka River –
Missowaja – A Useless Attempt – Awaiting a Reply –
An Extraordinary Permit

At four a.m. on 27 June we were again on the great ferry across the Selenga on our way to the left bank of the river, along which runs in a winding line the road to the Baikal. This time we found the boat engaged in ferrying to Verkhne-Udinsk a number of carts coming from the country. It was the same scene as the day before, only reversed. From the middle of the river we cried out to the moujiks and the Buriats to hold their horses very firmly. We had been obliged to recognize the decided dislike of the Siberian horse for the motor car. An encounter with a lion would not have caused these sweet-tempered beasts a greater horror or a greater fear. The poor brutes made desperate attempts to escape from harness; they neighed with fear, backed and reared, started violently aside, turned around, and almost invariably ended by finding themselves panting and trembling, with their faces towards the *telega* and in the position least favourable to flight. All this occurred without the astonished peasants doing a thing to prevent it. They had no eyes except for us. They looked at us with open mouths; often they greeted us, and always they let the horses do as they pleased. That is why we warned them from afar: 'Hold your horses! Look out for your horses!'

The air was quite wintry and chill. The moujiks and the Buriats were wrapped in their fur *armiaks* and had put on their big gloves. The breath of the horses went up like steam in the damp air. We crossed back over the little bridges of the day before, and then turned to the west. We now met no sign of life. The mud was slimy, and, however slowly we advanced, every few moments the back wheels of our car skidded. The car itself slipped aslant across the road indifferent to any amount of steering, and sometimes it would proceed for a little like this, all askew like a shying horse. As far as we could, we drove over the grass of the fields, where the wheels could get a better grip, and in this case we simply cut out our own way over the short plants. After an hour's advance we were on the point of turning back: we found ourselves before a short climb which at any other time we should scarcely have even noticed, but which today proved indomitable. This kind of obstacle always roused us to perfect fury. We should have preferred a river, a mountain, a precipice, any other respectable and considerable difficulty. Nothing of the sort! Here was a hundred yards' stretch of the most innocent-looking road. But it was covered with that greasy, slippery mud, on which even a man's foot is unsteady and slides with an irresistible tendency to go backwards rather than forwards, and our wheels felt the same tendency; they revolved in vain; the car was marking time.

'Let's get up speed,' we said to one another. Then we went back a little. The car would fling its whole might on to the assault, but at the very beginning of the incline it would stop and slide back, 'skating' down, as it were, with the wheels held still by the brakes. It would turn sideways, and sometimes even describe a whole half-circle, like a frightened animal. Then we tried going slowly, the prince and I pushing behind, and Ettore at the wheel. We found some pieces of wood which we put as wedges under the wheels, and so advanced sometimes for a little while inch by inch, but at a certain point the car would invariably come back, dragging down with it both the wedges and ourselves. We must have tried about a hundred times, now zigzagging, now in a straight line. The car shrieked, consumed precious fuel, smoked, got heated, seemed to feel the same irritation as ourselves. There was not a hand's breadth of road at the foot of this ascent which had not been furrowed by the wheels. It looked like a ploughed field.

'And to think,' we exclaimed, looking at the sky and anxiously searching for a bit of blue, 'to think that half an hour's sunshine would turn this into an excellent road!' The sun seemed to have resented all the harsh things we had said of him in the desert. The rain went on and on. Then we had an idea, that of laying large branches of a tree across the road – and we were soon intent in lopping off all we could carry, and laying the wet things across the road. The car backed a little, ran on to the branches, and with two swift revolutions of the wheels threw them back as a dog throws the earth when he is burrowing; then stopped, evidently quite satisfied with this charming piece of work, and came back by jerks, grumbling. We had exhausted all our resources; what could we do? Should we return to Verkhne-Udinsk to wait for good weather? Should we camp on the spot? Should we go to look for moujiks to come to our assistance? We were discussing all these plans when Prince Borghese proposed another one, namely that we should try and find out whether there was any means of doing without the road – going another way.

Now, to the left of the path was a thick, small forest, an impenetrable barrier of plants; to the right, higher up than the road, was a narrow field; and beyond the field a great precipice, at the bottom of which flowed the River Selenga. It was possible to enter the field at the foot of the steep end and to come out of it at the top, but the meadow slanted towards the precipice. Ettore took the machine up to it quickly. Near the top we saw him slacken a little, then turn suddenly to the right towards the void . . .

'To the left, to the left!' shouted the prince excitedly.

The car with a rapid movement had already thrown itself to the left and was coming on to the road. It had gone through that dangerous manoeuvre so as to gather up strength by following the downward slant of the meadow for a moment. We heaved a great sigh of relief. We looked down from the top at this obstinate enemy now at last overcome, and we shook our fists at it with the sincerest indignation before continuing our journey along the banks of the Selenga. The road now overhung the river – which becomes more and more swift towards the end of its course, almost as though wishing to hasten towards the endless stillness of the lake – and now proceeded on the same level as its wide, roaring waters. The valley grows increasingly narrow. The Selenga runs a narrow course between hills covered with thick forests of pine and birch trees. The railway, passing on the right bank, crossed our road at a majestic iron bridge, and thenceforward we travelled always near the line.

We seemed, indeed, to be constantly winding in and out round the railway line. We sometimes passed under it over flooded footways, sometimes we crossed it on a level; sometimes we left it, soon to find it again. We would sometimes think we were an immense distance from it, and then suddenly among the trees we would see its signals, its discs, the red roofs of its watchmen's houses. It kept us company. We could see from afar the little solitary stations with the high tanks of their reservoirs coated with timber and crossed by the tube of a warming apparatus, which in winter keeps the water from freezing. Now and then we found our road crossed by a gate; then we entered the territory of some village or the common property of a small municipality, or of a Cossack *stanitza*. By every gate there was a keeper, an old man huddled up in a neighbouring little wooden hut which was often covered with earth to make it warmer. But the keeper was not accustomed to the swiftness of a motor car, and he often would come out of his little place after we had opened and shut the gate ourselves and as we were swiftly flying off, and would remain dazed, motionless, looking at us.

A few of these watchmen made the sign of the cross. One of them, who had come out at the sound of the horn and of our voices, stopped hesitatingly.

'Open, if you please,' we said, stopping the car.

He began to rub his eyes hard, looked at us full of surprise, and began again to rub his eyes; he thought he was dreaming. Indeed, our thick, mud-coated furs made us look like something scarcely human, and that enormous roaring car which ran all alone seemed scarcely made to reassure a moujik concerning the nature of our flesh and blood.

'Please open.'

The old man, as if speaking to himself, exclaimed:

'What can it be, what *can* it be!'

The answer which he evidently gave himself must have been scarcely reassuring, for suddenly he drew back, and, swift as a chased hare, fled back into his hut and never reappeared again.

These episodes were amusing, but once we met a gatekeeper whose conduct did not indeed make us laugh after the first moment. He was a young man with a short, fair beard. He ran to open the gate with a hasty, uncertain, swaying movement. On hearing the sound of the approaching motor, he opened the gate impetuously, as if greatly afraid not to be in time, and threw himself to the side with a desperate bound, leaning, pressing with his arms against the open gate, as if anxious to leave all the room possible to this unknown, threatening monster. When we looked at his face we saw that he was blind. Opaque white eyes opened towards us with an instinctive, eager desire to see. On his pale face dwelt fear. He had felt that something swift and powerful and mysterious was passing by him, was almost touching him in the great, terrible, dawnless darkness. We felt a sense of remorse for that tragic fear which we had caused.

The villages on this road had a look of prosperity. The *isbas* were nearly all new, and we never failed to meet just at their entrance the 'outposts' of galloping cattle, which threw out splashes of mud on us in the impetus of their flight. But we were now familiar with the mud. The wheels of our car dragged it up by large pieces and threw it at us. About us in the air there was a storm of mud; both the car and ourselves were entirely covered with it. We had left off every attempt to clean our faces. We had grown resigned to be covered with a mask of earthy crust. We looked like clay statues only just sketched out: the statues of ourselves. Under that odd make-up, our grave and ill-tempered expression had something comical in it, which, however, at that moment we were scarcely disposed to appreciate or enjoy. We sat looking at one another. 'We *are* funny,' we said in exactly the same gloomy tones with which we might have said, 'How cold it is!'

Indeed it was very cold. The freezing wind blew in on us. I was sitting on the step that day, and I picked up so much mud on my knees and my legs that they seemed transformed into great shapeless things of enormous weight. Whenever I got down to open a gate I felt as if I had to drag so much lead after me. I shuddered under that coating of wet earth. I repeated to myself, just for comfort, that there really was summer *somewhere*. Fortunately, after the first hour or two of the afternoon, the rain ceased from falling and an easterly wind broke through the clouds. A little blue and a little sunshine came out at intervals, and as the sun was always hot it would dry up the mud and give us a feeling of comfort as if the warmth of the air revived us. We were far from any village, amid endless woods, travelling over a picturesque road covered with grass.

Since the construction of the railway line, those parts of the old Siberian road which cross uninhabited regions and do not serve for local traffic have been almost entirely abandoned, and nature has reclaimed them little by little. The woods spread again over the space of which men had robbed them. They thrust out new plants by the side of the road, decking themselves out in the fresh green of the spring, or holding over the ancient road the branches bent and broken by the weight of the snow. They throw upon it their dead trunks, crashing through rotten fences and breaking down ancient sign posts: they rush in on all sides.

From time to time we had to bend down to avoid knocking against the branches above us. The grass was the first thing to take possession again of its ancient haunts. That road is healing up like a great wound made by man into the earth. It is being cured by a cover of blossoms. We were in the midst of flowers: clumps of anemones, buttercups, primroses, and strawberry flowers – a whole feast of colour and fragrance surrounded us, peeping out from the shade of the trees. The Siberian spring has a vigorous, almost violent life, in compensation, as it were, for the long delay which its coming suffers from the ice. We enjoyed that silent triumph of the green. We were entirely caught up by the intimate charm of this place, where there was no trace of human activity except from many centuries ago. Here and there some natural watercourses caused by the recent thaw had crossed the road, devastating it, excavating it, dragging off stones and fallen branches, escaping from the old course dug out for them by man, and from the tyranny of ditches and bridges, and the bridges, worn out at their bases, unsteady, shook and creaked under our motor car. We had not yet learnt to fear them.

In the middle of the forest we came up again to the railway lines which we had left some hours before. Among the trees we caught a glimpse of the valley, heard the roaring of some water, and at the top of a short slope we saw a bridge. At that moment we heard voices calling to us:

'Stop, man, stop!'

The railway employee was making signs to us. When he saw us stop, he cried:

'There's no bridge now, it's collapsed!'

We got out. It was perfectly true. From below we had been unable to see that only one end remained of the bridge we were approaching. A rapid river ran below.

'How can we cross?' we asked the keeper.

'There is a ford down the valley. Follow the road, take the path that leads you into the forest, and you will find some one. There is a *stanitza* close by.'

'How deep is the water?'

'I don't know. This morning some carts passed over.'

'What is the name of this river?'

'The Bolshaia.' (The Great River)

We followed the path, fording a limpid little stream. With no difficulty we penetrated picturesque thicknesses encumbered with fallen trees, and came out upon the stony bed of the Bolshaia. We sought the ford in vain. The current was very swift and deep. During the thawing of the snows the Bolshaia must be a fearful river: it roots up trees and boulders from the mountains and carries them down, rolls them over, breaks them to bits. Its whole bed was full of gigantic tree trunks, and stumps and branches dragged there by the fury of the water. It seemed like a whole forest, dead, and thrown there in the grand disorder of a rout. On the other bank of the river we could see the roofs of some *isbas*. A young moujik, wearing a cap with a Cossack yellow band, came out of the wood by our side, driving a *telega*. He stopped to look at us, and said good morning.

'Where is the ford?' we asked him.

'I am just going to cross it. Come with me.'

He made us go up the bank for about half a mile, dipping now and then into the wood. Presently we went back towards the stream and he said to us:

'It is here. Look carefully where I pass. You must face the current diagonally until a certain point. Take care to follow me exactly.'

He had that kindly look of the Russian peasant, and the moujik's clear blue eyes.

'What's the bottom like?' asked Prince Borghese.

'Stony, like it is here.'

'How deep the water?'

'As high as the wheels of the *telega*.'

We thought of the Iro.

'Can we get any oxen?'

He shook his head. 'There are none.'

'Or any horses?'

'Yes. There are plenty of horses.'

'Could you get us six horses? We will give a rouble a horse, and one rouble for you.'

'Very good – wait for me here.' He crossed the bridge and disappeared.

An hour went by. We were beginning to grow impatient, when we saw a group of men on horseback arriving at a trot on the other bank. They were our men. They came over the ford, and when they were near us saluted us gravely, lifting their caps. They were beautifully strong types, each with a thoughtful brow. They were dreamy looking, like fair-headed saints, and had limbs fit for an athlete. Like all moujiks they wore their hair down to their shoulders. The whole Russian people perpetuates this fashion of the ancients, cutting their hair just by the nape of the neck, as though, if it were longer, it might still get entangled between helmet and cuirass.

They first carried our luggage across, loading it on to their horses' bare backs; the scene looked like a looting expedition. In the meanwhile Ettore, who wished to avoid taking out the magneto, was wrapping it up with rags covered with grease. Presently the six horses came back, and were tied to the motor car with those long ropes which had already served on many occasions. The men jumped astride their horses and one of them got on to the bonnet of the car. Ettore took the wheel. The car, bounding and swaying, entered the Bolshaia amid the cries of the men, the cracking of *nagaikas*, and the neighing of the horses. The water splashed and foamed around it, and the raging waves lashed its sides furiously. On the other bank we quickly got the car into running order again. That fallen bridge had made us waste three hours. We wanted to reach Missowaja, on the east bank of the Baikal, about one hundred miles from Verkhne-Udinsk, that afternoon. The moujiks put us on the right way, and now we plunged again into the woods.

There is only one region of Europe resembling the country we now crossed, and that is Scotland. We were surrounded by the same wooded hills, the same flora, the same picturesque and wild scenery as in Scotland, and in the distance was the sad northern mist which veils the colours in a shroud of melancholy.

Towards five o'clock, after thirteen hours of travelling, we saw at last the blue expanse of the Baikal sparkling in the distance, surrounded by the sharp black points of the fir trees. The lake seemed more luminous than the sky above it. In that dazzling blue we could scarcely see the mountains on the opposite bank fifty miles away. The waters seem to stretch indefinitely to the north and south. The Russians call the Baikal Lake 'the sea'; and as regards its length it is worthy of the name. The Sea of Azov is smaller by one-third. The name of 'sea' came to it by tradition: for two whole centuries it was believed to be a strange freshwater sea, and for two centuries Russian conquest halted on its shores. Then the longing for that other, the salt sea, urged the invaders on, and carried them to the shores of the Pacific.

The undulating road led along the banks of the lake. It took us sometimes so near the water that we could hear the rhythmic breaking of the waves on the sand. Suddenly the woodland was over. The trees here had been burnt, and there remained just a few charred trunks on the bare hills, dead bits of trees standing amid funereal squalor. Fire is the great enemy of the Siberian forest. It breaks out mysteriously, the wind spreads it, and the wind alone can push it back. We thought of the marvellous and terrible spectacle which that fire must have been on the shores of the Baikal. We tried to picture to ourselves that flaming devastation capable of devouring six versts of woodland; the great red light which must have shone through the darkness, mirrored by the waters and reflected by the sky, like an aurora borealis, as far as the banks of the Angara.

An hour later we entered Missowaja.

Missowaja is little more than a village: just one line of little wooden houses spreading over very broad streets, as muddy and stony as the bed of a torrent; pavements of rough wooden planks; a square covered with grass; a white church with a green roof; and military barracks. But this sleepy and almost abandoned village once had a period of great activity and importance. Until the railway reached the south bank of the lake, Missowaja was the eastern port for all the big steamers which crossed the Baikal. I remember it seven years ago, full of soldiers and employees,

with its customs-houses filled with people by the arrival of every steamer
or train, its station encumbered with goods, wagons, and travellers, its
port full of boats, and tugs, and gigantic ferries, which could hold four
convoys. In those times, the red and white lamps of its lighthouses were
lit every night, and the little hotel near the station was crowded with
people waiting to go by the evening train. Now, you could scarcely tell
that it is the same town. Its quay, one of the biggest wooden piers I have
ever seen, is falling to ruin. Its lighthouses are never lit; no boats come to
its shores. The lake all around it is deserted, the rails on the quay are lost
amid the grass; no one ever alights from the trains which pass by. All is in
decay, rusting, falling to destruction. None but a few inhabitants have
remained, and no one knows why these have not gone too.

At Kiakhta our friend Sinitzin had given us a letter of introduction to
the *starosta* of this town – its mayor, as it were – who organizes the winter
transit of tea across the frozen lake, and who is thus in constant relations
with Sinitzin. On arriving at Missowaja we, therefore, asked for the
starosta, who welcomed us hospitably in his wooden house – an *isba*
slightly larger than the others. He was awaiting us, he had something to
give us, and something extremely precious it was, arrived from Irkutsk
for Prince Borghese – oil, petrol, and grease! These were the victuals of
the motor car, now reduced almost to famine.

The *pristaff*, or head of the police, a man with an overflowing beard
and a portly figure imposing in his uniform, came to see us. He examined
our passports, and subjected us to a minute cross-questioning, intended
to discover the mysterious reasons why we had not come by train like all
respectable people. He poured himself out a glass of our tea, and
stopped there looking at us in silence. The lieutenant of the gendarmerie
also came; he questioned us cautiously, gave himself a glass of tea, and
stopped there to keep us company. After him came the Director of the
Telegraphs, and then more people, with uniform and without. The room
was filled. We had become the centre of a small assembly which looked
as if it would never adjourn.

The truth is that at Missowaja our means of locomotion had seemed to
the authorities entirely revolutionary. From the first, on our arrival
before the house of the *starosta*, a little crowd had collected to watch us,
and immediately some policemen had come, who said to two or three
people, calling them by name, 'You, all go immediately to your homes.'
The people so addressed had gone away with bent heads. They were
evidently political exiles, with whom the police feared that we might
have some understanding. But we had a magical document in our
possession, the letter of the Director-General of the Imperial Police,

and we now thought it was time to show it. This letter produced an enormous sensation. All suspicions were dissipated as if by magic. The deepest and most undeserved reverence of the authorities was suddenly bestowed upon us. The only use we made of it was to demand information concerning the road which goes round the Lake Baikal and towards Irkutsk. We thought it would be pleasant to travel to Irkutsk by that road.

In the programme of the Peking to Paris race the crossing of the Baikal had been put down as having to be done on a boat. That was quite fair, for rivers are crossed by a ferry, and the Baikal looks less like a lake than like a course of water crossing the road. But, since a road existed along the banks, we wanted to try it. The information we received was most unfavourable. We had already been told at Verkhne-Udinsk that the bridges over the principal rivers on that side of the Baikal had all crumbled, or were about to crumble, and at Missowaja we heard the same thing. But everyone seemed to be speaking from hearsay. No one had seen that road for about ten years, and we did not want to give up our plan without at least seeing for ourselves whether it could be carried out. It must be confessed that our crossings of the Iro and the Bolshaia had given us excessive confidence in the matter of rivers; we did not believe that the watercourses on the south of the Baikal could be so important as not to be fordable at one or another point of their progress. We therefore decided to start next morning for this hydrographic exploration. Our car was in excellent condition. Since our departure from Peking we had had no need to do more than change one tyre – that of the left rear wheel. We had fuel and oil sufficient for 600 miles, and provisions for three days. We could therefore risk an advance, even in entirely uninhabited regions. We slept on the floor, because the *starosta* possessed no beds. (A bed is a piece of luxury in Siberia, where in the winter one sleeps on the warm stove, and in the summer on the floor.) The following morning, 28 June, after bidding a friendly farewell to our host, we started.

We were destined to return only too soon.

The morning was clear and cold, like a beautiful fine February morning at home. The still lake, without a wave or a ripple, looked as diaphanous as the air; we seemed to be breathing it. The Baikal alone of all the waters I know has on clear days that appearance of ethereal transparency, that pale calmness as of a reversed sky, which adds to one's impression of its enormous vastness the other impression of an infinite and luminous depth. The bank, covered with woods, pushed out into the water little headlands crowded with vegetation, green and, as it were, dishevelled, and the water reflected them and made them look double and suspended in mid-air. Flights of great white birds like seagulls wheeled over the lake, and just showed us where the plane of its surface was, by skimming it.

We could not, however, indulge in admiration for long. The road absorbed all our attention, and we soon forgot the enchantment of the landscape.

The track here was not only abandoned, it was devastated. We went over little hills tortured and eaten out, through the ages, by the fury of the waters at each spring thaw. We climbed and descended regular ledges; we went down rugged slopes where we could not help working up excessive speed, and the car panted and chafed. It bounded over the asperities of the road, took the upward slopes with a run which raised its front wheels for a moment at the top of each steep climb, or at other times, when it had almost reached the summit, it stopped powerless, and we had to take it back again for a longer run which should give it more powerful impetus.

Elsewhere the road would be covered with grass and wild plant life, or encumbered with fallen trees and with dead branches carried down by some flood. At some point along the bank, the storms of the lake have done away with the fencing, have worked into the road and destroyed part of it through landslips. We advanced cautiously over the narrow brow of the lake, and beside us lay its calm, transparent waters.

The old post stations were uninhabited, half demolished; their roofs were crumbling, their floors everywhere invaded by the grass. They seemed to have been abandoned after a war and the sacking of the whole countryside. An indescribable devastation reigns over the ancient main road through Siberia. The road is gradually disappearing now, after once serving to carry Russian arms and authority to the shores of the Pacific Ocean. It is like a dead thing undergoing a process of dissolution. We could only see just a faint trace of this great road of conquest. It was like the dried-up bed of some great torrent – of a rushing torrent of humanity. That road saw once the passing of Muravieff Amursky, whose army gave to Russia in the Far East the finest possible vindication of her honour after the disasters of the Crimean War. It has witnessed the passing of exiles and emigrants, of all the pain and of the daring by which a nation has risen within the last fifty years between the lake and the sea. It has seen the passing of millions in gold from the mines of Blagowieschensk, and millions in silver from the mines of Nertchinsk, which have travelled over it with an escort of mounted

Cossacks. Over this road, once a very artery of the world's life, we were now occasionally obliged to make a way for ourselves with our hand tools.

The parapets of the bridges had decayed. Evidently no one had torn them up, for they were left there just as they must have fallen under the weight of the snow or by the violence of the wind. The bridges looked as if they were standing merely from force of habit, and we trusted ourselves too blindly to that force. We were careful in crossing the first bridges, but afterwards we no longer thought of the danger. We had grown convinced that these buildings were much stronger than they looked. Some of them shook and creaked under us, but with no disastrous results. We tried to avoid the broken planks, and those over which we passed swayed, but bore our weight. Once only, over a small bridge, we heard a crash. The car had a moment's uncertainty and a sudden slackening of its pace, but it bounded forward on to solid ground, while the few planks behind it crashed down, and, on the part of the bridge we had just crossed, a great hole opened.

After three hours' travelling we reached the first of the famous fallen bridges over the River Mishika. The current under it was broad and swift; the heights all around were still crowned with the snows of winter. We found a path at a certain point descending towards the mouth of the river. In following the path we arrived at a small group of *isbas*. We came upon a woodcutter sitting on the grass engrossed in the task of putting on an enormous pair of boots.

'Greeting!' he said to us, without seeming in the least impressed by the arrival of a motor car.

'Greeting! Where is the ford?'

'There is no ford, little father. The Mishika is deeper than a man's height.'

'Then how do you cross it?'

'By that boat.'

We looked in the direction in which he pointed, and we saw, tied up to a bush on the bank, a kind of peculiarly shaped canoe made out of a trunk of a tree. The bottom of it was filled with water.

'Are there no other boats?'

'Yes, there is another one like this.'

'Then how do you take the cattle across?'

'The cattle swim. Look down there now.'

Down near the lake, where the current was less strong, a number of horses were swimming towards the left bank of the river. They swam slowly, tacking a little.

'How can we get this car to the other side of the river?' we asked the woodman.

He thought in silence for a few moments, and finished putting on his boots. Then he got up and answered:

'The bridge might be mended. The suspension beams have remained, and would still do.'

'Are there any workmen here?'

'Any of us can make bridges. There are plenty of men and there is plenty of timber.'

'How long would it take?'

'A week at least, with six men.'

We began to discuss this plan. To rebuild a bridge was an attractive idea, and it would be quite bearable to wait here for a week. But we had been warned that we should find another fallen bridge over the Pereemna and another one over the Aososa, and another one over the Vidrina – without counting the smaller ones. We surely could not start rebuilding all the fallen bridges of the Russian Empire! The task would have been rather beyond the requirements of what was, after all, a motor race. Should we then abandon our plan of continuing our journey round the Baikal? No, not yet. There was one more thing we might try. Over these rivers there still remained some bridges, and powerful ones – the railway bridges. Could we not go over the railway, run along the track, cross the bridges, and then get down upon the old main road on the other side of the unfordable rivers? We had seen a station close by. Why shouldn't we make an attempt?

We started off again, full of rising hope. We arrived at the station, of which we had just caught a glimpse among the trees. It seemed deserted. We entered the little waiting-room, hung all round with great illustrated placards teaching first aid to the wounded; they were placards left there from the time of the war, when all the stations were full of troops. In the waiting-room there was no one. The doors leading out of it were closed. After contemplating for some time silently the medical placards, in vain hopes that somebody might appear, we began to call out, and brought a policeman on to the scene.

The policeman asked to see our passports – perfectly insignificant documents if you have a letter from the Director-General of the Imperial Police! We preferred to show the official this letter. He was an excellent man, that *gorodovoi*. He took a long time to read, spelling each letter out slowly. But at last he understood. And from that moment he became our friend. We had no idea at the time what an invaluable friend he was to prove to us a few days later.

The excellent man, having been told of our desire concerning the bridges, said to us:

'All right, this is my business. Now, we'll telegraph to my superiors. I will inform them concerning you, and everything will be all right.'

'But,' objected the prince, 'the railway authorities perhaps –'

'What have railway authorities to do with the permission to use railways? The police are charged with looking after the line. There are sentries at every bridge so that no one may destroy them, and nobody can use the line without our permission.'

The stationmaster also turned up, and took an interest in the matter; but he thought the difficulties of our plan much more considerable.

'For my part,' he said, 'I would allow you to do what you like. I should say to you, "Go at once." But I have not the power. Neither are the police competent to deal with this matter, and no railway authorities can arrange for anything to happen against the regulations. The government alone is master. You must ask permission from the Governor-General of Siberia, who lives at Irkutsk.'

We were discouraged, but we agreed to make a try. We would telegraph to the governor. If his permission did not arrive within two days, we would resolve to cross the lake by boat. Having taken this decision, we started back again for Missowaja. The return journey was a crushing business. There is only one thing in this world more oppressive than any great task, and that is the repeating of that task. It is humiliating to overcome great difficulties only to encounter them again, and, further, a road which is both bad and already known is doubly tiresome, for it lacks even the excitement of novelty – unless you consider it a novelty to have to climb where before you were descending, and to descend what before was a steep climb. The sky had now become vast and white like a sheet. One suspected that it was preparing for a good snowfall. A cold wind was blowing, and the waters of the lake were again beating against the shore in little waves, white as the sky above us.

The broken-down bridge gave us a great deal of trouble before we could mend it even provisionally, and it gave us severe misgivings as we crossed it. But it took us over for all that, and early that afternoon we were back at Missowaja, and again the guests of the excellent *starosta*, who received us as cordially as he had done the first time. We immediately sent off our telegram to the Governor-General of Siberia applying for permission to go over the railway. Nothing remained but to await his reply.

To wait at Missowaja means getting a taste of the bitterness of enforced exile. I must own that we placed very little trust in the likelihood of receiving an early answer. The governor would, no doubt, have to wait for due time and place to consult official personages around him; some regular procedure would have to be gone through – probably the matter would be referred to St Petersburg. There, the minister of the interior would refer it again to the minister of ways and communications, and the upper council of this department would form a commission to study the whole matter and report upon it . . . We felt as if we were facing the most serious difficulties, a great obstacle against which our whole 40 hp and all the strength which we had at our command would be perfectly useless – a thing like an immense grey, soft mountain, before which there was nothing to be done but wait, hoping to receive assistance from time and patience. Thus did we judge bureaucracy. But we were wrong. Russian bureaucracy was to accomplish in our favour miracles of swiftness and of independence of action, helping us during our whole journey from one end to the other of the empire.

We spent part of our time of waiting in exploring Missowaja. We walked along the shores of the lake, picking up onyxes and agates among its many-coloured pebbles; we recognized and classified the dead fish thrown up by the waters; we climbed about on to the falling pier; we stopped to look at the heterogeneous little objects shown in the dusty shop windows of a few stores. This latter occupation led us to make the acquaintance of the chemist of Missowaja (a vice-chemist, rather, from the German provinces) who invited us to come in among his jars, and there extended the most pleasing welcome to us. His shop became henceforth our favourite meeting place. We spent long hours there, sipping mysterious liquors invented and concocted on the spot, and listening to the hunting stories of our friend the chemist, who owned rifles, special cartridges, and bearskins, and kept them all mixed up among his medicines. He showed us an excellent thick skin of a bear cub. It was still fresh, and was laid out on a plank to dry. It had just been brought to him; a hunter had killed the animal with his knife. There were bears up the hill, at about three versts from the town. Now, why should we not organize a hunting expedition? We must; and there, breathing in the smell of medicinal essences, we planned expeditions.

From the chemist's shop we passed through the telegraph office to ask for news of our fellow-travellers. They had reached Kiakhta that day in good trim. They had gone over part of the road following the traces of our car, and on the banks of the Iro our good Mongolians, faithful to the trust we laid upon them, had gone themselves to offer oxen and to explain by wild gesticulations what means we had employed to cross the river. In the afternoon of that same day, on 28 June, the de Dion-

Boutons and the Spyker had left for Verkhne-Udinsk. Next day we learnt that at nine o'clock in the morning they had reached the Selenga near Novi-Selengisk (where we had come upon the first steamboat), and after crossing the river, had left at eleven. We calculated that they would reach Verkhne-Udinsk the following morning, 29 June, and Missowaja on 1 or 2 July.

What time we passed in the house was chiefly spent round the samovar, taking tea as one takes the waters at a watering-place, and indulging between whiles the delicacies of the *zakuska*, which is the Russian appetizer, and at which you eat a little of everything.

The *pristaff* came back, and the authorities of the town all returned, to keep us company in silence; while a curious but respectful crowd stood in successive groups at the door. Also our motor car received its visitors, while resting in the courtyard a friendly neighbour to the old sledges which knew the Baikal Lake during the ice months. The car was surrounded all the time by hairy moujiks, with their big felt boots, by Cossacks, and by little boys. Everybody who passed by came in, just to see it. Outside the enclosure there were always some horses and carts waiting.

We had great difficulty in curbing our impatience at this long delay, as we looked at the blue sky through our little window adorned with flowering plants. Our eye travelled through the green as far as the *isbas*, as far as the stony and deserted road, now dried up by the sun, and we looked at the endless sparkling horizon of the Baikal beyond them, and came back to sit down again, murmuring discontentedly:

'We are wasting some very fine days. Soon it will begin to rain . . .'

On the afternoon of the 28th, a Jewish merchant asked to see us. He wore the usual long, black tunic of the Russian Jew. He saluted us deferentially, then said:

'You want to go to Irkutsk?'

'Yes – that is, if we can.'

'I have an excellent plan to propose to you. I have a steamer here in the port. If you wish it, I can take you over to Listwinitshnoje for half the railway fare.'

'When is your steamer leaving?'

'It can leave tonight if you like. I have no load to take and it can go immediately. Or if necessary I can wait for you till tomorrow night.'

'We can't decide, for we're waiting for an answer which may be delayed.'

'Well, you can think it over.' And as he was leaving, he turned back at the threshold to repeat to us, 'Till tomorrow evening, then. Greeting!'

The whole day had passed without any news from Irkutsk. In the middle of the night we were awakened by a loud knocking on the outside of the *isba*. In these houses you don't have to knock at the door to be heard; you take a stone and you knock upon the wooden walls of the house all round, until somebody answers. It made an infernal racket. The sleepy *starosta* went to the door and came back with a telegraph messenger. He was holding a lantern and was armed with gun, bayonet, and pistol, and he held out the telegram.

'Why all these arms?' asked Prince Borghese, while he was signing his receipt in the light of the lantern.

'You can't go out at night without weapons,' replied the man. 'The whole countryside is infested with highwaymen. They assault, kill, and rob everywhere – the Sakhalin men.'

'The Sakhalin men?'

'Yes – the Sakhalin convicts, who defended their island against Japan. They were brought away on to the Continent after the end of the war, and in the confusion of things they ran away. Many were freed as a reward for having served. They scattered over the province of the Amur and all Trans-Baikalia. They attacked prisons there, and let the prisoners out; they broke into bank buildings, looted them, and disappeared. There is no safety now . . .'

This explained why the police had authorized us to carry not one but *two* revolvers; and that odd question which was so often put to us, 'Have you ever been attacked?' now became comprehensible and even reasonable. At Verkhne-Udinsk some police officers, who had come to the hotel, had said to us, 'At the first suspicious stirring of any one near you, especially by night, fire – fire immediately – and be careful of one thing above all . . .'

'Of what?' we had asked.

'Mind you, don't fail to fire, nor to hit your mark!' And they seemed really to be saying this in all seriousness.

The telegram came from Irkutsk:

The governor-general is at Krasnojarsk. We have forwarded there to him your application for a permit to cross the railway-bridges.

We went to sleep again on our floor, muttering some tolerably unorthodox words against the slowness of official doings in Siberia.

The next day, 29 June, we were lunching with our friend, the 'Chemist-so-to-speak', in his back shop, and we were talking about our famous future bear hunt, when the bell of the front door rang. Our host went to open it, and reappearing shortly afterwards with a mysterious manner, looked all round at his jars as if he feared they might report his words, and said to us in a whisper:

'There are two policemen – two policemen asking for you.'

'For us?'

'Yes, for you. They know that you are here and they say they must speak to you at once. I am sorry –'

We went to hear what the police might want. In the front shop two *gorodovois* awaited us. From the street, before the shop, a few people were timidly trying to see inside, through the shop window, without seeming to look. The arrival of the police is not always a good sign in Siberia; perhaps Missowaja was expecting those mysterious travellers, who had come from so far on a runaway engine, to be arrested. Prince Borghese was about to pull out his papers and show the famous letter. But this time the policemen were the first to show us a letter, bowing with the greatest respect. The longed-for, the sighed-for permit of the Governor-General of Siberia had come. Instead of speaking ill of the bureaucracy we were now full of enthusiasm for it. We lavished upon it expressions of our very greatest admiration and friendship. Indeed, the Russian authorities showed themselves on all occasions so courteous, so anxious to help, so entirely hospitable, that we shall never forget it. The permit which was now granted to us was an extraordinary, a quite unprecedented favour.

So we were legally authorized to proceed with our car on the railway line, and to cross all the bridges as far, if need be, as Irkutsk!

'What are we to do now? When can we leave?' we asked the policemen.

'You can leave when you wish. The employees on the line have all been notified, and at each station they will tell you when the line is free.'

Of course we decided to leave the bears to the peace of their forests, and spent the rest of the day in making preparations for an extraordinary journey among rails, junctions, and signalboxes, from station to station.

We were about to encounter the most dramatic adventure of our whole journey.

XIII

THE COLLAPSE OF A BRIDGE

∿∿∿∿∿∿∿

*By Motor Journey on the Railway Line – The Sixteenth
Sorting Station – The Old Bridge – A Collapse – Our Car
Overturned – the Rescue – Tankoy*

At half past four on 30 June, in beautiful, clear, but cold weather, we left
Missowaja for the second time and took the road over which we had
travelled on the 28th. We took with us, tied to our luggage, two long
planks which the *starosta* had let us have. We foresaw that we should
need them to pass over the junction of the rails near the stations during
our race along the line.

The idea of going in a motor over a railway line seemed to us so
extraordinary that we now spoke of it with some uncertainty as to the
possibility of its success. It had first struck us as a most natural thing, but
after thinking it over we ended by finding it absurd. The day before, our
only difficulty was that we had no permit; now, at the moment of
executing our strange plan, we saw a number of unsuspected difficulties.
Would the wheels not sink between the sleepers and remain wedged
there? How should we go over the parts where the line was being repaired? Could we come out of the track quickly enough if an additional
train were to come? Would not the iron pins of the rails tear up our
tyres, and even if everything went all right, would not the jolting of a
long journey over the sleepers have the most injurious and grievous
consequences for the machine? To all these questions we could only
reply, 'We shall see,' and we went on.

We wanted to come upon the line near the River Mishika, at the small
station where we had stopped before. We wished to start on our strange,
new way of proceeding at the very place where the idea of it had first
come to us. The next train for Irkutsk was to pass Missowaja at eight
o'clock, and the next train for Verkhne-Udinsk was to pass at midday.
There would then be time between one train and another to reach the
station of Tankoy at about sixty versts from Missowaja. Tankoy has
inherited the glory of Missowaja. It is a new port for the ferryboats,

preferred by them because it is nearer the western bank of the lake. The ferry journey between Tankoy and the station of Baikal, on the left bank of the Angara, is *only* about twenty-five miles. But there are rivers broader than this, such as the Para at Belem and the Plata at Buenos Aires. We partly repeated our journey over the solitary road we knew so well, so picturesque and so difficult, with its innumerable little crumbling bridges, its steep descents, and its upward slopes which had to be taken with a rush; now winding near the blue stillness of the lake, now plunging into the depths of the forest. We took advantage of the knowledge acquired a few days before. Prince Borghese's marvellous memory had retained all the landmarks. He said to Ettore, who was at the wheel:

'Now comes a dip – put on the brake . . . Now there's that bridge leaning over to the right – veer to the left a little.' But all this foresight did not make it possible for us to advance at more than an average speed of five and a half miles an hour, and it was only towards eight o'clock that we arrived at the little station near the Mishika. There we saw our friend the stationmaster, and the policeman – the one who wanted to telegraph to his superiors. The stationmaster had received no communication concerning our permit. The policeman had. The latter said to us that all the policemen and soldiers on duty along the line had received orders from Irkutsk to let us pass. The stationmaster declared:

'I make no objections – I know nothing – I will take no responsibility.'

The policeman declared:

'I shall accompany you, and you will pass everywhere.'

And we now had the most convincing proofs of the unlimited power of the police in Siberia.

So as to leave room in the car for this good fellow I climbed on to the piled-up luggage in the hind part of the body of the car, and there I seated myself astride, a little incommoded by the presence of the long planks, but delighted with my high seat which gave me an entirely new view of the things around us. The policeman sat on the running board of the car.

In order to avoid the junctions and signal joints which obstructed the line near the station we went about one verst further on, and found a junction between the old road and the railway. The railway bank was about six feet high, and the way to it consisted of a little ladder cut in the earth and used by the neighbouring watchmen, scarcely suitable for a motor car. But this was not a difficulty that would stop us. By means of some old sleepers which we piled up with great dexterity, and with the help of our two planks, we made a little incline, up which our machine went triumphantly with a bound. At last we were on the line. With its left wheels the car went over the right-hand rail. We took the planks aboard, tied them very securely and resumed our seats. I perched myself again on the luggage like an Arab on his dromedary's hump. We started.

The sensation of this motor journey was at first delightful. That superb, even, level, clear road was full of attraction after the ruts, the woods, and the ditches of the other. Narrow and high, this road gave one the idea of a slim line stretched over the country, of an immense, always varied, ribbon-like bridge, and this was perhaps the only reason why we liked it so much. We advanced slowly. The sleepers, though very near each other and covered with a layer of sand, made the car sway and gave it a motion as of a slight, gentle gallop, but if we went faster the gallop became violent and ended in a terrible jarring, a wild jerking and shaking which it seemed must break the machine. We were content, therefore, with 'galloping' very slowly at the rate of ten miles an hour. We came to the first watchman's house.

The man was, of course, no better informed concerning our journey than the stationmaster had been. We were apparently under the high and exclusive patronage of the police. The poor fellow could not understand this strange locomotive, which advanced with perfect ease without the rails. He looked on with an expression of great astonishment, and certainly ended by thinking the car some new sort of engine on a trial trip, for he rushed back into his little house and then returned immediately, armed with the flag that means 'no danger', and put himself in the orthodox position. The policeman gave orders to us to stop, got down, went up to the man and made him hand over the little red flag which he had rolled up in his waistband. The policeman, now waving that revolutionary emblem, came back to the motor car entirely pleased with himself and exclaiming:

'This'll do to stop the trains.'

We went across numerous little bridges of the same breadth as the sleepers, without parapets, slung over deep ravines, in the depths of which we could see the foaming water through the large spaces between one sleeper and another. These little bridges, built up of separate beams that seemed supported by the rails alone, looked fearfully light and fragile with so much empty space. We knew that they were strong, but we could not see it. The car advanced with its left wheels between the rails, and the right wheels on the outside – over the few inches of sleepers that stuck out. Over those bridges, then, our right-hand wheels travelled on the very brink of the abyss. It was a matter of an inch or so. The manoeuvre possessed no technical difficulties for a driver of unremitting attention and a steady hand, but it was impossible at these moments to help feeling a slight instinctive thrill which made you clench your fists, and keep your eye fixed on the front wheel as you went over the narrow way on the edge of those bits of wood hung over empty space. It was impossible to dispel the thought entirely from one's mind, that all our safety depended upon the faculties of one man, and that the steadiest of men might sometimes have a moment's weakness and sudden failing of strength, a sudden dimming of senses, or might be overcome by fatigue, by the very strain and tension of his whole being.

It was not long before we came to the great iron bridge over the Mishika. We saw it from afar, looking like an enormous reddish cage suspended twenty yards above the river. Guarding the bridge at each end were soldiers armed with rifles. All bridges of any importance are thus guarded by military forces. You felt as if you were going over a railway in wartime, near a theatre of battle, and that a sudden rush of the enemy might be expected. The impression produced upon one's mind was a sad one, and it was sad above all because this vigilance was necessary – and directed against a Russian enemy of Russia.

The river, which had stopped us two days before, passed roaring between the high pillars in the shadow of wild, high tufts of trees. We were glad to cross it now; we seemed to be taking our revenge. When we had passed the bridge, we ran for a certain time along the banks of the lake, which the railway follows, dominating it from above. Then the lake seemed to recede from us, and we got into woodland again. The evenness of the road, which had been so pleasant at the beginning, began now to oppress us. An even and flat road should make up for its monotony by allowing high speed, and this one did not. At a certain point we found the line under repair. A band of workmen were levelling a curve, the sleepers were all isolated, and the galloping of our car became furious, although it was not swift. We could not proceed at a lower speed than we had done so far, because there would have been the danger of being caught fast between the sleepers, and our car was rapidly leaping over them, passing from one to the next with a jar of the tyre against each. At every moment we thought a tyre would burst. Fortunately, after a few hundred yards of this horrible dancing, we came back to the normal road, and to a station.

It was now a quarter past nine.

The station has no name, it only has a number. It rises on an entirely uninhabited tract of land. It is a 'service station', built like so many others at the time of the war with Japan, in order to increase the power of the line by adding to the number of shunting places. It is called the 'sixteenth sorting station'. None of us three will ever forget the 'sixteenth sorting station' of Trans-Baikalia.

The stationmaster, a well-built, fair-headed, courteous young man, warned us that the train from Missowaja would soon be passing, and that therefore we could not continue our progress on the rails. In point of fact there was more than half an hour before the train was due, but the man's warning was cautious and therefore wise. We drew aside to wait. The stationmaster advised us to continue our way to the old main road which it was still possible to use, and to proceed as far as some level-crossing where we could rejoin the railway. The man, in the absence of direct official orders to himself, was really doing all he could to prevent us resuming our journey on the rails from his station, and was kindly but firmly pushing us out of his jurisdiction. We took his advice. It was a question after all of a very few miles, and we had covered hundreds of miles of that road. We faithfully followed the little path which he pointed out to us, and a moment later we were speeding over the thick grass of the abandoned road.

There, too, as on the tracts we had crossed, no sign was to be seen of recent use, no footprint of any living being. The road led through thick woods. We immediately lost sight of the station, and found ourselves in the green, blossoming solitude. We had been scarcely more than half a mile when we came to an old wooden bridge. It was about twenty-five paces long and four paces broad. It was not quite as wide as the other bridges, and looked different from them both because of the different order in which its planks were arranged, and on account of its remarkable roughness of construction. The road bridges usually preserved signs of a great solidity of building, and retained something of the appearance of an ancient ship, even when they were rotten and undermined and half demolished. This bridge looked as if it had been built up again with the timber of another bridge which had previously fallen on that spot. There was no trace of a parapet; the bridge was rather crooked, and had the irregularities and the carelessness of a temporary construction. But we had crossed several temporary bridges which had been in appearance no better than this. This one went over a little torrent about ten feet deep, whose banks were so thickly covered with bushes and shrubs that they seemed to be stretching out towards one another with a desire to join hands.

Ettore slackened speed and stopped for a few seconds to look. Before every obstacle he always made a halt to reconnoitre. We used to inspect the road without stirring from our car; we rapidly gauged the best speed to adopt, and came to a decision in an instant. Our eyes and our minds had grown accustomed to the thousand problems of the road so similar to, and yet so different from, one another. We judged them in a minute by analogy with past experience. We applied with great assurance the methods learned through practice; we knew where impetus was needed and where caution would be necessary; we could tell by intuition on what points the wheels could pass, and could guess which would be the most resisting part of a plank, or the depth of a piece of water, or the possibilities of a muddy stretch. In this spot we had a moment's hesitation, a fleeting foreboding of danger, but it was only for a moment. Every doubt was completely overcome, and we adopted our usual odd way of reasoning in face of a difficulty. We said to one another: 'Let's just try.'

The policeman had jumped out. He had not had our experience on the subject of old bridges, and was using his judgement with virgin common sense. He thought it necessary to observe cautiously, to get down into the torrent and look at the planks. He was saying to us: 'Wait, wait', and was preparing to reconnoitre . . .

Prince Borghese gave the order to Ettore.

'Go on, slowly.'

The car advanced on the planks, which trembled, cracked a little, swayed as so many others had done under the weight of our machine. We were not greatly alarmed. Yet during such crossings one always has an indefinable sense of suspense and expectation. One follows the progress of the machine intently; one concentrates upon it the whole force of one's thought, almost as though one could endue matter in its arduous task with the energies of mind, as if one could help, uphold, push, direct it by the powerful tension of one's own will. I do not remember that we ever exchanged a word at such times.

The front part of the car had already traversed more than half the bridge. It was drawing near to the inviting grassy bank on the other side. Every danger seemed over . . . Suddenly we heard a frightful crash. The planks had given way under the weight of the hind part of our machine. They were sinking in, they were drawing us under, the whole bridge was opening out and crumbling. This collapse seemed to us, who were in the midst of it at that moment, almost like a cataclysm.

The engine was silent. The car, at the same moment in which it stopped, fell in backwards with a sudden heavy movement, and knocked its body on the broken edges of the planks. Then, continuing its rotation with a continuity which made it impossible for us to grasp the situation, it raised its front wheels up in the air and plunged with its back towards the abyss, and, describing a huge see-sawing movement, took up a vertical position. In this manner it plunged deep into the torrent – to the very bottom of it – carrying all three of us down amid a terrible debris of broken, wrenched, smashed planks and beams. When it had reached such a depth that the main tank was in the water, it still did not stop, but continued its revolution upon itself and turned over. It would have fallen upon the seat, had it not been held up by a beam jutting out above it; and there it remained almost overturned, with its wheels up, and the top of the seat towards the ground, showing only its lamps and its radiator among the debris and the remains of smashed woodwork. All this had come about in a few seconds. With the slowness of some uncouth great animal, the car had accomplished a kind of backward somersault. We only succeeded later in disentangling our ideas as to what had happened. At the moment of the fall we could only see things confusedly: all the faculties of our minds were concentrated upon the present. The field of our observation was restricted to the immediate neighbourhood of our own persons; each one of us was engaged in his own adventure, his own struggle, his own hand-to-hand fight with mortal peril. Afterwards we told one another our experiences. In my mind there remains more vividly the remembrance of sensation than that of vision, of feeling than of sight. There comes back more clearly to my memory what happened within me than what was around me. I was astride over the luggage, therefore my fall was the farthest. On hearing the first crash I thought it was only the partial sinking of the car and a catch of the wheels in the hole of some broken plank, and imagining some tiresome and tedious trap, I exclaimed:

'*Ci siamo!*' (Now we are in for it!)

The next instant I was under the bridge in sudden and ominous shadow, catching on to the ropes of the luggage; the car was still falling and breaking more timber. I felt as if I would never arrive at the bottom. I just allowed myself to be dragged along, bending under a storm of broken wood which beat upon me, principally on my shoulders, splintering with a continually increasing, crashing noise. I remember noticing with a certain satisfaction that I felt no great pain, and I remember thinking several times, 'So far it is all right.' I thought I had just escaped danger, when I saw that the great back of the car was slowly reversing itself over me. The part destined to hold the oil, and situated just under the feet of the driver, was now perpendicularly above my head, and was flooding me with warm oil. I was soaked in it, I could feel it pouring over my face. Just at that moment I noticed that the two seats which the prince and Ettore had occupied a minute before were now empty.

Conscious of the danger in which I stood of being crushed under the automobile, I attempted to escape, but escape was impossible. I was wedged in between the luggage and the fallen timber. In vain did I gather together all my strength to save myself from the danger. Fortunately one heaven-sent construction beam had stopped the car in its slow overturning. I heard just above me cries of pain coming from Prince Borghese. I saw his feet kicking desperately above my head, and also dripping with oil. His cries ceased almost immediately. At that moment Ettore appeared at my side, exclaiming:

'Come out! Come out from there!'

'I can't,' I answered.

'But come out – run away – come!' he kept repeating anxiously and quickly. 'If the beam breaks, you're a dead man.'

'I cannot,' I replied. 'Give me a hand.'

He caught me up with great strength under my arms and pulled me out of the trap. We all three found ourselves on our feet facing one another, each asking the other how he had fared, and exchanging expressions of great relief. Looking back at the position in which the car stood, we exclaimed: 'It is incredible – surely we were saved by a miracle!'

Prince Borghese, at the last moment, had, with an instinctive movement, turned round, taking hold of a beam, and had remained thus suspended in mid-air until the machine, turning over on its back, had come to rest actually on his shoulders. He was thus jammed between the beam and the engine of the car, crushed by it, unable to breathe. It was at that moment that he had uttered the cries which had made me look up. With the strength which comes to men sometimes at a crisis, he somehow raised the car for an instant and freed himself. He has never succeeded since in remembering how he had been able to turn back from his seat and catch hold of the plank; the incidents of that decisive moment have not remained impressed upon his memory. The awful pressure of the motor car upon him had produced heavy contusions on his back and chest. He felt a sharp pain if he breathed deeply, and he quietly expressed his opinion that he must have broken some of his lower left-hand ribs.

Ettore had only a few scratches; he had remained at his post of driver, hanging on to the wheel, till he ended by finding himself head down and feet up. Then he had let himself fall outside the debris of the bridge, and looking round him, he had seen me still in the midst of danger and had run up.

I had received some mysterious injury from my fall. At every movement I felt a diffused pain along my spinal cord, and I could no longer lift my legs properly: they refused to obey me. I dragged them after me in small steps. I was soon obliged to ask for support, and for a fortnight I still moved with great difficulty, dragging my feet, and was only able to climb stairs with great difficulty and with a sigh or two between every step. During this time I fear I must have caused some disturbance to my travelling companions. My face was peeled here and there, I know not why or how; I only mention the fact because it seems useful to say that the machine oil served most excellently to heal the skin. All these contusions in no way detracted from our happiness – the happiness of still being alive.

We felt an exhilaration after our anxiety. The danger had passed, leaving in our minds the impression of a nightmare. When you dream that you are being hurled from some great height, it often happens that you awake and feel a great and unusual delight on remembering that it was only a dream. We felt at that moment an inexpressible joy. We smiled, looking at the overturned car as if it had wanted to play some trick on us, and we took photographs of it from all points of view, pointing out to one another the positions which it was scarcely credible we had been in shortly before.

'I was there, like this.'

'I was under those beams.'

'I passed through there.'

'If that beam had not been there!'

'We should have been simply crushed! . . . Ha, ha! . . .'

The policeman had not waited to see the end. He had run towards the station shrieking out for help, and we could hear his voice in the distance repeating an agonized cry.

Prince Borghese's first thought was for the motor car. He looked at it keenly, and cried:

'I see no serious damage – have a look, Ettore.'

And Ettore remarked, 'She seems quite safe.' And he smiled with joy.

He set to work at once to undo the ropes which bound the luggage, and carried off bags, portmanteaus, cushions, and tents. The fuel was oozing from the upper joints of the tanks which were now in the position of lower joints; he tightened the screws and saved what still remained. The shovel was doubled up like a piece of paper; the pickaxe was broken; the iron flagstaff of our railway banner was twisted; the case for our spare parts was dented here and there. The fuel tank at the back also had deep dents; the straps which held on our spare tyres were broken; the planks we had brought from Missowaja were reduced to splinters; but the engine itself was unhurt. One of the long iron cranks which supported the differential was a little bent (it had bent at the moment when the under part of the car had come down upon the floor of the bridge), and the copper tube leading the water from the two cylinders to the radiator was slightly twisted. That, I think, had probably twisted itself on the shoulders of Prince Borghese. No other damage.

This immunity from breakages was due to several fortunate circumstances. First of all, our fall had been rapid, but not headlong. We had been going slowly, and the bridge gave way because of the weight of our machine, not because of its speed. The collapse of the timber, although sudden, was in stages. The car had to break through a number of beams and planks on its downward way, and although the timber which it found in its descent had not sufficed to hold it up, it had somewhat broken the impetus of the fall. What really had protected it were the spare tyres which were bound on to the back of the car; for, after raising its front wheels until it stood in a vertical position, the car had plunged backward into the void and had fallen precisely upon these tyres. It had found an indiarubber cushion, as it were, which had lessened the jerk. Yet that jerk must have been tremendous, for those providential outer covers were completely embedded in the bottom of the river: so deeply embedded, indeed, that we were afterwards obliged to dig them out. If the beam had been just a little further off, or the tyres had been strapped elsewhere, our race would have been over. One wooden beam had saved us, and a few extra tyres had saved the car. We gave greater importance to the intervention of the beam – and deservedly so.

Not many minutes passed before a good many people arrived, running from the direction of the station. In front of them came the policeman, voiceless by now. His face shone with a smile of pleasure when he saw us alive. He expected, no doubt, to come upon a scene of appalling disaster. Immediately after him ran the stationmaster, poor man, full of remorse. He greeted us with effusion, almost as if he were grateful to us for not having died in the accident, and from that moment he gave himself up entirely to our service. He gave us the work of his hands and of his mind, and also the support of his authority. He would not leave us until the evening, and as long as the day lasted he helped us, accompanied us and guided us. He had brought with him a band of workmen whom we had seen along the line – the men we had met shortly before coming to the station. They were about twenty Siberians, great, strong, rough, disciplined, clever men, and the crowd presented a characteristic appearance, with their long, red smocks, their wide, loose trousers, their high boots and their dishevelled fair heads of hair. They carried ropes and hatchets. The Siberians, the tamers of the forests, the fellers of giant trees, are true masters in the use of the hatchet. We saw them now at work. The rescue of the vehicle began.

The stationmaster directed the manoeuvres. Ropes were bound round the casing of the engine, and then tied to trunks of trees so as to ensure that the motor car should not change position. Then the workmen finished pulling down the bridge. They demolished all that still remained standing of it, accompanying their labour with the singing of slow chanties. The beams fell rapidly one after the other under the powerful and accurate blows of the men's hatchets, and they were carried away and piled up on either side of the torrent. And now the car was isolated. Then the men divided themselves into two bands and caught hold of two ropes, one in front and the other behind the car: one to pull it up and the other one to hold it steady; and at the word of command all of them very gently brought the machine again to its normal position. It was now standing properly upon its four wheels at the bottom of the river-bed. Now we must pull it on to the road, and so the second phase of the rescue work began. The most ingenious means of effecting it were devised. Behind the car, that part of the bridge which the car had crossed (and which had remained intact) was easily reduced to a slanting plane by the destruction of the supporting scaffolding – of its pillars, so to speak. Then two ropes were tied to the back part of the chassis; our good Siberians took hold of the ropes, and by the strength of arms, singing all the while, they pulled the machine slowly up the inclined path as far as the road. The work had lasted three hours.

All these good people seemed as happy as ourselves concerning this rescue, both out of ambition and also because one always grows attached to things which give one trouble. They were taking a lively interest in the condition of the car. They wanted to know whether it could advance – whether it 'was still alive', as they said, with a picturesque turn of expression. We, too, were very anxious to find out. Had appearance deceived us? Was the machine really undamaged? We wanted to hear the sound of it at once. Ettore put the engine and the carburettor and the ignition in 'marching order', and began to work the handle.

Not a sound was heard. All round us was tense expectation as at some judge's courtroom sentence. The handle turned once, twice, thrice; the machine remained dumb. Ettore tried again in vain several times. He put all his force into it; he put some anger into it too – the engine remained still. Ettore exclaimed:

'Perhaps there is some oil in the cylinders, then ignition will not take place. Let us see.'

He opened the bonnet, removed the cylinder covers, and wiped the ignition points with a rag so that oil, which is an insulator, might not interrupt the electric current. He put everything back in its place, tightened the screws and went again to turn the starting handle. At the second turn of it the car began to snort. Its usual hum broke out suddenly, loud, triumphant, making the whole machine shake as with a violent movement of impatience. This was the answer to the unspoken question which was in everyone's mind. The motor had spoken. 'Hurrah!' cried our kindly Siberians, waving their caps.

The preparations for departure were long. Ettore required a whole two hours to put the vehicle into order again. He insisted upon examining the whole of it minutely. In the meantime the stationmaster offered hospitality to the prince and myself in his own house, and he led me there step by step, supporting me in a brotherly manner because of those tiresome, disobedient legs of mine. He gave us tea, milk, steaming *shi* – the rich national soup – and offered us beds. At two o'clock the car was ready. We waited for an engine to pass which had been signalled from Missowaja. It went by like a flash of lightning and we turned to the railway road. The stationmaster insisted on accompanying us, so we left the policeman behind. He did not seem deeply grieved to abandon motor driving after having made so close an acquaintance with its dangers. The stationmaster took the place on the step, the prince sat on the back of the seat; Ettore drove, and I was lifted up on to the seat beside him.

Two of the strongest men stood at the back of the car with their feet on the projecting part of the planks, and hanging on to the luggage ropes like footmen behind a state carriage. Six persons and a load of things were on the machine but she seemed not to notice it. We advanced as in the morning along the rails. The stationmaster consulted his watch at every moment. He was expecting two trains – one from Tankoy and one from Missowaja. When we came to a level-crossing he made us leave the railway to follow the old road. Perhaps he wanted to prove to us his honest conviction that the advice he had given us that morning was the best. At every bridge the workmen got down to examine it carefully. When their verdict was uncertain, the stationmaster cried:

'Forward, top speed!' And we plunged forward with all our might. Over the flat bridges the advice was excellent. In two or three seconds we were on the other side, and it must be remembered that the resistance of a plank or beam stands at inverse ratio to the time during which a strain is placed upon it. Each part of the bridge only supported for an almost incalculably small length of time the weight of the car, and so had actually no time to break under it. After the crossing of every bridge our guide would noisily manifest his satisfaction, clapping his hands, and giving out orders like an officer on the battlefield:

'Forward! Courage! Full speed!'

Over a little stream we had to build ourselves a small bridge. It was done in about five minutes. We heard the Missowaja train pass by, and shortly after we came to another level-crossing. The stationmaster wanted us to continue on the old road, but the two workmen who were sent forward to explore came back saying that on that track all the bigger bridges had collapsed. We began to 'gallop' again over the sleepers of the line. We were now approaching Tankoy. At another level-crossing, a keeper came out making signs. When he came up within speaking distance, he cried out to us:

'Leave the rails! The train is coming, it has left Tankoy.'

The car tried to leave near the signalman's little house, but at that point the sleepers were uncovered, the wheels became embedded among them, and all the efforts of the motor were powerless to move the heavy car. The men began to push, but in vain; it would have been necessary to lift the machine. We heard the whistle of the approaching train, which was hidden from our gaze by a turning. There was no time to lose. With some old sleepers, piled up there beside the line, the men feverishly tried to make a little inclined plane to help the wheels to come out of their holes. In the meantime we heard the roaring of the train, and we saw its smoke in the distance among the trees. Prince Borghese cried to me:

'Get down now – you can't jump – get down!'

But my legs refused for the moment to lend me their modest but necessary service. Fortunately one collective and powerful shove brought the car out of the place where it had sunk, and out of danger. We let the train pass. It was a lowly goods train, absolutely unworthy of the honour of running over us. We continued our journey along the line. An hour later we reached Tankoy, a new town which offered us a beautiful sight of flaming red roofs. It was late. The sky had become grey, cloudy, and dark, and it was cold.

The people here were already aware of our adventure on the bridge, and they had come to see us arrive. Everyone saluted us gravely; a few younger men went so far as to applaud. The road was kept free by soldiers armed with rifles. The police officer approached us, saluting, and delivered a document to the prince. It was a formal permit from the Governor-General of Siberia for us to go over the whole railway line as far as Irkutsk. It was this permit that had been sent by telegram to

Missowaja, just to spare us the trouble of waiting there for the post.

We took up our quarters in the station buffet, and before a good and well-earned bottle of champagne we discussed our plans. Should we continue over the railroad? We had gone over nearly forty miles of it. A journey like that presented no difficulty; it would present the most humdrum safety. From Tankoy onwards we should not have even had the excitement of trains coming upon us, for our car would have been officially reckoned in the service as an additional train. We inquired whether it would be possible to use the main road from Tankoy, but the information we gathered left us no hope. The road, to all intents and purposes, no longer existed. All the bridges over it were destroyed. Now, the railway track offered one means of doing the thing easily, and the ferryboat offered another. Seeing that we could not follow the ancient main road, we were obliged to have recourse to one or other of these aids; why should we take the railroad rather than the boat? There were only before us less than twenty-five miles of water; we could surely go across that short distance as we should have crossed a river! So we decided to embark. But against our taking the boat on that small piece of the lake there stood a great difficulty. The port of Tankoy is only a military port.

Ever since the railway was finished round the south of the Lake Baikal, passengers are no longer allowed to embark on the great ferryboats of the State. They are obliged either to go by train, or to use the private boats outside the ports of Baikal and Tankoy; and that line of navigation, with its great ice-breaking steamers, remains for army transport alone. The law will not admit of exceptions. Ships and landing craft become immediately 'military secrets'. It is forbidden even for officials and their families to draw near the ships. Could we, strangers as we were, expect to be given a special permit? We tried for it. We wired again to Irkutsk, and began to fear that we might prove somewhat importunate, but after all, it was the fault of the bridges.

We received at our quarters many calls from small dignitaries, kind, obliging, ready to run on our behalf to get information for us at the telegraph office. They, too, asked us if we had ever been attacked, and on our replying that we had not, they showed a pleasure not entirely free from surprise. This question was henceforth put to us everywhere over the whole of Siberia, even by governors of provinces, and everyone was surprised that we had not at the very least been robbed by our moujiks. I believe that the Russian upper classes do not know the moujik. I believe they are so separated from him as not to know how he lives or what he thinks, and that they only have traditional – and false – ideas concerning him. They speak of the moujik as of a stupid being and one to be feared, an animal, which is to be frightened in order that he may not frighten you. We came into contact with moujiks much more than many dignitaries do who govern them, and this is why we felt affection and esteem for them. And there is one more thing that I believe: that Siberia itself is not rightly esteemed in the official world. Its statistics are known, but its character is not. Its features are known, but not its qualities. The Siberian of yesterday is confused with that of today, and no real conception is formed of the Siberian of tomorrow. Siberia is preparing a great surprise for us. The assertion of cultured Siberia that 'Siberia is the most advanced part of the Russian Empire' may become a true dictum. It is a land peopled with exiles, that is, with intelligent men; with emigrants, that is, people full of initiative; and with Cossacks, that is, with bold men. These are the constituent elements of a select people. It is a people that will receive modern machines and ideas. The Trans-Siberian Railway, constructed solely for the purposes of conquest, thought of as a military road alone, produces in the provinces which it traverses a slow and unexpected revolution . . . But I am digressing. To return to the buffet of the station of Tankoy.

Into that buffet at a certain moment there came a group of about fifteen men, whom you could tell miles away were not Russians, notwithstanding their thick coats of local fashion, their Cossack shoes, and their skin caps. How could one help recognizing their nationality at once, when one looked at their dark, bright eyes, their expressive faces, and their impetuous movements? We turned to them surprised and delighted.

'How ever did you get here?' we asked, greeting them. 'So many Italians in this distant corner of Trans-Baikalia!'

'We are working in a coal mine near here – we heard of your arrival, and we have all come to greet you. *Bravo! Viva l'Italia!* Hurrah! Long live Italy!'

Questions and answers followed haphazardly.

'A hard journey! Have you come from Peking? I was there when I was working on the Pao-ting-fu railway.'

'*We* know the Chinese roads – we worked a whole year building bridges on the Manchurian line.'

'Building bridges?'

'Yes – railway bridges.'

'But aren't you working in a mine?'

'Yes, we are. We are waiting for the building of the Amur railway. They say it will begin soon.'

'The mine is a poor one.'

'We have worked for this line too – mason's work.'

'And tunnels.'

'But how ever do you come to be now in eastern Siberia?'

'We were working on the Romanian railways, then on those of the Caucasus, then in Turkestan, then in Siberia, then in Manchuria, then in central China. Do you know anything about the Amur railway?'

'Are you not going back to Italy?'

'I should think so!'

'That's what we're working for.'

'Some future it'd be to remain in Siberia!'

'To get our noses frozen!'

We conversed with this band of modern-minded men, of adventurous masons, who are travelling over the world building railways, as six centuries ago other bands travelled over Europe building cathedrals. Then we went to the local theatre, to sleep.

To sleep in a theatre is a pretty widespread habit, but it is usually done during the performance. With us the matter stood differently. The little wooden theatre of Tankoy was closed at the time, and the police, in the absence of an hotel, had had three beds, destined for our accommodation, made up on the stage. The theatre was illuminated with electric lights, and was all decked out for a coming performance of railway men, who were drama amateurs. The curtain was raised, the footlights flooded us with light (we had to hunt an hour before we could find the place to turn it off), and amid all that splendour we three undressed to go to bed, sighing and moaning because of our bruises which hurt at every movement. We seemed to be acting some scene out of a farce.

Outside, armed sentries paced up and down. Tankoy was watching as if it expected an assault that night from 'the men of Sakhalin'.

XIV

IN THE PROVINCE OF IRKUTSK

*Across the Baikal – On the Banks of the Angara –
Irkutsk – A Country Covered with Flowers – Over the
Rivers – The Convicts – Zima – The Motor Car and
the Telega – The Old Post Station – Nijni-Udinsk
– Difficulties with the Telegraph*

Permission to cross the lake on one of the state ferryboats was granted to
us by telegram. At three in the afternoon of 1 July we sailed on the great
ice-cutting steamer *Baikal*. It was still raining. Tankoy soon disappeared
from our sight in the grey mist. From the bridge of the boat we looked at
the high wooden pier, the white lighthouse, the great mooring machinery (which connects the boats with the bank and the rails of the large
quay with the railway), the new roofs of the barracks and of the
government buildings surmounted by a tall telegraph pole without
wires, looking like the mast of some great ship. Obedient to the law, we
had buried our photographic machine in the bottom of our box. We had
been warned that it was strictly forbidden to take pictures of military
buildings, of harbour constructions, of boats and bridges and railway
works, and of other things which everyone can easily see for himself if
he goes there. A strange country, this, where photography is a forbidden
thing and firearms are allowed! Since the war with Japan there has
remained a kind of terror of espionage. The most extraordinary stories
are told about Japanese spies endowed with strange powers of transformation, and it has more than once happened to us that, in spite of our
build and our faces, we have been taken for Japanese by some moujik
whose sincerity could not be doubted.

The cold and the rain drove us away from the bridge of the boat, and
the captain, a Russian giant from the Baltic provinces, invited us to take
tea with him in the stateroom. We were the only passengers on board,
and the crossing only lasted two hours. At five o'clock we were on the
left bank of the Angara, moored to another pier and near a railway

station. We were at Baikal. The road to Irkutsk lies to the right of the
river. You pass from one bank to the other by great transport boats
towed out by tugs. Our car, landing from the ferryboat, crossed the
railway lines by its own power, passed many a coal and timber storage,
and landed, with a difficult and skilful manoeuvre, on board a raft just
about to leave. It was followed by a crowd of soldiers, porters, moujiks,
and beggars, full of curiosity. There were some strange types among that
crowd; one could never have guessed where they came from or what
they were; beggars with the appearance of gentlemen. One of these gave
us information about the road we were to follow.

'As far as Krasnojarsk it is passably good. In some parts it is excellent,
as between here and Nijni-Udinsk. Near Tomsk it is bad; further on,
good. Between Omsk and the Ural Mountains it is almost entirely an
excellent steppe –'

'How is it that you know it so well?' we asked him.

'I know it inch by inch, the Moskowsky Trakt!' he insisted. 'Step by
step, I do – I have done it all on foot.'

The crowd all around us laughed. A few voices said, 'I too.'

'To come here?' we asked.

'Oh, yes; I would willingly not have done it.'

And the laughter was renewed.

'What is your trade?'

'My trade now? Whatever chances to come my way. I am a porter,
a woodcutter, a railway worker . . . just anything for bread and
butter.'

'And before?'

'Before? I have forgotten!'

And he shrugged his shoulders in that characteristic Russian way
which means *nitchevò* – 'What does it matter?'

It was half-past six when we landed at Listwinitshnoje on the other
bank of the Angara, which is the great emissary of the lake, bearing its
waters to the Yenisei after a course of about 1300 miles. Listwinitshnoje
appeared before us in the mist, enclosed between dark woody hills and
the lake, spread out on the shore, part of it penetrating into a narrow
little valley, with its small wooden houses. It looked like a Japanese city.
We had landed, and were about to leave in the direction of Irkutsk, sixty
miles away, when a young lady pushed through the crowd which had
gathered round us, and cried to us:

'*Ah, messieurs, messieurs! Vous n'allez pas repartir tout de suite!*'

'*Mais oui, madame.*'

'*Impossible!* You must stop an hour at least – just an hour. *Voyons!*

Oh, see – the flag!' she said, hesitating a moment. 'Are you not French?' she then asked us.

'No, madame – we are Italians.'

'Oh, Italians . . . ! Oh, stop at least one moment!'

She seemed very much saddened at learning our nationality. She was French, a governess with a rich Siberian family. She was waiting anxiously for the arrival of the motor cars, with a feverish anxiety which only those know who live far from their own country. We tried to comfort her for the disappointment which we had unwittingly occasioned her, and which seemed to grieve her as a national disaster, by explaining to her that our being the first to disembark at Listwinitshnoje had really nothing victorious about it. We told her what we knew about our colleagues – that is to say, that they had spent the night at Kabansk, a village situated between Verkhne-Udinsk and Missowaja; that perhaps by this time they were already on the shores of the lake; and that probably the next day they would disembark and advance towards Irkutsk, where no doubt they would catch up with us. We had indeed wasted four days in our attempts to cross the lake, and from Tankoy we had thought it better to warn our colleagues by telegraph of the uselessness and the risks of the enterprise.

The lady smiled again, and said, 'Thank you, thank you very much . . . Do wait a moment!'

She went running off, and reappeared with a great bunch of flowers, which she gave to us, exclaiming, 'I picked them myself in the forest – please accept them. And now goodbye! *Bon voyage!*'

A minute later we were speeding on the way to Irkutsk with our car full of blossoms. But at a short distance from the village we found our way closed by a gate, watched over by a customs-house official. At the gate the special scale of lower tariffs enjoyed by eastern Siberia comes to an end. We were stopped and questioned by officials. They had received no order to let us pass. Kiakhta had communicated nothing to them. We possessed no document to prove our right of being exempt from toll. With a kind manner the officials asked us to wait till the next day to continue our journey, until the Irkutsk customs officials could furnish information concerning us. All our arguments were useless. Our passports were shown, and they left the customs officials of Listwinitshnoje perfectly indifferent and unmoved. We tried one last resource. A miracle! The gate was opened, the guard stood at attention. The officials smiled ceremoniously, saluted with their hands to their foreheads, saying, 'Pass! *Bon voyage!*'

What had happened?

Prince Borghese, without speaking, had shown two slips of paper – our two magical papers – the letter of the minister of the interior and that of the director of police! We gave them no time to reflect for fear that they might change their minds, and we fled at full speed.

The road was good, as the commander of our tugboat had told us it would be. 'Government officials coming from Irkutsk to Listwinitshnoje on business concerning the port and customs-house travel that road daily. Where government officials use the road it is always kept in excellent order,' he had said.

We ran along the green banks of the Angara, whose strongly drifting waters have given the Lake Baikal two qualities most unusual in Siberian rivers: they never freeze, and they remain, summer and winter, at a constant temperature of four degrees. We moved quickly, but we were stopped for a minute by a rather unpleasant incident. As we were going down a slant, Ettore remarked:

'I can feel the engine straining.'

'Really?' said the prince. 'The road is downhill, and the engine ought to be scarcely pulling.'

'I believe the brake is on.'

'Stop – let's look.'

The brake was on with a vengeance. We were suddenly surrounded by a cloud of smoke and a strong smell of burning oil. The grease of the brake was alight, and the flames were surrounding the gearbox. This mishap was perhaps due to some damage brought about by the fall. The footbrake would no longer obey accurately, and had remained on, so that by its friction so much heat was developed that the grease was set on fire. Fortunately there was water in the ditches, and also in the puddles of the road, and we were able to put out the fire at once. We loosened the brake and went off. It was still raining, and we were being coated with mud as we had been on the way to Missowaja. The day was slowly waning. At nine there was in the sky that strange white light of the polar zones which seems like that of an endless sunset. An hour later we could still see the road stretched between shadows of great trees. On a steep slope, the car stopped. We were six versts from Irkutsk, whose lights we could see from afar – a dim, starry tract in the night.

A piece of road covered with deep mud was holding us back. We went back and tried in several ways to overcome that obstacle. We put the car on the low gear. We tried to advance zigzagging, but in vain. The car slid back, just as it had done on the road to Verkhne-Udinsk. We had been half an hour fighting that obstacle when we saw some conveyances advancing over the high bank which bordered the road. We could see the heads of the horses and the *dugas* outlined against the sky. There were a good many carriages and they stopped. Above the sound of the motor we heard voices calling us by name.

'Kniatz Borghese, Kniatz Borghese!'

'Who is it?' asked the prince.

'You cannot advance upon that road. Go back as far as the bottom and take your machine on to the bank. On the road you would sink.'

'Thank you. Who are you?'

'We come from Irkutsk. We have come to meet you.'

Shortly after we were shaking hands with somebody in the darkness, and listening to the heartiest and friendliest welcomes. A gentleman offered himself as our guide and installed himself in our midst. He was called Radionoff, and was one of the richest merchants of Irkutsk, the owner of steamboats on the Baikal and Angara, and one of the most enthusiastic members of the Russian committee of the Peking to Paris race. He took us through Irkutsk and then through the deserted roads of the city, where the light of the few and scattered street lamps was reflected in the mud; he led us to a white enclosure with a green gate and called out to somebody. A regular giant appeared and opened the gate. We went into a kind of garden, where we dimly saw some trees, and we stopped before a beautiful white house, pierced with windows which threw a strong light over the foliage outside, and just as you find in fairy-tales, Mr Radionoff got down, exclaiming, 'It is here.'

'Where are we?'

'You are in my house – that is, *your* house. The bath is ready, your rooms are prepared, and the dinner is being cooked.'

We were given the most sumptuous and friendly welcome in that white house: the full and free hospitality of one who offers all that he has, and offers it willingly. At midnight some friends arrived for the dinner which was being cooked. The hour must seem rather unsuitable to anyone unacquainted with the Russian summer, that relentless season of light in which at eleven in the evening it is still daylight, and by two o'clock the next morning it is daylight again. Officers, tradesmen, and dignitaries appeared, and we felt among them as if we had known them for years. There is something in the Slav character which makes it resemble the Latin one – a certain demonstrative affability and generous trust.

At Irkutsk we indulged in a delightful period of repose. Repose is really a rather exaggerated expression, but to rest often means no more than changing your occupation. We ran over Irkutsk in all directions – on the great roads with their uneven paving stones, flanked by great showy state palaces, over the huge squares made shiny by the mud, over the market-place all built of wood, and with numerous booths as though for a continual fair. We went from bank to shop, from shop to telegraph office, from telegraph office to government buildings. We had information to ask for, bills to pay, a hundred things to provide ourselves with for our personal use, as our present clothes had been ruined by the oil of the engine. We watched the movement of that city curiously. It has a little the air of a capital, and is, in fact, a central town. It governs a country twenty times as vast as France. It rules over a people of all races. In its streets there are Buriats, Trans-Baikalians, Kirghese from the Steppes, Tunguses from the Tundras, Circassians, Tartars, Armenians and Jews, mixing with the native Slav population. It is a city both western and eastern at the same time, and in which matters of business are up to date and the fashions are old. The ways of ancient Russia are found there intact, preserved by men full of new daring.

The members of the cyclists' club had prepared a reception for us at their clubhouse near the bicycle course on the other side of the Angara, which we reached by crossing over one of the longest footbridges existing. The rain and the cold spoilt the entertainment, but were not sufficient to damp the generous enthusiasm of our hosts. The flags and banners, obviously put up in our honour, drooped sadly under the cold rain, but counteracting the effects of this unpleasant dampness there was a generous wine coursing down our throats, and a warmth in our hearts. A few valiant men found courage enough to get on their bicycles and go through the racing programme, while a military band played the most martial war songs, which were echoed by the distant banks of the river. And when night came we were still doing the city. We were taken first to the theatre, then to the *café chantant* (in Russia the *café chantant* only begins its performance after midnight), and then to supper – for so the local custom demands, and 'when you are in Rome you must do as the Romans do'. After having been given Moscow shrimps and caviare from Kazan, we were taken to another café concert to hear some famous Russian choirs – some songs of the Ukraine – and when the choruses were over why, thought we, should we not ask for the folk-dancing of the capital of Little Russia? So we saw the dancing. The day was well begun when we were given the 'stirrup cup', so called, no doubt, because it is precisely what makes you lose your stirrup and your head! We returned home in an *iswoschik* at dawn, on 3 July, just as the city began to stir. Our 'rest' at Irkutsk was over.

A few hours later, at eleven a.m., we left Irkutsk, surrounded by a bodyguard of cyclists. The car had been provided with full supplies, and had become transformed by a careful external *toilette*. Ettore had washed it with a powerful firehose, and all the muds of China, Mongolia, and Siberia had yielded and fallen before that impetuous stream of water. But the car, even when washed, had not acquired its original colour. It was weather-beaten, and like ourselves, had taken on a darker shade; it had changed skin, it had lost its lustre and smoothness, showed cracks and indentations. It was uglier, but looked mightier. Prince Borghese, meaning to embellish it, ordered a sign painter to write upon the sides of the machine, the words, 'Peking-Paris' in large white letters. But this inscription unfortunately looked like a shop sign. The damaged car coating would have been better. At Irkutsk we did away with part of our luggage, and the third seat, the one behind originally meant for myself, was cleared and made available. But it was taken by M. Radionoff, who wished to accompany us over part of the road. He climbed on to it (this was not an easy thing to do, for you had to vault over the tanks), pressing against his heart a large paper parcel, which was afterwards discovered to contain food. Our friend had seen noon-time approaching, and he was not accustomed, like ourselves, to forget his lunch.

Just before our departure a telegram from Missowaja brought us the last available news of the other cars. They had reached Missowaja the day before, and at that station had taken the train straight for Irkutsk.

We crossed the great boat-bridge, travelled over a couple of versts of uncertain ground, in which our car threatened several times to sink – the bridges of Siberian towns are always very badly kept – and towards midday we arrived at the beginning of the good road, as far as which all the cyclists and all the *iswoschiks*, which carried our fellows in comfort, had, to our shame, preceded us. We exchanged greetings. There was some clamorous cheering, and all caps were raised and waved vehemently in the air as our machine started upon its swift flight.

We should have found that new phase of our journey exceedingly enjoyable if the cold had not been so sharp; but the cold that year was unusual, even for Siberia, in those months. The road was such that we could keep up an average speed of eighteen to twenty miles an hour. We were following the left bank of the Angara, an imposing river with swift, clear waters. Irkutsk disappeared little by little in the even, fertile valley, and we ended by seeing no more of it than its tall and enormous churches: a crowd of cupolas, spires, and pinnacles, which still showed up white in the green distance when the city dwelling-places had already disappeared from sight.

The landscape grew softer and sweeter to our sight. Here the country gently sloped down, following the incline of the Selenga. The suddenly rising mountains and hills, which surround Lake Baikal, here lost themselves in ever slighter and slighter undulations. You could feel that they would soon be lost in the endless plain of central Siberia. We left behind us the steep mountains lying in a slope like great breakers on the horizon, just as when we were nearing Mongolia. They looked like some suddenly petrified storm. The road began to travel along straight, level tracks, over which we could fly at the speed of twenty-five or thirty miles an hour, on verdant and prosperous prairies, bespangled and streaked with yellow and white wild flowers, starred with the same vivid colours as the Alps, and peopled by herds of cattle and droves of horses in the care of men wearing the long Mongolian tunic and the fur Cossack cap. The tending of cattle is still down there the exclusive occupation of the semi-barbarians and the mixed populations, which are at least a quarter Mongolian. M. Radionoff, who was now being initiated for the first time into the inebriating joys of velocity, was uttering cries of wonder and enthusiasm. At every longer flight of the car he fervently reaffirmed his intention to get a motor himself. He would have one at once. He would order it as soon as he got back home. He would telegraph for one. He would have one identically like ours. After a little while, his enthusiasm seemed to abate. Our excellent companion seemed to have become taciturn: he had opened the luncheon parcel. And now, without saying anything, he passed us food. We suddenly saw appearing near our faces a hand with an enormous sandwich, which we would take with a sign of thanks and would immediately devour. As soon as the sandwich was gone the hand would reappear with a fresh supply. It was like the hand of providence, and its bounties must have been inexhaustible, for our appetites were sated before the end of them was seen.

We passed through numerous villages surrounded by palings and protected by gates which crossed the roads. Beyond the wooden roofs we could see the slender poles by the wells, all alike, tall and sloping. They looked like long lances, lying outside of the doors too small to receive them. Some of these villages were Cossack ones. Over their houses flew little red or white flags with numbers. Every window had its flowers. The black *isbas* were all decked out with them in honour of the brief spring. The inhabitants of Siberia worship flowers, and, however poor, the Siberian house always has pots of geraniums and pinks, and oleanders, which prosper by the heat of the stove. And the flowers relieve the bareness of the *isbas*. They are loved because they are rare, and also because those plants which you have to tend keep you company in the long, silent, white months of winter, when the cold and the snow interrupt all outdoor work, and confine each family to its own house. The moujiks delight in giving constant care to the embellishment of their homes. They spread their carpets over the floor, they cover the walls with bright pictures, with icons, with the crests of the Imperial family. They keep everything in fine order, place their shining samovar upon a table near the window, so that it may be seen from the street. Around the samovar are placed glasses and small plates. Spread over a specially honoured piece of furniture are all the family treasures: porcelain pots, painted dishes used at the wedding feast, and a votive lamp which is always lit. The windows are adorned with little print curtains. There is in these Siberian homes something intimate and cosy and happy, which does not exist in lands where the house is not constantly dwelt in, because the sun is warm even in winter, the climate temperate, and one can be happy outside.

We arrived at the right bank of the river – the Suchuja. This is a double river, divided by a bank of earth running down the middle; half can be forded, the other half must be crossed by boat. There are a good many Siberian rivers like this, deep on one side and shallow on the other. On one side they are treacherous, and on the other benign. Some of these have a bridge over the better side, and a boat over the other, and all the dangers and all the furies of a strong current gather in the latter. One long bridge could not stand against the floods. Here it was a large boat that ferried us across. It was not easy to place the motor car on it. We had to strengthen the little landing-stage, and Ettore drove the machine swiftly over it, with the same firm hand and steadiness of judgement which he had displayed on the Selenga. We ended by growing accustomed to these somewhat anxious embarkations. We had to cross by boat, and sometimes on old and rickety boats, a number of other rivers both great and small – the Ospin, the Bjelaja, the Salarin, the Oka – all of which were driving down their waters to swell the Angara in its advance towards the Yenisei. On the bigger boats, *telegas* coming from the neighbouring markets were taken across at the same time as our car, and so we found ourselves amidst typical groups of Siberian countryfolk, who saluted us respectfully and exchanged curious remarks among themselves. It was on one of these boats that the question was actually put to us, whether we were Japanese. The man who had expressed that suspicion about us explained:

'I thought you might be Japanese, because these sorts of machines do not exist in Russia, and you are coming from the other side.' He motioned towards the east. Then he added, 'They say that the Japanese have all the machines that have ever been invented.'

Over the Oka an old moujik said in a low voice to the boatman:
'We shall soon have the war here again.'
'Why, little father?'
'They are here inspecting the country,' and he pointed to us, shaking his head in a concerned manner.

I wonder what were his thoughts concerning ourselves and our journey. I should like to know what idea all these passive villagers had of the automobile. Some expressed the greatest surprise: they seemed stunned, and let their tools fall from their hands in their astonishment. Others ran gaily to look at the car, as a crowd runs to look at some harmless but strange phenomenon, or at a troupe of itinerant mountebanks passing by with their caravan. A few fled. The women often laughed, holding their sides, just as the Mongolians had laughed near Urga, and this might be used as an argument to prove that woman is slightly less civilized than man, and that her soul is still a little uncouth. But when we stopped, everyone was reassured and approached us, and a moment later they would treat both ourselves and our car with the most friendly familiarity, the younger generation admiring the machine, and putting very pertinent questions to us concerning its speed and its strength.

At times we found our way stopped by railway works. A double line is being built over the Trans-Siberian Railway. Travellers using the present line are probably not even aware of it, because it is an entirely independent line, following a path of its own, and intended to be worked independently of the other, doubling the advantages of the railway, and avoiding the dangers of a double line with occasional meeting points. If the bridge of one line over a given river crumbles, the bridge of the other line will remain intact, and nothing is likely to interrupt the communications entirely. The new line will have its own stations, its own telegraph service, its own signal stations, and its own watchmen.

At a certain point we came upon an impressive spectacle. There were hundreds of men in grey uniforms working on the new railway. We took them for soldiers, and thought we recognized the uniform as that lately introduced into the army, but when we came close to them we saw that each had a chain from his waist to his feet. Sentries, armed with fixed bayonet, wearing the military cape thrown over their shoulders, kept watch, smoking cigarettes. When we passed near them the grey-cloaked men halted in their work, and all of them raised their heads to look at us in silence. Then they gave us greeting, raising their caps. Half of their heads was shaven; they looked like clowns with a wig, and gave one a sense of horror. We had a feeling in our hearts like the grip of an iron hand as we stood before this sad revelation, and murmured, 'The convicts!'

They were still looking at us. We were far away, and they still looked on. We felt pursued by their fervent, silent attention. To their minds we represented flight and freedom. I thought of those terrible pages of Dostoevsky in *The House of the Dead*. Who knows what great event our passing was in the terrible life of that herd of men, outcasts from society, with no name but a number?

We arrived at seven that evening at Zima. It was wet. We had done about a hundred and fifty miles that day. In the buffet of a neighbouring railway station we were able to get a *borsch*, seasoned with some cream, and some cutlets, which we declared to be the most excellent we had ever tasted. We found our fuel supplies in the house of a Jewish merchant who was the representative of the Nobel firm, and in his house we spent the night. Zima in Russian means 'winter'. As for ourselves we found the name distressingly appropriate. At Zima the cold was almost unbearable. We said to one another, smiling, 'July will come.' The odd thing is that our host, the merchant, assured us that only two days previously the weather had been unbearably hot. It really seemed as if the cold were doing it on purpose, accompanying us across Siberia to do the honours of its country.

At four the next morning we were already on the march. Of course the sky was covered over, the air was damp and frosty; our furs were not sufficient to keep us warm, and we had to add to them overcoats and raincloaks. We were as round as Eskimos. For several days now this wretched meteorological phenomenon took place regularly. We started with a most lovely dawn; at sunrise a little mist showed up to the west; then it rose, turned into a cloud; it grew, it invaded all and began to dissolve into rain. The whole cycle was gone through in something like half an hour. The sky undressed at night and clothed itself in the daytime with a quite excessive sense of propriety. With perfect regularity the west sent us a daily storm. Was *this* its welcome to us? Ettore, who at dawn was always the most firmly convinced of us three that we would have 'a splendid day', could not understand or put up with this change. He exclaimed from time to time, pointing to the west:

'What is it? Is it a line of clouds? Will they never come to an end?' And he added sadly, 'What a country!'

There were many villages on our road and we met a pretty constant traffic. We had to be very careful about the horses, so as not to cause mishaps. Their drivers were paralysed with astonishment, and irresistibly funny scenes took place. A horse which was drawing a *telega*, terrified by the presence of the motor – although we were going at a snail's pace, as we always did when we met horses – began to rear, upset the *telega*, overturned the load and also the moujik who was looking at us, and took flight. The good man, finding himself sitting against his will upon the cold ground, yet continued to look at us, smiling as he had done before his fall, without a thought for his cart or his animal, and looking as if he did not even notice his own sudden change of position. He was absorbed in the contemplation of ourselves; he looked bewitched, and when we got up to him he addressed us:

'Greeting! Where do you come from?'

'From Peking.'

He clasped his hands and remained seated in open-mouthed admiration.

A peasant on a horsecart was overwhelmed with laughter at the sight of us. Suddenly his terrified steed made a turnabout and threw him from his seat. He got up, still laughing, and said to us, wittily:

'Ha, ha! Better a cart without a horse than a horse without a cart. Ha, ha, ha!'

I must confess that, notwithstanding all our caution, the quantity of *telegas* we overturned was overwhelming. The horses seemed afraid of the car, even if it stood still. They thought it some strange devouring monster, and the *telegas*, which are made narrow in order that they can pass everywhere, high so that they can ford, and light so that they cannot sink in the swamps, had all the characteristics necessary for an easy overturn. Moreover, the horses of the peasants in Siberia have no bit. They are guided by a very simple halter. Add to these circumstances the men's astonishment which incapacitated them, and you will understand the reason for these disasters. The men were probably occupied with one thing alone – with trying to understand what in the world this great swaying, bounding, grey monster, which they found hurtling along the road, could be. They seemed to hear nothing, neither shouts nor advice, and very often we had to stop, to get down ourselves and lead their horses some distance onward. We met a public mail carriage, a big *tarantass*, in which everybody, driver and passengers, were fast asleep. The three horses, terrified at our approach, were unanimous in their wise resolve, and all turned back. We passed the *tarantass* with no mishap, and several miles further on, from the top of a hill, we still saw it in the distance behind us, continuing at a steady slow trot to retrace its steps. We could not help laughing at the thought of how surprised the travellers would be when they awoke, after so much travelling, to find themselves probably at the very place from which they had started the day before.

Often great herds of cattle took up the road, and we had to wait for all the animals to go by, one by one, distrustful and afraid, urged on by the goad of the cattle drivers, who were galloping here and there to keep these animals all together when they tried to escape. There was great variety here in the nature of the road. For many miles we advanced among lonely woods, fragrant with resinous gums, and we felt as if we were passing along the avenues of some great park. All was blossoming; the meadows and the clearings were full of silent, beckoning shade. Whenever we saw a little valley before us we were sure to find a village there.

The villages took refuge in the valleys, so as to be sheltered from the impetuous winds which blow down from the icy plains of the tundras in the north, and also for the sake of the running water. *Isbas* collect by the side of limpid streamlets, on whose banks huge flocks of geese spend their days until the time comes for them to be killed and frozen and sent to the big winter fairs in Russia. At either end of the row of houses stands a pole painted white and black, and on it is nailed a notice-board, bearing the name of the village, the distance which separates it from the next one, the number of its homes and its inhabitants – in short, a regular extract from a statistical book for the use of government officials passing to gather the taxes or enlist soldiers. There is a plate to show the house of the *starosta*, another one at the Zemstvoskaya Dom, that is, the place where those officials travelling on governmental business have the right to lodge. There is a look of military occupation in all this, and the houses themselves seem to belong to some regiment, to be counted and drawn up as soldiers, and like the tents of an encampment they looked as if they must be ready at any moment to move at the first word of command from their superior. They look as if they owed their origin, not to the common wants of men, but to some command that they should be built. The villages are scattered at almost equal distances, every twenty versts or so, and they give one the idea of great patrols of sentinels placed over the Moskowsky Trakt. And in point of fact they were regular halting places before they became villages.

A few years ago, before the railway was laid across Siberia, each of them marked the end of a day's march for the convoys of exiles, whom the trains now carry in prison vans with little barred windows. At one end of each village there is still a halting station for these 'transported' men. It is a large wooden building, low and square, with high, inaccessible windows, strongly barred, and lying beside a yard surrounded by an enclosure. Within the enclosure are a few buildings for common use, previously stables, offices, and dormitories for the soldiers. Around it are the sentryboxes. But now the doorways are sealed with planks; no one is allowed to enter. Everything is crumbling. Roofs are falling in, and the sides of the buildings are warped and rotting. These empty, dilapidated buildings are as lugubrious to look upon as haunted houses. They seem not only abandoned, but avoided. It seems impossible to look at them and remain indifferent. They were built to harbour nothing but grief, and if you think of all the suffering and the anguish which they witnessed for so many years you feel as if some part of pain must be still there, and as if the strong sense of sadness and repulsion which they give you as you pass by could come only from something living and heartsore in the air itself – some mysterious emanation of weeping, some indefinable echo of disappearing voices given out by these things and heard by the soul.

Every village had a little river, and therefore a bridge for us to pass, and naturally the bridge was wooden. After our accident we felt for bridges in general a respect full of mistrust. We always tried to pass them at the greatest possible speed, not so much for fear of seeing them collapse under us as out of a desire to avoid the sound of the creaking wood.

There had remained with us an invincible dislike for that sound. It was an entirely physical sensation, the strong effect of an automatic link of memories. The creaking of a piece of wood under our wheels always had the effect of a danger signal. Our minds might be elsewhere, and might even continue to remain elsewhere, but our bodies, ever on the alert, started at the sound. And over the bridges, and especially over the greater bridges, those high ones which crossed deep ravines or swift rivers or precipices, we felt an odd kind of satisfaction and negative pleasure. It was the mere pleasure of not being precipitated below. We said to one another:

'If this bridge were to give way?'

'We should not survive to tell the tale!'

'They would find us in bits . . .'

And we seemed delighted not to be down there in the deep chasm which we saw if we leaned to look over the side of the bridge, as we always did by some uncontrollable attraction, delighted above all not to be down there already.

About half past two in the afternoon of 4 July we reached Nijni-Udinsk, about three hundred miles from Irkutsk. We were received by the police, who had prepared us a lodging in their own headquarters, an honour vouchsafed only to great men and criminals. A policeman made tea for us, another policeman made up our beds, and a third one cooked our dinner; this was the Force become domesticated. Just imagine yourself ordering your menu from a *gorodovoi* standing at attention! The extraordinary thing, too, is that the dinner was excellent.

While Prince Borghese received the visits of the chief of police and his officers, while Ettore, who had found our deposit of fuel and lubricants, was cleaning and stoking our machine, I was engaged in a heroic struggle at the Nijni-Udinsk telegraph office, from which I wanted to send my newspapers an account of recent events. Since the opium-smoking clerks at the office of Hsien-wan-fu, I had not come across more singular officials than here.

'What language is this in?'

'Italian,' I replied.

'We do not telegraph in Italian.'

'You are obliged to by the International Convention.'

'But who can assure us that it is Italian?'

'I do.'

'That is not sufficient.'

My patience was about to give way, but I just recovered it in time, and I observed with great restraint:

'Get the telegram read by someone who knows Italian.'

'No one can understand Italian here.'

'Oh, come!' I cried, 'will you transmit it, or will you not?'

'We will transmit it as a code dispatch.'

'Very well.'

'Words of more than ten letters pay double fee.'

'Very well.'

'Please give us the code, and the translation in Russian. The law demands this for code telegrams.'

This was really too much. I went to search for assistance, and I found Mr Radionoff, our good travelling companion, who having started with us just to see us out of Irkutsk, apparently did not intend to leave us again. I dragged him to the telegraph, I infected him with my exasperation, and we combined our oratorical powers, but in vain. Then I had a good idea. I took a telegraph form, covered it with an indignant protest, and had it sent off at once as an urgent message to the Director-General of the Siberian Telegraph at Irkutsk. An hour later the Italian language was officially recognized at Nijni-Udinsk. But how I wished I had to deal again with those little Chinese clerks isolated in their distant mud offices in the Gobi desert, those good pigtailed telegraphists, who had to write on my telegram: *No. 1*, and who then forwarded it without error or delay across all the empty spaces of the east.

In the evening our friend Radionoff resolved that he must leave us. The wind and the splashes of mud had given him a sudden cold in the eye, which prevented him from appreciating any longer the pleasures of too long a motor journey. We bade farewell to this delightful person with some considerable regret. He wished to take the night train back to Irkutsk. In saying goodbye he announced to me with a satisfied, confidential expression:

'Do you know that I am something of a journalist too?'

'Indeed?'

'Yes. Today I sent a telegram to the Irkutsk papers. It ran like this: "On Borghese car. We reached Nijni-Udinsk at 2.35 p.m. Splendid journey!"'

'And was that all?'

'Oh, no! I signed it too.'

XV

IN THE BASIN OF THE YENISEI

On the Taiga – *Kansk* – *The Chained Wheel* – *Krasnojarsk*
– By the Power of Two Documents – *Crossing the*
Kemtschug – *Atschinsk* – *We Founder*

Nijni-Udinsk is no more than a big village on the banks of the Tshuna, one of the many tributaries of the Angara. We travelled through its muddy streets at four o'clock in the morning, scattering in rapid flight sundry peaceful families of pigs which were stretched out in the water of the gutters along the walls of the houses. A few early risers looked out at the noise, opened their windows on hearing the sound of the car, and looked at us with a sleepy, distrustful eye. Our car was preceded by a police *tarantass*, mounted by an officer and driven by gendarmes, who were coming to show us the way to Kansk, 150 miles away. At a level-crossing over the railway, the *tarantass* stopped.

'Now the road is quite easy,' exclaimed the officer. 'You simply follow this path. *Do svidania!*'

'*Do svidania! Spasibo!* – Goodbye – thanks,' we cried.

And the car got up speed, hastening eagerly towards its new goal. We ran through a thick, icy fog, which bathed our faces and covered our furs with dewdrops. For a little while we hoped that the sun would disperse it. The sun did show at intervals, very white behind this veil, and we cried words of encouragement to it.

'Courage, good friend, courage now!'

There seemed to be a struggle waged in that state of the weather between the sun and the mist. The victory inclined now to the one, now to the other. We, of course, took sides with the sun. Ettore sympathized with it.

'Poor thing,' he said, 'he is doing all he can.'

But the sun was ignominiously routed. He fled and we never beheld him again that day. The mist rose only to fall again in the shape of rain, and that whole day we were tormented by water, wind, cold, and mud. The roads were not nearly so good as they had been near Irkutsk. We were obliged at times to deviate from our course, so as to avoid holes, deep puddles, and suspicious-looking stretches of mud. We met no traffic now; the region was becoming more and more deserted. The fields and prairies were supplanted by a tree-covered tract of land. We were entering the region of the *taiga*, the interminable Siberian forest. At nine that morning we were already in a dismal half-shade.

The road had been artificially cut through the forest. Men have made a way for themselves, but over long tracts the forest is virgin on every side. The regions of the *taiga* stretch from the meadows to the tundras. They are as vast as an empire. Mankind has only succeeded with all its labour in acquiring a right of way over the greater part of this world of green giants. We ran over miles and miles amid an imposing dark crowd of fir trees, of pine centuries old, of white-stemmed birches. When we came to a height, the endless green stretch of woodland reached the very farthest horizon before us. A painful sense of isolation was slowly creeping over us and this solitude was oppressive, because it was shut in by the great barrier of shade which ran by our side, darker and more fearful-looking by reason of the dim light which came from the stormy sky. That great population of trees seemed to have a life of its own, and a strange, hostile feeling towards us. It stood in a silent attitude of defence. It seemed to have the will to enclose and imprison us. At the turnings of the road the plains always seemed to close before and behind us, to stop our advance and cut off every way of retreat. You would have thought they were moving as we looked at them. At every moment the road disappeared in the green growth, and seemed conquered and destroyed. The trunks of the pine trees, straight, reddish, prodigiously high, had a solemn majesty of columns in a cathedral. Thick shrubs in a wild entanglement invaded the sides of the road, and formed long, impenetrable hedges, which seemed to stand there on guard over the virgin majesty of the forest. Suddenly a wolf, frightened by the swift advance of the motor car, crossed our path, running. We were breaking into the primordial life of the *taiga*.

Sometimes the wood was less thick. We found openings and then meadows, and in the little valleys solitary villages living in the forest and on the forest, surrounded by enormous piles of timber, destined perhaps for the building of the railway. They were little, happy-looking villages, satisfied with the small knowledge they had of the world, and with being their own world; inhabited by athletic-looking, fair-headed woodsmen. These men are at the same time the friends and the enemies of the *taiga*. They love it and they fight it; they pull down its gigantic trunks, and they believe in the most poetical legends of the forest: the trees around them are both their companions and their victims. Near the *isbas* are long lines of enormous carts standing with their shafts up like beseeching arms. These are the carts used to carry away the trunks of the trees, and all around graze horses which our car frightened and drove into a long and anxious gallop.

A surprise awaited us. Suddenly we saw some telegraph poles among the branches, and shortly afterwards we were by the side of the railway line. There was a long whistle and a train came up behind us with its quick, sharp panting. For a few minutes we raced side by side with it. From the windows of the carriages the travellers greeted us, then cried 'Goodbye' to us. But soon our path left the side of the railway, and we found ourselves alone again in the primitive stillness. This was for us like a fleeting apparition of the world we had left, joining us for a moment here in the wild solitude. Mankind had come to give us a short cry of encouragement, in the vast silence of the forest.

In the afternoon a violent storm burst, flashing and thundering with a continuous roar from one valley to the other. The road was streaming with water and the pouring rain veiled everything from our sight. Near the village of Taitisk we crossed the River Birussa by boat. The Birussa is a tributary of the Tshuna, which we had crossed in the morning at Nijni-Udinsk, impetuous, turbid and swollen like a great torrent. The storm abated in violence, but a few hours later, as we were descending into the valley of the Kan, another tempest overtook us. We crossed the Kan in a boat of about the same size as that in which we had crossed the Selenga at Verkhne-Udinsk, while this second furious storm was at the height of its violence and lit up our way with livid lightning.

The Kan was the first river we crossed that flows directly into the Yenisei. We had now definitely left behind us the basin of the Angara and were entering into that of the Yenisei. We were on the outskirts of central Siberia. Kansk, on the banks of the Kan, appeared like a great city, but this appearance of grandeur was due to two things: to the mist which dimmed and broadened the outline of the city, and to the presence on the bank of the river of a large industrial establishment. A young man, who looked something like a university student, and who was travelling on the same boat as ourselves, understood by the word 'factory' that we were talking about this building and had noticed its high chimneys. We had already said goodmorning, so now he said to us:

'No, it is not a factory.'

'Then what is it?'

'It would be better for Kansk if this building did not exist. It drains the country instead of enriching it. It is a terrible thing. It is the ruination of Russia.'

'What is it?'

'It is a government vodka distillery . . .'

We were as wet as if we had had to swim across the river. We found the roads swamped and deserted. A few scattered *iswoschiks* passed by us, splashing. We took up our lodging in an old wooden inn, the best in the place, and they brought us there the supplies which had arrived for us. There were no other customers sleeping in the hotel, and its rooms had the chill of uninhabited places. But the billiard-room on the ground floor was full of officers, of sound, and of smoke, and during the night, through the endless dripping of the rain, we could confusedly hear the shouting of the players and the click of the balls.

At three the next morning we were up. We wanted to reach Krasnojarsk early, and that was nearly 150 miles. Shortly before our departure a police officer came to offer us the escort of some armed soldiery.

'It's quite impossible, thank you,' remarked Prince Borghese. 'They couldn't follow us.'

'Take them with you on the car,' advised the officer.

'There is only room for ourselves.'

'We have been notified of the presence of some bandits in the wood. A short time ago some rebels delivered a surprise attack on the barracks at Krasnojarsk. They made off with arms and ammunition and opened the doors of the prison. In the prison there were seventy criminals, all of whom escaped, and only thirty were recaptured.'

'And what happened to the other forty?'

'The other forty, divided into little bands, are scouring the country round the Yenisei. They are constantly seen here and there, but we have not the necessary force to pursue them. They often assault people passing over the trakt in the wood. Fortunately now there is a railway, and the few people who have to go by road, if they are people of importance, are granted an escort.'

To stop a motor car is not an easy matter, especially for people who have never seen one before. Only a trap could betray us. Besides, there was no means of taking soldiers with us, and we could not, for fear of a chance meeting with bandits, take seven days over our journey to Krasnojarsk so as to be accompanied by an escort on foot. As for the bandits, they had been a constant subject of conversation between our hosts and ourselves from Missowaja on, and we were becoming somewhat sceptical concerning this kind of danger on the main road. The escort was therefore declined with thanks. The officer shrugged his shoulders, as if to say, 'Very well, it's your own business.'

Instead of having the escort, we asked to be taken outside the town, as we had been at Nijni-Udinsk, and put on to the right road. It is not so difficult to arrive at a city in Siberia as to come away from one. The officer, with great courtesy, got on to the *iswoschik*; he gave a sharp order to the coachman and was off at a quick trot. We followed him.

Outside the city the officer left us, saying:

'Be on your guard.'

That day, 6 July, was one of the worst days of our whole journey. We were pursued by a continuous downpour of rain, a regular deluge, which flooded the roads over the plain and worked itself a bed down the roads of the hill. It was impossible with 40 hp to work up any speed at all. The car slipped, skidded over the greasy mud; the wheels sometimes could not bite and revolved madly, whirling round with a wild, shrill sound, and throwing up mud and water.

It is impossible to give any idea of what a Siberian road is like with such rain. In the villages, where the hoofs of the cattle work up the ground, the mud is deep and soft. Our wheels disappeared in it as far as the axles, and the liquid mud splashed all round in a fan shape. Over vast tracts of land we found the so-called 'black earth', which certainly is one of the most fertile soils of the world, but it is also the most hostile to motor travelling. This black earth is, as it were, a pulp, into which for thousands of years the dead grasses have been worked. It is a kind of peat, an ex-swamp, which, under the rain, turns into swamp again. It is saturated with organic material, soapy, thin; when it is wet there is no more difficult feat than to walk on it keeping one's balance. The car stopped on it and gave signs of the most deplorable rebellion against being guided. It turned round, it threw itself aside; and we often had great difficulty in stopping it on the very edge of a ditch.

We were not very far from Kansk when we came to a little slope covered with this black earth. For more than an hour we tried to climb by all the methods which experience had taught us might succeed. But the thing was impossible. Tired and exasperated, we decided to go back. A few versts away, there was a level railway-crossing, with a little watch-man's house. We asked the watchman for shelter, and we left our machine out on the road. There was nothing else to be done. We should have to wait until the rain stopped and the road was a little drier.

The watchman's wife lit her samovar. We hung our furs and raincoats round the hot stove, and we sat down in this little room, silent and gloomy, like people condemned. Ever since we had entered Siberia we had had bad weather, except for one day, and that day, when the sun was shining, we had fallen through a bridge! Surely there must be something like an evil spell working against us. From time to time we glanced out through the window. It was still raining. The sky was dark and low. It was not a question of hours: it was a question of days, of weeks perhaps.

The hour of midday arrived. The watchman put on his coat and his cap, took down the signal flags from the wall and went out. His wife ran to shut the gates of the level-crossing, and shortly after a long train passed swiftly by, making the window-panes rattle and the house shake. It came from Kansk. The watchman came back, took off his coat and his cap, filled his pipe, and said to us:

'There is no change in the weather.'

'Is summer always like this in Siberia?' we asked him.

'There has not been a summer like this here within the memory of man. For two months it has rained now, almost all the time. Never have we had such cold and such rain in July. It is impossible to work in the fields. In the territory of Yeniseisk a great many crops are entirely spoilt. We shall have a hungry winter in Siberia.'

We could not stop for ever here, smoking cigarettes and watching the trains pass through the station. Surely we must find some means of overcoming that dreadful black earth, some ingenious way of preventing the wheels from slipping. For such roads as these we ought to have had studded wheels.

Ettore went out and began to rummage round the machine. This meant he had some plan in his mind. He was the Man of Resource. In fact, we saw him take the chains of the hauling-tackle and twist them round the left driving wheel. It was a stroke of genius. We applauded it enthusiastically. 'Let's try now!' exclaimed the clever chauffeur, putting down again the chain wheel, which he had lifted with a screw-jack.

'Let's try.'

We jumped on to our seats and off we went. A few minutes later we were within sight of the enemy. The car speedily tackled that climb which had so often repelled us. About half-way up the machine had a moment's hesitation, but it was only a moment: the chain was digging into the ground like a claw, it reached the hard substratum, and advanced foot by foot. We reached the top and never stopped again. We had, however, to put up with a great nuisance, and bear it patiently and resignedly. The chain picked up the most extraordinary amount of mud and kept throwing it over the car and ourselves. Everything was covered with it, and nasty, slimy, greasy stuff it was. We could scarcely keep our eyes open, and in the villages it would pick up bits of wood, little sticks all covered with slime, and stones, and would throw them all on the top of us, with perfect indifference, but we were advancing! We had now no more fear of this constant mud.

The rain, driven by a frozen, violent, biting wind, beat upon our faces.

For many miles the road took us again on to the *taiga*. The clouds, lowering in the darkened sky, often came down and enveloped us in a strange mist, through which the trees of the forest seemed to take on bizarre spectral forms. The masses of fir trees outlined against the sky, dark, fantastic profiles full of tall, slender points which looked like spires and pinnacles: the fantastic outlines of some Gothic city. We could never see the horizon with any clearness. Everything round us was dim and pale. There remained in our memory an impression of those regions, as inexact and confused as of things seen in a dream. We could remember clearly only the impetuous rushing of the torrent, the rustling of the rain upon the trees, the streaming of little courses of water along the sides of the road: a picture entirely of raining waters. The little torrents were swollen and turbid, the rivers were all overflowing, but everywhere we found bridges; we crossed one over the Kizbna, near the village of Kiebfska, which was very long, and shaken by the strong current which drove against its pillars.

In the wood, after hours and hours of solitude, we suddenly saw three men, armed with guns, standing still upon the road. They were dressed as moujiks.

'Could they be the famous bandits,' we wondered on perceiving them. 'Or simply poachers?'

Poachers or bandits, whichever they were, we got our Mausers ready and watched their every movement. The three men also watched us, motionless. You could tell they were filled with astonishment at so strange an apparition in the heart of the *taiga*. When we were about fifty paces from them, they waited no longer: they fled full speed between the trees and then stopped to look at us with a terrified expression. They seemed so stunned that we could surely have demanded of them with perfect success 'their money or their lives'!

During our short halts we were a prey to whole clouds of insects, which bit us till they drew blood. We suffered greatly from this well-known Siberian plague, especially in the forest. The local inhabitants, in order to defend themselves, swathe their heads in long black veils which cover their chests and their shoulders. All men, women and children, wear this lugubrious garment. It gives the sinister impression of some sign of mourning worn by a whole people.

*

It was six o'clock when, coming out of the wood, we saw in the far-off distance the white gleam of a river. It was the Yenisei, and an hour later we were on its right bank, facing the blue domes and tall spires of Krasnojarsk. A splendid river it was, between steep banks, vast and swift, looking almost eager to make up for its long hibernal stillness; furrowed by steamers and other boats, crossed by the slight and quaint local *pirogues*, a special kind of canoe, made of a single hollowed-out tree trunk. Before reaching the city the river is divided into two branches, which we crossed on large, solid boats; some police officers expected us and took us to an hotel, leading us through almost deserted streets. Krasnojarsk was resting in the endless clearness of the Siberian night.

We stopped for a whole day at Krasnojarsk: a long and tedious Sunday, which we spent in the hotel. Outside it was raining; the shops were closed, the streets were silent, and the city had a desolate look as if its people had fled at the threat of some mysterious danger. We went down into the yard now and then to have a look at our car, which was undergoing a general clean-up, of which it was in dire need. The mud had penetrated to such an extent in the honeycomb of the radiator that it prevented the free working of this lung of the motor, and we attributed to the mud the incident of the overheated brake, an occurrence which had stopped us again since our last halt.

Thanks to the police, we found at Krasnojarsk, as we had done in the other cities, our supplies of fuel and oil. It was always the police who took upon themselves the duty of finding where our supplies were, and of getting them delivered to us by day or night.

Around the car was always gathered a chosen public of dignitaries and officials, for the courtyard was inaccessible to the crowd. Here we found, not without some surprise, Englishmen, with whom we entered into the most friendly relations out of a certain sense of western affinity. They were engineers, retained in Siberia by that employment which most of all seems to cast a spell upon man – gold-digging. At Krasnojarsk there is the same talk of gold that there is in Alaska. It appears that under the rich layers of fertile land used for fields and pasture Siberia hides other and greater riches. In the basin of the Lena, of the Yenisei, of the Amur, and of many minor rivers, there are abundant deposits of gold. As regards gold production, Siberia is second only to the United States, Australia, and the Transvaal, and the gold veins have not yet been properly explored. The gold-bearing sands and alluvial deposits are being gathered together and washed by the most primitive methods. But for some years now more reasonable methods of gold producing have been inaugurated. For machines, engineers, and directors, England has been drawn upon like a land of masters in the art of finding gold.

Krasnojarsk also has another history of relations with England, a curious history, which very nearly succeeded in turning that city into a naval port. An English navigator called Wiggins had the bold idea of profiting by the few weeks – only six or seven – during which the Arctic Ocean is not icebound, to come over the Kara Straits and penetrate the estuary of the Yenisei in search of a new route of communication with Siberia. In 1874 he tried this experiment with a ship called *Diana*, and it was successful: a most unlikely naval connection was in fact established between England and Siberia. A second attempt was made in 1875, and proved equally successful. In 1878 this idea was put at the service of commerce, and goods were landed at the mouth of the Yenisei and the Obi. Seven years later an English company was formed to regulate and work this summer navigation. But if England wanted to export her goods, Siberia was not yet ready to receive them; business went badly, and the company was dissolved. A second company was formed for the same purpose a few years later, when it looked as if Siberia was beginning to develop, and might soon need iron machines, but this plan also had to be given up. Siberia was not yet ripe. But in 1895, when the railway brought the first awakening of trade to that vast continent, a third English company was formed, and during the summer of 1896 not one, but three ships sailed up the Yenisei as far as Turukhansk, where they deposited their goods, among which were seven railway engines, which were put on to smaller boats and towed up as far as Krasnojarsk. In the following year, the English steamships which anchored at Turukhansk, increased to the number of six, and several of smaller tonnage penetrated the Obi. This time business was doing excellently. In 1898 a regular commercial fleet arrived, but the Russian government, which had encouraged this enterprise by reducing or cancelling duties, now ceased the granting of any favours, and thus this summer navigation came to an end. Krasnojarsk will never be a seaport again.

That evening the hotel was noisy and gay with one of those great Siberian banquets which preserve the pomp of ancient feasts. The waiters in white smocks came running from the kitchens bearing steaming dishes held high in both hands. We went to sleep among the echoes of full, loud laughter from the banqueting hall, and with the quick step of the servants passing before our doors and making the wooden floor shake. From the road came up from time to time the heavy sound of men marching, reinforced patrols passing by. We had seen the sentries take up their posts in the streets of the town. There was a report that evening of some mutiny which had taken place in barracks, but no one had any accurate information, nor seemed to care, about it. They spoke of these things as one would talk of the weather.

At four a.m. on 8 July, two of our English friends got into an *iswoshchik* and showed us the way out of Krasnojarsk; needless to say, it was still pouring. At about one verst from the last houses we bid our guides a friendly goodbye and went on over the most horrible roads, over slight grassy undulations among which we sank and on which we rose as a boat does in the hollow or on the crest of the waves, and a journey began for us exactly like that of the day before and the day before that. We crossed prairies, woods, narrow cultivated zones surrounding villages. All was wet, dark, and sad. The hours went by and the miles went by, slowly. The little incidents of the way, the comical look of surprise among the moujiks, the fright of the horses, our arrival in the midst of Russian fairs, the cause of the most ludicrous rout, availed no longer to distract our attention or engage our conversation. We were gloomy and almost resentful.

For one does end by feeling real resentment against an evil fate pursuing one like an enemy. These were not inevitable obstacles such as the mountains of Kalgan, or the bed of the Iro; no, they were difficulties which might have been nonexistent an hour before our arrival and might not exist an hour later. They seemed placed one after the other on purpose to fatigue us, to delay us, to exasperate us. This was usually a season of horrible drought, and this year there was not a moment's interruption to the rain. Those roads should have been excellent, but they were impassable; one day's sunshine would have made them good, and the sun would not appear. All our calculations, all our forecasts were upset. We thought we could go from Krasnojarsk to Tomsk in one day, and we found it would take us three, or perhaps four. Siberia showed a kind of obstinate resistance to our journey, and we felt our own will growing obstinate; after all, obstinacy is simply an irritation of the will.

About nine o'clock we reached the bank of a river, the Kemtschug – a tributary of the Tschulym, which in its turn flows into the Obi – near a small village, which is called *Great*: 'Bolshaia.'

We asked for the ferryboat, the usual *paravieda* which takes *telegas* across.

'It was here,' answered the peasants who had gathered round us, 'but the flood overturned it and it sank. It went down about half a mile down the river.'

We asked whether there was any bridge in the neighbourhood. We were told that the inhabitants crossed the river by a tiny little improvised footbridge about two feet broad, and which was already unsteady and dangerous.

'There was a bridge,' they said to us, 'but the flood swept it away.'

'And what about the chances of fording it?'

'No, the river is deeper than a man's height in the middle, and there is no ford across it.'

We then thought of crossing by the railway bridge, as we had done in Trans-Baikalia.

'Where is the railway?' we asked.

'It is down there, about ten versts off.'

'Is there a road to it?'

'No.'

'A path?'

'No. It is all forest, and you can only go on foot or on horseback.'

We were in a quandary. A tiny river like the Kemtschug now seemed about to block our advance completely. We tried to find out how long it would take to build a large and solid raft – at least two days' work. Then we fell back upon our last resource. We sent for the *starosta*.

He was an old, white-bearded moujik dressed in an *armiak* of embroidered velvet, which gave him an appearance as of an old boyar or Russian nobleman, come to life. Prince Borghese put before him the official letters which had been given to us by the minister of the interior and by the director of the imperial police, and which enjoined upon all authorities the duty of giving us every possible help and protection, and he solemnly said to him:

'Do read these . . .'

Unfortunately the *starosta* could not read, and he solemnly considered these documents, holding them upside down. But a youth who was wearing a military cap took them from his hands, and read them aloud to the crowd round us.

The *starosta* made a deep bow. What seemed to impress those good people most of all was the title 'prince', and the description of Prince Borghese as an Italian deputy.

'He belongs to the Duma of Italy,' was repeated on all sides in tones of great admiration.

'He is a Kniatz!'

'He has a *podorojné* from the government.'

'He is like a courier of the tsar.'

The *starosta* asked what he could do for him. The prince said that he required most urgently to reach Atschinsk that evening. He must cross the river as soon as possible. A short discussion took place among the moujiks, and after this the old man declared with a polite bow that he hoped to have us cross the Kemtschug in a few hours. In the meantime he invited us to wait in his *isba*, where his wife offered us tea in her best Sunday porcelain.

In a moment Bolshaia was up in arms: the peasants, armed with hatchets, ropes, spades, and pails, gathered on the banks of the river. We watched their doings with great curiosity from behind the double windows of the *starosta*'s house. The *starosta* was in command of the manoeuvre. Those pails puzzled us; but we very soon understood his plan, and therefore also the use of the pails. The idea was to pull the foundered boat up again. One end of it was still jutting out of the water. Some men went into the river, tied heavy ropes round the boat, and by these ropes pulled it up close to the bank, then with their pails they emptied it, and set it afloat again; this job lasted several hours. Then some planks and beams were quickly carried to the shore, and with the extraordinary cleverness in timberwork always exhibited by the moujiks, a solid landing-stage was built in a very short time.

When everything was ready, we came down, our car was hoisted on to the still-moored boat, and the somewhat rehabilitated ferry, drawn, pushed, accompanied by men through the water, began its journey across. The rope which moored it was now thrown to the other bank, where a long chain of men started pulling it. The actual landing was easy to manage. The car came on to the bank like a triumphal chariot, drawn by a multitude streaming with water and perspiration but aglow with the joy of success.

After distributing a well-deserved remuneration among the good moujiks of Bolshaia, we continued our journey at twelve o'clock amid hearty shouts of '*Do svidania!*' The road was now slightly better. Here and there we came again upon steppe land. By three o'clock we were within sight of Atschinsk, which is at a distance of about 130 miles from Krasnojarsk.

Atschinsk appears quite suddenly before one coming from the east, and it presents the most picturesque sight. You cross little woods of birch trees, then the wood slopes down, and on the slope among the trees you see the cupolas and belfries of the town. Shortly after, its little white houses appear, with their roofs sloping gradually towards the river, the Tschulym, beyond which an immense plain spreads as far as the eye can reach.

Before we entered Atschinsk we were met by most of its inhabitants. They had tied their *tarantass* among the trees and were waiting for us by the roadside. A police officer began to make signs to us, waving his handkerchief, and when he suspected that we might not understand his words, he began to make violent gesticulations to express eating, drinking, sleeping, with a mimicry which appeared to cause great amusement among the public. We begged the officer to take a seat in our car and to lead us to the place where you could eat, and drink, and sleep. He seemed extremely surprised to hear us address him in Russian.

Our arrival had been rumoured all over Atschinsk; people looked out of their windows, came to their shop doors. We passed before some low, strongly barred buildings, guarded all round by sentries; these were well-known prisons. Even behind bars the great piece of news had been heard, and the convicts were expecting us. Behind the window railings there crowded shaven heads, one upon the other, as in a heap. Dozens of hands were nervously clutching on to the bars, and even farther back, where the light was dimmer, you could see a sparkling of eager eyes.

We lodged in a poor wooden hut, which had taken to itself the proud title of Hotel; and it was the best hotel in the town. In the night a group of men arrived and knocked at the door. No one opened, for it appears that we were the only ones in the *gostinitza*; a lad had come late the evening before, to bring us our dinner, and then had gone off. The men shouted, said that they would barge in, and in fact did come in, by the light of a candle, and imperiously demanded sleeping accommodation. They were merchants, from somewhere or other, wrapped in furs and covered with mud. We succeeded in convincing them that they must look for lodgings elsewhere, and they went off still shouting. At three in the morning, the same lad of the evening before appeared with a lighted samovar, to make our tea.

That hotel – if I remember rightly it called itself *Hotel d'Europe* – certainly had the most original arrangements for its service. If we had not been taken there by the police we might really have believed that we had fallen into some trap.

At 3.30 we left the place. Getting up and out was quickly done, because in the small towns we had to sleep with our clothes on, and only the larger hotels in the principal towns have such things as sheets. Siberian travellers take their bedclothes with them, just as they carry their samovar, their little bag of tea and their tiny bag of sugar. That custom of carrying your bed with you has a flavour of nomadic life; it is perhaps a last relic of the tent. It is true this habit may be derived from nothing more than a habitual distrust of the beds of the *gostinitzas*, and the distrust is certainly not undeserved. I was saying, then, that we slept with our clothes on, wrapped in our furs, lying on bare planks, with a bag for a pillow; the next morning we made up for it by thorough ablutions in the yard, to the great surprise of the Siberians, who are accustomed to wash under a kind of measuring glass which takes half an hour to drip out one glassful of water. As for the moujiks, when they think it might be advisable to clean their faces, they fill their mouth with water so as to warm it, and spew it out a little at a time into the hollow of their hands and wash . . .

The police inspector, in whose house we had taken tea in the evening after dinner, had warned us that besides the usual bandits, another danger might be feared: namely, swamps. We had to be very careful not to miss the Marinsk road, for we wanted to spend the next night, that of 9 July, at this place, and we were anxious not to get lost in the watery expanse which extends over the Tschulym Plains. To save us from this mishap, the inspector offered to send a lieutenant with us as a guide, to lead us on to the safe road, and the next morning the lieutenant, in a *tarantass* drawn by two splendid horses, started off.

The sky was full of rain, and it was cold. Just past the city we crossed the Tulim by one of the usual Siberian ferries, consisting of a platform held up by two boats, like one large raft; we rode off over the low grassy plain, denuded of any trees, and the reeds and the regular clouds of insects betrayed its swampy nature. The road was muddy, but not very difficult. We were quite annoyed at having to go slowly, to follow the *tarantass*, and we were about to overtake and pass with a greeting the bearded officer who led us, feeling quite sure that we could brave the swamps of the Tulim, seeing that we had come out of those of the Chara-gol, when our car suddenly stopped, and slowly leaned over to one side.

We were in for it! The swamps of the Tulim claimed our respect and attention.

XVI

TOMSK THE LEARNED

*On the Way to Marinsk – 'Where is the Verst?' – In the
Mud – Our Friends the Moujiks – Jerks and Joltings –
Discouragement – The 'Big Beast' – We Run Around
in the Wood – Tomsk – Towards Kolywan – The Obi
and its Bogs – Kolywan*

The back wheels of the car were sinking deep. Ettore, who was at the
wheel, remarked in regretful tone of voice, 'If I had been going faster
perhaps we should have got through.'

And convinced of his guilt, he wanted to get out of the difficulty
without outside assistance by driving the engine with a sudden increase
of power and with jerks, now backwards, now forwards, but the wheels
slid, revolved in the ruts they had dug out for themselves, and sunk
deeper, throwing up on us (we were trying to push the car on) a thick
spattering of black mud. It covered our faces like a mask.

'It's no good – we'll have to ask for help,' said Prince Borghese.

The officer went back in the *tarantass*, galloping towards the city in
search of men and planks. An hour later we were surrounded by
policemen, and by soldiers who had been drawn from some regiment on
guard, all armed, commanded by a huge bearded sergeant who looked
like a sapper in Napoleon's army; and Tschulym boatmen also appeared
on the scene carrying planks. It took this good band of assistants two
hours to lift the machine and pull it out of the mud.

What a lot of different people we had seen at work round our car,
pushing it, pulling it, raising it! In how many tongues had the same ideas
been expressed with panting breath; how many human wills had joined
their efforts to ours! That group of Russian soldiers – wearing their
characteristic cloaks, with hoods that looked like monastic cowls, and
their traditional flat caps and high, rough boots; with their cartridges at
their belt, a long sword by their side, all intent upon managing that big,
grey machine, ready to obey the commands of the huge sergeant, and

working together at the spokes of the wheels – they all seemed to be enacting a war scene. It made one think of some episode in a battle, of the rescue of some strange new gun.

We crossed the vast plain without further misadventures and entered upon a great undulating stretch of little hills, now bare, now wooded. Gradually, as we advanced, the road became less practicable; it was nothing but hills, ditches, and ruts. It had been given up by *telegas* and carts, which had found another passage for themselves, leaving capricious traces of numerous paths zigzag across woods and meadows. This suggested that any road would be better than the real road; the bridges, however, were still firm, and at the near end all the paths converged, parting again at the other end of the bridge. The old main road was covered with grass and brambles, and it would have been almost impossible to detect where it lay if we had not seen the traces of its original ditches, and if alongside there had not always been at every verst a peculiar sign post painted with white, red, and black spirals, bearing the record of the distance which lay between that point and the nearest postal station: lonely placards which no one now uses.

Those sign posts guided us. We constantly said to one another: 'Where is the "verst"?'

And if we could not see it we went back to look for it.

We ran along little country roads, leaving the marks of our wheels over the grass and the brambles. We passed from one to the other with that continuous illusion which never seems to fail to comfort man, that the place where he does not find himself at any given moment must always be better than the one where he is. Envy is a fault which probably arises from this illusion.

Sometimes we lost our way, and we had to go back to the last village and try to find another road. We were always upheld and comforted by the hope of coming at any moment to that good main road which all the topographical maps promised to us, and which we had been seeking for over a thousand miles. 1000 miles of disillusionment! But the longer its approach was delayed the more we felt sure we must be getting near it. The very distance which we had covered without coming across it seemed to us an unanswerable argument in favour of our being near that promised joy.

The landscape was becoming oppressively monotonous: all prairie, all clumps of willow and birch trees, all stagnant little pools. But sometimes the path was bordered by tiny yellow flowers, and then it would present a charming sight which made us forgive and forget all our ennui. While we were passing one of those flowery tracts we had to stop and change a tyre, and a few moujiks who happened to be passing with their *telegas* gathered round us. They stood by, watching the operation with the greatest interest. They felt the tyres, they conferred together, and then pressed them again. When they saw us pumping them up they expressed the liveliest approbation. It was in listening to them that we were informed of the most extraordinary idea we had heard about the car since the Chinese idea of the hidden horse. We were to meet again with the opinion which we now heard; and we found it to be one of the ideas most natural to the mental constitution of the moujik. The thing in the car which most strikes the moujik's eye is the thickness of the tyres, and he insists upon attributing to them that fine secret power which makes the car move. In the tyres is speed and strength; they contain the wonderful machinery which makes the wheels go round; this is why they are so large. The Chinese mind is given to abstractions, the Slav mind is simple; the former imagines more than is necessary, the latter less. The moujik always goes more by appearance, and in this matter he seemed almost to have an intuitive idea of the dynamo.

Suddenly we saw a group of men standing still in the middle of the road and waving their caps to us as a signal to stop. These were peasants who had seen us approaching and had come to warn us that a little bridge further on had collapsed. Fortunately, it was only a question of a small bridge crossing a ditch, and with their assistance and by using the fallen planks we were able to build a temporary one very quickly and continue our journey a few minutes later.

At five that afternoon we were ferrying across the Kija near the town of Marinsk. With all its grand air of a mighty river, the Kija is only a tributary of the Tschet, which is in its turn a tributary of the Tschulym, itself a tributary of the Obi. It was indeed a *tributary*, a feudal dependant! But it was just now flooded and appeared before us as a thing to be reckoned with. Near the bank was a crowd of people, and in front of all the *pristaff*, a splendid old man, wearing the decoration of the Order of St Andrew. He welcomed us with a solemn greeting and begged us to go across the place very slowly, very slowly indeed. Prince Borghese reassured him; we would see that no accidents occurred.

'No, no, I know,' said the *pristaff*, with a polite smile. 'I am only begging you to go slowly so that my dependants may admire you at leisure.'

The entreaties of this paternal dignitary were absolutely unnecessary, because the streets through Marinsk were in such a condition that there was no choice for us but to proceed at a very solemn processional pace. The crowd surrounded us, boys always in front, and among the people were men on horseback and also *iswoschiks*, bearing the aristocratic representatives of the town. We were escorted to a Zemstvoskaya Dom, one of those houses which exist for the purpose of giving hospitality to Russian officials in places where there is no hotel. The house was decent enough, and our hosts certainly showed themselves very eager to please us. The dinner too was fairly good. The police located our supply of fuel, and our car was refilled and housed in the large shed close by.

The crowd stopped there for some hours looking up at our windows, waiting for some strange thing to happen. Then they dispersed slowly.

From 3.30 that morning to the present time, 5.30 p.m., that is to say, in fourteen hours of unbroken march, we had covered about one hundred miles – less than eight miles an hour. True, we might have covered even less, and so it proved the next day.

We got up at two o'clock and left at three. We were making our start earlier and earlier, so as to take advantage of the fine weather which we had in the night (for the weather continued to be wet by day and clear at night), and of the unbroken Siberian light. That day, 11 July, we wanted to reach Tomsk (about 160 miles away) by about one or two p.m., so as to take a little holiday; but Fate, alas, had decreed otherwise, and her laws are unalterable!

Our road had begun by being moderately good, but ended in a most horrible track. I have already written that it is almost impossible to imagine, without having seen it, how evil a Siberian road can be in the rain. And yet, from the point of view of motor driving, there is something even worse than that, and that is a Siberian road *after* the rain. When the rain is falling, the mud is deep, but liquid. The wheels skid in it, they do everything except advance, but at least they do not remain stuck. When the rain has ceased and the road is beginning to dry up, this mud slowly consolidates. From viscous it becomes gluelike, and the car sinks in it and remains clogged in it, held there and imprisoned. Sinking is much worse than skidding. We had divided the less pleasant situations of the journey into four categories in order of importance: being overturned; sinking; clogging; skidding. Sinking was a second-class misfortune. On the road to Tomsk we had no less than eight experiences of it; and it was always the fault of the sun!

In the morning we hailed joyfully the change we saw in the weather. The western wind became northerly and then changed to the east; the clouds that rose on the horizon broke, and were swept away in white flakes over the blue sky: the sun rose resplendent, untarnished, scorching. But about five a.m. the mud was already beginning to threaten us. We could feel the efforts which the car seemed to make not to be caught in a trap, and we could find no other way of preventing it except by getting up speed. We went by bounds, but in the villages, where it is impossible to go very fast because of the obstacles in the shape of planks and animals, and where the mud was very deep, we sank with the most exasperating frequency, remaining on these occasions swamped for a long time among the *isbas*.

At Tomsk an official worthy of credence had told Pierre Leroy Beaulieu, the well-known student of contemporary Russia, the story of an ox drowned in the mud before its own door at the time of the thaw. I am quoting my authority because the story might seem incredible, but in point of fact you need only cross Siberia to realize it is quite possible. In the mud of these villages our patience was certainly drowned. The local inhabitants, in order to make for themselves some kind of a path, put planks along their houses, now fronted by characteristic and quite indispensable little platforms; and in order to facilitate the progress of vehicles, they throw branches, faggots, and straw over the mud in the middle of the road. But these things, although they will hold the weight of Siberian light carts, are completely submerged under the weight of an automobile. Some of the local roads, and the best ones no doubt, have tree trunks laid across them, one close to the other, forming a kind of primitive pavement. We sometimes met with this arrangement even far from the villages, and our poor machine bounded over it as if it would disintegrate any minute. In the villages, fortunately, we found the remedy close to the evil, the remedy being the population itself, which was always kind to us, very willing and ready to help.

If the moujiks were really the thieves they are said to be, they could have robbed us a hundred times with perfect ease. We found them always entirely friendly, full of good nature, self-sacrifice and simplicity, intelligent and indefatigable. When they saw us push our machine they would join forces with us without being asked or encouraged to do so, calling to one another for extra assistance. In five minutes the whole population of the place would be round the car, and the press would be so great that you could only see the banner and the luggage standing out from a crowd of fur, caps, and fair heads. Some women thought that our car must be moved by the devil, and one crossed her upper lip rapidly with her thumb. But the men showed they had no fear of the devil, especially when they found that he offered them a means of earning a few roubles.

'Come, come,' said some, quite sensibly. 'If it is the devil that moves it, why doesn't the devil pull it out of the mud?'

Why indeed? The argument was convincing, and the moujiks, even the more timid ones, arrived by crowds, splashing into the mud with their big antediluvian boots, pushing our car and helping their work by singing in unison. There was no want of timber, and when the strength of men proved insufficient we could always get long beams brought to us to build powerful levers which raised the machine and made it possible to put stones or wood under the wheels. These efforts for the release of the machine always took a few hours. In some villages, after the men, the women would come too, and often the prettiest maidens of the place would gather together to sing a chorus for us, no doubt following some ancient patriarchal and poetic custom of honouring guests.

When we were far from the villages, without any hope of prompt assistance, our position was extremely trying. We went over the most horrible paths, which we knew might be excellent the very next day. The ground seemed to be all overturned mud, hardened where it jutted out into relief and very soft in the ruts. We ought to have gone slowly so as to avoid dangerous jerks, but we were obliged instead to go at full speed so as not to sink. The car often knocked against some hidden obstacle (stones or roots or tree trunks buried under the mud) and then it would sway suddenly, tilting its front wheels and falling back sideways. There were moments when we had to hang on very hard to some part of the car so as not to be thrown on to the road. We were constantly falling against one another. The springs seemed to be yielding, and the chassis was continually coming down over the differential axle with hard, dry knocks, which made us bounce up from our seats. The luggage straps were bursting and the luggage continually fell, or dropped its contents. But we could not stop until we were out of the worst spots, because stopping would have meant sinking; we lost some field-glasses, a tub, and a few other articles.

We were stunned and bruised. We feared at every moment to hear the crash of some irreparable damage or the breaking of the wheels. The whole car was so covered with mud that the air could not come in through the radiator, and the engine, impeded in its work, grew heated, and sent out a burning blaze. It seemed as if it would melt. And even amid so much mud, we could not find any water to fill the radiator, which was panting and steaming from the vent. When this funnel was opened, in the hope of cooling the water-jacket, a great column of steam came out with a sudden gust: a real geyser, which made us draw back to cover our faces with our hands. We had to dig holes in the mud and to wait for a little water to dribble into them, and then took up one glassful at a time; with that kind of muddy substance we filled our radiator. The fuel consumption was at this point enormous; the accelerator was in constant action, and we were continually surrounded by clouds of white, acrid smoke.

We crossed over the ditches, getting up speed, for we feared to land at the bottom, which was always covered with deep mud; and on these occasions the car would always run up the opposite bank with its front wheels uplifted, and then they would drop again sideways. On one of these leaps we heard the sound of broken metal. It was the back part of the car, which had crashed on the ground with so much force that the earth, grazing the fuel-tank, had loosened and torn off its whole cover, as if it had been orange-peel. For hours at a time we spoke not a word. The first misgivings were beginning to cloud our hopes of victory.

We had so far cherished the illusion that each difficulty or danger we encountered would be the last. We had thought that the beginning of our journey must be the worst part of it, and that presently everything must become easier, but now we seemed to find that obstacles grew and multiplied before us. We had never found so bad a road as this, and we were scarcely midway through Siberia! Every day, without a moment's rest, we were at it in an unbroken stretch of sixteen or eighteen hours, and we only achieved the paltriest mileage. We intended to continue to use all our energies tenaciously and obstinately, but would our strength and our will resist the strain, and would the car be able to stand a job for which it was not quite meant? The engine seemed still intact, but the body of the car with all the shocks and jolting had cracked here and there, was loosened at the joints, and swayed, while incessantly we could feel under our feet the gaping of the planks; the reserve tanks, too, seemed to threaten to part company with the seats to which they were fastened. I asked Prince Borghese:

'Can we go on for a long time like this?'

'No,' he replied.

'How long do you think the car can stand this sort of road?'

'300 miles at most.'

In those moments of discouragement we were convinced that thousands of miles of road like this stood before us. Well, then, we should have to give up the race!

We watched over the working of the car with an anxiety that was not unmixed with affection. We had ended by loving that obedient machine which carried us. We considered it almost as a living being; we called it 'our big beast', and cried out *bravo!* to it when we got out of a difficulty, and pitied it when it got caught in the mud. We spurred it on with encouraging words up the steep ascents as if it had been a horse. For a month now we had not left it for even a minute. We lived the same life with it, and it seemed as if the machine must be consciously sharing the trials and the fatigue of our journey. This close intimacy had made us grow to know the machine so well that all the noises and sounds of its movements were familiar to us. We noticed at once the slightest irregularity in its operation; we were constantly listening to the roar of the engine with the greatest anxiety in our minds, watching lest there should be any first symptoms of some irremediable sickness.

By seven o'clock that evening we came upon our first tract of good road. We had not yet given up all hope of reaching Tomsk, and now we took courage again. We were fifty versts distant from it, and by nine, or ten o'clock at most, we could be in one of its great hotels. But we came to a little swamp at the bottom of a large natural ditch, and there was no means of avoiding it. To the right and left of it was a thick wood of birch and fir trees, the last kind of extension of the *taiga*. Prince Borghese got down to examine the road, walked into the mud, and immediately his feet stuck in it. The only thing to do was to try to cross it at the highest speed of which our car was capable.

The car backed up, then made a spurt down the ditch, cutting through the mud with its four wheels and up the other side with one of its terrible tiger-like leaps. We thought we were free from the danger – when we found ourselves suddenly standing still, and the engine still roaring. The machine had not all come out of the mud. Its hind wheels had sunk as far as the axle. They were caught and held as in a vice, and no effort of the engine or of our arms could succeed in moving them.

Three versts away we knew there must be the village of Tarunta-yeva; so Prince Borghese left us to look after the car, and went off to get help. An hour later we saw him appear again accompanied by ten moujiks and four horses. These peasants had at first refused to follow him, but he had shown the village *starosta* our famous miraculous documents . . .

The horses were harnessed to the car and began pulling. The men pulled with them, but every effort seemed useless. It was necessary to lift the car first by means of levers. So the moujiks went off into the woods to chop down trees and make beams of them.

It was 9 p.m., but the sun was still high on the horizon, huge and red, lighting the tops of the forest trees. The blows of the hatchets on the trunks echoed in the vast silence, and we could hear from time to time the crash of a falling tree as it broke through the foliage and branches round it. We lit a fire in a little clearing, and crouching round the boiling kettle we waited for this Cyclopean work to come to a successful end. We were absorbed in the thought of the distance which we still had to traverse before reaching our goal, and the distance and its obstacles seemed insuperable. We felt as if Siberia was holding us, never to let us go again.

About 9.30 we resumed work. With the aid of the levers our manoeuvre became easy. In little more than half an hour we were able to continue our way along a downward slope, paved with tree trunks, which took us to the village of Tarunta-yeva; we spent the night in the house of an old peasant woman, and were offered brown bread and milk.

Notwithstanding the lateness of the hour, the priest of the village came to see the car. This was the first Siberian priest who manifested no horror for that machine. He was a fair-headed, calm-looking young man. He greeted us with a dignified motion of the head, and went off again without speaking a word.

We laid ourselves down to sleep on the floor of the *isba*, but for several days now we could not sleep quietly. Our dreams were agitated. Even the fatigue we felt was not sufficient to make us rest soundly. Every hour of halt seemed to us a wasted hour. We longed to be running all the time, not exactly in order to make a record, but because we wanted to go far and fast, and to be soon again amid our own friends and back to the life on our native soil.

It was just a month to the day that we had started.

We left Tarunta-yeva at three in the morning. After about twenty versts we came to the large village of Khaldeyeva. Before crossing it we went to examine its roads, and we found them impassable. Rather than make a certainly unsuccessful attempt to force our way through with the car, we decided to ask for assistance beforehand. The village was still wrapped in sleep. We knocked at the *isba* of the *starosta*, and begged him to provide us with five strong horses. The good man went to requisition them. Khaldeyeva was up in no time. The horses came and with them came the inhabitants, among them many Khirgese, so strongly resembling Buriats and Mongolians that they could almost be described as Muhammadan Mongolians. We harnessed the horses to our car with the usual long ropes. Two moujiks, formerly Cossack artillerymen who fought in the last war, got on to the two first horses like postilions, and led them admirably to the attack at a quick trot, whipping and directing them with their *nagaikas*. The whole population watched this strange race through the village.

In the meantime a *tarantass* drawn by two horses approached us, and from it alighted a police officer, who asked us eagerly whether anything had happened.

'At Tomsk there is a rumour that you have been assaulted. The governor, Colonel De Nolcken, has sent word to me tonight to start immediately in search of you, and here I am. I am glad to see you well and safe.'

'Our delay is all due to the roads.'

'Oh, yes, the roads are execrable.'

'What are they doing with the money that they take from us,' murmured a moujik near us, 'if they do not even look after the roads? They devour us like wolves . . .'

The car seemed about to come out of the mud when we suddenly saw it sink and stop with its wheels almost buried. In vain did the horses, urged on by cries and lashes, redouble their efforts. The car would not move. We had to send for some beams, and were obliged to repeat the old lever manoeuvre, lifting the car in this way. Then we put more ropes on to the chassis so that men could pull too. More than thirty men held the ropes. Others came behind to push the car, and at last we were able to lead it to a safe place outside the village, and then we continued on the still difficult road.

Two hours later we were within sight of the sparkling gilt and enamelled cupolas of Tomsk, rising against the dark background of the forest. Mounted messengers came to meet us, and when they saw us from afar they turned, galloping as fast as they could to announce our arrival. The town garrison was encamped outside the city, according to the custom of the Russian Army during the short summer months. A whole crowd of soldiers came running forward to look at us. The chief of the police, surrounded by his officials, awaited us at the entrance of Tomsk.

'The governor expects you. He wishes to see you at once.'

'Like this?' and we pointed to our muddy clothes and our faces covered with dust.

'Yes, just as you are. He wants to bid you welcome. I will take you to him, just follow my carriage.' And he got into a resplendent coach which was standing a little to one side, driven by a great big coachman clad in a blue *armiak* according to the Russian fashion. This part of the journey was frightful. The roads of the principal city of Siberia were no better than those of Khaldeyeva, and several times we ran the risk of being shamefully clogged by the mud. But, notwithstanding its treacherous roads, Tomsk seemed to us a wonderful city, elegant and imposing too, perhaps chiefly because of the contrast it presented to the monotonous *taiga* we had just crossed. At first we went through market-places full of people like those of Irkutsk, but gradually, as we approached the centre of the city, it seemed to lose the characteristics of a Siberian town. It grew more refined, and we came to modern palaces, great shops and stores, and then to a sumptuous modern hotel, were we were to stay.

Tomsk seemed to us like many cities of European Russia: the life we saw in it gave us almost the illusion of being in some suburb of St Petersburg. We were surrounded by the little, swift *iswoschiks* with those quaint seats with no backs to them, on which you cannot sit two at a time without holding one another by the waist for safety. There were also bicycles and great carriages as large as ammunition wagons; and we also had the unexpected pleasure of seeing elegant ladies in their summer dresses. Tomsk seemed to us really to deserve the fame it has as a fashionable city.

The Trans-Siberian Railway has left Tomsk to one side, damaging its trade perhaps, but leaving its real life uninjured. This city is the great intellectual centre of Siberia. Its beautiful university is hidden away in a picturesque birch wood, where the students' little houses, as pretty as Swiss chalets, can just be seen among the trees. From the whole of Siberia young people come to the technical school and to the great library of this university. For this reason the city goes by the name of 'Tomsk the Learned'.

The governor welcomed us with effusive hospitality, inviting us to lunch and to dinner. During that day we spent many hours in his palace, in whose fine halls were open fires as in mid-winter, and the cordial affability of Colonel De Nolcken and his family eased us after the discomforts we had suffered in the rough solitudes. He showed us his bears in the garden; his son took us to see his splendid horses, which are bred locally and are famous all over Russia; and Baroness De Nolcken made us admire her stags, which were so tame that they would take food out of our hands. By the palace gate stood a group of supplicants, gypsies who had been wounded in a fight, moujiks who wanted to make complaints – quite a little crowd, full of curiosity, silent, patient and obstinate. They would not hear of speaking to functionaries or officials, but insisted upon seeing the governor himself, and stood waiting for the hour when he would give them a hearing. The governor came to the door, heard their complaints, and then sent everyone away, saying, 'We shall see what can be done' – and the group dispersed, pleased with their success in having spoken to *him*.

Baron De Nolcken's face – he is an attractive type of cultured man, German, I believe, by origin – is covered with scars. They are the traces left upon him by revolutionaries. Two years ago he was Vice-Governor of Warsaw. Whilst holding office there he received threatening letters, and once he found on his table a death sentence pronounced upon him by some anarchists. Finally, one evening he was attacked and left for dead upon the public road. He had forty-two wounds, but he recovered, and to this adventure of his he owes his nomination as Governor of the Province of Tomsk, which covers an area equal to that of the German Empire. The posts of governor in Siberia, formerly given as a punishment, are now the most sought after, and are granted as a reward. They are not without their own dangers: the Governor of Omsk was killed last year in broad daylight, together with two policemen of his escort, but still they are less dangerous than those of European Russia, where governors and public officials are so constantly done away with. The chief of the Tomsk police (who also comes from Warsaw) has had his own encounters with the Nihilists.

'Warsaw would be an excellent place to live in,' he said to us, as he told us his stories, 'but in that blessed country they shoot people too often – much too often!'

And he seemed to imply by his remark: it wouldn't matter so much shooting a man only now and then!

We asked the governor for information concerning the road between Tomsk and Omsk. What he told us was scarcely encouraging. According to him, for two-thirds of the way at least, we should find no better roads than those we had traversed yesterday. And, alas, this was official information!

Not far from the governor's house are the remains of a great palace, which has been burnt down; it was a splendid theatre, presented to the town by a rich merchant. Two years ago the soldiers in revolt destroyed it by fire; not being able to touch the governor's palace they just set fire to something near it. There was a moment after the war when it seemed as if the whole empire was going to pieces. The outside world heard nothing but an inexact and distant echo of that beginning of ruin. At Irkutsk, at Krasnojarsk, at Tomsk, and Omsk the telegraph and postal services were interrupted. The trains were driven by soldiers who had remained loyal, and the troops returning from Manchuria brought back to their native land the fury of war. Trade was at a standstill, shops and houses were barricaded, the great cities seemed dead, and all this happened, not for the triumph of an ideal, but for a paltry political struggle. It was not a revolution, but a much less complex phenomenon. It was simply a question of hundreds and thousands of men who had learned during the war to kill and to destroy, and still continued to do it after the battles were over.

Late that evening, as we were returning to the hotel, we encountered

in the deserted road, lit by the rosy pallor of the Siberian night, some
regiments returning from a field exercise. The soldiers marched on
singing in a chorus, and on the barrels of their rifles were tied little
bunches of wild flowers.

We left Tomsk at four in the morning of the next day, 12 July, under a
still threatening sky. Two Cossacks preceded us at a gallop, having been
sent by the governor to show us the road out of the town. A whole group
of cyclists and motorcyclists formed an escort for us.

At that moment we had no hope that the sun would come out again.
To reach Omsk, a distance of nearly 700 miles from here, seemed a goal
perfectly unattainable in no matter how long a time. We had been given
by Colonel De Nolcken information concerning the principal villages on
our journey where we might halt for the night. We reckoned only upon
covering just about a hundred miles a day. Who would have thought that
the sun, first so timid and pale and hesitating, the kind of sun that goes
back in hiding the moment it has had a peep through the clouds, would
accompany us from the beginning, and would grow bolder and more
burning until it produced a torrid heat, capable of drying up the mud and
hardening the roads and of preparing us a safe ground for our race?

We sped over the deserted road of Tomsk, following our Cossacks.
Sleepy faces looked out behind the windowpanes, attracted by the
unusual sound of galloping horses, of bells, and of our motor. The
singular cortège left the city and stopped a few minutes after on the right
bank of the Tom, which lay before us wrapped in the mist.

'Halt! *Regardez ici, Messieurs*,' commanded an imperious voice
addressing us.

It was a photographer, looking just like a retired cavalry officer, who,
assisted by his wife, had set up an enormous photographic machine, and
was awaiting us at an opening, heaven knows since when. We looked *ici*.
He changed the slide, giving orders to us again.

'*Ne bougez pas.*'

'But we're in a hurry.'

'*Moi aussi.*'

He got through the preliminaries, photographed us again, and then,
pointing to the camera, said to us in solemn tones:

'*C'est la gloire. Adieu!*'

We crossed the Tom on the strangest boat in the world, pulled by four
horses, which by turning round and round on the bank as they would
round a mill, drove a lazy, and primitive paddlewheel.

At five we left that extraordinary horseferry, and began to run southwards along the left bank of the Tom. After about twenty versts of hilly and dull country we found ourselves in a magnificent wood of gigantic fir trees, the last of the gloomy, imposing, and sinister *taiga*. For a while, now, our road (which was the road to the town of Kolywan, about 150 miles from Tomsk, where we hoped to encamp that afternoon) was the same as that leading to Barnaul, near the interminable Barabas steppe; so that we were trying to find the parting of the roads where we should change our direction for the west. We questioned the few moujiks who passed by us in their *telegas*, but they did not know in what direction Barnaul or Kolywan might be. They only knew their village and the way to Tomsk.

We began to feel that we must have passed the branching point, and to have completely lost our way. We felt as if the forest had enveloped us, and would hold us bound in the intricate labyrinth of its paths. Four hours passed like this. Finally, the dense trees through which we drove grew less thick, and after a little we saw straight before us on the grass a post marked with a faded number. This was the long-looked-for sign of the right road (which is not, however, to be taken to mean the good road). We were now on the Moskowsky Trakt, on the ancient main road which used to connect Moscow and Irkutsk, two capitals: the mother and the daughter. The only remaining signs of the trakt's ancient life were those sign posts, and some ruts, scarcely visible now in the grass, and left by a traffic of long ago between east and west.

We were leaving the *taiga* further and further behind us, and sped on in the light of the early sun. The groups of trees around us became more and more scarce, and scattered over the green monotony of the prairie they looked like the last cloudlets of an abating storm. The land before us became increasingly flat, less and less varied, and almost deserted. We passed a few villages surrounded by windmills. But thinking of the road only from the utilitarian point of view of the speed it would allow us, we rejoiced at the disappearance of its more picturesque features.

Suddenly we saw from afar a group of mounted men coming at a gallop towards us, almost as if they meant to intercept our path. We looked carefully, and thought that the Mongolians were with us again. Those riders were wearing a costume exactly similar to that of the Mongolians; they had the same general characteristics, and they rode with their saddle almost on the horse's neck, just as we had seen the Mongolians do. They were Kirghese. These men had an indefinably wild and warlike air. They made us think of scouts, or of some advance guard sent on far in front of some Asiatic army on the march from the southern steppes.

When they came within a short distance of us they stopped their horses suddenly, and looked suspiciously at the car, bending over their saddles. Then they broke into a long and most cheerful burst of laughter. The thing seemed to be a source of the greatest amusement to them. They went off at a gallop after saluting us, and turned back to look at us several times, laughing. The Kirghese seem to have been enemies of the picturesque just as much as we were. They live where no trees grow, and where there are no hills. The plain is their native land. They love vast horizons, and the freedom of running everywhere without meeting obstacles. They want to feel masters of illimitable space. They have, on terra firma, a sailor's instincts.

That day was some Slav holiday. In the villages the people were wearing showy clothes. Men and women gathering together outside their houses, sang in unison, and accompanied themselves with their balalaikas and accordions. When we passed by they interrupted their singing, and a great shout of surprise rose, happy and merry, as at the passing of some beautiful carnival masque. But the shout of a crowd, even when it is one of delight, seems to have a threatening ring about it. It is too strong, too formidable, even when it wants to be playful, and we would on these occasions turn to see whether the faces were smiling or serious. People ran after us sometimes, crying:

'Wait a minute, wait a minute – let us climb on.'

'Take me for a little ride, and I will stand you a glass of vodka.'

We arrived at the bank of the Obi, a much vaster, slower, lazier, and straighter river than the Tom. The banks of the Obi are so far from one another that at this point it looks like a green streak on the horizon. The ferry, which was also driven by horses, took a long time to carry us across. The boatman warned us that we should find about forty versts of not yet dried-up swamp, produced by the Obi. We crossed that insidious zone of water plants in a most singular and extraordinary manner. When we landed on the other side of the Tom we found that the *pristaff* of Kolywan had come there by order of the governor, to serve as our pilot. A *tarantass*, with the horses harnessed as they would have been to a *troika*, driven by a Kirghese coachman, stood close by, waiting. The *pristaff* got up on it and begged us to follow him with the greatest care.

'If you swerve one step,' he said to us, 'you run the risk of sinking. I promise you that I will take you quickly.' And he kept his word.

The Kirghese coachman, wrapped in furs as in winter, and wearing a fur cap, began whipping his horses without mercy; the *troika* set off at full speed, and we after it. It looked like a desperate pursuit over the high grass, among which shone large expanses of stagnant water. After about five minutes we saw a path near us, which looked so much better than our own. We swerved into it, and we sank.

Fortunately, we were still near the Obi, and after many attempts, all of which proved useless, to 'float' our machine by using only the three horses of the *tarantass*, the coachman went back swiftly to the river and called some men. Moujiks and boatmen came up, and in less than half an hour we were out of the swamp.

'I *told* you that you must follow me, Kniatz Borghese!' exclaimed the *pristaff*; and from that moment we followed him like a dog to heel.

The *troika* made fantastic turns upon the road. There were moments when it disappeared behind bushes, behind tufts of marsh-plants and of dwarf willows, of reeds and rushes. Our only guides then were the tinkling of the bell which hung from the high-arched *duga*, over the middle horse, and the whip and fur cap of the Kirghese coachman, which we saw passing as if in a flight above the tops of the plants. Often the water splashed out under the wheels, and we felt the car slightly sinking, but the speed at which we were going saved us. That swift flight had something romantic about it, and we felt almost the pleasures of the chase.

Every ten versts or so the *troika* found a new relay of horses and a new coachman. The change was done with lightning speed; one could scarcely say that we stopped for it at all. All was in such readiness that there was hardly an instant's halt. We crossed the little river which ran into the Obi by an old rickety boat, and we had to join some moujiks and the *pristaff*, and work hard to build up again a little landing-stage which had threatened to break under the weight of the car. On the other side of this little river the ground began to rise and fall. The swamp was passed, and at about seven o'clock we saw some tall spires showing against the low line of the horizon; half an hour later we arrived at Kolywan.

Here we were expected, and the population gathered to look at us as it had done at Marinsk. Everyone seemed to have come out of the town, either on horseback, on foot, or in a *telega*. The chief of the police was there, and everybody stood at a respectful distance from him. As soon as he saw us he came forward to meet us, but a unique incident provided a sudden interruption to our triumphal entry.

Hundreds of oxen were returning from the fields to their stable with all the haste of home-loving animals . . . But I should first explain a special custom among Siberian oxen, which bears witness to a great development of social instincts among them. The pastures in Siberia are nearly all the common property of a village or town under collective ownership. In the morning the inhabitants open the doors of their stables and all their oxen go off to graze together on the common green. At nightfall the great herd comes back together to the village as if the oxen were boys coming back from school, and when they get among the houses each ox separates from his companions and goes home by himself quite quietly. He finds the stable door open, goes in, and the general herd diminishes until the only ox left disappears into the last house in the village.

We happened to be entering Kolywan just at the evening home-coming of these citizen oxen. Frightened by the car, they precipitated themselves among the houses, and they entered the principal street just as we did. The people fled. The chief of the police disappeared with half his greeting unsaid. We found ourselves in a great cloud of dust, surrounded by a herd of scampering, lowing animals. We might have been in the midst of a Wild Western stampede. We ended by reaching the Zemstvoskaya Dom, accompanied by that cortège.

Shortly afterwards the chief of the police rejoined us there, and was able to end his interrupted speech of welcome. He afterwards remained with us a little, telling us of the misfortunes of Kolywan.

'The city is done for,' he said. 'It was rich and now it is poor. It was peopled and now it is deserted.'

'Whose fault is it?'

'It is the fault of the railway.'

Kolywan had been left deserted to the north of the railway. Every-body emigrated to the nearest railway-station, Novi-Nikolajewsk, which gathers together the commercial activity of Kolywan and of Irkutsk, which has become a great city, and which will be in a few years even more beautiful than Tomsk itself. It has already 20,000 inhabitants. Mushroom cities do not exist in America alone: Siberia has many examples of this very significant phenomenon.

The mistress of the house, a woman with energetic movements and vast proportions, took us under her most effective protection. She sent away importunate visitors, and then said to us, as a person full of good sense, without awaiting our orders, 'I thought you would be hungry, so I have had your dinner prepared immediately. It will be ready very shortly.'

'Thank you, madame.'

'A *vhi*, some cutlets, a few roast chickens, white bread, beer, and tea . . .'

Oh, Kolywan, land of delights . . .

XVII

ON THE STEPPES

~~~~~~~~~~

*The Steppes – The Telegraph Station at Kainsk – Our
Brake on Fire – Omsk – Siberia Awakening – Our
Fatigue – The Steppes Again – A Fire on the Prairie –
Ischim*

Our car had found at Kolywan – as it had with great regularity found on
the other halts since Missowaja, and continued to find to the end of its
journey – its daily portion of petrol and oil. We never quite filled our
reserve tanks, because we were anxious not to increase the weight of our
machine too much, but at every start we took with us enough fuel and
enough lubricant for about 500 miles.

At four a.m. on 13 July we were running towards Kainsk, which lies
about twenty-two miles from Kolywan. The sky was clouded and
threatening. An hour after our departure the rain began to fall heavily.
But it was only a short shower; by seven o'clock a fine easterly wind had
swept away the clouds, and the sun shone out of the bluest sky in the
world.

The road which we followed would in Europe not have even been
dignified by the name field path. But it was hard, flat, and level, and to us
it seemed wonderful, notwithstanding the marshy ground which ran by
the side of it, covered with very tall and thick grasses. From these grasses
rose from time to time flocks of birds: white herons, snipe, moorhens
with their awkward flight, and clouds of grey-breasted rooks, which
sometimes, startled by the speed of our car and fluttering about like
maddened things, ended by knocking against it and falling with an
agonized flutter.

All the same, we could not help enjoying the delight of swift flight
which we had not had for so long. Watch in hand we counted the verst
poles which seemed literally to fly past us. There were points when we
went at a speed of thirty-five to forty miles an hour; but the little bridges
caused us to slacken speed. There are crowds of these bridges, and you

can see them from afar because they have little wooden sides painted white, red, and black, and sometimes they almost produce the illusion of groups of men standing motionless in the middle of the country. These bridges were so tiny that sometimes when our front wheels reached the further end of them, our back wheels were only coming on to the bridge on the near side, and it often happened that the lower part of the car, when standing in that position, struck the planks of the bridge. To avoid this we had to use the greatest caution.

We passed through the few and scattered villages on our road very rapidly. This was apparently another saint's day. We met processions of moujiks in gorgeous clothes, with shirts of all colours held in by belts adorned with worked metals. Before them walked their priests, wearing church vestments, a pluvial or a dalmatic, and crowned with their mitres, which remind one by their shape of the Russian imperial crown; and at the back of the procession the women, with their heads covered with red kerchiefs and wearing short skirts and boots like those of the men. This procession, carrying crosses and icons, filled the road and advanced in slow disorder, praying and singing. We stopped so as not to disturb the sacred ceremony, but our precaution was useless. Prayers and hymns ceased; the pious people, including the priest, forgot heaven for a moment, and stopped to look at us ecstatically. All the icons turned towards us, showing us the black faces of Byzantine images with golden haloes, and only after a little interval did the procession continue its way and the songs start again louder and fuller, as if to make up for the momentary neglect. I fear that our car was a great hindrance to devotion. When we passed, the bellringers, who were merrily pealing their bells as custom demands when a procession is taking place, left off ringing and took advantage of their high position on top of the belfries, to follow with their eyes the automobile speeding afar with its train of dust which blew back over the meadows.

In the afternoon we came to the real regions of the steppes – the steppes of Barabinsk, which now and then reminded us of the Mongolian prairies. This was, however, a greener land than Mongolia and richer in water. It was chequered by little clumps of dwarf trees and by lilliputian woods. We laughed at these plants, and especially at the birch trees which lord it over the *taiga* but grow humble in the steppes, and look like paltry caricatures of themselves, desiring to hide and turn into grass again. Great stagnant pools and lakes sparkled from time to time confusedly on the line of the horizon, and we felt, when we saw them from afar, as if we must be running into some unknown sea. All that endless plain seems full of mirrors of water. The blue alternates with the green, the movement of the wave with the stillness of the land. We coasted for a while a picturesque lake called the Lake of Ubinsk: one great blue stretch. We crossed enormous rivers by commodious ferry-boats – the Tschulym near the big village of Pulym (another Tschulym, which has nothing to do with the one near Atschinsk), the Kargat near Kargatsk, and other lesser ones. In the steppe we found *yurtas* again. These were Kirghese, but differed in no way from Mongolian *yurtas*. These little cupolas probably represent the only form of building capable of standing against the impetuous winds of the plain. They always seem to crown the houses of a people who love space and solitude.

Towards seven o'clock we reached Kainsk, surrounded by dozens of windmills whose vast wings, motionless against the far horizon, looked like the great crosses of a giant cemetery. At Kainsk no one expected us to arrive so soon. We entered almost unobserved because there was a fair going on, and in the middle of the fair a horse circus, a drinking booth, a great tent of living freaks, the music of organs and of fanfares. The criers were calling out, and all the people, grouped round this wonderful enclosure, were turning their backs to the road up which we arrived. But some soldiers saw us and they turned round and called to their companions, and in a moment the crowd stood as if obeying an order, with its back to the booths and admiring faces turned our way. The barrel-organs and the fanfares stopped in the middle of their tunes, and the criers, from the height of their platforms, looked at us with hostile curiosity, as people look on a fortunate rival. We wandered about the deserted roads in search of an hotel and found one – the worst and dirtiest hotel in Siberia.

I did not succeed in getting into the telegraph office at Kainsk. I was sent away from it as if I had gone there to leave not a telegram but a bomb. I was accompanied by a youth who had offered to show me the way. The door of the office was closed. We knocked, and heard an irritated voice crying behind the door:

'Who is there?'

I gave my name and described myself.

'Come back tomorrow.'

'I cannot. I am leaving at dawn and I have a telegram to send off.'

'Go away!'

'Open up, and I will show you my papers. Don't you send off telegrams?'

'Yes, but I don't know you.'

Was it, then, an office for friends alone?

'I have to send a telegram to the Governor of Tomsk.'

'Go away.'

The voice had grown threatening. I insisted. The man the other side of the door called out something which I did not understand, but which the youth who had come with me understood and answered by precipitate flight, making a sign to me to follow him. I asked him:

'What is the matter?'

He replied, still running away, with the action of one firing off a gun, and with these two eloquent monosyllables: 'Boom! Boom!'

My paper must be left that evening without news of our race. 'Well,' thought I to myself, 'better without news than without a correspondent.' And I went back to the hotel.

We crossed the Om at Kainsk, a little way from the town itself, by a curious wooden bridge, which had sunk, perhaps because of alluvial deposits, until it was nearly all under water. We called it the 'ford bridge'. It was four a.m. on 14 July. We took up our swift flight again over the immense plain, which we should not leave now until we reached Europe. There were no other heights until we came to the Ural Mountains.

When we started the weather was threatening; two hours later it was pelting with rain. The road became suddenly almost impassable. When we came to a level railway-crossing we asked the watchman to shelter us for a little, just as we had done between Kainsk and Krasnojarsk. We were rather anxious not to have to chain up our wheel again to get the best of it against the mud, for I have forgotten to say that this last resource of the chain had some special drawbacks. The chain cut into the tyre, and what was worse, it strained the spokes of the wheel, weakening the point where they are attached to the rim. The left driving wheel was beginning to give us some cause for anxiety. Where the spokes fitted into the rim it was cracked here and there, and sometimes it creaked. To have a broken wheel meant to be irremediably left on the road; we had to be cautious.

Besides, Siberia had taught us to check our impatience. It had given us a little of that fatalism which is at the bottom of the Slav character, and which is probably derived from men's constantly finding themselves confronted with the insuperable difficulties of an unfriendly climate. No matter what the urgency, no matter how great one's need, when the weather says 'Stop!' you have to resign yourself to stopping. The need of bending to this violence and waiting for an indefinite length of time ends by making you give up your own independence with a certain calmness.

Submission to a superior will becomes an instinct. You bend your head immediately and without a groan before the storm as before a ukase, before a flood as before an order from the police. To both you say '*Nitchevò!*' The chief autocrat over Russia is not the tsar; it is the climate.

How long should we have to remain there waiting? The sky was dark and heavy with rain, as if no rain had ever fallen from it before. The railway watchman told us that we should find about sixty versts of very bad ground, but that the road would always be good even under the rain, because it was sandy. After about an hour's waiting we saw that the clouds did not scud any longer from west to east, but were retiring in a fantastic flight towards the south: the wind, then, had changed direction. We ended by knowing more about Siberian winds than a compiler of almanacs need know. West wind, a storm; south wind, variable and misty; north or east wind, fine weather.

It was still raining, but we were as cheerful as if the sun had already appeared. We began to be serene before the sky was. We got on our car without waiting any more, and were off.

Not an hour had passed before the weather became glorious. The road was good, and in many places excellent. We went on quickly. We reckoned our speed at times as over thirty miles an hour. We kept up quite comfortably an average speed of about twenty-five miles an hour. The endless panorama of the steppe spread out on either side of us with monotonous persistency. The villages were fewer, and consisted of small *isbas*. Timber is scarce in these regions, and the poorest huts of oriental Siberia and of Trans-Baikalia would here look like palaces. We saw tiny dwelling-places, within which these great moujiks must certainly be always sitting, like the saints in Giotto's pictures. The heat of the sun was becoming intense.

We had hopes of arriving at Omsk without interruptions, but about midday we found ourselves confronted by unforeseen danger, one which might have had the most disastrous consequences. Suddenly we smelt burning, and, turning round, we saw that the car left a thick streak of smoke behind it. This smoke came from underneath the car.

'The brake,' we cried, 'the brake is on fire!'

We were already too familiar with this kind of occurrence to have the slightest doubt concerning its origin. We stopped the car and leapt to the ground. The flames broke out. This time the matter was extremely serious. The great speed at which we were going had prevented us from noticing it at once, because of the draught which we made. The fire must have begun long before its smell reached our nostrils. The flames, which had so far been kept low by the draught of our motion and by the very powerful action of the swiftly revolving flywheel, now flared up roaring in the stillness. The cause of this fire was the same as on previous occasions, namely, it was the friction of the footbrake, which would not release its grip owing to some injury which we could not discover without taking the connections to pieces. This time, not only had the grease round the brake caught fire, but the wooden floor of the car was beginning to feed the flames. We feared at any moment that the petrol would be set on fire, and we had 200 kilogrammes of it. The slightest imperfection in the tube between the feed-chamber and the carburettor, which passed at very few inches from the flames, would have sufficed to bring about this catastrophe.

'Water, water, quickly!' we cried to one another.

Lately we had had no difficulty in finding water near us. I took the saucepan and ran to the ditches by the road. They were dried up. I sought in vain even for some mud among the grass. The sandy ground was perfectly arid. About fifty paces before us there was a little bridge; surely there I should find a pool at least. I ran to it in hot haste: not a drop! For a moment we all ran about excitedly.

'Never mind,' we said to one another, 'let's throw some sand on it.'

'Some rags!'

'Are there any rags?'

'Our clothes!' and Ettore threw his raincloak over the flames, Prince Borghese his furs.

The grease which had caught fire went out, but the timber of the car was still alight. We took up some planks from the floor, put out the flames from them by throwing earth over them, and we scratched the pieces that were alight with our penknives, making all the burning parts of them fall off in sparks. At last the flames were under control; with a few rags damped by the little water which was dropping from the radiator we extinguished the remaining sparks. We watched anxiously for each little column of smoke, and stood there until we felt quite sure that the danger was over. Then we gave a great sigh of satisfaction and looked at one another smiling, just a little dazed.

'Safe again!' we exclaimed.

'How awful it would have been to have taken our car so far and then to have seen it blown up like a firework in the middle of the steppe!'

'It was lucky we saw it in time.'

'If the petrol had caught fire we should all three have been blown up.'

'Let us get on now and be off; it is getting late,' said the prince.

'To Omsk!'

Ettore had already completely detached the footbrake, deciding never to use it again on this journey. There was still the handbrake that could be used. It was not so quick in its action, but it was certainly equally effective. So we continued our journey.

Near the village of Jurjewo we found ourselves at another little river. The peasants feared, perhaps, that our car might sink the little ferry-boat, for they would on no account let us cross by it. 'The boat,' they said, 'is for men, horses, and *telegas*. This is not a horse and not a *telega*, therefore it cannot pass.' All Prince Borghese's eloquence did not suffice to convince them. What then? Well, the precious ministerial letter was brought out again, and a quarter of an hour later we were on the other side of the river.

At a short distance from Omsk we had to cross the Om again. A crowd of moujiks in Sunday clothes witnessed our short water journey from the opposite high bank of the river. Our appearance and our methods of travel evidently aroused the deepest suspicions of I know not what authority in a neighbouring village. This man was a sort of peasant wearing an official cap, and he took advantage of a brief halt, which we had to make for the purpose of refilling our radiator with water, to go and arm himself with a register, and then come back with great speed. We were just starting.

'Stop!' cried the man imperiously.

We looked at him with a sort of indifference which must have greatly wounded his dignity, for he cried, angrily, 'Stop, I tell you, stop!' Not a bit of it! We knew these little village despots by this time, who give themselves airs as if they were put there to direct even the course of the rivers and the blossoming of the meads, who take advantage of their position of authority in order to give all possible annoyance to their neighbour. They are ignorant and greedy people, who on other oc-casions had asked us our name, surname, profession, nationality, demanding explanations of every kind, and transcribing our answers solemnly in a little notebook, and looking at us with the severity of judges. A stranger, from the mere fact of passing over their territories, is treated by them as a criminal. No, the good man might cry as long as he liked. We had no intention of increasing, even by this one, the number of unforeseen halts. We did not mean to go through a stupid cross-questioning, and show our papers and give satisfaction to that micro-tyrant.

He ran in pursuit of us, crying:

'Stop, in the name of the law!'

I got up on my feet, turned round, and seriously, gravely, looking over our luggage, made the most horrible face at our persecutor. Just the worst face I could remember having learnt in the far-off time of my earliest school career. He stopped, disconcerted by so much daring, and we gaily continued our way.

At four p.m. we reached Omsk, lying in a sandy plain, interspersed with tufts of rushes. Just outside the city rose great and curious wind-mills, with their many wings standing out like spokes in gigantic wheels, and they made one think of some strange, unknown engine of war. We were expected by the police officer, who, getting on to an *iswoschik*, took us to the hotel. In a little more than twelve hours we had come over 250 miles. This had been the best day of our journey.

We happened to enter Omsk at the hour of the people's Sunday airing. Along the wooden pavements moved the peaceful crowd of the citizens, walking with the peculiar gait of people wearing their best clothes and anxious not to spoil them. Officers and people in brilliant uniforms passed by with their families, holding their children by the hand. There was the quiet atmosphere of a provincial town taking its rest. From the churches, with their many-coloured cupolas, came the sound of bells. Everyone stopped to see us, and turned round to look. We interrupted by our passage that lazy, vast movement of the crowd. We crossed the beautiful bridge over the Om near the mouth of the Irtysch. A mounted policeman signed to us to slow up: the bridge had to be crossed at a footpace.

Along the banks of the river stretched the long lines of docks and landing-stages. By the little platforms some of those large and elegant passenger steamers were anchored which from this station go down the Irtysch to Tobolsk, and up it as far as Semipolatinsk, covering nearly 1000 miles of the river's course. Near the steamers the large barges were being laden by means of cranes. The whole thing had an aspect of modern activity. This was quite a revelation to us; we felt as if we were in the heart of Europe. We had found in Irkutsk the political capital of Asiatic Russia, in Tomsk its intellectual capital, and now in Omsk we found its commercial capital.

Omsk is the centre of an enormous commercial output. By its position it dominates all western Siberia. It gathers the riches of the most fertile land by the way of the rivers, and launches them upon the European markets by means of the railway. There is a talk of surrounding it by a local branch of the Turkestan railway; it will then become the heart of central Asia. This ancient city, which a breath of progress has rejuven-ated, presents the aspect of a pioneer city, of a city rising now, and urged on its way by haste; of a new city in a new land, with no traditions to break and with no customs to be respected. The sign of its activity, which is now developing independently of any bonds with the past, is chiefly apparent in its widespread use of machinery. On the stages along the river we saw nothing but machines by the thousand, ready to embark upon the virgin steppes of Kulundinsk and of Naiman. There were the most recent agricultural machines; the same machines which a dislike of novelty still keeps out of so many civilized parts of Europe. It is more difficult to change than to create, and Omsk is now creating. Great stretches of black earth, which had never been touched by human labour, are now opened out by the American double plough, are made fertile by the most perfect machinery for sowing and cultivating, with the help of the most ingenious implements invented for this purpose by human civilization.

Omsk yearly receives and distributes over the fields 100,000 pounds' worth of agricultural machines. The Kirghese, who have never handled more modest agricultural appliances, sail up the Irtysch as far as Omsk in order to get machines from there. They begin by using the best we have yet reached. Many industries, which were yesterday almost unknown, are now rising down there, and beginning to have importance in the markets of the world. A special train with refrigerators crosses the confines of Siberia daily, carrying westward loads of fresh butter, two-thirds of which end on English tables; and in the past year the butter exported from the region between Omsk and the Kurgan has amounted in value to five million francs. The Siberia known to tradition, the desolate land of exile, the frozen land of hunger, exists no longer, if ever it did. Siberia reveals itself as a bolder and richer country than Russia. In face of this, the spectacle of its first awakening, no one can say what the future may reserve for it.

At the hotel we met with a cordial reception from the local committee of the Peking to Paris race – a strange committee consisting of English, Germans, and Norwegians, the representatives of great commercial firms, to whom much of the impulse of the new life of these regions is due. From a balcony of the hotel some one cried out '*Viva l'Italia!*'

We looked up, and saw a gentleman waving his hat. After having greeted us thus from above, he came down and welcomed us from a lesser distance. He was an English correspondent sent to meet us by the *Daily Mail*, a congenial colleague, who from Omsk forward, followed us by railway on the rest of the journey, and became a pleasant companion on our long halts.

We decided to stop two days at Omsk; we were in need of rest. So long as we travelled, we were kept up by the nervous tension of continual vigilance: driving so fast was feverish kind of work, even if no accident occurred. But when we stopped, we were suddenly overcome by an inexpressible prostration. All the past watches and efforts seemed suddenly to crowd back upon us. They seemed to be claiming their due of rest. The average of our sleep had been four hours a day. When we arrived at a halting place every evening, after a short toilet, we had a great deal of work to do. Prince Borghese, with the aid of the police, devoted himself to searching for our deposit of fuel; Ettore cleaned up the machine and prepared it for the next run; I had to write my telegrams in my best handwriting so as to ensure their correct transmission, and, a longer and more difficult thing, had to induce the telegraph clerks to receive and transmit them. The length of my telegrams seemed to frighten the employees. To send a telegram of one or two thousand words seemed a madness which they absolutely refused to comply with, and they found innumerable pretexts to make me renounce my desire to telegraph. We scarcely ever had any food before ten o'clock at night. We often slept on the bare earth, and by two or three in the morning we were up again. There was besides in our work something more unnerving than this physical strain – there was anxiety. Times of uncertainty, often of great strain, attended our progress; then, there were the continual vivid impressions we received; our discouragements and our moments of buoyant hope; times of obstinate resolve, the ups and downs of an apparently useless struggle. For all these reasons we had decided to rest for two days at Omsk, so that we might start again feeling fresher and more certain of ourselves.

Among the qualities which most called out my admiration for Prince Borghese was his power of resistance; a resistance which was physical and, to even greater extent, moral. He was tired, but he knew how not to look it. He took a special pride in never appearing tired to strangers. He held himself thus much in hand: if there were guests or friends he seemed to forget about bed. He fortified himself in the smiling impassability of a diplomat, and stood the test for an indefinite length of time. As soon as the strangers were gone the diplomat was also gone, and Prince Borghese fell asleep, murmuring that he was quite finished. I must own that at Omsk I felt myself assailed by fatigue as if it had been an illness; like those famished people who, out of sheer excess of hunger, can no longer eat, I had become unable to sleep. But a reaction came about, and in the strangest manner.

On the evening of 16 July I was going back to my hotel, when all of a sudden I felt my knees bend under me and was conscious of walking like a drunken man. My eyes clouded over and the sky looked green. All the passersby seemed to be livid in the face and then black: a great darkness was gathering round me. I knew I was being looked at by the crowd with curiosity. I leant against the wall, passing a hand over my forehead. In the meantime a disengaged *iswoschik* came my way. I gathered together all my strength and called it, '*Iswoschik, iswoschik!*' I had a confused vision of the carriage approaching me in obedience to my call, then I remember nothing more, but what happened is not difficult to guess, seeing that when I came to myself again, I was on the ground and in the same place. I had fallen, out of sheer heaviness and fatigue. I woke up thinking I was in bed, and when I opened my eyes I was very surprised for a moment to see shod feet moving in the immediate neighbourhood of my head. Then I remembered at once, and I got up again, dazed and ashamed. The *iswoschik* was still there and had been awaiting me. How long had I been there unconscious? Who knows? And why had no one helped me to get up? Ah! This was due to the special customs of the place. If you had to pick up all the men who fall asleep by night along the streets of a Siberian town you would have far too much to do. I had been simply taken for an honest drunkard. Drink is so common a vice in Siberia that it has become respectable, and is, therefore, respected. The crowd might look at me with mistrust or contempt while I walked amongst it, but when I lay down everybody had no alternative but to esteem me. I acquired, as it were, the right of citizenship.

I got into my cab. The coachman turned round, and said to me in dulcet tones, 'I will go slowly, master, but you would do well to take hold of this firmly,' and he pointed to the iron bar at the back of his seat.

The car, except for the damage to the brake, which was immediately seen to, had no need of further repairs. Even if it had needed them, really important repairs would have been impossible. In organizing the race the prince had ordered some extra spare parts to be sent to Omsk, but the Russian custom-house – or the Austrian one, we never knew which – had kept them back, heaven knows where. The tyres of the front wheels – they had covered the entire road from Peking to here – were changed, and the machine was cleaned from head to toe and minutely inspected. Ettore waxed enthusiastic about that car, which was still in perfect condition, notwithstanding so much rough work and so many vicissitudes. But if the car had been an intelligent thing, enthusiasm would have been its own attitude towards Ettore, who was lavishing such intelligent care upon it. His patience and conscientiousness went so far that at every halting place he went through minute and difficult inspections which chauffeurs usually make only at considerable intervals. Every evening he unscrewed the gearcase which surrounds the pinions of the change-speed and differential gears, so as to verify whether the working of these parts had been normal, and so as to renew the oil and the grease with which these gears must be always coated. The body of the car, which, as we have seen, had been more than disjointed by the horrible road near Tomsk, was reinforced here with little steel plates and screws.

At Omsk we decided upon the route which we were to follow for Kazan. There are two routes, one short and one long. The shorter one was, of course, that chosen by the committee of the race at Paris. It runs thus: Omsk, Kurgan, Tsheljabinsk, Ufa, and Kazàn, and it goes very nearly along the side of the railway. But the Russian Committee, formed at St Petersburg to further the race, had advised us to follow the longer way because it was the better one, namely, to go via Tjumen, Ekaterinburg, and Perm. This road turns northward, reaching as far as 58° latitude, while the other road scarcely reaches 55°. That great arc up 3° did not really attract us as much as the straight line which, as geometry tells us, is the shortest way between two points; but we deferred to the wisdom of the St Petersburg Committee, which had provided us with the most beautiful tracings of roads, designed expressly for us. On these tracings only the itinerary chosen by St Petersburg was completely traced, with the altitude and the distances, measured in versts between each village, and carefully marked. This was a work of great patience and accuracy which proved extremely useful to us. We were grateful for these efficacious aids provided for us by the Committee of St Petersburg, and to the endless courtesies which were added to it by the lesser committees formed for our reception in the smaller towns. Everywhere we felt surrounded by an open and spontaneous cordiality. You would have thought that the Russians, being unable to do away with the obstacles and the dangers of their roads, were doing all in their power to make us forget them.

On the 16th we received the news that the de Dion-Boutons had reached Marinsk.

We were piloted out of Omsk at three a.m. on 17 July by a tiny, ancient motor car, resembling more a perambulator than any other means of conveyance: a rare relic of Siberian automobilism. It was driven by two of our most recent friends, who were members of the Omsk Committee. One of them, a pleasant Swedish man of colossal stature, wore a quaint white raincloak, which looked very like a woman's garment because it had ruching round the hood. He would have looked like a lady wrapped in her opera cloak, if we had not seen, whenever he turned round, his most beautiful and imposing beard.

The town was still asleep. The Om, touched with the rosy pallor of the dawn, seemed motionless; the dark shadows of the boats, with their high, now smokeless funnels, stood in strong, still groups along the banks which had been so busy in the daytime. When we were out of the inhabited parts on the road to Tjumen, when we could not possibly mistake our way, our little guide drew aside to let us pass, and we exchanged farewells. In his enthusiasm the opera-cloaked Swede pulled out his pistol and emphasized his hurrahs by a vivid accompaniment of shots. After this naval salute our car began its rapid flight over the steppe, which lay before us like a calm, green sea.

The sky was clear and limpid; we should have thought it was an Italian sky if the keen air had not bitten our faces. The sun was just coming over the flat horizon. We were dipping again into an even, endless, melancholy landscape, like that we had left two days previously. Grasses, shrubs, dwarf birch trees, rushes, nothing else. But we were glad of it; we asked for nothing better. For us now, the best landscapes were those which furthered our swift flight. We put the car sometimes in third and sometimes in fourth speed. We had to bend down cutting through the air, which filled out our garments, made the little flag before us flutter with a noise, and roared impetuously around us. We felt intoxicated, like prisoners newly freed. We felt as if we were at last enabled to continue a great flight begun down there in the Mongolian plains.

From time to time we met long lines of *telegas*, whose drivers were still asleep, deaf to any call of ours; they only woke up when we passed quite close to them. Then they rubbed their eyes, thinking perhaps that they were dreaming, and like all Siberian drivers they remained so stunned by the sight of us that they did not even hold in their shying horses when the animals tried to run away.

The villages were scarce; there is not enough timber here to build them. Some little huts were made with intertwined branches; they looked like great baskets, and it was curious to hear the cries of wonder which came out of those 'baskets' when we passed by. With a three hours' run we were on the banks of the Irtysch, on which navigating marks and Russian buoys floated in the current. The steamers used that watercourse as far as Tobolsk. On the banks of the river we found a large caravan of peasants returning from Omsk, where they had been to buy American harrows and reaping machines, and now awaiting the ferry to take them across. These were all emigrants come from the German provinces, and they presented, indeed, an appearance much more akin to the Teutonic than to the Slavonic type. They pronounced themselves very satisfied with their new country; to a great extent the rapid transformation of Siberia is brought about by the men of this race.

We crossed the Irtysch on a boat drawn by four horses like that crossing the Tom. This team was under the orders of a splendid bearded captain, who rode on the horses and incited them by reins and whip to keep at a trot. We started running again. The hours went by and verst after verst flew past us. We passed through little villages, with huts entirely covered with grassy sods of earth, and roofs all blossoming, so that it looks almost as though their little houses had sprung out of the ground, bringing up with them bits of the meadow. At ten o'clock we saw on the horizon a great column of smoke.

It was an immense cloud, white at the edges where the sun shone upon it, and dark as with a storm near the earth. It massed and seemed to disappear towards the west. As we drew nearer we saw it increasingly high, thick, and vast. What could be burning? We could not doubt that some great fire was destroying a village. We looked in the direction where the cloud was and then consulted our map. The fire seemed to lie straight before us on our road. Perhaps Abatsk was burning. We made up our minds it must be that. Abatsk lay just down there.

We watched eagerly and anxiously, without a word, that tragic cloud, which grew larger and larger and occupied, little by little, half the sky, and from time to time oscillated slowly here and there, dispersing on one side and thickening on the other. Half an hour later we saw it was a prairie on fire. The dried-up grasses and shrubs fed the flames inexhaustibly, which were pushed towards the west by a light breeze.

We found Abatsk still safe, but threatened by the flames. The sun had disappeared; clouds of smoke filled the air, and formed above us a sinister reflection like that over an eruption. There was a gloomy light like the foreboding of a great disaster. Outside every house were receptacles full of water: pails, pitchers, jugs; groups of people were ready round the wells. The village was in a state of defence. Everybody watched motionless; they looked as if they had been expecting an assault and were there awaiting the enemy. A little way from the houses, some men were at work making a ditch. Numerous *telegas* arrived from the neighbouring villages, bearing peasants armed with spades, hoes, and other tools, but there was in all this an orderliness as of a long-prepared defence – fires in that season must break out pretty frequently over this tract. The villagers must have a plan of war to hold the fire back, for when the flames approach them they execute their plan with the steadiness of men not taken by surprise. In a few minutes we were out of the smoke again, in the clear air. The monotony of our journey recommenced. We passed a few sandy stretches, which reminded us of our arrival at Kiakhta, and in the afternoon we came upon some birch woods. The birch tree was here reacquiring its natural proportions. Near those little woods was Ischim, the place where we had decided to halt that night: a white, silent little city. We reached it at three o'clock, having made about 230 miles.

Ischim is small, isolated in the plain, and it looks uninhabited. Once every year it becomes a great city; many of its buildings do not open and are unused except on that occasion. It is celebrated as the site of a great annual fair, which equals in importance, or so its inhabitants say, the fair of Nijni Novgorod; but we came upon it during the long period of its rest.

A rich merchant wished to give us hospitality in his house. Here we found again the same patriarchal generosity that we found at Kiakhta and Irkutsk, a free table and open door for all friends and local dignitaries. While we did our best to show our host our delight and gratitude, somebody came to tell us that the people of Ischim desired to see us. The people must never be kept waiting, neither at Ischim nor anywhere else, and especially when they ask for so slight a boon. So we went out.

A great crowd had invaded the courtyard, and was besieging the car. On our arrival a hearty applause burst out. Having received this applause with the dignity demanded by the occasion, we were just about to go back into the house; but no, the people were not content. They wanted to see us moving in the car. We had arrived so suddenly in the town that no one had seen us pass; it was now our duty to make up for this regrettable want of consideration. We got into the car, and in five minutes we went through all the streets. Our entry into the yard was a most glorious and triumphant thing. Popular enthusiasm knew no bounds. I was taken by violence down from my seat and lifted on the shoulders of the crowd, and carried about in triumphant procession. The people of Ischim had taken me for the prince.

I shouted out that I was not the prince, and so was allowed to get down free. But I remained unavenged: Prince Borghese had already taken shelter in flight.

XVIII

THE URAL MOUNTAINS

From the Car to the Troika – *Tjumen – Farewell, Siberia! –
Kamylschow's Salute – Ekaterinburg – From Asia to
Europe – The Ural Forest – Our First Minaret –
Perm – A Damaged Wheel – And the Cure for it*

The steppe – always the steppe.

At five a.m. on 18 July the church spires of Ischim disappeared from our view. We left the little birch woods, which form as it were an oasis of high plants on the banks of the River Ischim (a tributary of the Irtysch), and we came again on to the green flat plain.

Our chief amusement was to watch the flying past of the verst poles, which stand all along the road between the villages. We reckoned up the mileage we had covered, and varied these calculations by reckoning up the mileage still before us. After the first few hours, our advance was retarded by stretches of deep sand, which we tried to avoid whenever possible by running on the grass by the side of the road. From time to time there were slight undulations in the ground. We were almost imperceptibly beginning to leave behind us that absolutely flat plain, that ocean of earth over which we had travelled for nearly 1000 miles; and trees, really big trees, could not now be very far. They were not yet within sight, but we met people carting pine trunks away. By midday we had passed some dunes, which were very trying for the motor, and we arrived at the sizeable village of Zowodonowskaja.

At the end of the village stood some magnificent *troikas*, whose splendid black horses made their silver bells tinkle by the impatient jerks of their nervous heads. On their *dugas* the little bells sparkled. The coachmen, with long hair and flowing beards, were clad in gorgeous Circassian *armiaks* with showy belts, and they wore clothes padded after the ancient Russian fashion, which makes the stylish coachman look like a mastodon: enormous, more broad than high. The servant of a great house is expected in Russia to be fat, to show the opulence and generosity of his masters. Those *troikas* were waiting for us; a very rich Siberian merchant, the owner of the surrounding mines, wanted to offer us lunch in his place close by. We accepted. The car was left in the village, and we joined our host and his friends in the *troikas*, and off we went at a relentless speed between clouds of dust, putting our arms round one another so as to prevent the violent jerks from upsetting us out of those little carts with seats and no backs to them.

Usually the strictly Russian carriages are not exceedingly comfortable; it requires great skill to balance oneself on them. It seems almost as if the Russians tried to add to the attractions of the seat in a carriage the attractions of the saddle as well. You have to be acquainted with the secrets and the resources of horsemanship before you can use those carriages with impunity. But they are especially created for swiftness, and they give you by their very simplicity, and by the lightness of their build, the full pleasure of racing. The mode of harnessing a *troika* has something classical about it – it could be the harness of a Roman chariot. The horses are placed there in statuesque symmetry; in the middle of them the leader, and by its side the two wings galloping. And they do gallop, turning their heads aside, outwards, kept in that position by strong traces. The three horses are placed like horses in a triumphal Roman chariot.

We were going at a furious speed over sandy roads; then we entered woods, and half an hour later the steppe was changing wonderfully before our eyes. Thick pine woods and orchards rose before us in succession; then came a shady path by the side of a calm, limpid stream, and among the trees were the roofs of sheds, of little villas and stables, and a factory worked by water power.

We were given luncheon in the open air, in the shade of the trees, with the openhearted and simple hospitality of olden times; and we seemed to be living many ages ago, in some colony forgotten by the world and forgetful of it. The ladies' styles were in the fashion of forty years ago. My venerable neighbour, with her grey hair done up in ringlets, spoke to me fluently in a kind of literary French, which sounds now almost like a dead tongue. Our host's brother, a gigantic-looking man, was dressed in the old Siberian costume, with a silk shirt covered with embroideries, and a lovely waistband covered with silver. Our hostess herself was a type of the great heroines of old-fashioned novels, and she was fond of dressing as a Cossack, of arming herself with a gun and a *yatagan*, riding astride like a man, and galloping off on a hunt through the forest. Her children were all dressed in the national costume like little moujiks. The servants about the place were very numerous, and both men and women among them came to look on with a respectful kind of familiarity. We took our lunch under the eyes of a picturesque, many-coloured, bare-footed crowd. One old woman, by way of greeting her master, kneeled before him and touched the ground with her forehead; fair-haired maids came and went ceaselessly, bringing food and drink.

This sort of banquet would have lasted heaven knows how long, if after three hours of it we had not remembered that we were to sleep that night at Tjumen, about 210 miles from Ischim. We had to resist the most pressing invitations to remain, and to insist with firm courtesy upon having our own way, or we should have been kept there as permanent guests. As we approached Europe we were coming to regions where we should be met by many of those pleasing obstacles which are called invitations. In order to advance at all the prince had need to show more unwavering strength of will amid this hospitality than had been deman-ded of him by rocks and bogs. The day before, at about one hundred versts from Omsk, we had also been hindered by a luncheon invitation which, however, did not stop us so long.

The *troikas* were made ready again, and we galloped towards the village. At four o'clock we were again on our way to Tjumen. We crossed the Tobol at Jalutorovsk, and a few hours later the Pyschma at Bogandinsk. Whenever we passed through a town we found people awaiting us in the streets to cheer us. We were preceded by the news of our coming. Even in the open country we were often recognized. At a parting of the roads once we asked a young man to tell us the way, and he, after having told us, cried to us just as we were leaving:

'From Peking?'

'Yes.'

'Prince Borghese?'

'Yes.'

'Hurrah!'

And he waved his cap. These spontaneous individual greetings gave us a special pleasure; they called up in us sudden response, as if they cried to us, 'We are friends!' And on these occasions we would turn round to respond with effusion and gratitude.

We reached Tjumen at eight p.m. There was a committee at Tjumen, and they came out to welcome us at the entrance of the town. With the members of the committee came also some photographers, and with the photographers some Russian newspaper correspondents. Thus were we welcomed, portrayed, interviewed. One of those colleagues fastened himself with great insistence upon me. Armed with a large notebook and a well-sharpened pencil, he stood by me like my own shadow. He stood by my side while I was writing dispatches; he stood by my side at the telegraph office, and then again during dinner (I had not been able to go with Prince Borghese to a banquet given in our honour); he was near me when I went to bed; he came to knock at my window, which was low and near the street, even while I slept. He was a small, thin, obstinate, immovable man.

He said, 'Tell me something.'

'I have nothing to tell you. I am sorry . . . The journey has been excellent. That's about all.'

'Tell me something more.'

'There is nothing more to tell.'

'Try to think of something.'

I sat silent, I did my work, I busied myself, I forgot his existence. Then all of a sudden I would hear his voice:

'Have you thought of anything?'

He was still there – ever there, implacable! I tried to pass him on to Ettore, but in vain; he was firmly convinced that I would reveal some wonderful thing about the Peking to Paris race.

Tjumen has all the appearance of a city in European Russia, with great paved streets, palaces built no longer of timber, but of stone, trees along the principal roads, and that special wealth of placards and notices about its shops which is always a sign that a certain percentage of the passersby know how to read. In Siberia the shop signs are much more numerous than the inscriptions, even in the large towns; round the shops you see many pictures and few words. Ideas are chiefly conveyed through colours and design. You see hats, shoes, samovars, clothes, carriage wheels. You are still in the heart of the age of hieroglyphics. At Tjumen you begin to feel that you are in a land more familiar with the alphabet.

We were, in fact, almost on the political boundary line of Europe.

We left again at four a.m. on 19 July for Ekaterinburg, over 120 miles away.

At Tjumen the steppe comes to a definite end. Already in the neighbourhood of the town it changes little by little insensibly. We could see the shrubs and bushes around us growing, as it were, broadening out, thickening, becoming trees again, and rising upon ever stronger and taller trunks, I might almost say towering trunks. We were approaching the forest again. It slowly took possession of the land around us and overwhelmed the steppe.

We found ourselves, almost before we knew it, in the shade of gigantic birch trees flanking the road. They stood at first like two beautiful, immense lines; then they grew thicker and turned into a wood, a flourishing, vigorous wood, through which the road made a way for itself. Amid the birch trees were some firs; then an enormous army of pine trees, with their long, slender trunks looking like reddish columns. Signs of traffic almost disappeared on the road covered over with grass. We almost felt as if we were entering the *taiga* again. Here, too, the railway – a short, local line between Tjumen and Ekaterinburg – condemned the main road to disuse. The thick foliage almost met above our heads; we could only see a little streak of sky, and a slender sunbeam here and there. We had to lower our speed and advance slowly in the cool, green shade, fragrant with resin, thyme, and mint, and flowers. The grass was dotted over with little ripe red fragrant wood strawberries.

We were at fifty versts from Tjumen, when in the depth of the wood to our left we saw two sign posts, near one another, painted with the usual white, red, and black bands. On their arms was painted the Imperial double-headed eagle with open wings and with the sceptre and globe in its claws. Below this eagle was some washed-out lettering. We slowed down to see if we could read it. One bore the words 'Province of Tobolsk', and the other 'Province of Perm'. We gave a loud shout that echoed in the silence of the forest.

'Farewell, Siberia!'

We were entering European Russia.

This was not really Europe yet. Europe proper begins at the Ural Mountains. We were only now crossing an administrative boundary, but Siberia, the true Siberia, was already far behind us. We had left it when we left the steppe. For a little while our minds travelled back over the roads already covered. We sat silent, looking absent-mindedly before us. And the eyes of our mind saw Trans-Baikalia, with its landscapes so varied that they give an idea of disorder, with its violent little rivers, and finally, that great lake, which in its stillness seems like an abyss of blue sky. They beheld green prairies and the herds grazing on them, and the Buriat shepherds; and the dark and grand *taiga*, a countless people of trees on their defence. We saw again the broad, interminable-looking Siberian rivers, rising from the torrid centres of Asia and dying in the ice-bound seas: rivers which carry amid the mud of their beds gold dust worn out of the remote and almost unknown mountains of the Altai and Changai chains, where are perhaps hidden the richest deposits in the world: the swift Yenisei, the majestic Obi, the busy Irtysch. We saw the endless chain of obscure, isolated little villages with their rough *isbas* made out of tree trunks, and picturesque cities, and innumerable white temples with their blue or green cupolas – and the steppe, which seemed endless before us. We almost forgot all we had done and suffered, and as we crossed its boundaries we felt that we had grown to love Siberia a little, precisely because we had suffered there. For all the energy and the emotion which had been called out in us on our long journey across it were a living part of ourselves, and they seemed to bind us with curiously intimate bonds to this foreign land.

There had been moments when we had hated it, but that was when it was strong, when it seemed about to stop and conquer us; now, in leaving it, we proved the conquerors, and we felt for it a new liking derived directly from this sense of victory. One's generosity towards the conquered is, after all, little more than gratitude: nothing is sweeter to the heart than the memory of a battle fought and won. We love most the things which have cost us most, which we acquire with difficulty. So we loved Siberia for her fallen bridges, for her clinging muds, for her bogs, her sand, for all that in her to which we owed what was highest and fiercest in the triumphant joy of this moment. We thought, too, with sweeter emotions, of all those whom we had met down there; of all the friends we had left almost as soon as we had made them, and all the kindnesses from unknown people which had served to further and comfort us. We felt that our thoughts must be answering to the thoughts of others for us, and that Siberia was following our steps with a thousand thoughts . . . Farewell, Siberia!

For another thirty versts we continued to run through the wood. Then its thickness diminished, its plants opened out; we came to clearings, then among meadows, then among fields, over which the horses, in twos and threes, dragged the plough and the harrow, driven by boys, and followed by flocks of croaking rooks. Villages followed one another in rapid succession, with more elaborate houses built more carefully with cut timber, ornamented with carvings, and with their shutters painted over with bright flowers. The moujiks all wore those red shirts which are so favourite a costume with Tolstoy.

But, alas, we met no longer with the same good-natured friendliness as in Siberia! These men received us with a certain hostile astonishment, as if we represented the arrival of some unknown enemy. A few of the men fled; the others looked at us sullenly, and stood in an attitude of defence. Some women went through a strange ceremony of protection against evil, spitting in our direction. This alone would have sufficed to prove to us that we were among people of another race, or at least most assuredly of a different temperament.

The landscape became more and more varied; it had slight undulations, with short slopes and short dips. We could not yet get up speed
again. The road continued bad even outside the forest; it was interrupted by little depressions full of puddles; it traversed unsteady little
wooden bridges. In drawing near to a town we found some people on
the road. Rather, I should say, it was the presence of some well-
dressed people, ladies, officers, students, standing still in the shadow
of the pine wood among the carriages which had driven them there,
by which we knew that we were nearing a town. This was the crowd
drawn from small Russian provincial centres: they were waiting for
us.

On seeing us approach, these people drew near and cheered us. As we
passed by them they shouted out good wishes to us. The men took off
their hats, the ladies waved their handkerchiefs. A young man on a
bicycle started pedalling on before us, making a sign to us to follow. We
went down a slope, and the city came in sight, with its roofs showing
here and there among trees, and the gilt spires of its temples; it was
Kamyschlow. We followed our cyclist faithfully, and he piloted us
through streets and squares, then through a market-place, then over
a bridge, and there left us, after having shown us the right way to
Ekaterinburg. Without his guidance, and following what seemed to be
the continuance of the main road, we should probably have made
a mistake and gone towards Irbit. That passing through Kamyschlow
was rapid, and left us only a confused impression of the graceful little
city, for which we had a feeling of gratitude on account of the welcome
it gave us, unexpectedly, in the open country.

The weather was rapidly breaking. We had left Tjumen under a
beautiful clear sky, but had found rain when we came out of the forest,
and every now and then a regular downpour alternated with an hour's
sunshine. After we had passed Kamyschlow the weather seemed satisfied with remaining threatening. Towards the west, the sky was stormy:
since the early part of the afternoon the most violent thunderstorm must
have been raging on the European frontier. We were going straight into
that black west.

The road no longer bent to right or left; it would not pause to turn
round; it seemed to be in the same haste as ourselves, and to wish to run
straight up against the Ural chain; it went up and down on the slight hills
like a ribbon laid upon the earth. It was a better road, too, and we could
go at greater speed.

Our car made and left behind it in the still, heavy air a thick cloud of
dust which did not settle for miles behind us. We could see that streak

from the top of heights now and then, still there in the distance, as if it had been the smoke of some fire we had caused in passing.

About three o'clock that afternoon we came upon a tract of wild land again. The villages were few and far between. We went for long hours without seeing any. Then the forest closed again about us with the ancient magnificent pine trees typical of the Ural Mountains. The road ran as if sunk between them; it seemed cut into a valley of majestic trunks, but here and there were a few clearings, and in these clearings stood prosperous-looking villas, and groups of elegant ladies cheered us from their verandas. The primitive look of the landscape spoke falsely to us; we were near a great city, and a rich one. Ekaterinburg was approaching – Ekaterinburg, the capital of the mines of the Ural regions, the great market for gold and coal.

It was seven o'clock when from the brow of a height we saw a crowd of waving arms. We came up to it and were welcomed by loud hurrahs. Ekaterinburg too had sent its greetings to meet us.

Followed by bicycles and carriages we entered shortly after into this elegant city, under a regular downpour, and it was here, surrounded by the most hearty and welcome hospitality, that we spent the last few hours of our life in Asia, which had begun in Peking about 3000 miles away.

We crossed the geographical boundary of Europe on 20 July at 5.17 a.m.

Near the road, and in a little clearing in the middle of the forest at the crossing of a valley in one of the highest mountains of the Ural chain, stands a marble obelisk; facing the east it bears the word 'Asia'; facing the west, 'Europe'.

We had eagerly looked forward to this point. We had often talked of the moment when we should pass from one continent to the other, that fleeting and yet significant and memorable instant when we would end our journey over Asiatic soil. That instant was bringing to its close our journey across the whole of Asia, from its most distant point on the Pacific Ocean. In forty days we had travelled over the whole of that immense continent, step by step we now knew one of the greatest roads of human traffic, the greatest perhaps which from time immemorial has seen the ebb and flow of races and civilizations, has borne towards the west the Tartar hordes, and towards the east the Slav invasions. A royal road of conquest and ideas, of religions and riches, of legends and trade, of armies and of gold. We had felt breathing around us all the mysterious fascination of Asia, especially down there in Mongolia in the vast stillness, amid a people of dreamers, wrapt in the thought of endless cycles of existence, and looking upon this present life as only an episode, as the passing of a wave in the ocean: a people living for the sake of death. And we had wondered whether there could be in the air or in the water of that Asiatic centre, some mystic power to draw men away from the world. The greatest among religions rose in Asia; they came like sparks out of the flames of that land of ideals destined to spread over all the world. The conception of the soul, which is perhaps the highest conception ever attained by man, and in which lies the origin of conscience, virtue, and goodness, is an Asiatic conception. Our sceptical materialistic civilization, flowing back again into Asia, beats against a great contempt of worldly things like the waves of the sea against the rock. It meets not hostility only, but indifference. Even the indifference of the moujik, that serene readiness to be content, which is the only obstacle to progress in the Slav temperament, is probably inherited from Asia.

In the awakening of Siberia it is the foreigners who communicate a feverish activity to the dreamy soul of that fair-haired people. We had felt Asia in all the things around us: in the neglect of the roads, in the indifference and resignation of people in every circumstance of life, in the very hospitality offered to us, which welcomed us and would fain have kept us there, because it did not understand the value of time, and could not realize our eagerness nor the very fact of so long and useless a race as ours being run. For us, our crossing of Asia had represented more than a mere succession of landscapes. We had been in constant and intimate contact with its inhabitants, passing from Chinese to Mongolians, to Buriats, to Slavs, to Kirghese; passing from Buddhism modified by Confucius to the Buddhism of the lamas, from the fetish-worshipping Christianity of Trans-Baikalia to the 'orthodoxy' of western Siberia, and to Islamism; we had felt innumerable shades of difference between races and consciences; we had noticed relationships in nature and in character, affinities between tongues and opinions; and without understanding it we had yet perceived a slow movement of races, an incalculable coming and going of emigrations, a continual stream of people, with all their apparent immobility, away from their common land in the heart of Asia, and had watched them, as it were, returning transformed. We had had a dim vision of a movement which goes back into prehistoric times: Asia, that silent, sleeping, ancient Asia, that seems almost like a continent now dead, had shown itself to us, on the contrary, full of an activity too vast to be either measured or accurately perceived: that great mother of peoples, from which our own race came, had revealed itself to us still young, surrounding a new fertility with quiet and stillness. This is why we thought, with a certain awe, of the moment when we would definitely cross her boundaries and leave her behind us.

And seeing that this point marked also a further stage on our homeward way, we had decided to stop and drink to the occasion on this poetic threshold of our native continent. In the toolbox had been put away, by a forethought upon which I pride myself, a good bottle of champagne destined for this very purpose. But I know not why, when we got to that point we remained silent, and by an instinctive agreement we went on running, each one of us wrapt in his own thoughts which blended with a sudden emotion. At that moment the ceremony we had thought of seemed a paltry thing. To stop for a toast in that place would have been a kind of profanation; nothing would have been so worthy of the spot we were crossing as our present recollection was.

The car slid on rapidly down the gentle slopes of those slack, low hills which go by the name of mountains. The Urals seem high and imposing only to the men of the steppes. They are mountains because they rise between two plains; but for ourselves, accustomed to the imposing lines of the Apennines and the Alps, we had come upon the Ural chain without being aware of it. When we reached Ekaterinburg the day before, we thought that their peaks were hidden by the storm clouds. Then in the early morning, as we went up and down among the woody undulations, we thought that we were only on their outlying counterforts: but we were, on the contrary, passing among the highest peaks of that mountain system.

The road, very broad and good enough, went on without swerving for a very long stretch: an endless looking white furrow in the thick of woods where no sun ever shines. The interminable pine woods seemed to us full of darkness. At a sudden point a stag leaped out of the wood, stopped on the road for a few seconds, with its tawny body ready to take a spring, surprised by the lightning approach of the car, turned its fine nose and slender neck towards us with a look of fear, jumped back, and disappeared among the undergrowth at the foot of the great trunks. We often came upon fallen trunks, beaten down by lightning or by a storm; a few of these prostrate giants encumbered the sides of the road.

We advanced for two hours in this primordial landscape. We could never have believed that we were in one of the most industrial regions in Russia, if we had not seen from time to time in the fold of some valley smoking chimneys of factories, mines, and foundries, showing above the tops of the trees. The wealth of this country is not above ground, but lies hidden in the bowels of the earth. It would be a vain work to clear the woods; if you come upon a mine, you make a road for the transport of the mine's produce, and that's all. The country round it may remain perfectly wild. We were now frequently obliged to slacken our speed, or even stop, to let pass long caravans of hundreds of *telegas* laden with wood, with coal, with copper, and directed towards Ekaterinburg, whence a short local railway line carries these products of the Urals to Ischeljabinsk, to the main railway line. A line is just now being built between Ekaterinburg and Kazan, and several times in that morning's journey we came upon the railway works, which blocked our road, and which obliged us to go over little banks of earth or unsteady provisional bridges. The cart drivers of the Ural provinces insulted us, but we felt rather pleased than offended. Those insults were the most unfailing sign that we had reached European soil. The landscape might quite well have been Asian. It was just as well that we should see that there was *something* different. The patience and calm friendliness of the inhabitants had remained on the other side of the border.

About ten o'clock we were again in the plain. It was raining; we had left Ekaterinburg with a promising blue sky, now we were threatened with a regular deluge. The road outside the region of the mines became bad, muddy, and difficult; the distances seemed to us endless. We were delayed by rebellious ascents like the one near Krasnojarsk, but after a few attempts to master them we nearly always found the means to avoid them by going over the grass in the fields.

We were beginning to get quite coated with mud; it splashed up so continuously upon us that we had to forgo even the necessary comfort of food: we had scarcely taken out our modest lunch, before it was covered with mud. That ceaseless pouring of mud upon us, which penetrated into our mouths, and our eyes, humiliated, overwhelmed, and irritated us like an insult. We were tired: usually, we felt our fatigue more when we were furthest from the place chosen for our next halt. It was a curious phenomenon by which the road we covered tired us less than that which remained before us. And this day we had a great deal of it remaining before us. We wanted to reach Perm, the seat of the governor of the province, about 250 miles from Ekaterinburg, by four in the afternoon; we had as yet covered barely 160 miles.

A little later the rain ceased, and we were able to increase our speed. In the monotony of the road we all three felt as if an unconquerable drowsiness weighed down our eyelids, when a singular vision appeared before us. Cupolas, gilded, silvered, enamelled, large and small, and belfries of every shape and size rose before us, grouped above a little town – Kungur. Kungur looks like one of the most beautiful of oriental cities; it has the aspect of some legendary place, with all that sparkling of precious metals. It must hold some great sanctuary, must be some great centre of faith, for to look at it it has more churches than houses. Sacred images and tabernacles and votive chapels, whose semi-darkness is bespangled with little flames of lamps and candles, abound in its streets. The moujiks, as they pass by, uncover their heads and bend their knee.

A few hours later we received another surprise concerning religion; we saw the first Tartar minaret at Kojonowa, at thirty versts from Perm. It was an accommodating minaret, which tried to look almost like a tower, with a crescent instead of a cross, and standing over a wooden mosque with windows like those of an *isb*; a Russianized mosque, in short. It is not until you come south of Kazan, in the province of Samara, that you meet those beautiful white, slender minarets which Islam has implanted on its regions like white lances marking a conquest.

The Tartars ran festively towards us, smiling upon us with their good Asian faces; they wore many-coloured coats with that artistic careless-ness common to Oriental people. Behind the panes of little windows we caught glimpses of the dark faces of their womenkind, adorned with necklaces like gypsies; they reminded us of real gypsies, whom we had several times met upon our way.

The gypsy represents another mysterious race. We met numerous families of them, even at Tomsk and over the steppe, with their tents pitched in the midst of their caravans and horses. How did they reach so far? Where do these people come from? Who are they? If musical gifts really represent a sign of intellectual aristocracy, from what noble ancestry may not this fugitive race be descended, a race which in its wanderings and wild life has preserved the instinct and the love of melody, and knows how to put into song inexpressible sorrows and passions.

Not far from Perm the road penetrates into fir woods and becomes sandy. On putting down the accelerator, so that the car might go more easily without sinking into the sand, we became aware of a very dangerous thing: the left driving wheel was breaking asunder.

I have already mentioned that the chain which we put round the tyre of that wheel so as to prevent it from slipping in the mud, between Kansk and Krasnojarsk, had done some damage to that part of the rim where the spokes fit into their sockets. It was obvious that on that occasion the chained-up hoop had suffered too great a strain, and the joints in it were loosened. It was at the time a question of cracks no larger than a fraction of a centimetre, the sockets were increased in size by fractions of a millimetre. We could scarcely see the tiniest crack round the end of each spoke, and this crack disappeared entirely when the wood was swelled by the rain. But in the sunshine the wheel began to creak, and Ettore, when he fed the radiator with water, had formed the habit of throwing a pailful on to the sick wheel. The remedy seemed efficacious; but this was between Omsk and Ekaterinburg.

And lo! as we came near Perm the wheel began to creak as it had never done before; we got down to look at it; the crack had considerably broadened, and the spokes were moving in their sockets, opening them more and more. Ettore, however, the man of resource, immediately had an idea. He took some strong string and wound it tightly round the spokes, pushing it into the cracks, thereby ensuring a sudden stiffness in the wheel. The creaking grew fainter.

We reached Perm about eight o'clock that night. It was still broad daylight; the streets were crowded and the trams full of people. These trams were most pleasing to behold; they were the first that we encountered on our journey. Each city seemed to reserve for us a new surprise, something which would bring suddenly before us a vision of the distance we had covered, some unexpected sign of the approach of our goal. At Perm it was trams that we looked at with the same attention with which the crowd looked at us.

Some cyclists came to meet us. They were good young men representing some sporting association of the city. They were charming and courteous, but the moment we came into the town, covered with mud as we were, tired, with one wheel of our car nearly broken, and just at the end of a run of over 250 miles, they led us to their racing course! And they did it for the purpose of seeing us speed round it. Such things did not happen in Siberia. When we reached the hotel, our care was immediately directed to the wheel. It was unlimbered and carefully examined. We held a consultation. The case was rather grave. There was no doubt but the spokes threatened to break away *en masse* from the rim. Prince Borghese suggested putting some new and dry string round the spokes, fixing the ends of these strings into the open cracks, and then to soak the wheel all night. The wood and the string would swell because of the dampness, and the wheel would no doubt become strong and firm again. Ettore approved of the plan and set to work. Two hours later the wheel was bound up, and the only thing remaining to be done was to put it to soak: surely the easiest part of the business. Not at all – it proved the most difficult. There was not in the whole city of Perm a receptacle large enough to contain our wheel. Our researches were long and anxious. They began with the hotel, and gradually spread over our whole quarter of the town. The people who had gathered round the motor car, and who had witnessed Ettore's work, took an active interest in the success of our researches, and were busy trying to remember the largest vats or tanks they had ever seen, that might serve our purpose.

A big man in official uniform had a sudden stroke of genius. He approached Prince Borghese and said to him:

'Excuse me. You wish to bathe your wheel?'

'Yes.'

'Then why do you not send it to a bathing establishment?'

We should have thought it a joke if the big man in uniform had not remained perfectly serious and unmoved under Prince Borghese's scrutinizing eye. Prince Borghese smiled, not quite knowing how to receive this suggestion.

'You mean . . .'

'I mean that you ought to send your wheel to a bathing establishment. You ought to hire a bathing box, and have the wheel put into the bath and send for it tomorrow. In this way you will also make quite sure that no one touches it.'

'What bathing establishment?'

'I know an excellent one on the Kama. If you wish it, you can simply put your wheel on to an *iswoschik*, and I will give the coachman the address.'

'Excellent. And will it be open at this time of night?'

'It is always open.'

Thus it came about that a sick wheel of a motor car was sent to a hydro to take the waters.

Next morning by four o'clock the wheel was at its post again, ready for work.

'How is it?' I asked Ettore, pointing to the wheel.

'In excellent condition,' he replied, perfectly delighted. 'It has come back much stronger.'

Oh, sad delusion! Serious illnesses often follow this course of treatment. They give the illusion of sudden swift progress. Our poor wheel was breathing its last. A few hours later it was done for.

XIX

FROM THE KAMA TO THE VOLGA

Our Car, Milk and Eggs – A Storm – Our Wheel Breaks –
The Rebuilding of the Wheel – A Timid Village – A
Damage to the Brake – 'Postowo!' – Melekeski –
The Labour of the Fields – Kazan

The citizens of Perm on the morning of 21 July must have suffered, and with some surprise, from a great rise in the price of milk and eggs. Very little milk and few eggs on the market that day! And we suffer under the reproach of having been the innocent cause of that profound economic disturbance. Motor car driving in countries not yet accustomed to this form of sport has the most unexpected results. It has consequences absolutely impossible to foresee. This is what had happened.

We had scarcely left the town in the face of a threatening and lowering bank of clouds, when we came upon a long line of *telegas*. They were bearing country produce to the market of Perm. The peasants, both men and women, drove their horses with their usual nonchalance, sitting on the edge of the *telega*, with their legs dangling. For the moujik has two ways of driving a cart, one for when he is going to market, the other for when he is coming back; and when he is coming back it is his head that dangles, and his legs are inside the cart. For the moujik never fails to turn most conscientiously into vodka a good part of the money he has earned; nor does he fail to drink that vodka with the same conscientiousness, to the last little drop. But that morning, as I have said, the peasants whom we met on our way were *going* to the market, and their *telegas* were therefore driven according to method number one.

When we approached, the first horse leading the line showed signs of terror, and then of frenzy. Horses in the province of Perm are, owing to some mysterious and unaccountable influence, the most irreconcilable enemies of motor cars. We had found a great difference in the behaviour towards us of the horses of the different provinces which we traversed. The horses of Trans-Baikalia were hostile, those of Irkutsk were mistrustful, those of Tomsk indifferent, those of Omsk variable, those of Perm irreconcilable. I may also add, for anyone who may desire to study the inscrutable connections between the characters of horses and the religions of men, that the horses of the Buddhist and Muhammadan people were the most friendly toward us. Even in the neighbourhood of Perm, the horses of the Tartars looked at us doubtfully, like tolerant brutes not claiming the undivided ownership of the road, and who will run and let run.

Well, then, as I was saying, the first horse in the line of *telegas* began to shy. We slackened the speed of our car to walking pace, but this was a useless precaution, the horse jerked to one side, and its *telega* was upset. The *telega* was carrying milk and eggs: little white and yellow streamlets coursed all about the road. We were just about to try and make up to the man for our involuntary misdeed when, like a flash, this panic fear spread to the other horses one by one. The second *telega* was upset, then the third; there is nothing more contagious than bad example. In a moment all the *telegas* were overturned, milk was flowing everywhere, and the peasants, encouraged by their wives, were throwing themselves in our direction. What was to be done? What can you do when you are on a 40-hp motor car, and threatened by a crowd of moujiks anxious and able to fall upon you? The matter becomes simple: regretfully, but firmly, we put down the speed lever, and our machine took to its heels, and was soon far out of reach of the peasants' sticks.

We had not gone one verst before we saw before us another long line of *telegas*. This time we decided to stop altogether and let it go by. Surely, that seemed the best thing to do. But a motor car standing still does not frighten Perm horses very much less than a motor car on the move. When they came near us, the horses began to prick their ears and toss their heads, to snort and to neigh, and suddenly the first one stood up on its hindquarters and turned right about, forgetting that it was harnessed to something. The *telega* immediately overturned, the second did the same, and was immediately followed by the third and fourth. *Tableau!* Milk and eggs on the road, sticks up in the air, and our car racing off at top speed.

From that moment we changed tactics, and with good success. In passing near carts we went on, full speed, and no more milk flowed in rivulets. The horses had scarcely time to see the passing of our monster before the monster had disappeared, and they went on their way completely reassured. The only thing that happened was a slight movement of fear on their part; it was over in a second. We were, after all, adopting the same tactics that had served our purpose on insecure bridges. The horses had no time to shy, just as the bridges had had no time to break. The critical moment was reduced to a second, and the peasants cheered us enthusiastically, smiling surprised at the sight of that lightning speed.

A few hours later we were entering some great pine forests, and one of the most violent storms I have known was breaking over our heads. An impetuous wind, moaning and shrieking, swept over the trees, making them sway; the darkened sky seemed to skim over their black and violently tossing heads. Through the darkness overhead scarcely any light came, and it was as dark as if the night had fallen, except for a blinding flash of purple light now and then. The thunder roared continuously above us; a deluge of rain poured down everywhere like water of a great cataract, inundating everything, flooding the road, filling the seats of our carriage, penetrating through our raincoats, beating against our faces violently enough to cause real pain, as though the water were a solid thing. So big were the drops and so hard were they driven by the wind, that we had to advance slowly; the ground could no longer be seen – it was covered with running water and veiled by a sheet of falling rain. The car was naturally giving way to all those moods of ill behaviour by which it usually protested against such weather; it skidded sideways, it went all on one side, and manifested an irresistible propensity towards turning back. It was disobedient and capricious.

The storm went on for four hours. At 9.30 we had scarcely covered fifty versts since Perm, and we had done nearly six hours' travelling.

We arrived on the banks of the Kama. It was still raining, but much less violently. Low clouds still passed overhead, broken into by the trees of the forest which coasts the river, but out towards the west was a streak of blue. We crossed the broad river – the chief route in east Russia after the Volga, of which it is a tributary – by a boat towed by a little steamer. It was a little old tug, pieced up again, and mended everywhere with varnished sheet tin, and to which we immediately gave the nickname of the *Coffee-pot*. The *Coffee-pot* was in no hurry; it boiled against the grain; it spent all its breath in giving long whistles to signal its presence to the deserted banks, and it certainly showed itself in no way preferable to that comfortable horse propelled towing machine adopted by the Siberians for the ferries over their broadest rivers. We landed on the next bank, fording over a part of the way inundated by the storm, and we continued our race through the mud; sometimes we had to get down and push the machine when the driving wheels persisted in revolving without advancing.

While still in the neighbourhood of the River Kama we crossed the little city of Ochansk, where we began to see some wooden houses built after the old and picturesque style of Russian architecture, with the corners of their gables rounded off into the shape of an inverted heart, adorned with reliefs and perforations as graceful and naïve as Byzantine ornaments; and we went assiduously on our way as best we could, hoping to be able to reach Malmysch before night. But Malmysch is on the River Wjatka, a tributary of the Kama, and it lies at nearly a hundred versts from Kazan. We had decided to cover 230 miles that day, and we reckoned upon being at Kazan early the following morning, but things were to happen very differently indeed. On certain journeys it is better never to settle things. Any settling of plans is a deplorable act of presumption; it is an attempt to limit and direct Fate. Fate would avenge herself and humble our pride.

About eleven o'clock we had done about thirty versts the other side of the Kama. The road grew better and was drying up; the weather had cleared. We took advantage of these favourable circumstances to increase our speed. Our sick wheel began to creak; it was groaning hard. We went on – what else could we do? – and the groan changed into a shriek. A few yards more, and then came a crash. We stopped. Prince Borghese jumped down to look at the wheel, and uttered an exclamation of real grief.

'What's the matter?' I asked him.

'We're done for. We can't move another foot.'

The spokes of the wheel had now completely parted company with the rim. As the wheel turned they went in and out of their sockets; they went into the sockets in the lower part of the wheel, being pressed into it by the weight of the car, and they came out again as they found themselves on the other side.

It would have been difficult for anything worse than this to have happened. We were now stopped, and for an indefinite length of time, in the middle of an uninhabited tract of land, hundreds of miles from a railway. We had a moment of real consternation; we stood there silently looking at the broken wheel with hostile glances, full of vain resentment.

'And now?' we asked one another after a few minutes.

'So many obstacles overcome,' sighed Ettore, 'only for this . . . !'

'We cannot even have it dragged by horses,' I remarked, 'minus a wheel!'

Prince Borghese was thinking hard, and then, as a sensible man, he said:

'Let's think it out. What is the most urgent thing of all? To arrive at the nearest inhabited place. To begin with, we cannot stop in the middle of the road; after we have done this, we shall think of the second thing to do. Let's look at our map.'

We consulted the map of the province. The nearest village was eight versts away.

'Well,' said the prince. 'Now we must find the means of going eight versts. For that distance we can repair the wheel here.'

The prince was always energetic and calm, which means resourceful. We invented a very ingenious provisional kind of repair, capable of resisting for a little way, providing the way was covered with due caution. This was to fit in some bits of wood between the nave and the rim of the wheel, after the manner of additional spokes, put alternately with the real spokes and tightly bound with ropes. Ettore started working with great alacrity. With a hatchet he cut down some strong branches from a tree; he smoothed the necessary lengths of it, and put it in well measured pieces between one beam and the other of the wheel, keeping the latter raised with a screw-jack. Then he bound them tightly to the wheel itself. The wheel took on the strange appearance of a singular bundle of wood surrounded by a large tyre. While we were at work an old moujik came by, pushing on a calf before him. After looking at us with attention, he said: 'Greeting.'

'Greeting.'

'You will have to get a new wheel.'

'Ay, yes.'

'There's a man close by who knows how to make one.'

'A wheel like this one?' asked Prince Borghese in a tone of unbelief.

'A wheel like this, little father,' answered the old man. 'Just like this. He is the best sledge and *telega* builder in the whole province. You won't find such a good one even in Perm.'

'But this is a very complicated *telega* which can go of its own accord . . .'

'I can see that it isn't like ours. However, Nikolai Petrovitch is clever enough to copy your wheel exactly.'

'Where does this man live?'

'Six versts away. You go this way. You find a little white house. To the left of the house there is a slope down and then a little bridge. You go over the bridge and you are at his door. You can't make a mistake. His *isba* is the only one in the whole countryside.'

'And will he work today? It's Sunday.'

'He works only in the morning, but if you are in a hurry . . .'

We thanked the kind old man, who continued his way preceded by the trotting little calf. And we started slowly and cautiously to go to the house of Nikolai Petrovitch. After a few turns, the wheel began to creak, to moan, to groan. We expected at every moment to hear the sound of a definite breaking, and to feel the car going down on one side. But the wheel, though complaining all the time, held out. We took more than an hour to go to the cart builders *isba*. It was a comfortable-looking house, made out of beautiful planed timber, and standing by an enclosure over which were a number of shed covers. Outside in the sunshine, numerous sledge beams stood in lines, with one end kept at the required curve by strong rush ropes.

We called out. Immediately afterwards the gate of the enclosure was opened and a man came out.

'Nikolai Petrovitch?' we asked.

'I *am* Nikolai Petrovitch. Greeting.'

He was a fine-looking man about fifty years of age. He wore a long grey beard; his face had the peculiar mystical expression common among Russian peasants. His long hair, parted over his forehead, came down to his shoulders; he was of a big make, like a giant, and wore the red shirt of the moujik, open at the neck; he was bare headed. His assistants followed him. They too had a peculiar patriarchal appearance. Their athletic arms looked capable of pulling down a tree.

'Look at this wheel,' said the prince to the *telega* builder.

He looked at it for a few minutes.

'We can give it new spokes,' he said. 'The rim is still excellent. You deepen the sockets . . .'

'Can you make the spokes again?'

'Yes.'

'Good, strong ones?'

'I'll make the wheel stronger than when it was new.'

'I want it at once.'

'With half a day's work it's done.'

'Very good.'

The car was taken into the rustic courtyard, all full of shavings and splinters, and cumbered with beams, sledges, carts, iron hoops. In a corner stood a *tarantass*, freshly varnished, supported on two stands. Our wheel was taken out of the axle, unscrewed, dismounted. Its spokes, taken out of the nave and of the rim, served as a model for the fresh ones. A few moments later the yard echoed with ringing blows of the hatchet. No other tool was used by the men, but they wielded this one with the most marvellous dexterity. The hatchet becomes in the hands of the Russian peasant a wonderfully exact tool. To mark the point where the hatchet is to fall, those men made no lines, put no leading marks. They laid their left hand upon the wood and the blow fell almost grazing their thumb. The position of the latter indicated to the eye and to the hand the place where the blow was to fall. The new spokes came one by one out of the big stump of an old pine tree, pared off with great powerful blows, which made the splinters fly all around. The workmen took their measures by putting the old spokes over the new ones, and they had need of nothing else. They copied identically little grooves one millimetre wide with a sure eye and hand, and with hatchet blows brought down with a full swing, as if instead of so delicate a piece of work they had been making the boarding of a raft.

While we were watching that picturesque group of rough-bearded men, leaning attentively over their tiring work, one of them turned towards us and calmly and seriously addressed us in Latin. Our surprise was so great that for a moment we looked at him full of astonishment, unable to reply a word.

'Where have you learned Latin?' asked Prince Borghese.

'I have studied it by myself at home in the winter,' the man replied gravely.

And this reminds me of another Latin scholar whom we met upon our journey: a Chinese cart driver near Hsien-wa-fu. He was a Christian Chinese in the service of a Roman Catholic mission in the Shan-si Province, and was returning from Peking carrying some provisions for his Fathers. But the occurrence is not so very unusual in China, for Latin is there the living tongue of Roman missions, and many converts come to use it with most admirable precision. Just as there is pidgin-English there is in China pidgin-Latin to the glory of the Faith.

Our moujik's Latin was somewhat Russianized, but it served well enough to let us know that if we were tired we could go into the house close by, where we would be able to rest and take some milk. And we found there not only milk, but good little white strawberries, which the wife of the master eagerly offered to us.

By four o'clock all the spokes were made, and the most difficult part of the work – the setting together of the thing – began. It took two more hours of unceasing work to put the wheel together again. It seemed almost impossible to do it. At last, however, the wheel was complete, and nothing more remained to be done than to fix the screwed bolts which hold the steel nave and other accessories (the brake and so on) in their places. The wheel was taken to a primitive kind of forge close by, for Nikolai Petrovitch – like all cart builders – was also a smith. A fire was lit, and with long, red-hot pokers the spokes were pierced where the screws were to go. It was another long hour's work, done in clouds of smoke, which came up wheezing from the burned places in the wood. At last the screws were put in, the nuts were tightened: the wheel was ready.

The new spokes were certainly not very well polished or elegant. Made of strong, rough wood, the only delicate bits of work about them were their joints; they gave the wheel a look of rough solidity. It looked like a medieval wheel but it was strong enough to resist any shock and strain.

In less than it takes the say so, Ettore put the wheel back in its place on the machine; it was seven p.m. when we got on our way again, and came out of the yard on to the road. The workmen followed us waving. They smiled, very pleased, wiping beads of perspiration from their calm brows.

At the moment of our start they held out their good hard hands, which we shook affectionately and gratefully.

'*Do svidania!*' they cried to us as we went off.

'*Salve!*' exclaimed the Latin scholar among them.

Their voices followed us for some way, and looking back we saw our kind rescuers waving their hats, until the trees hid them from our sight at the bend of the road. They must have been a little proud of that powerful speed of our machine; they must have felt that a little of their will, of their cleverness, and their strength, was helping us forward to reach our goal.

We wanted to advance so long as the daylight lasted. The roads were now dry, and we were going at nearly twenty miles an hour. The region of the white nights was finished, the darkness was late in coming; but now it came. An hour after our departure the sun was setting. We kept saying one to another: 'We will halt at the next village,' but the desire to make up for lost time was too strong for us, and at the 'next village' we went on without even stopping a moment. In the inhabited places the Sunday crowds grouped before their houses at times greeted us festively, shouting good wishes to us, and at others looked at us with suspicion and hostility. The explanation of these different modes of behaviour lay in the telegraph. The villages which had a telegraph were friendly; they knew about us, and in some places were awaiting us. From one telegraph station to another the clerks communicated to each other news of our arrival, and the news was spread about the streets, circulating from mouth to mouth. We never failed to see telegraph clerks looking out of the window; they were always the first to greet us.

The sun had gone down long ago, and by nine o'clock even the twilight was fading. We came to a village, and there definitely decided to stop for the night. Many *isbas* were already shut up, and the streets were solitary. Country people go to bed early all the world over. A few people looked out of the window at the sound of our passing, and drew back their heads immediately when they saw the monster fleeing in the semi-darkness bearing those furry beings. The hour was late and propitious to fear. We found two young men walking together on the flags of the wooden pavement. We caught them up and stopped our car to ask the way to the Zemstvoskaya Dom, but we had scarcely opened our lips before they, having looked at us for a second with staring eyes, made the sign of the cross and fled full speed without a word or a cry, running on tiptoe, almost as if they feared to draw us after them with the sound of their footfall. Obviously it was a case of a village without a telegraph station. The situation was becoming difficult; we could not do without stopping in a village because our provisions were long since exhausted and we had taken no food since Perm the evening before, excepting only the strawberries of our good *telega* man. We went on slowly, putting the silencer on to our exhaust so as to make less noise and not arouse alarm. We used to call that 'gagging' our machine.

On the threshold of a house we at last saw some women; they saw us too, and we stopped. Prince Borghese made a movement as if to alight and enter into conversation.

'For heaven's sake,' I whispered to him, 'with those furs you'll make them run away at once. Let us talk from here.'

We had already noticed that our clothes, either furs or raincloaks, often produced a disastrous impression upon the peasants. When we wanted to get down to ask them something we always had to be careful to take off these cloaks; therefore we now spoke from the car.

We said good evening to the women, softening our voice so as to seem less diabolical. The prince found the most dulcet tones in which to say:

'Good evening. Will you tell us the way to the Zem –'

It was no good going on. The women had gone into the house precipitately, shrieking and banging the door behind them.

'Ah!' we murmured. 'The best thing that can happen to us will be if we are allowed to sleep without food in the open air.'

We passed before a well-to-do looking house, all painted blue, with white window sashes.

'Here there must be somebody of a certain position,' said the prince. 'Perhaps he will give us a better reception.'

We knocked at the door. Perfect silence. We knocked again. No one answered.

'The house must be empty!' we exclaimed.

No, it was not empty. We heard a whispering, a sound of precipitate footfalls on the wooden floor; a knocking of doors violently closed; a creaking of bolts.

How could we break through this wall of fear which surrounded us? We soon saw that the inhabitants of this house were awake, and that, coming down upon the road, they were peering at this mysterious car. It was scarcely pleasing to remain like this, also because the chance was not altogether unlikely that someone among these people would think it a virtuous and praiseworthy deed to fire a shot at the devil. Prince Borghese remarked:

'If only one of them would come near I could show him our official letter, and we should immediately be received with all honour.'

Then, struck by an excellent idea, he began to address those timid people who were pressing in a hedge fifty paces away, ready for a prompt retreat. He started with explaining the motor car.

'This,' said he, 'is a machine like the boats on the Kama, and like a railway. Come forward – there is no danger. It works by means of . . .'

The boldest among them came near, the others followed, and soon a circle of people stood around us, gradually growing convinced that we really were men of flesh and blood. Now the distance between us disappeared entirely; they touched the car, at first with a certain timidity as if it might have burnt them, then with confident security. Two peasants invited by us heroically accepted the offer of getting on to the car and of being taken for a drive. They grew so enthusiastic that they would not get down again. Now everyone wanted to be driven. The crowd pressed around us on all sides. The priest of the village arrived, and expressed the desire to be taken next morning to the neighbouring village.

The ice was broken. All these people became our good friends. The blue house unbolted its doors and gave us shelter. The samovar appeared upon the table, and in its wake came eggs and milk, and bread and butter. And we satisfied our hunger. The car lying quietly in the yard was surrounded by the admiring population.

We received visitors until midnight; the people came and went freely, after the manner usual in Russia, without asking anybody's permission. They wanted to see us close up; they looked in at the door, took off their caps, gazed upon us silently, and went off again as pleased as Punch after murmuring a nervous greeting, twisting their caps in their hands. At twelve o'clock we put out the light, we wrapped ourselves in our furs and lay down upon the floor; the last visitors went off on tiptoe to announce from the door of the house: 'The strangers are asleep!'

On the following morning, 22 July, at four a.m., we started our race again over a changeless country: great forests, a few prairies, and a few cultivated fields made prisoners by these majestic woods, which still occupy so much land untouched by the labour of man.

We crossed by boat the little River Uschim, then another wider one, the Wala, both of them tributaries of the Kama, itself the main road of commerce for steamers down to the Volga, which is in its turn the chief artery of Russia. Unfortunately the waterways are here so numerous and so commodious that they cause overland ways to be neglected, so that we found most execrable roads, and had to advance with the most irritating slowness, while our car was subjected to the same terrible strain which made us so often despair between Marinsk and Tomsk. We were afraid that the springs could not hold out any longer. We felt them give way much more easily to the jolting, and we had no new ones to replace them with, as, feeling sure that we should have no need of them, we had left our spare springs at Kalgan because they were too heavy. They were probably at this moment still in the office of the Russo-Chinese Bank, as a souvenir of our passing.

To have an idea of the ground we were traversing, you must imagine yourself going by car over a well-ploughed field, and seeing before you hundreds of miles of the same sort of road. Of course now and then it also rained. We crossed little tiny, quiet, sad, solitary villages, with little wooden houses just like those in the fields, except for a gay coat of white paint; we felt oppressed by a great melancholy as we thought of their monotonous, silent life. They seemed towns in exile. They would suddenly appear in a valley behind a wood on the bank of some little stream, isolated in the monotony of an uncultivated country, dark with fir and pine trees of a funereal shade of green. Some of these villages have names that are not Russian, but Tartar or Bulgarian.

A few names remain as relics of that strange Bulgarian race which once had its empire here, and which has left the magnificent ruins of its capital town on the banks of the Volga. It had been so long forgotten that it was lost, and the forest had covered its ancient site. It remained as a tradition, when, under Peter the Great, its majestic ruins were found again in the heart of the forest. Those ancient Bulgarians were lovers of the great watercourses; they shared the Volga and the Danube between them. 'White Bulgarians' were those of the Volga, 'Black Bulgarians' were those of the Danube. But they were swallowed up; the one by the Tartars, the other by the Slavs. Just names have remained of them: Bulgary on the Volga, and Bulgaria on the Danube. Their race exists no longer.

In the afternoon we found ourselves again in the most serious straits. The road across these interminable woods had become so bad that we could advance only at the rate of about nine, or sometimes, six, miles an hour. The body of the car was creaking; it swayed at every shock as if it had been about to fall to pieces. The footbrake – that blessed pedal which had caught fire three times in Siberia – was no longer burning, it is true, but neither was it working. It was completely spoiled, and we were left to the handbrake alone, which, as is well known, acts only on the driving wheels. Suddenly down a steep slope, while we were using the only brake left us, we felt the car giving a violent heave, and we heard a metallic creak in the fore part of the machine. It stopped, all askew.

We jumped down and looked.

'Now, what can we do about that?' we exclaimed, full of anguish, seeing the damage done.

The brake, whose action was too violent, had caused the kind of stirrup which holds the springs to the axle of the wheels to break, and the axle of the driving wheels was entirely cut off from the springs, which means, from the chassis. We had some spare links, but they were too short. Fortunately Ettore, diving among his tools, found some screws and nuts, with which, after long and patient work, he was able to put together and join wheels and axle. But a still more serious damage appeared: the back springs were about to give way. Out of the nine leaves of which they were made up, three were broken on the left side and five on the right. All our hope lay in the power of resistance of the big spring, the longest and thickest, at the end of which are the joins, and which is made of the finest steel that can be had. It was, however, a very slight hope, and we knew that one big bump would suffice to do away with it.

Night was falling, and our work still went on in the wood. It was a sad evening for us. The doubt came back to us again and again that the car could not resist, and yet only external breakages were threatening to defeat us – breakages of things which are scarcely taken into account. When the engine, the transmission gear, the pinions, the differential, the joints of the chassis, all the real machinery is perfect, new, strong, and working smoothly, who thinks of anything else? When the heart, the digestive organs, all the vital parts of a man's body are strong and in perfect condition, who thinks of his feet? Yet it was exactly the feet of our car that were now sick, and this becomes a serious matter when you want to walk.

We heard the tinkling of bells, and a few moments later a *tarantass* appeared on the brow of the hill. It was a public one, a diligence. The postilion took advantage of the fact that he had no traveller on board, to stop and talk with us. The man was drunken and talkative. He had a hairy face and looked like a bear, an intelligent bear – well, no, scarcely intelligent: let us say good-natured. He was wrapped in a fur *armiak*: old, greasy, torn. He wore felt boots, and on his fur cap shone a large brass badge with the Imperial Eagle. He patted his badge with his open hand to show us his dignity, and by way of introducing himself he called out '*Postowo . . . postowo*.' (Postilion)

He came down from his seat and walked staggering round us in great glee. He might have found his dearest friends again after a long parting; he came up to each of us as if he was going to tell us some secret, and then pointed to his badge and cried out '*Postowo, postowo*', with a look as if to say, 'What! can't you remember? *Postowo*.'

'Where are you going to?' we asked.

'To Melekeski.'

'Is it far?'

'Fifteen versts.'

'Can one lodge there for the night?'

'What! Can one lodge at Melekeski? – there's an excellent relay station,' and beginning to tap his badge again '*Postowo . . . postowo*.'

'All right,' we said to one another, 'then let's go to Melekeski.'

And as the repairs were done, we started again slowly with the greatest precaution, and we arrived after more than an hour at the post station. We had some eggs, we drank some milk, and went to sleep on the floor.

The station was little more than an *isba*, and as you see would not allow us very great luxuries. The chief, a kind of moujik who could read and write, did not possess an abundance of anything except icons and regulation tables – both of them hanging on the walls.

Next morning we were awakened by the clattering of horses' hoofs in the yard, and by the cries of the postilions harnessing them to their *tarantass*. We had some tea and then went off. It was four a.m., and it was raining.

We came, little by little, into a more prosperous and more beautiful region. The landscape changed, but alas, the road was no better! We passed Malmysch – the same Malmysch which we flattered ourselves to be able to reach the same day as we left Perm – a little town near the River Wjatka, which if you cross in a hurry looks as if it were inhabited only by a dozen officials, by a chemist and two policemen. Life cannot be very cheerful at Malmysch. The road grew worse, or else it seemed to do so because of our increasing sensitiveness to the irregularities of the ground, due to the state of our springs. We advanced slowly, preferring the grassy path.

We were, however, cheered up by the sight of the magnificent country around us. We saw at last again, after a length of time which seemed to us longer than the memory of man, the richness of field labour. When we came out from the woods we looked out at last upon European land; everywhere, among the green, rose villages, Tartar and Christian, with minarets and belfries, crescents and crosses, mixed together in the great peace of the fields. Nothing spoke any longer around us of past struggles. Dissimilar in every way as are the Tartars and the Slavs, in look and in character – one is fair, the other is dark; the fair ones are tall and the dark ones are little – yet they are alike in one point: in their tolerance.

Each village has its own customs, kept up unaltered through centuries. We were surprised, full of admiration, as before visions of far-off times. Picturesque garments of old Russia, now no longer worn where there is constant contact with modern progress, are to be seen down there, far from the railway line.

The people seemed dressed for some great holiday; this was the season of haymaking. The people scattered over the fields stood there like great living flowers. Among the high grasses and the ripening harvest were red, yellow, white clothes, women's curious headdresses like mitres, covered with embroidery; beautiful silver-braided garments, strange capes and shirts, little necklaces of coins, golden waistbands, silk sashes. In this crowd of colours gleamed whole lines of sickles with a slow, even motion. We heard the echoes of songs. Hundreds of carts and horses, in groups over the fields, gave the scene a certain military fierceness as if these were fantastic bivouacs.

The diversity of customs you meet with at every turn in Russia is really surprising. You feel that under the two names of Russian and Tartar are hidden other races mixing but not blending. The religions are different and their origins are diverse. The people of each insist upon preserving their distinctive characters; they wish to distinguish themselves from one another and to endure. They could not wear certain uncomfortable and extraordinary clothes for centuries, for any other purpose than for that of maintaining their own individuality, of wearing a uniform of their own race, of knowing one another and being able to defend one another in a common medley. There is an instinct of preservation in those traditional fashions. Each village is a little state living aside and in peace, as different from the others as if it were separated from them by the widest distances.

At twenty-four versts from Kazan a little surprise awaited us. A road paved in the European fashion, laid with stones: rolled, white, and perfect. This was the first road practicable for carriages that we had found since leaving Peking. But the peasants returning from the town preferred not to take their carts over the road, but drove them out all together, into the mud of fields. The moujiks say that those roads spoil the wheels because they are too hard, and they avoid them. In order to oblige them to pass there, local authorities build ditches and trenches by the side of the road. The peasants pass along the bottom of the ditches and on the top of the trenches, profiting by the least space sufficient to hold the narrow wheels of their *telegas*.

It was about three o'clock, when coming down the valley of the Kasanka River towards the west, where the sky was blue after a long rain, we saw the sparkling of a long line of water: the Volga. And in the luminous mist there stood up before us the outline of a great city. At last we were coming to Kazan, with its towers, and the cupolas of its sixty churches, with the minarets of its thirteen mosques!

We entered the town through vast streets full of movement and sound, among the coming and going of the *iswoschiks*, and the roaring past of the electric trams. We were observed curiously, recognized by many, and sometimes cheered.

A lady turned her grand-looking carriage to follow us and see us better. She caught up with us. She was a lady with gold-rimmed spectacles, wearing a man's hat and smoking a cigarette. She asked us:

'Are you from Peking?'

'Yes, madame.'

'Oh!' and she looked at us with deep astonishment as her carriage drove by our side. 'And now, where are you going?'

'To the hotel, madame.'

'To which hotel?'

'Hotel d'Europe.'

'Do you know the way? Would you like me to show it to you?'

'Yes, please. Thank you.'

The carriage started on before us and we followed it. We passed by some churches and gardens, and came down the principal street. Here some men ran forward with outstretched hands, panting and smiling; they were Italians. They cried: 'Welcome! . . . *Evviva!*' We loved them!

At the end of the road we had a glimpse of the Kremlin of Kazan and the grand Spaskaja Tower, which looks like an ancient menace facing the modern city.

XX

FROM THE VOLGA TO THE MOSKWA

~~~~~~~~~~

*In Siberia Again – A Hostile Village – A Miller's
Hospitality – Nijni Novgorod – A Telegram's
Adventures – The Road – Vladimir – A Voluntary Halt –
Moscow's Reception for Us – On the Banks of the Moskwa*

At Kazan our springs were repaired. The thing was done quickly in one
night. A carriage builder promised to renew the broken leaves in ten
hours, and he kept his word. At nine a.m. on 24 July we were able to
leave Kazan with our machine in perfect order. We passed by the severe
walls of the Kremlin: that ancient Tartar citadel, whose history is one of
the darkest histories of fire and blood, a citadel which saw the massacre
of the Christians, ordered by Makh-met-Amin; the massacres of the
Tartars, ordered by Ivan IV; the massacres of the nobles, ordered by the
Cossack rebel, Pugatcheff; which saw the town below it sacked and
destroyed four times. We came to the distant suburb of the Admiralty
and then to the fort on the Volga.

That great river – the greatest river of Europe – vast, slow, majestic,
proud, was covered with ships, great steamers which sailed as far as the
Caspian Sea, with rafts, with tugs, with passenger boats. It was particularly crowded at that time, because the fair of Nijni Novgorod was
approaching. Some of the busiest traffic of the world passes over the
waters of this river: it connects central Russia with Persia, the Caucasus
and Turkestan. A most motley crowd was gathered upon its banks
between the landing-stages, and the latter, built entirely of wood,
were crowned by sea-like waving of signals and pennons. There were
Tartars, Armenians, Circassians, Kirghese, mixed with the multitude
of Russian peasants. Some steamers were just leaving for Nijni
Novgorod.

We embarked upon one of the smaller boats which travelled backwards and forwards between the two banks. This boat which carried us

was different from the bridges or boats or rafts by which we had travelled across the other rivers. This was a regular steamer, and seemed to us as grand as a transatlantic passenger liner. Some Cossacks, sitting near the prow between horses and *telegas*, were singing and playing the bala-laika, that strange triangular musical instrument which the Slavs have brought as far as the Adriatic Sea.

In a few minutes we were on the right bank, hilly and green and scattered over with villas, and we went on quickly climbing among hills, from whose heights we admired the beautiful spectacle of Kazan all white, raising to the sky the sparkling cupolas of its Cathedral of the Annunciation, the first church risen on the ruins of Muslim domination. Next to those cupolas, and in strange contrast to them, we saw the high, old, dark Tartar tower of the Siumbeka, named after a Tartar princess who (according to tradition) climbed the tower when the besieged city was about to yield to the victorious Slav army, and threw herself down into space to perish with the freedom of her country. In the lower Kazan, which is still all Tartar, minarets rose among the little houses, sur-rounded by their gardens, and near the river was a strange panorama of round buildings: enormous tanks for the petroleum which the ships carry from Baku on their way up the Volga. Kazan is one of the greatest petroleum deposits in the world. Presently everything was left behind, disappearing in the distance, and soon all was hidden behind a hill, and we were alone again in the solitude of the country.

We advanced southwards some time till we came to a parting of the ways. To the left was the road to Saratow, and to the right that of Moscow. We here resumed our road towards the west. We ran along abandoned, uncertain paths, all covered with grass. We were obliged to be content with the very lowest speed, and vaguely felt as if the great city we had just left then, with its vast boulevards and their electric trams – that populous, animated, noisy modern town – had been a dream, a hallucination come to us in the heart of Siberia.

For surely this was Siberia again around us. There were places where the water had so hollowed out the road that it had made for itself a course like a deep ravine, along the edges of which we went in search for a passage. We entirely lost our way here, as we had done once before in Mongolia. We came to a place where no trace of road or of path was in the slightest degree visible. Here we began to stop looking for a good road, but rather for a man to serve as our guide. Every attempt we had made to find a way by consulting our map and the compass had brought us to some insurmountable obstacle. We saw two peasants cutting the grass in a meadow; one of them consented to come on the car and be our

guide. After about ten versts we came to a muddy little path flanked by
the line of the telegraph poles.

'Now follow the wires,' said the man to us, and he left us.

How long it seemed since we had had that unending line of poles for
our guide! And was this near Moscow? All overland traffic down there is
restricted to the winter alone, when the snow serves admirably to level
everything and to provide a way for the swift sledges. It would therefore
be useless to keep up costly roads. In the summer there were bridges. In
olden times, before steam navigation was invented, there was in this
place a magnificent road, of which the only traces we now could find
were a few birch trees in a line, unsteady little bridges and, in the marshy
places, a few bits of paved road now hidden and spoilt by the grass.
When the peasants want to go from one village to another, they now
prefer not to pass any longer over that deserted road. They follow their
own caprice over numerous paths, which cross and recross as in a
labyrinth. This labyrinth was our despair. We seemed to meet again with
all the same difficulties that we had met with in Siberia. We came out of
them slowly; but still, we found that the practice we had acquired in
overcoming them was now of considerable assistance to us.

About one o'clock we were crossing a small village when, on the little
green which always surrounds the white church of a Russian village, the
car, although going very slowly, frightened a horse which was harnessed
to an empty *telega*. The horse began to run away, and a boy of about ten
years old who had only just got down from the *telega*, tried to stop it. He
caught the long halter which was dragging behind the cart and tried to
pull it. But, unfortunately, the halter got entangled round his leg and he
fell. We cried out in fear; we could already see in our imagination the
boy dragged after this terrified horse, and encountering a most horrible
death. But we had not taken into consideration the size of Russian
boots. The boy had scarcely time to fall before the rope which had
wound round his leg simply took off his boot, leaving him perfectly
unhurt! The horse stopped before the church enclosure. This incident
made the whole village rise up in indignation against us. In a moment a
large group of peasants was gathered together, and taking advantage of
our somewhat slow advance, they began to run after us. As they went,
more and more joined the crowd. They took up stones and came to the
assault, shouting furiously 'Stop!'

The runaway horse alone would not have been sufficient to justify so
much indignation. Even a Russian peasant could surely tell that this
incident was not our fault! But a few days later, at Moscow, we heard an
explanation of the popular fury we had met in that village, and also of

the silent hostility which had received us in so many Russian villages. It appears that the motor car has been used on various occasions by revolutionaries for their deeds of violence, and for distributing their illegal proclamations. Certainly in many places in Russia the idea has obtained that motor cars are vehicles exclusively used by the enemies of religion and the tsar. The runaway horse, then, was in our case simply the spark which caused the open burning of a latent fire.

Our pursuers did not seem prepared to let us escape. The road helped them; for just past the church we came to a steep descent full of ruts and holes. We had to slacken our speed and use the brake, or the machine would have broken up in the jolting. The peasants were led by a fair, red-shirted young man, who ran lithely before the others, shouting something to egg them on. The distance between us was diminishing notably. We were coming to some stones; a few seconds more and we would have been caught. Then I made up my mind to do something, which put an immediate stop to the pursuit. I made quite a simple movement with my right hand, a slow gesture, getting up and facing the crowd. The crowd stopped suddenly, ceased from shouting, backed away, let us go free. I should say that in my right hand was a Mauser pistol, cocked and loaded.

A little later we were sunk in the mud near a small river called the Zimylskaja. We got out of it with three hours' work, and with the assistance of three moujiks who were going by. We crossed the river by an old bridge, leaving the picturesque little city of Woronowka to our left, and off we were again over the uncertain and insidious roads. In the meantime the weather had grown threatening. From the west there came up a black storm, which overtook us while we were in the middle of a big forest of oak and beech trees, and it spoilt the pleasure we had in meeting with friendly trees. We were tired of fir trees and birches. Firs are certainly among the most beautiful trees – they have a kind of architectural severity given them by their dark, cathedral spires – but after a while they end by palling, by becoming as tiresome as a crowd of closed umbrellas upside down. The oak trees seemed full of enchantment. They had such a free, varied, familiar look. They seemed to be gesticulating with those twisted and irregular branches swayed by the wind; they were home trees.

It was raining cats and dogs, and with the usual accompaniment of thunder and lightning; it was the rule now that it had to rain every day. We had ended by considering this fact as a quite inevitable circumstance during this journey. We watched the storms coming, without saying a word or expressing the slightest annoyance. We did not even have the trouble of putting on our raincloaks when it began to pour, for we now wore them permanently. There might be above us the bluest sky and the most glorious sunshine, but we would not part with our precious garments. We never trusted the fine weather much; we knew beforehand that it was just a playful little trick of the sky.

Of course, the roads, already bad enough in the fine weather, now became impracticable. We went on as we could, slipping, skidding, sometimes getting down and putting our shoulder to the wheel up some slimy ascent, and we had to stop now and then to get water out of the ditches for our radiator, which continually exhausted what it had through the great friction which heated the engine. We had to cross pools of water that looked like ponds, and had to walk in them first ourselves, to make sure that the bottom would hold us. We went at a rate of five or six miles an hour. Night overtook us in the middle of a solitary plain. On leaving Kazan that morning, we had hoped to reach Tschebokssary, one hundred miles away; but at eight that evening we had not been more than fifty miles, so we decided to stop at the next village. The darkness, however, which fell sooner because of the covered sky, prevented us from seeing the way clearly. Suddenly the car leaned right over to its left side and stopped. We had sunk. Ettore had not seen a deep, muddy depression in the road, and two wheels had sunk into it as far as the hubs.

We looked all round for signs of a village. Nothing. We were in a little deserted valley. At the bottom of it there ran a torrent, now swollen with rain. Prince Borghese and I, leaving Ettore to look after the machine, went off to the top of the hill to see if any inhabited place came in sight from there; but nothing was to be seen. There was just the dark countryside, an undulating prairie, broken here and there by little clumps of trees: nothing else. We resigned ourselves to spending the night in the car, wrapped as warmly as we could in our furs and cloaks. The torrent roared below us. We were just coming back, when through the rushing of the water we heard the sound of wood – a rapid *ta-ta-ta*.

We stopped to listen.

'You would almost think there was a mill,' we said to one another.

But there was nothing to be seen.

We looked more closely down the torrent; we searched its banks with our eyes.

'Down there! down there!' I exclaimed. 'There's a roof – in that little clump of willows to the left of the bridge.'

We walked in that direction and soon found a path; it *was* a little mill. We went in. At the door of an *isba* was an old woman who, on seeing us, fled terrified. Two men appeared and, addressing us in anything but a friendly way, asked:

'Who are you?'

Prince Borghese explained who we were. He spoke about the car, promised them a reward if they would help us, and ended by softening their hearts and inducing them to come and look at this wonderful machine sunk in the mud.

'We shall have to go to the village,' they said, after looking carefully, 'to get more help. There are only four of us at the mill. How much are you willing to give to get the car up again?'

'Five roubles,' said the Prince.

It was a starting sum, as in a public auction.

Five roubles! The mill folk were dazed by the promise of so much riches. Five roubles! They looked at one another and exchanged a few words. They had suddenly acquired gigantic strength and the courage of lions. They wanted to have them all for themselves, those five roubles. They were ready to raise not one, but ten motor cars.

'There's no need to ask for any help from the village,' they exclaimed. 'We can do it ourselves. We have beams, planks – everything.'

They went off, came back running soon after with two more companions who had remained at the mill, and they went to work. We helped them with all our strength and with the experience we had gained. By levers and screw-jacks the machine was raised up in half an hour. By good fortune this incident had occurred on a steep slope, so we dug out the earth before the wheels, then Ettore started the engine and took the wheel, and a good push was enough to send the car off. It ran to the bottom of the valley, passed over a little wooden bridge, went down the path, and stopped exactly in the yard of the mill. The miller himself had offered us the hospitality of his house. He interrupted the work of the grinding wheel. They wanted to have a holiday that evening at the mill. The women busied themselves; there were just the two (the mother and the wife of the miller). The other men there were bachelors. They brought us some eggs, milk, and bread; they lit the fire and all the lamps of the house; one of the assistants arrived an hour later with an enormous bottle of vodka, which he had been to the village to buy. It was our five roubles beginning to turn into drunkenness.

Those big, fair men gathered round us, and began to drink our health. They swallowed glassfuls of the terrible spirit, after having crossed themselves three times with their glass in their hand, and having said a short prayer. It might have been a sacred libation: their drinking bout began with the solemnity of a rite. The women looked on, sitting aside sadly and silently. Some dirty little children played alone in a corner. A votive lamp was burning before the image of the Redeemer, hanging from one of the rough walls of the *isba*. The interior of those rough timber houses, cemented between the planks by dried musk, with a low ceiling and tiny double windows which cannot be opened, make one think of a stowing place of some ancient ship.

It was not long before the vodka produced its effect. The miller suddenly found out that he loved us; he looked at us with tenderness; his blue eyes filled with tears of emotion. How he loved us! He could not desist from telling us again and again. He embraced us one by one, reverently kissing our brows. His men expressed their approval by solemnly bowing their heads and speaking in a convinced manner. It was right to love us, they said. We *should* be loved. Their love soon extended to our country. Why had they never met Italians before? they asked one another in surprise. A most adorable people! All the blessings of heaven were called down upon our heads. The younger woman, who had a serious and almost sorrowful face, took advantage of a moment when her husband was engaged in his demonstrations of affection to carry off the big bottle of vodka without his noticing it, and to hide it away in a corner under some rags.

When we showed a desire to rest they all went out and left us alone. The women and children slept in a passage on the floor. The men stood for a long time on the floor of the *isba*, and we heard them for hours singing their sad Slav songs, as solemn as prayers. Then, when the cool night air had got the better of their drunkenness, they went back to the mill, and we heard it working again. *Ta-ta-ta* . . .

We had stretched ourselves out upon the floor. I could not go to sleep. There were big rats racing around the room. Suddenly I felt a breath of cold air upon me. I saw the door was opening gently, gently; somebody wanted to come in without being heard.

I raised myself up on my elbow and strained my eyes in the dark. From the narrow opening in the door came just a ray of light, by which I saw, or rather guessed, the person who was entering so furtively into our room. It was a woman, the younger one; I could see the white patch of her smock. After she had opened the door she stopped upon the threshold, listening. What could she be wanting? I looked at her with intense curiosity.

Reassured by the stillness, she came in. She was walking barefoot and made not the slightest sound; she seemed a shadow. She walked straight up to a corner and began to search there. Then I remembered: it was the place where she had hidden the vodka. In fact I heard, by a slight sound of glass, that she was taking the bottle. After a moment I heard the faint gurgling of liquor, long, interrupted by sighs . . .

She was drinking.

We started off again at six o'clock the next morning. The roads were dried up and were better. For long stretches we found ground like that of the steppe, and were able to go full speed upon it. We crossed Tschebokssary at the market hour. It was an old provincial town, as sleepy and restful as a retired pensioner. We passed through a village where there was a fair, striking, with its great crowd of people all dressed in black and white – a crowd that might have been in a convent. By midday we were at Wassilsursk, a pretty little town on the right bank of the Sura – a tributary of the Volga – lying at the mouth of the river, coquettish looking, amidst the green of the woods, and straggling down the slope of the hill, almost as though its little houses had been suddenly arrested in their course as they were racing one another down towards the river. We crossed the Sura by a raft, itself drawn by a tug. The road to Nijni Novgorod starts again on the left bank, two or three versts away. So on we went all day, and on, coming from time to time to the bank of the Volga, whose vast, slow windings, covered with boats, we could follow with our eye over the plain; on, over the land, still wet with rain, picturesque with its veil of mist.

In the afternoon we began to pass by comfortable-looking villas, dotted about among the woods, and we occasionally met parties of villagers. We were approaching the great city of Nijni Novgorod. About the hour of sunset we saw, far away in the distance, those vanguards of the modern metropolis: some tall factory chimneys. On the brow of the hill were standing some *iswoschiks*; when we came up to them we were welcomed with a loud cry, '*Evviva!*'

The shout came from some friendly compatriots, the Italian commercial representative in Russia (a kind of trade diplomat, Signor Fumasoni), a secretary of the Italian consul of Moscow, a consular agent, and other Italians. We were now entering within the radius of official Europe. We received our post – letters, papers, and telegrams; it was the renewing of old links. Our great loneliness was coming to an end; it *had* come to an end.

Bottles of champagne and glasses were brought out and we drank a toast, shook hands again and again, and asked for news of our world. Then we were seized with a sudden impatience, an imperious desire to come to the end, to run and run without stopping, like that legendary person who made himself two mechanical legs with which to run, and having started them is running still, because he forgot to provide them with a mechanism that would stop them.

'Aboard! Aboard!' we exclaimed.

We felt no more fatigue or sadness. All was forgotten. 'All aboard!' and shortly after the superb panorama of Nijni Novgorod was displayed before our eyes. Since Kazan we had covered about 280 miles. It was night before we entered the broad streets of the ancient capital of Russia, the 'Lower Novgorod', which was the real cradle of the great Empire. The eleven towers of its famous Kremlin, high up over the city, were still lit with the rays of the sinking sun. They showed proudly like flames above the golden cupolas and the wide towers of the town. We looked upon those eleven conquerors with a certain sense of pride, thinking that they have something Italian in them. They were built by an Italian architect, Pietro Frasiano, when the Kremlin ceased from fighting and thought it was time to adorn itself. It was around that fort that the armies which conquered Kazan from the Tartars were formed; and later on it was from there that the army started which went to expel the Poles from Moscow. The 'Lower Novgorod' must be a sacred spot for the Slav.

We had scarcely arrived before we were given an invitation. The élite of the city, headed by the governor, wished to offer us a public banquet in the open, in a large garden of the 'higher town'. The air was balmy, the sky blue. We could see the Volga, just where the Oko joined it, vast and pale, flowing in the valley below us, scattered over with a thousand lights of anchored boats, like a Milky Way spread over the earth. There was a band among the trees. We stopped there late, won over by the sweetness of the still night. During the banquet I was sent for.

'What is it?' I said to the waiter who brought the message.

'Have you sent a telegram?'

'Yes – two hours ago.'

'Well, the telegraph office send word that it cannot be dispatched. If you would like to speak to them over the telephone –'

I ran to the telephone and was put into communication with the telegraph office. My telegram could not be dispatched because it was not written in Russian.

Ever since Nijni-Udinsk I had heard no more of the preposterous objection. Fortunately for myself I had close at hand the most important person in the town, who telephoned for me, went to the telegraph office, brought the office to terms and came back triumphant. The telegram would be dispatched.

'Everybody here does what they please,' he said, by way of commenting upon the event. 'They thought the telegram was too long –'

'Ah! our good old times!'

It was long after midnight when there came a knock at the door of my room in the hotel.

'What is it?' I asked.

'Did you send off a telegram?'

I jumped out of bed in a rage and went to open my door.

'Yes,' I cried to the *maître d'hôtel*, whom I found there. 'I sent it four hours ago. Four hours!'

'Calm yourself,' said the man softly; 'your telegram has gone. It may have already reached its destination. The telegraph clerk only wants to know something –'

'What?'

'He wants to know whether the words of your telegram should be read going down the page, one under the other, or across it from left to right.'

I stood there stunned. Then I fell upon a chair, exclaiming in aggrieved tones:

'My telegram was not Chinese, nor was it in Japanese. I can swear to it. I wrote in a European language. Only Chinese and Japanese are written and read in columns down the page; telegraphed in columns, too!'

'All right, all right. I will tell him at once. From left to right, isn't it?'

'But since you say that it has already been sent off, how did they send it? How?'

'Reading it down the page, sir.'

It was ten o'clock next morning when we continued our journey. With the kindest forethought our friends had adorned our grey, peeled car with bunches of flowers. The people along the streets cheered us in a friendly manner, came out of the shops and crowded to see us. We crossed the Oko by the 'fair' bridge, the splendid wooden bridge which connects Nijni Novgorod to the *Jamarka*, the place where is held the famous fair of Sts Peter and Paul. This was two days before the fair was opened; the *Jamarka* was preparing to receive the four hundred thousand strangers who journeyed there every year. The great river was crossed by countless brightly coloured steamers and boats; it was full of sound and movement, light and songs.

Whole mountains of merchandise were piled up on the banks, crowned with a fluttering of flags; enormous boats moored to the bank supported provisional buildings, floating cafés and restaurants, all decked out and festooned with flowers; a theatre and smoking lounges, for it is forbidden to smoke in *Jamarka*. On the left bank of the Oko we crossed the vast ground where the fair actually takes place, with its six thousand stores, its shops, its market-places; a whole city sleeping during ten months of the year and flooded in the spring, of which we now saw the noisy awakening. Its strange population left off their work for a minute to crowd round our passage. There is a little of everything at the fair of Nijni; but the motor car has not yet come.

Among the serious and thoughtful Slav population we saw some strange people around us; there were many Tartars wearing a Turkish kaftan, or a blue kulmak; Kirghese, who had come from their steppes (we had met very many of them on our way), and had driven their horses for thousands of miles, bound to one another by straw ropes by which they also drew the *telega*. There were Circassians, covered with showy weapons; Persians, wearing their tall fur caps, who had come up the Volga from Astrakhan; Armenians with stern faces; Siberians from Tobolsk, laden with precious furs. Word went among the crowd that we were coming from Peking. The people looked at us with great surprise, and put us a thousand questions which we did not always understand. We passed before the splendid palace which the governor inhabits during the time of the fair. Then we entered into the Moskowskaja, the Moscow road, and came by the carts, flanked by workshops: beautiful, vast, massive, flat, and straight.

We put the machine at its greatest speed. The city and its *Jamarka* were left further and further behind, the road grew more lonely. Soon we were quite alone, and we expected to come within a minute to one of those same wretched paths which until this day had been our running track. This time, however, the path did not appear. The straight, solid road went stretching on evenly before us, and it never left us again. We had come to *the road*, the real road!

At last! After nearly 5000 miles of journeying, after forty-six long days of work and anxiety and suffering and discouragement! We had been looking for it, sighing after it ever since we came out of the Mongolian desert. We thought we should reach it at Kiakhta, then at Irkutsk. At every halt our courage had been sustained by the hope of finding it. In describing our journey I have called it road, so as to give a name to the strange and varied tracks which we followed. In point of fact we had proceeded nearly always upon untouched soil, more or less good, upon sand and mud and stones and stubble. The road was beginning only now, preceded only by the short outposts of Kazan so far away. It was beginning here at Nijni Novgorod, the memorable place which marked for us the beginning of the last stage of our journey. It seemed to us to mark the beginning of civilization.

The boundaries of Europe are not, as geographers would have us believe, and as we certainly had believed, at the Ural Mountains. No. Europe begins at Nijni Novgorod, with that straight line over which we were racing: a broad, metalled, endless ribbon which, starting from there, binds all nations together. Now, now only, did we feel as if we had triumphed over every difficulty. We should now no longer have to climb rocks, descend into abysses, bound over trunks of trees. We would no longer now sink into insidious swamps, nor should we have to find out our way with difficulty among water plants and forest trees. The road would lead us. It was our friend and our guide; it would comfort us, and accompany us to our goal.

We gave a cry of joy when from the brow of a hill we saw it running as far as the horizon, and yet there still remained in us a doubt, a vague anxiety. We had been too often deceived, and we still feared that it might disappear and abandon us; we could not grow accustomed so quickly to the idea of a change so complete and sudden, and so beautiful!

It was, perhaps, to make the change a little less radical for us and to put a certain gradation into it that even the Moskowskaja showed us a certain hostility, at least, at the beginning, with her bridges. The bridges were old and unsafe. We could hear the abhorred creaking under our wheels. Once, as we were running swiftly, one of those little bridges gave way under the weight of the car and a plank broke. Prince Borghese cried to Ettore, who was at the wheel:

'Full speed!'

The engine roared powerfully, and the car, which seemed about to stop, bounded forward on the sloping bridge. It was safe. Behind us we heard a falling of wood.

After about fifty versts we passed the confines of the territory of Nijni Novgorod; we found excellent roads and new, firm bridges.

The car leapt forward full speed. We, bending low to pass more swiftly through the air, flew over long tracts of road, tasting again after so long an interval the joy of unbroken flight. We crossed picturesque woods of beeches, of pines and birch trees, which seemed to be Crown property, for there were keepers watching over them from high wooden towers which looked like old-time engines of war. We passed cultivated land, and there fled confusedly before us villages and fields, quiet pools covered with flowering water plants, golden corn, and solitary *isbas*.

We breathed in deeply the scent of the hay, the resin and the flowers, which give out their breath to the warm air. The road runs in wonderful, long, straight stretches as far as sixty versts long. If we had not been kept back by the works over bridges under repair we would have reached Vladimir, our next halting place, at more than 150 miles from Nijni Novgorod, in five hours. We took eight hours over it.

It was the hour of the promenade when we entered into that delightful little white town under the shade of the great thick trees, in which you half feel already that you are nearing the sacred capital of the Empire. You feel this by the number of churches, of funeral monuments, and of shrines scattered over the country, where in the evening shine solitary lights, and before which the passerby bows with bended knee.

We took our rooms for the night in a little hotel. For the first time, not even our fatigue gave us the relief of sleep. Moscow was only a few hours away.

By seven o'clock next morning we were passing the turreted Vladimir gate and were speeding towards Moscow. The road, flooded with sunshine, was excellent, as straight as if it had been made by gunshots, through steppes and woods, fields, rivers, and ponds. There is in this straightness of the road something grand and hieratic: a road so wonderful as this can only lead to the supreme goal of the Holy Place of the empire.

We are spurred on by the desire to arrive soon. We fly over the country. Our car seems to understand; working evenly and silently and answering obediently to the slightest pressure of the pedal or accelerator, it bounds forward or restrains its ardour according to the movements of Prince Borghese, who holds the wheel. It balances itself lightly over the tyres with gentle, lulling movements. By eight o'clock we are crossing a little city.

The people come out of their shops, they run out from the little side streets and cheer us. Even a big, smiling policeman gives us a military salute. In passing by him, we ask:

'What is the name of this town?'

'Pokrow.'

We are greatly surprised. Pokrow lies at about eighty versts from Vladimir. If we go on at this rate we shall reach Moscow before ten o'clock. And this must not be: we are not supposed to arrive before two p.m. Why? Out of courtesy. We had received a telegram from Moscow asking what would be the time of our arrival. And the prince, accustomed to unexpected obstacles, had allowed himself ample time for all eventualities, and had replied: 'Two o'clock.' Here we are, then, obliged to hold back. We decide to while away the time by having breakfast.

Half an hour later we stop at the principal hotel of Bogorodsk. We sit down with the gravity becoming to our first return to civilized breakfasts, and we indulge in the second bottle of champagne of this journey; we had taken the first one at Tankoy. Since leaving Peking during our marches, we have never breakfasted with a tablecloth before us. We have taken our food in the car, and often have forgotten to eat altogether.

We are feeling very happy, almost childishly happy. The weather has broken up again and it is beginning to rain, but we can now laugh at the weather, and we deride this downpour. It cannot now stop our progress! It is vainly endeavouring to show us hostility too late in the day. Our obstinate old enemy is overcome.

In a moment the news of our arrival spreads through the town. The public crowd round the car in our courtyard, and stop in the road to look at us through the windows. Officers, functionaries, the more important people of the place, all come to call upon us. We receive all sorts of invitations; Prince Borghese has to protect himself, or he will run the risk of arriving at Moscow at two tomorrow! We cannot help accepting a little light refreshment in the house of a lady, the proprietress of some of the most important cotton factories of the province. She has come to the hotel in a sumptuous-looking carriage to invite us, with so much courtesy that we are not able to refuse. The workers crowd at the entrance of their factories to cheer us, as we pass on our way to the little timber villa of their mistress.

At twelve, we take our seats upon the car again and get up speed so as to make up for the stop, which has been rather too much prolonged. We are at thirty versts from Moscow when we meet two splendid mounted soldiers whom we take for Cossacks from the Kuban, picturesque-looking in their traditional Circassian uniforms, with their fine cartridge cases on one side of their tunic, a great dagger at their waistband, and high fur collar. They are standing still, facing one another, by the side of the street. As soon as we are past, they turn their horses' heads and follow us at a gallop. At every hundred yards other Cossacks guard the road in the same way, and then join the cavalcade which we rapidly outrun. It is not long before the conclusion is forced upon us that this guarding of the road is done in our honour, so that we may be sure to find the way free from any other traffic, which the sentinels keep to one side of the road. These soldiers belong to a new police regiment instituted at Moscow since the revolution of 1905.

We find a strange thing, and that is that the cart drivers are no longer angry and insulting; on the contrary, they bow to us effusively. But this is not the end of the surprises we are to encounter. At a quarter past one, on coming to the boundaries of the Muscovite territory at a place called Kordenky, we see a crowd round some shining objects, which, on our approach, we recognize as so many motor cars in a line. Other motors arrive in quick succession, tooting their horns. These are the first big cars that we have seen since we left Peking. They have come to meet us. From round them is roused a loud salute – Hurrah! We are surrounded by friends, and shake a hundred hands which are held out to us.

It is an indescribable moment.

On Prince Borghese's diplomatic countenance I see a vague shadow of emotion. We are still 2500 miles from Paris, but we feel as if we had already arrived. We are now joining our world again, our own life. This is really the close of that long break in our existence represented by the loneliness and the difficulties of this hard trial.

With our hearts somewhat full, and with our eyes reddened, not alone by the wind and rain, we got down from our car amid this brotherly gathering. The President of the Moscow Automobile Club, M. Giraud, who has been the promoter of this delightful welcome, imparts us the news of our nomination as honorary members of the club, and gives us beautiful gilt and enamel badges, which we immediately pin upon our muddy travelling caps. Then follow the introductions. We have a few minutes' conversation with the French Consul-General Lebrun; with the Belgian Consul Zenker; with the Italian Consul Dutfoi; with the Italian Commercial Agent Fumasoni, whom we had already met at Nijni Novgorod; with the members of the automobile club, of the cyclists' club, and of the Italian colony. I find myself surrounded by numerous colleagues, among whom is the correspondent of *Le Matin*, who has come to congratulate Prince Borghese on behalf of the paper he represents, and from whom came the inspiration for the Peking-to-Paris race. Here I find again my colleague of the *Daily Mail*, who is following us by rail from halt to halt, and many foreign correspondents. There are some ladies; one of them, by way of a most delicate gesture, places a bunch of roses upon our car, almost as if to fête the machine too, to which the triumph of our arrival is so largely due. The president of the automobile club offers us refreshment in an *isba* close by – a rough little wooden house, whose inhabitants watch this unusual and elegant invasion with the greatest astonishment.

'To Moscow! To Moscow!' we cry.

At two o'clock we continue our way, followed by all the motor cars.

The fantastic spectacle of this cortège recalls to my mind another swift cortège; the one which followed our car when we took the Chinese Governor of Mongolia about the streets of Urga. And I see again, in my mind's eye, the furious galloping of those fierce Mongolians, with their many-coloured clothes and their conical-shaped hats, which made us feel as if our car were being pursued by all the barbaric populations of Asia. Here it is *we* who represent the barbarians, dirty as we are, covered with dust and with mud, travelling on a rough, dull car of the colour of the earth, also coated with mud, and laden with old ropes and chains and rusty spades. Behind us there is a shining of the furbished metal and of varnished, aristocratic motor cars, over which blow about in the wind summer dresses, all fresh and festive with feathers and flowers and ribbons and veils. Suddenly there appears upon the horizon our first vision of Moscow.

It is a sparkling of gold domes over a white, diaphanous expanse of buildings; an amazing apparition, like a dream.

We arrive in its suburbs, so full of factories, bristling with tall factory chimneys. These are new suburbs, full of the sound of labour, surrounding the ancient quiet of the sanctuary.

What is happening? A great crowd appears down the street. It is all the workmen running out of the factories by hundreds and thousands, both men and women. The windows are all crowded. From the suburban railway line, which we cross too, more crowds of men come running. What is happening?

When we come close to them, we understand. A formidable cheer greets us. This is the salute of the people, rung out by the great voice of the multitude. The salute is renewed, and spreads. It follows and accompanies us. We are not aware of having deserved it; but our soul is filled by the impetuous wave of this popular emotion. We hear the Italian cry, '*Viva l'Italia!*' There is loud clapping. In the public trams the passengers stand up and wave their caps. Coachmen and omnibus conductors, even policemen, salute us.

Prince Borghese can scarcely refuse to answer with a gesture of his hand, and he murmurs in the meanwhile, full of surprise:

'But what is it, after all, that we have done?'

We cross in this manner the suburb of Novaya Andronovka, and we pass under the Ragoiskaja barrier. There is a special cordon of police to keep the road clear before us; swiftly we plunge into the heart of the city, where we find stillness. The greetings offered to us here are noiseless. Over the great boulevard we arrive finally at the proud, ancient walls of the Kremlin. Here no one knows us, and people stop, looking on with a questioning expression, watching our cortège, and surely surprised to see so many beautiful motor cars preceded by one so old and dirty, driven by people dirtier still.

We alight at the hotel and fall immediately into a kind of captivity. The race committee takes possession of us. They wish to fête us, and two days at least are necessary for the accomplishment of the necessary ceremonies. Our fatigue prevents us from rebelling against the committee's ukase.

'Well,' we say to one another, discussing the future programme, 'let us stop. We will try not to yield to the seduction of further rest anywhere else. We will make one long spin from Moscow to Paris.'

And what about St Petersburg? St Petersburg, too, is expecting us. The itinerary of our race, it is true, did not include the Russian capital. It is too far from the straight course. By having taken the Perm route and by going to St Petersburg, we are adding considerably to the length of our course. But the St Petersburg committee has arranged the distances between our supply depots, has provided us with road maps, has organized numerous sub-committees in the big towns to welcome and refresh us. It has certainly done us more service than any other committee, and we could not now refuse its invitations. We must then go to St Petersburg, but we also must not remain there more than a few hours, for there is Berlin to reach, and from Berlin we have had invitations by telegram ever since we reached Tomsk . . .

Moscow gave us all the dinners, suppers, and breakfasts we had missed during our journey. Our constitution, which had withstood the strain of so many labours and privations, began now to give way under the reaction of this welcome which we could not oppose, so great was the cordiality with which it was offered to us. We were the guests of the Italian colony, who insisted upon presenting us with some valuable souvenirs, certainly in no sense necessary to impress indelibly upon our minds the memory of these moments.

We were also the guests of the automobile club, of the Italian consul, of old and new friends. We drank toasts, listened to orchestras and concerts and songs, passed through all the best and most renowned restaurants of Moscow, from the Métropole to the Hermitage, from the Mauritania (hidden in the thick shade of the Petrowsky Park, and famous for its cosmopolitan choruses) to the elegant Yard, where the concerts begin at midnight and end at sunrise with the break of day.

All the cars in Moscow were placed at our disposal for us to see the city and its picturesque surroundings.

Thus, we were taken to see the sunset from the historical Vorobievy Gory, the 'Sparrow Mountain', on which Napoleon is said to have stopped to admire the wonderful panorama of Moscow on the evening of 14 September 1812. The sun lit up this superb, immense city as with a light of fire, its gilt domes gave out fiery flames; everything was merged in a light which seemed unreal. The spectacle was sublime. We were taken to see the celebrated Moscow trotting races on the magnificent racecourse, which is the finest in the world. From the monumental grand stand, we followed the phases of those endless competitions between Russian and American horses; competitions which take place every day even in the winter, when the track is covered with snow and the horses are harnessed to some swift sledges. In short, we were made to live during those few hours the singular and manifold life of this unique city: the true capital of Russia without mysteries; both modern and ancient, a working city and a sacred one, whose amusements are not interrupted by the present 'state of small siege', which causes you to see guards watching over the movements of grand private carriages, armed with rifles and with their bayonets fixed, while Cossack patrols pass by with their carbines at their side, trotting between the carriages.

It is not rare to see over the great roads all the carriages draw aside at a sudden order given by the guards, and a line of three or four carts, preceded, flanked and followed by Cossacks, passing by swiftly. They are only convoying the money belonging to the State; danger has raised the rouble to sovereign honours.

In the meantime, the car had performed its *toilette*. It had been well washed and cleaned. It had also been carefully looked over, but there was no need of doing anything else to it. The examination of its machinery had been witnessed by motorists, sportsmen, newspaper correspondents, chauffeurs; this examination had taken place in the garage of the Hotel Métropole. Even we were surprised to find that even the parts which usually have to be frequently changed in a car, because they are by the nature of their work subject to exceptional wear and tear, were intact; e.g., the sparking-plugs; the little eccentric cams which revolve from 1200 to 1400 times a minute; the inlet valves, which rise and fall from 2400 to 2800 times a minute; the change-speed gear, and the bearings and the transmission shaft, which many judges believe to be less strong than a transmission chain.

The only thing that had to be changed was the wheel made by the moujik between Perm and Kazan, because it was found that it was badly centred and was straining the tyres.

We were sorry to leave it behind. We owed a great debt of gratitude to that big wheel.

XXI

WE LEAVE RUSSIA

~~~~~~~~~~

On the Way to St Petersburg – Novgorod – In the Imperial Parks – St Petersburg – Towards the Frontier – Unexpected Hospitality – The First German Salute – Königsberg – Approaching Berlin

On the morning of 31 July, at four a.m. precisely, our car left the garage at the Hotel Métropole, looking much more slender through a notable diminution of baggage. We were leaving in Moscow the exploring outfit which had made our car look so singular: we were leaving behind the ropes, chains, pails, spades, and pickaxes.

In the course of our progress we had dropped little by little all useless and heavy things. We had left two mudguards at Kalgan and two over the Mongolian prairies; we had scattered provisions of corned beef and iron tools. We had dropped our ballast, like balloonists, for the sake of lessening the strain upon the springs. On leaving Moscow the car carried a few spare tyres and a few of our personal belongings. It had put on an air of resolve. It seemed to have stripped like an athlete for a race.

Followed by the escort of other motor cars, we swiftly crossed the not yet silent town. Dawn is an hour of great movement in Moscow, when people are returning from restaurants and concerts: thus we received on our departure the farewells of the people who play, after having been welcomed on our arrival by the greetings of the people who work. Out of every carriage that passed by us men with white ties saluted us warmly; from the club balconies we received ovations. We passed through the elegant Twerskaja Gate near the Smolensk station, and we entered into the St Peterburgkoje Avenue, over which the versts are no longer marked by numbered sign posts, but by monumental obelisks. To our right spread the Petrowsky Park, where carriages, returning from more distant cafés, still passed us. In those carriages we saw showy fashions somewhat dishevelled, and top-hats balanced somewhat uncertainly on nodding heads. Greetings came to us still, hoarse but cordial. We were immediately recognized, by the strange shape of our machine, which was known through the illustrated papers, and by the Italian flag, which floated from our car.

Over the silent, severe landscape was a veil of mist; then, with the rising of the sun – a dim, pale sun it was – the mist became thicker. We ended by being unable to see anything beyond the actual borders of the road. We were travelling through a grey fog, in which even the other cars near us were hidden from our sight.

At six o'clock, the sun begins to pierce here and there through the gloom; the horizon appears, flat and endless. We see white church spires above the green of dimly outlined woods, then little by little everything grows clear again; we find unchanged the same landscape which has accompanied us for weeks. We reach the little city of Klin, for the most part built of timber; we exchange rapid farewells with the other cars which have caught us up, and then continue our race alone, listening to the even, slight rhythm of the engine, and enjoying the cool morning air.

At eight o'clock we come to another town with the characteristic oriental outline of gilt or blue or many-coloured domes. It is Twer, the city of the forty churches, the point of departure for navigation on the Volga. The crowd stops to look at us. We receive good wishes and greetings from them as we pass. And now we cross the Volga for the second time, over a new and splendid suspension bridge. But this Volga is so much smaller and more modest than our first friend, that we can scarcely recognize in it the immense river of Nijni Novgorod and of Kazan: as broad as an arm of the sea.

Towns and villages and prosperous monasteries, isolated among pine woods, vast steppe-land and fields, all pass in rapid succession; we have a long road before us, so we are going at a high speed. We want to spend the night at Novgorod, nearly 300 miles from Moscow. Some peasants, busy with the harvest in a little field, come running upon the road when they see us from afar, holding their scythes up in the air. One of them, a fair-headed youth, cries to us:

'Are you from Peking?'

'Yes.'

Then all of them wave their caps and shout, 'Hurrah!'

We smile. That prerogative of finding an amusing side to every event, and that light-hearted scepticism, a little irreverent sometimes, which are a constant feature of the Latin character, begin now to blend with our emotion.

We reach Torshok at ten o'clock, and there find fuel awaiting us. The prepared distribution of supplies was to have come to an end at Moscow, because, in organizing it, Prince Borghese, although uncertain what road he would follow, was sure that he would easily find fuel between Moscow and Paris. The Nobel firm, however, when questioned by telegram, had taken upon itself the responsibility to send us some more regular deposits from Moscow to the Russian frontier.

At the entrance of the town, there are men on the road, awaiting us with barrels of petrol and of lubricating oil. In a few minutes we fill our tanks and are off again.

This is the first time that we run on at high speed over such a long stretch of road. We are going at thirty miles an hour. We are urged by an ever stronger desire to hasten. The versts fly past. We consult our maps, and reckon up our distances. We pay comparatively little attention to the landscape; yet we notice that now it is changing and becoming picturesque. The country houses take on a more characteristic aspect. They begin to be adorned with wooden sculptures, and with more elaborate windows; they are covered with traditional designs of ancient Slav art; in some cases there is a medieval wealth of ornament about them. But we have no care except for the road, almost as though we would fly over it before the machine can do so.

But, alas, as soon as we are out of the province of Twer, the road changes for the worse! We have to slacken our speed until we are reduced by a sudden, violent storm to covering only fifteen miles an hour. This is the daily storm. To think that not a drop of rain fell whilst we were stopping at Moscow!

Roads, landscapes, medieval houses disappear; all is rain around us, just as in the morning all was mist; a rain which is not going to leave us till we reach Novgorod on the banks of the Volkhof, near the still and vast lake of Ilman. No town has yet produced upon us the same impression of sadness as Novgorod now does. You would think that it wears mourning for its lost power and glory. There is a Russian proverb still extant: 'Who can fight against God and Novgorod?' In this world, alas, a few words last longer than an empire!

We have only one regret, that of covering some ground that takes us no nearer to our goal; for we are now running northwards, and this diversion to St Petersburg represents a real interruption of the journey; we are deviating from a straight line. Here at Novgorod we come into the regions of the clear northern night again, but it is now reduced to a pallor like that of a moonlit night. This light shows through the windows of our rooms at the hotel until the morning. We can hear the rain fall over the sleeping town . . .

*

It is still raining when we leave Novgorod at six a.m. a fine, persistent rain, coming relentlessly down from the wintry sky. The road has become all muddy through it.

We cross the Kremlin, around which the sparsely populated little town presses as if for shelter, as if it were still seeking the protection of the strong crenellated walls; and we depart from Novgorod by the Bolshaia Petersburgskaja, the 'Great St Petersburg Road', and we find ourselves at last in the open country.

We endure long hours of ennui silently, with the rain beating down upon us, but comforted a little by the thought that St Petersburg is near. Soon we begin to find little villas, gardens, parks, all the signs heralding the approach of a great metropolis. Then we see a dense, low, black cloud of smoke on the horizon. That comes from the factories. A milestone tells us that we are at twenty versts from Tsarskoe Selo. It is now eight o'clock, and we have covered twenty versts in two hours.

Suddenly we come up to a car standing still in the road. It is waiting for us, and has been sent to guide us. It bears, in large characters, the words 'Peking – St Petersburg'. This is a little 12-hp racing car, capable of going at a good speed, and which has come from Paris driven by its proprietor, M. Efron, one of the most active members of the automobile club of St Petersburg. It has come from Paris, and tells you so, to make sure that you know it.

A rapid exchange of greetings takes place, and then we follow our guide through the large avenues which lead towards the seat of the empire. The rain has ceased.

We cross the ground reserved for military reviews, which has rung so often with the sound of Cossack voices while the regiments filed at a gallop before the emperor, shouting the song of loyalty. Today it is deserted, lifeless, sad . . . We plunge amid the green of the parks. We cross little lakes, pass along flowery gardens where the colours are all the brighter for the rain that has fallen. Amid the trees we catch a glimpse of the beautiful Imperial Villa, guarded by sentries. We run silently over the sand of the road, and the cars fly in mutual pursuit.

We meet a group of mounted Cossacks of the imperial guard; the officers recognize our car and salute us. We come out of the parks, and are running towards St Petersburg, when, at a turning, we are stopped by an enthusiastic shout of 'Hurrah!' A line of cars is awaiting us. We alight, and are immediately surrounded by a joyous crowd. We shake hands with the Italian military attaché, who has come to bring the ambassador's congratulations to Prince Borghese.

Other cars arrive in continual succession, bringing us fresh greetings.

We are a little early. All the motorists had agreed to come to this place to meet us on our arrival, but we have come in before the time, and are witnessing what should have been their preliminary gathering. We were expected at one o'clock, and instead of that it is not yet midday. As happened in the case of Moscow, Prince Borghese's calculations, on being requested by telegram to state the hour of his arrival, have proved too . . . too Siberian! We have arrived so soon that, in order to keep the programme of events more or less as it stands, our friends actually beg us to go back a little.

So, instead of continuing for St Petersburg, we re-enter the shady avenues of the imperial park, followed this time by all the other motor cars. The task of showing us the way has been assumed by a motor belonging to the automobile club, and this car flies a kind of signal banner. It is a strange coincidence; this banner is white, with a red disc in the middle: it is, in fact, the Japanese flag. Our lively procession advances till it comes to the little station of Tsarskoe Selo, where we all come to the decision that one best way of spending the time will be to take lunch.

We invade the buffet: toasts are given, and champagne flows.

At two p.m. we decide it is time to return towards St Petersburg, and we are off.

An enormous public motor bearing the representatives of the Italian colony has broken down, and is waiting for us on the road, lying halfway across it. While we pass by, loud, hearty shouts of 'Viva!' come from this car, and the echo of them follows us until we reach the neighbouring black suburb of Putilov, roaring with the sound of its smoky and immense metal foundries, so sadly famous. When these factories are not working, it means that there is a mutiny in St Petersburg.

We enter the capital by the Narva gate – the gate where most of the famous massacres took place. We go down through the Peterhofsky Avenue. The trams stop, the crowds wave greetings to us from the pavements; from the car which heads our procession comes the lusty sound of bagpipe tunes, played on an instrument with four notes. Now we come to the heart of the town, to the Great Morskaja, the fashionable part of St Petersburg, and to Maria Square, where stands the monument of Nicolas I, guarded by hoary veterans wearing the ancient uniform of the Grenadier Guard. The cathedral of Isaac towers above us with its imposing mass of granite, and we run by the foot of it towards the Square of Peter the Great, where the crowd presses around us and impedes our progress for some moments. We are in the heart of St Petersburg, and in the heart of the Empire, among the palaces of the

Holy Synod, of the senate, of the war office, and of the admiralty – the seats of Russia's power. This is one of the grandest places in the world, and I have never felt its grandeur as I feel it now, when I came to it almost suddenly from the endless, unpeopled, grey land of the steppes.

We continue our way along the Neva. We see on the opposite bank of the vast river, the high, bold, pointed, gilt steeples of the cathedral of Sts Peter and Paul, rising beyond the bastion of the citadel of the political prison by the same name. We pass near the reddish Winter Palace, then we break out into the Nevsky Prospekt – the great artery of the town – and amid the pressing crowd of carriages and trams we reach the grounds of the Automobile Club. As soon as Prince Borghese sets foot to the ground, a member of the club pronounces the traditional form of welcome, and offers him bread and salt, according to the ancient Russian custom, as a sign of hospitality. A great crowd of people comes round us and cheers.

So the ceremony is finished, and we are allowed to withdraw from popularity and to become private people in the Hotel Europa. But for a few hours only; a great banquet awaits us . . . !

It is the morning of 2 August, and we have left the capital since 4.30, with the same cheering as a farewell which was granted us as a welcome. We are still a little dazed by our early rising, as we have had only three hours' sleep.

We cross at high speed the city of St Petersburg, which is now deserted and hidden under the veil of its endless mist, and we retrace our steps over the road of yesterday, which we remember so full of crowd and movement and of sound. The streets seem larger in this stillness. We go out through the Narva Gate, pass again through the Putilov suburb, and then make our way straight towards Gattschina to the south, following a broad road, flanked, as all roads are in the immediate neighbourhood of St Petersburg, by little woods and chalets, which make the outlying districts of this town look like one great park.

Half an hour later, turning back, all we can see of the great city we have left is a few sharp spires piercing the rosy mist and lit by the first rays of the sun.

At six o'clock we cross Gattschina, a little new, clean, tidy, silent town. It seems built by order and neatly bedded out, so symmetrical is it. We just catch a glimpse of the famous castle which is the favourite residence of the dowager empress: around it are grouped buildings that look like barracks, as if they were mounting guard.

We go at a good pace, profiting by the fair weather and the good road. But suddenly, towards ten o'clock, there rises again from the west the same wind which has pursued us from the day on which we entered Russia at Kiakhta. Thick black clouds rise on the horizon. We put on our cloaks, preparing for the downpour which, alas, does not give us long to wait, and which comes in a torrent, accompanying us with more or less persistence during the whole day! We are obliged to slacken our speed owing to the mud, and also because the rain, at the moment of its severest fall, beats against our faces so strongly that it gives us real pain, as if it was of hard hailstones. This is due both to the speed of our travelling, and to that of the wind.

Suddenly, an incident occurs which stops us completely: the right back spring breaks! It is partly the fault of the Kazan steel, which has not been well tempered for the work, and partly our own fault, for we have heaped up the weight of all the spare tyres at the back of the car, thus increasing the strain on the springs to excess. At Moscow we did take the precaution of providing ourselves with a spare spring. But now, at the moment of substituting it for the broken one, we found that it is too short by an inch or two. I do not know by what miracle Ettore achieved it, but I do know that he pulls in some way a spring hinge at the back of the chassis, and succeeds in putting on the shorter spring. It is somewhat strained, it is working under somewhat abnormal conditions, and gives way more than the other spring does, but still it allows us to continue our journey. In order to diminish its work as far as possible we move the spare tyres and the luggage to the back seat (*my* seat), and here we are again, all three of us as we were in Mongolia and in Trans-Baikalia, sitting in the fore part of the carriage – the seat on the step being brought into honour again.

We cross Luga, scattered over graceful pine woods: a town which seems composed of little villas almost hidden among the trees, a picturesque, attractive little place. It might be a town of people all in search of quiet and sheltered places of refuge – a haven for lovers. In the afternoon we reach Pskow, surrounded by thick woods.

On the road some people are awaiting us. We find there the kind governor of the town, who invites us, some gentlemen who offer us a brief stay in the country at a neighbouring castle, and a number of good people who do all they can to persuade us to stay at least to dinner, at least to drink our health. It is impossible; it is getting late. Russian hospitality is such that, if we accepted all the invitations we are offered, we should not reach Paris for many years to come.

We continue, getting up speed again whenever the rain abates its violence. We mean to spend the night at Dwinsk, five hundred versts from St Petersburg. And now we perceive that today is a holiday all over the province. The peasants in their Sunday best return singing from the villages to their scattered houses. We meet long trains of carts crowded with women dressed in showy colours. These vehicles already resemble more the German carts than the Russian *telegas*. The horses harnessed to them carry also a little saddle, over which their drivers are seated like postilions. The latter cry, flick their whips, and sing. We see types of Letts, of Poles, and of Jews. We are rapidly leaving the older Russia behind us. In many villages the Orthodox Church is confronted by the Catholic Church, and then a little further on, in many other villages, the Catholic Church, with its Gothic spires, stands alone. The Muscovite domes, with their oriental outline, become scarce.

During a short stop which we are obliged to make to change a tyre, we offer cigarettes to the peasants who have gathered round us. This is the greatest present you can give a moujik, for the moujik is an incorrigible smoker, who, unable to indulge in the extravagance of buying cigarettes, smokes the most horrible tobacco, wrapped up in bits of paper which he always carries in his pocket. He finds an old newspaper very acceptable for this purpose. But to our great surprise these special peasants refuse our gift. They belong to the sect, until lately so badly treated, of the 'True Believers', a kind of iconoclastic, puritanical sect which has taken refuge here *en masse*. We have already met co-religionists of theirs, but exiled in Siberia. We are thus nearly out of the land of orthodoxy; we are among people who seem to have been pushed back to the gates of the Empire. Near the boundaries are the hated races; you might think they have settled here so as to be ready for flight.

Evening comes, and we are seventy versts from Dwinsk. Our fatigue daunts us and we would like to stop, but the country around us is deserted.

Near a solitary wood we find a luxurious motor car standing still. A liveried servant, seeing us arrive, comes forward from that motor, signs us to stop, and offers a letter to Prince Borghese. The letter is from a rich proprietor of the neighbourhood, who offers us hospitality. The car which is there waiting has been sent to pilot us. We accept, and are soon running along the avenues of a beautiful park. We come to a little group of comfortable-looking villas, surrounded by gardens all abloom on the banks of a beautiful shady, quiet little lake.

Our host is an engineer, a Pole named Kerbedy, the promoter and constructor of the Trans-Manchurian Railway, and director of other great railway companies. As in a dream we see ourselves transported from the rain and mud of the road to warm, comfortable apartments. We are waited upon by liveried servants and made happy by the smiling cordiality of this hospitable family, who (and this is the best surprise of all) speak to us in good Italian.

And we speak of Italy, and so, of course, of sunshine.

In the most wicked December weather we continue our journey again next morning, 3 August, at four o'clock, shivering with cold, under a fine, continuous drizzle.

Dwinsk is still asleep when we traverse it. How sad these silent cities are, as we visited them during their sleep! They seem dead; we shall never know what they really are like. The only picture we have of them in our minds is one of desolation.

We cross the vast Duna by the railway bridge, which is used for trains, but also for carriages and foot passengers, and we enter the splendid military road of the frontier. Here is one practical advantage of war. The nations, in order to be ready to fight, lay out near their boundaries the most beautiful roads. Here we find the way so good that, notwithstanding the persistent rain, we are able to go at twenty-five miles an hour.

The impressions of this day of our journey can be described by two words – storms and crosses. Every half hour it looks to us as if the blue were coming, and then instead a great storm breaks out, blinding, and so violent that it is difficult to hear ourselves speak. The wind howls among the foliage of the trees along the road, and the rain pelts down in a perpendicular line. And over the landscape you see nothing but enormous crosses. Crosses by the pools, in the fields, at the entrance of the woods, at the approaches of the towns. These crosses are sometimes richly sculptured, adorned with naïve coloured reliefs. They stand in these places as the solemn affirmation of the Catholic faith of the Poles and Letts, an affirmation occasioned by the religious persecution they have suffered. A faith is always strengthened by persecution, and these people once raised their crosses, as men raise their flag on the battlefield.

By four p.m. we are in sight of the bastion which crowns the fortifications of Kowno. By these military works we feel the approach of the frontier line. They stand almost like sentinels, watching the movements of the stranger.

Now Kowno, with its little red roofs, suddenly appears before us from the top of a hill; we see it lying softly along the green banks of the Njemen. The city is full of hotels called by Italian names: Hotel Venezia, Hotel de Naples, Hotel d'Italie. I do not know the reason of this strange love of Russian hotel-keepers for my native country.

Along the road we meet a car, surmounted by a white flag covered with Polish words, and crowded with gentlemen, who shout warm

'*Vivas*' to Italy. They are Polish journalists who have come on purpose from Warsaw to meet us, and wish to accompany us as far as the frontier. They are giving vent to their feelings by cheering Italy, partly because of the sweet taste of forbidden fruit which this shouting gives them. Italy is worshipped in Poland because it was an enslaved nation, but has revolted and fought, and is now free. Our colleagues tell us at once of their 'adventure with the flag'. It is forbidden in Poland to carry a flag without a special permit from the police, so the gendarmerie had stopped this car, demanding to be shown the permit for that white standard.

'But it is not a standard,' answer the Polish journalists.

'Then what is it?'

'It is a shop sign. Are shop signs prohibited?'

'But it looks like a flag.'

'It *looks* it because it is a sign made of cotton instead of being made of wood or tin.'

'What do these words mean?'

'Read them.'

'They are in Polish. We do not know Polish.'

'We are very sorry. In Poland we talk Polish. If you come here you ought to know it.'

'Very well, what are your names? You shall be called to account to the police for this offence.'

The inscription upon the banner reads simply 'Warsaw Automobile Society'.

Whilst we went towards the hotel a panting officer caught us up.

'Kniatz Borghese!' he cried. 'Come, I entreat you! Madame the Governoress awaits you at the charity fair of the Red Cross.'

A charity fair was taking place under the high patronage of the governor's wife in a garden not far away, and that kind lady had thought of increasing the takings of the fair by showing our car and ourselves for the modest entrance fee of ten copecks. The idea was, no doubt, excellent; but we refused as politely as we could, and withdrew to our hotel.

We had come 520 miles from St Petersburg, and we were at a few hours from the Russian frontier. In a very short time our surroundings were rapidly changed: manners, tongue, and customs – all was different. Accustomed for more than a month to travel amid the interminable sameness of the Russian land, we felt as if we had covered in the last few hours an immeasurable stretch of road.

It seemed scarcely possible that at dawn the day before we were running along the Nevsky Prospekt. St Petersburg seemed already far away among the memories of the past.

Twenty-four hours later, the Russian Weirzbolow, the neighbouring German Wirballen, Königsberg, Elbing, Marienburg, Stargard – all these cities had passed before our eyes in rapid succession, in a confused phantasmagoria. We were only a short day's march from Berlin. We had travelled nearly 270 miles that day. Our good 'Big Beast', as we called it among ourselves, had bounded on at thirty miles an hour over the excellent Prussian roads. This was unlooked-for speed. We seemed to find in our machine an intelligent haste, a powerful desire to reach the winning post, to devour at one fell swoop the last few thousand miles which separated us from the goal.

We had left Kowno in the early dawn. A few stars still shone in the firmament, and a slender crescent of the moon shone blandly over the domes of the cathedral. But our haste in leaving before it was day was ill rewarded. In the darkness we and our Polish friends with their car and their flag mistook the road and got lost among the labyrinth of the fortifications, being driven back from one sentinel to the other. About four a.m. we at last found the right military road to the frontier. It looked so strange a road, with its great chalked stones symmetrically disposed among the grass pavements or among the trunks of the trees, that it seemed lined with tombs. By six o'clock we had covered the ninety-four versts which separated us from the German Empire. There stood Weirzbolow, the last Russian city!

We had taken forty-one days to cross the Empire of the Tsar, on whose soil we encountered the worst obstacles of our journey. We left it now without regret but not without a certain affection for it. Many a time we should have been obliged to get down to abandon the car, and renounce all our plans, if we had not always met with goodness, patience, and hospitality from the people around us. We could not think of the most critical moments of our journey without the serene, majestic, gospel-like image of a moujik arising before us, with his fair beard, his long hair – always helping us out of some difficulty, saving us from the mud, or from the swift current of a river, or sometimes from hunger.

The frontier between Russia and Germany is marked by a little bridge. Two coats of arms face one another, one at each end of the bridge. They are supported by poles, painted with the national colours. The two eagles confront one another, one double-headed. A chain is drawn across the entrance of the bridge. We stop.

Our passports are examined in a moment. Orders sent by telegram have prepared everything, so that we shall have no trouble. The Russian customs-house grants us immediately the necessary certificate. We start again.

The chain is lowered before the car, which advances slowly and solemnly between two empires. The *gorodovois* that are mounting guard give us a rigid military salute. The chain is drawn up again noisily after us. We are in Germany.

Two German policemen, wearing their spiked helmets, salute. Immediately we hear the roaring of a motor engine approaching us, amid the festive sound of horns. Three cars come up swiftly over the German road. In a moment they are near us; they stop, and we receive from them the first Teutonic welcome, a three-fold German '*Hoch!*', rising up in unison from ten voices, while ten caps are waving in the air. These are members of the Imperial Automobile Club of the Königsberg branch. We reply with some emotion. From this moment we are under the aegis, as it were, of the imperial club, which accompanies us with its protection from town to town, and offers us the great assistance of a cordial and friendly greeting.

At Wirballen, too, the customs-house formalities are gone through very quickly. A number is put on to our car, and Prince Borghese receives a regular permit for free transit over German soil, accompanied by a formal chauffeur certificate, which they grant him without examination! By seven o'clock we all leave for Königsberg, about one hundred miles off.

The road is quite wonderfully good. We fly over it in the shadow of two long lines of trees. The sun, though pale, is shining, and our machine gleams fitfully as its beams filter through the branches. We cross Stallupönen, with its vast red barracks full of helmets with sparkling spikes, then Gumbinnen, Insterburg, Waehlau, all of them little cities which we scarcely see in our flight: tidy, neat little places, looking fresh and new as if they had just been built. At last comes Königsberg, which we reach at ten o'clock. It looks elegant and picturesque with its old houses, with its gabled façades and its sharp-pointed roofs, upon whose top the friendly stork sits in motionless meditation . . . Königsberg, with piercing spires and its ancient fortifications, surrounded by drawbridges, which are now never raised. All these things pass as in a vortex before our eyes, like the vision of some enchanted land.

We are entertained at lunch in an hotel, which I do not think I could find again without guidance, by our colleagues of the Imperial Automobile Club. The crowd gather round the exit; a solemn and disciplined crowd, who salute us with a '*Hoch!*' at measured intervals: quite a choral '*Hoch!*' A little girl timidly gives us flowers and then runs away.

At two o'clock we are again under the shade of the trees in the great main road and the giddy vision of a landscape, which we have no time to register on our memory, continues.

We pass little villages, as graceful as if they had been made for some artist purposely to put in pictures; little lakes, ponds which reflect the green of the woods, and canals full of boats. Suddenly we give a great cry of astonishment; down there on the horizon is the blue line of the sea! It is the Frische Lagoon, an iridescent lake like a great shell. Far off, beyond it, is the Gulf of Danzig. In a dim blue we see boats sailing, like tiny white specks suspended in mid-air. We joyfully greet this sea, whose waters come from the Atlantic. We cry to it: 'Welcome, old sea of our land! The Pacific Ocean sends you his greetings!'

At three o'clock we pass through Braunsberg; half an hour later through the holiday-making Elbing. Everyone here is keeping Sunday by promenading about the parks. At four o'clock there stands before us a kind of medieval dream. It is Marienburg, with its fantastic-looking castle, so beloved by Kaiser Wilhelm – an impressive reflection of ages seven centuries distant – imposing, grand, and strange, half cathedral, half fort, surrounded by old houses with sloping sides which look as if they were stretching out towards the Nojat to mirror themselves in its calm waters. In a few moments Marienburg is far away behind us. It disappears. And now comes Dirschau, all modern, with its monumental bridges thrown across the Weichsel. At last comes Preussen-Stargard, a modest little town which seems to invite one to rest. It is late; the still-ness of the place is so attractive that we decide to spend the night here. We are a little less than one thousand miles from Paris.

XXII

NEARING THE GOAL

~~~~~~~~~

Visions – Landsberg – The Burden of Popularity – Berlin –
From the Spree to the Rhine – Crossing Belgium

The ancient town clock of Preussen-Stargard was striking six on the morning of 5 August when we got on our machine in the deserted square of the town.

It was late; we had not rested till so lordly an hour since leaving Moscow; but the excellent roads allowed us here to lie a little later abed, feeling quite sure that we should soon reach our next halting place. That night we were to sleep at Landsberg, about eighty miles from Berlin. A whole programme of events had been arranged on this understanding. Next morning at nine o'clock we were to reach Küstrin, where many cars of the imperial club would come to meet us and escort us to Berlin, which we were to enter at midday exactly. At one o'clock the public luncheon would take place at the quarters of the automobile club, etc.

And instead of this we found ourselves in Berlin the very same day! We travelled too fast. To keep your host waiting is bad, but it is still worse to arrive too early. We had to remedy our serious offence, which upset the whole plan of reception, and so we considered ourselves therefore as not yet arrived in that capital of punctuality. Officially, we were still on our journey towards Berlin, and the official programme remained unaltered for the morrow; only the solemn entry was irremediably *râtée*.

Our journey from Preussen-Stargard had been an exquisite pleasure. The sky was blue and brilliant. We had not had such a clear sky for a long time, having been pursued by rain for nearly six weeks! This was also the first day since we had left Mongolia that we had not suffered from the cold during the early hours of the morning. Coming swiftly towards the south, we felt ourselves plunging into the summer warmth. What a new and delightful sensation was that return to our own natural surroundings, that sweet homecoming; with what joy we put away our furs into the luggage! From six to eleven o'clock we ran continuously at the rate of forty miles an hour, rejoicing in the wonderful poetry of that countryside covered with blossoms and harvest, scattered with little woods, from which rise the sharp red roofs of villages wrapped in shadow and quietude.

I do not know how many little towns we crossed. The strange flight of things only half seen before they were gone continued around us: a confusion and chain of visions passed like a flash before our eyes during this giddy flight, which made our ears buzz with the wind.

Lines of trees, often laden with fruit, speed past by the roadside, and the road plunges sometimes into the thick of forests which remind us of the *taiga*. There were plants which, warmed by the sunshine, give out a fragrance like that of incense. We are now back again for a short tract in uncultivated land. There! a stag crosses our road bounding, with the same lithe movement as those other stags in the woods of the Urals. A few minutes later the shade breaks up and the forest disappears behind us. Our car travels over sunny fields where peasants are busy at the harvest, wearing large hats adorned with ribbons as a sign of joy. This is the pagan festival of the harvest. Great carts pass by us, laden with hay and sheaves of corn, on which are gently rocked joyous parties carrying their sparkling scythes.

We pass through Czersk, Konitz, Flatow; all villages that look like little towns, and this is one of the most striking differences between Germany and Russia, where many towns look like large villages. We pass through Deutsche-Kronen, reach Landsberg at eleven, and both these places have already a 'Berlin look' about them. While we are slowly travelling through the principal road of the town, a panting voice calls out to Prince Borghese. Someone is running after the car.

Prince Borghese recognizes his pursuer as one of the directors of the Itala firm. Hatless, out of breath, full of emotion, this man speaks to us effusively. His eyes are red with emotion. He is followed by a fairheaded colleague of the *Lokal Anzeiger*, also hatless. These two men, in a car, had spent the whole night looking for us from town to town. They had been as far as Dirschau vainly inquiring after us. Twice they must have passed under the windows of our little hotel at Stargard, where we were soundly sleeping incognito. They had at last come to believe that some terrible catastrophe must have occurred, and that we must have been annihilated with our car, when lo! from the inside of an inn they suddenly saw us pass.

The news of our presence spreads immediately to the crowd, which forms a thick hedge around us.

'It is *the Chinese!*' they cry. 'It is *the Chinese!*'

Newspaper correspondents and photographers appear as if by magic. The trams stop, and the passengers look at us through the little windows with astonishment and admiration. The conductors forget their duties, and lean out of their platforms; the police come to maintain order. As for ourselves, we, covered with dust as we are, wearing our horrible goggles (only adopted at St Petersburg), which make us look like frogs, feel so little worthy of admiration that we take refuge inside the inn, begging for beer and peace.

We decide to leave for Berlin, and by one o'clock are again flying over the open country. A few hours later we meet three cars, flying their colours. These are Berlin Italas, full of motorist and journalist colleagues. Among the latter are the correspondents of the principal papers. For whilst we were busily imbibing our beer at Landsberg, the wires have communicated the news of our arrival to the journalists of Berlin, and they are come to meet us. There are greetings and hand-shakes and shouts of '*Evviva!*' Then, altogether, we start upon our way.

We halt at a large place – Münchberg – and suddenly remember that we have not had any breakfast. So we stop at the little restaurant, and sitting in the shade of a vine trellis we devour Frankfurt sausages, drink iced beer, and face interviewers, while a whole circle of cameras stand around us, taking pleasure in registering our likenesses. An artist is sketching us from all points of view. We cannot move without irritating some photographer or other. One asks us to show our profile, another one begs us to look at him full face. We wish to leave. Not at all! We are given orders, 'Stop, one minute. So!' Popularity certainly has its draw-backs: there is a good side even to the Gobi desert.

Finally, when all slides and all films are exhausted, we become again free citizens of a free country. We resume our places upon the cars and start off. We speed towards Berlin amid a thick cloud of dust, unable to see anything before or behind us, advancing in the same way as we had done in the morning mist of Siberia, when the road, a few steps distant, was hidden from view in a grey dimness.

Anyone seeing us pass surely could not guess that the splendid motors which precede us are sisters of our own, that they come from the same hands, I would almost say, from the same family. Among these sisters, ours is a Cinderella.

We have unfurled our little flag, which for the last few days we have kept wrapped round its staff for the sake of preserving it. It is still the little modest bunting sailing flag, given to us by the Italian Marines garrisoned at Peking. It was so fresh down there, and its colours had flared up in the sunshine. Now it is torn, faded, soiled, impossible to recognize. It has lost threads in all the winds, and some colour in all the rains. And yet it is very dear to us. Its vibration, its pulsation, in the air close by us, rings in our ears like the music of a friendly voice.

By four o'clock we cross the great band of factories which surround Berlin with their high smoking chimneys, and which look, in the distance, like some gigantic naval squadron ready to sail. At last, after gardens and parks, we come to a broad road flanked at the beginning by small, almost diminutive-looking houses: the Berlinerstrasse. We run over a vast boulevard: the Frankfurterallee. The buildings around us are now majestic, the road fills with an increasingly active traffic, its life presently becomes feverish. We are in the Königstrasse, in the heart of Berlin.

Many among the crowd guess, by the strange look of our car, that we come from Peking. A few salute us. We run under railway bridges, and the trains pass shrieking over our heads. We now cross the monumental part of Berlin. Here are the Courts of Justice, now comes the Imperial Castle. We thread our way into the famous Unter den Linden, proud, aristocratic, filled with life. A crowd is in expectation before the Bristol Hotel. Above the crowd shine the knobs on the helmets of the Guards, stationed here to keep the road clear. As soon as Prince Borghese alights he is surrounded, welcomed, pressed upon, followed by the crowd which penetrates into the hotel with us, and invades the yard, the drawing rooms, the offices; till at last we succeed in reaching the lift, and are taken to the longed-for privacy of our rooms.

The banquets are kept back according to the programme. At midday on 6 August, the Imperial Automobile Club entertains us in its beautiful reception-rooms with an elaborate luncheon, which is as solemn as an official ceremony. The same evening a less severe gathering of our compatriots fêtes us with the most delightful cordiality at a dinner. Between these two ceremonies we are given refreshments (why ever are they called refreshments? Our speech really has sometimes expressions full of the most ingenious irony!) by our French journalist colleagues, who have come from Paris to meet us. Parisian hospitality and *reportage* have pushed out as far as this, and in a motor! The most important among these Parisian brethren is certainly the correspondent of *Le Matin*, M. Des Houx, who, besides being possessed with brilliant qualities as a writer, recently displayed so much religious activity in attempting to create a Gallican Church, and was, indeed, for a few days the sovereign pontiff of it. He is, of course, the leader, I would almost say the spiritual director, of this brotherly journalistic escort.

Our car, meanwhile, has a foretaste of the glory awaiting her. Crowned with flowers and laurel, she is exhibited in the large showroom of the Itala on Unter den Linden. The crowd presses round the window to see her. The door of a shop has had to be locked to prevent an invasion. The police are obliged now and then to clear the road and tell the crowd to move on.

We are supposed to find our 'Beast' there. Her unsuspected pride grieves us and moves us to indignation. She is suddenly advertising herself!

On the morning of 7 August, before the waiter of the Hotel Bristol knocked at our door to announce that the hour of departure had come, we had been awakened by the beating of the rain against our windowpanes. We now expected another long, wet day, but instead the weather, with quite unusual consideration, seems to have merely desired to water the road and lay the dust for us.

At the moment when we get on to our machine some blue shows here and there in the sky. The macadam of the vast Unter den Linden, all wet, reflects this well-promising blue. Near to our car there are the other cars of the imperial club waiting to escort us to Potsdam, also more private cars come to witness our departure, and many public motors hired by the curious. The gathering round us represents elegant motors and workaday motors, the aristocracy and the democracy of the motor car.

By five o'clock the correspondents of the French papers arrive. They mount upon three Italas bearing side placards 'Peking-Matin', which is the formula into which this brilliant organ of the Press has transformed at the last moment the usual 'Peking-Paris'. Everything is ready. The cars set off.

A warm shout of 'Hurrah!' bursts out around us. A considerable crowd has collected, chiefly composed of Italians. Several ladies have had the courage to get up at dawn; numerous gentlemen have not yet gone to bed, and come from their clubs in evening dress.

'Viva! Buona fortuna!'

The cries are repeated. We shake hands with a quantity of people who are holding out theirs. Hats and handkerchiefs are waved aloft, and now the cortège of the cars goes off swiftly over the deserted avenue, on which the trees stand like soldiers in a line through green shadows.

Now and then some of the cars, putting down their accelerators, came out of the procession to our side, to repeat their greetings and good wishes, and to throw flowers at us. We have by now learnt not to protest, and accept all homage. We are no longer even surprised, as we had been at Moscow, when we heard the first applause. We take our popularity as an unforeseen phenomenon, as an unexpected and most unmerited recompense for our past loneliness; but this atmosphere of friendliness which surrounds us touches us deeply. The brotherly benevolence of the crowd, even though undeserved, reaches our hearts. We listen with deep gratitude to this continuous, and, in a sense, solemn voice which says to us 'Welcome home!'

The disorderly groups of cars, over which German and Italian flags are floating, passes under the triumphal arch and continues along the celebrated Avenue of Victory, where among the vigorous green of the Tiergarten flash the white marbles and the statues of great and famous Germans, standing there as if they were in a line for some fantastic review, and a few moments later we find ourselves in the still, deserted streets of the outlying districts. The cars awaken the echoes of these streets with the continuous and discordant sound of their horns and trumpets, making a barbarous kind of music, like some extraordinary modern *hallali*.

Soon domes and pinnacles disappear from our sight. We enter a region of villas and gardens; Berlin with its solemn splendours is now behind us, together with St Petersburg and Moscow among pleasant far-off memories.

There are no more capitals before us until we reach Paris.

To Paris, then!

Prince Borghese presses down on the accelerator. Not all the cars can follow us. The last salutations are lost in the distance, as those who find it impossible to keep up with us send their cry after us. We are left with the cars of the automobile club which precede us, and with those of our French colleagues who follow us: seven great motor cars in hot pursuit of one another, going in a line at forty miles an hour!

At 5.30 we cross Potsdam with its low white houses, padded as it were by little green woods, standing there as if they had been put to guard better the silence which becomes an imperial residence, and surrounded by sad-looking little lakes and canals on whose clear waters heave small white yachts. We are in an aristocratic countryside which will not put up with being tilled.

But very soon the vision round us changes. We are again amid the wealth of the fields. At 6.30 we pass Brandenburg, where we meet groups of workmen arriving from their little country houses on bicycles, all pedalling hard together, with their sacks over their shoulders and their long clay pipes in their mouths. We are often obliged to slacken our pace to let little milk-carts pass, drawn by a man and a dog together.

A battery of artillery on its way to the manoeuvres now closes the road before us. For a few moments we march at the same step as the horses, among soldiers with their shining helmets, amid the sound of the artillery carriages and guns. Some of the soldiers recognize us and smile, unable to salute us in any other way without breaking the rules. They whisper something about us to their companions, who turn round; then all make way to let us pass.

Later, we meet a patrol of Hussars standing on the watch, motionless on their saddles, leaning upon their long lances reversed, so that the fictitious enemy may not see their little white and black streamers fluttering in the wind. We are evidently traversing the ground of some practice battle. Presently, we see in the distance the dust of a squadron of cavalry passing at a trot. No other soldiers are to be seen from here.

When at eight o'clock we reach Magdeburg, we are stopped by another military incident: a regiment of infantry on the march. The soldiers are singing a war hymn in a full-voiced chorus, and we feel to the depth of our souls the impressiveness of this music coming from this strong, solemn, formidable voice of an army.

One moment more and the scene is changed. We are crossing the market of Magdeburg, all bright with colour and with movement, dotted over with the white headdresses of the peasant women; an old church casts over the crowd the slender, solemn shadow of its Gothic spires.

We are not content until the gear lever is put into top and our car bounds forward, cutting through the air like a meteor. Prince Borghese wants to go as fast as possible. He intends to reach Paris on the 10th, the date fixed upon ever since we reached Moscow; but he prefers to take a few days' rest near the goal rather than to shorten our marches here. He is suddenly seized by the strange fear that now, really at *this* point of our journey, he may meet some obstacle to prevent his arriving; and he wants to make sure. All three of us have caught the fever of arrival.

The sky is darkened. At nine o'clock we cross Helmstedt with its old picturesque gates, then Königslutter, of which I only recollect the window-boxes and walls covered with green; then Braunschweig, large and noisy. Just as we are entering this town a violent storm suddenly bursts over us, and the wind rages furiously among the trees. The rain beats hard upon our faces. But as we approach Hanover the sun comes out again, hot and burning.

At a bend in the road we find some cars, and they welcome us festively. Some members of the automobile club, with many of our compatriots, have come to meet us. At two o'clock we start again amid lively cheers, after a most excellent lunch, given to us we scarcely know where or by whom, but certainly delightful.

We meet along our way a number of boys going to school with their bags under their arms, beautifully disciplined and marshalled, serious, covered with green caps. They recognize us. Evidently they read the Berlin newspapers. Everywhere, indeed, we find that boys are our most assiduous admirers. These now improvise a demonstration, divesting themselves of their gravity for a moment. Our journey must appear to these youthful imaginations enormously greater than it really has been.

We go towards Minden, which, however, we do not touch. We describe a curve near it as soon as we have crossed the Weser. Of the city itself we see no more than the gardens and the pointed roofs behind the trees. We pass small cities, villages both large and small, without even trying to find out their names upon the map, because it would interrupt the swiftness of our flight. Besides, a little vagueness of thought concerning them adds a mysterious enchantment to the things which we see. In certain small towns we descend through little streets, where high old gabled houses thrust out their upper floors over the street as if their windows and balconies were stretching towards the light. They look like medieval habitations and they bear sculptured upon their wooden façades dates of three or four centuries ago, and old proverbs, and figures of armed knights. The latter seem to look with great surprise at the swift car which passes by, breaking their long tranquillity.

At five we are at Herford, a spa with excellent mineral waters. A newspaper reporter leaps on our car and has a moment's interview with Prince Borghese. The guests of the hotel come out and applaud the prince. On all sides you see sick people in bath-chairs. One of them half raises himself painfully, and cries '*Evviva!*' All the other unfortunate men near him, seized by the same enthusiasm, cheer us, half raising themselves painfully. We smile back, but this greeting from pain and weakness to the triumph of health and strength leaves us silent for some time.

By seven we reach Bielefeld. Here we stop for the night.

Our first care is to make a simple arithmetical calculation. We spread out our maps: we measure the distances from town to town and we proceed to make an addition: the total of which wrings from us an exclamation of joy – the total is this: 425.

We are 425 miles from Paris!

Next day, 8 August, we cross the Belgian frontier at Eupen at six p.m. and we reach Liège by night. Thus in one day we pass from the Westphalia to the Rhine, and from the Rhine to Belgium. Our flight is so swift that the things round us change hourly, and the day seems to us as long as a lifetime. Impressions succeed one another so rapidly in our minds, they thrust one another back, away from the front ranks. The events of the morning seem by nightfall a far-off memory.

Perhaps this sensation is partly due to our own excitement, to some vague and unspoken eagerness which comes upon us now near our goal, now that we are expecting almost hourly the realization of many months' dreaming. Our whole mind stretches forward with a kind of longing. The highest speed seems too low for our desire, and we live not so much in the present as in the future. This is why the past fades away. There happens now with our thoughts what happens with the images which we perceive on our way; they are scarcely formed before they are hidden in a cloud of dust in our wake.

It is scarcely necessary to mention that at Bielefeld Prince Borghese was offered a banquet. I suppose that even if we had stopped in the middle of a wood, there would have immediately appeared before us a beautiful laid table and a local committee to do us honour with cordial and exquisite hospitality. In Germany every branch of the Imperial Automobile Club insisted upon welcoming us; and at Bielefeld, there being no local branch, we were met by the members of the Cologne club, who came up on a racing car. They left Cologne intending to meet us wherever we might be.

Their swift car served as our guide from Bielefeld on, but this 'guide' went with the most bewildering speed at something like sixty miles an hour and dragged on, in a furious and desperate race, both ourselves and also the other cars in which the Paris journalists were riding. The 'guide' passed on over the plain in a cloud of dust, like some apocalyptic vision.

To make up for this tremendous speed, fairness demanded that our pilot should mistake the way several times. On one occasion, near Wiedenbrück we were obliged to look for the right road driving over some fields. Thus we showed our companions a mild sample of the best Siberian roadways.

At 10.30 we were already among the hills of the Rhine, climbing up and down winding roads which spread through an uninterrupted chain of villages and boroughs, all bristling with black factory chimneys and full of the sound of machinery; a network of rails forced us to slacken our speed every moment at a level-crossing.

We come to a town over which lies a stormy-looking cloud of dense smoke: Barmen, with its mines, its foundries, lifting towards the sky enormous machinery that looks like the monstrous engines of some fabulous ironclad. How distant now are the idyllic landscapes of Prussia and Pomerania, the picturesque little cities of the Brandenburg, old and neat, in whose medieval squares you meet with gigantic and naïve statues of Roland, watching over the quiet market-places.

At eleven we suddenly see from the brow of a hill the luminous valley of the Rhine spreading before us. The magical river sparkles in a serpentine line, pale and vast below us. On its banks, in a blue mist, rises up a forest of spires and belfries. It is the city of Cologne, overlooked by the two gigantic twin pinnacles of its cathedral.

At the foot of the hill we find the members of the Imperial Automobile Club and many compatriots awaiting us. So we make a kind of triumphal entry into Cologne, with a large cortège of motor cars. We cross the swift, clear Rhine over a bridge of boats, and we run along the vast boulevard to the club house, where we find a sumptuous lunch and many toasts awaiting us. Prince Borghese has to reply with a speech, which I believe is his fiftieth speech since we came into Europe: whence may be seen that in order to win a motor race from Peking to Paris, you must be not only a motorist, but an orator as well.

At three p.m. we continue our journey. Our swift pilot car of the morning heads the start again, intending to show us the way to Aix-la-Chapelle; but near the village of Müngersdorf its flying speed causes it to assault a house, and enter it precipitately through its demolished outside wall! – fortunately, with no loss of life. I do not know exactly how the accident occurred. On arriving at the village we simply find the car overturned near a gaping house, and modest furniture showing through an enormous breach in the wall. We also find the driver all smiling, unperturbed by the wrath of the poor peasant, saying to us with a satisfied air, pointing at all the ruin:

'*Messieurs, regardez ce que j'ai fait!*'

We therefore continue our way alone.

The news of our passing has been spread by the telegraph over all the country we are crossing. In some small towns the masters have brought their school children on the road in a line, to see this car which has come from Peking: an excellent incentive to the study of geography. The children cheer us with clear, bright voices. Rows of fair-headed little schoolgirls clap their hands enthusiastically.

At five o'clock we enter the suburbs of Aix-la-Chapelle. When we stop to take glasses of fresh beer before a café the crowd gathers round us, and shout *Vivas* and good wishes. We find another guide full of good intentions, but he too mistakes the way and leads us towards Bruxelles. We notice it and leave him alone, directing ourselves towards Liège. We are now swiftly approaching the frontier. After so many enthusiastic welcomes we receive at last a less benevolent greeting. An old peasant woman, looking out from a window as we go at a footpace through her village, shakes her fists angrily at us, crying in spiteful tones:

'*I* know you, *canaille!* It was you who ran over my hen last Thursday. Pay up!'

The accusation is entirely undeserved, but we are just able to bear it, and continue our feverish advance.

And now we come to the confines, an unpretentious sort of confine, with no chain. We should scarcely notice it were it not for a modest sign post, which indicates the limit of German jurisdiction. The customs-house is at some distance from the road, and it takes us half an hour to find it.

Our entrance into Belgium has the popularity of a joke. Here for once the telegraph has not announced our arrival. The way we are to follow is not known. To those who meet us we are simply three very odd-looking creatures upon a most extraordinary motor car. Our black and dusty countenances and our ragged clothes appear exceedingly grotesque. At Verviers a portly woman, sitting outside her shop, exclaims on seeing us:

'Oh, *les laids!*'

Shortly after, a car driver also exclaims convincedly:

'Oh, *les laids!*'

And he stops his car to see us better.

It feels almost as if the cry were being passed along as a new kind of welcome. It spreads; on all sides we hear voices saying:

'Oh, *les laids!*'

We do not doubt for a moment that the exclamation is profoundly sincere. All stop to look at us, and laugh as if they were beholding the most comical carnival masque. There must be something singularly humorous in the contrast between our looks and our means of loco-motion: no doubt we look like three beggars riding in the king's car.

The children run after us: they can easily follow us, because here cities and villages are so frequent that we are scarcely for a moment out of sight of houses, and there are numerous placards up, enjoining motorists to drive slowly.

At a certain point a policeman, whose suspicions have been aroused by our strange appearance, stops us and looks at us severely. An exquisite bit of dialogue ensues between Prince Borghese and him:

'Who are you?' he asks the prince, who is at the wheel.

'I am Prince Scipione Borghese,' replies the prince with deference.

The policeman, who has not the slightest doubt that he is being made fun of, puts on a terrible frown and thunders:

'You! you – a prince – *you?*'

Prince Borghese makes a gesture, as if to say, 'Alas, I cannot help it!'

'It is not true!' continues the policeman with great energy. 'You are a Belgian chauffeur – *I* know you!'

He knew us, too – like the old lady with the hen!

'*I* know you – do you understand? And I will immediately summon you for excess of speed. You know the regulations – eight miles an hour,' and he pulls out his notebook, licks the point of his pencil, and commands:

'Your name and address?'

Prince Borghese, quite calm, replies:

'Prince Scipione Borghese. Address: Palace Borghese, Rome.'

'What! again? *Assez de plaisanteries*. Show me your papers.'

The papers are taken out and shown. The policeman examines them and exclaims with a deeper frown than ever:

'They are not yours. You are a chauffeur. Why pretend to be a prince? . . . In that get-up! Are you ashamed to be a chauffeur? *Chacun gagne son pain comme il peut*. Where do you come from?'

'From Peking.'

'From . . . Peking . . . Borghese . . . Ah!'

The policeman's face is illuminated by a ray of intelligence. He remembers, now: he understands. He falls into an attitude of deep regret. He passes from severity to deference, salutes and says obsequiously: '*Passez, Monseigneur, bon voyage*.'

Half an hour later we enter Liège, just as the street lamps are being lighted.

XXIII

PARIS

*Along the Banks of the Meuse – On the French Frontier –
Rheims – Relic Hunters – Meaux – A Sleepless Night – The
Last Hours – At the Gates of Paris – On the Boulevards –
The Race is Ended*

At Liège we discover that our motor car is being gradually covered by
signatures, like an album: signatures written in pencil over the fuel tank,
over the spare parts chest; nearly all of them unknown names, followed
by the dates of Moscow, St Petersburg, Königsberg, Berlin. Ettore in
cleaning the machine has respected these writings, which represent so
many sympathetic good wishes and so many modest attestations of
friendship from people whom we had never seen before and shall never
see again in our lives.

Ettore does not cease one moment from tending and caressing his car,
which indeed owes it largely to those caresses and those cares that it has
come so far. Ettore never leaves it now: he sleeps by its side. His love has
become jealous. He confesses that he thinks only with pain of the
moment when he will have to part with that machine.

At 5.30 a.m. on 9 August, after examining again the screws, the
mechanisms, and the tyres, Ettore starts the engine, the prince takes the
wheel, and we are off for Namur. We cross Liège swiftly through the
roads still clear of traffic, as far as the Meuse, from whose banks
commences the most enchanting part of our journey. We coast the
beautiful river for about ninety miles.

Under a clear fine sky the Meuse is clear too, and its shimmering
waters reflect as in a picturesque mirage the thick green of the hills, the
arches of the bridges, the rigging of boats and yachts. The Meuse has
sudden bends which make it seem no longer a river, but rather a long
lake in a park, broken here and there by the thick shadow of clouds of
smoke given out by the numerous coal-mines which surround it and
which are always like a volcano in eruption.

Paris lies a little under 250 miles away.

At a quarter past six we traverse Huy. At ten minutes past seven we are at Namur, overshadowed by the white walls of its ancient citadel, and climbing up a hill over which the city unfolds the zigzag line of its bastions, now inoffensive amid verdant woods in whose shadows the people take their walks. Large boats go up the current, towed slowly by great horses, which are walking upon the same road as ourselves and often stop the way. Then we slacken our speed, and looking back we see the line of the four Italas closing up behind us, for we are still followed by the representatives of the Paris press, cheerful and delightful travelling companions. When the valley grows narrow, we seem to fill the whole of it with the thick dust which rises up towards the hills like mist. By eight o'clock we are at Dinant, whose old cathedral with its vast stained-glass windows and its strange dome seems to be lying under shelter, at the foot of an immense rock which looks down over the water.

A quarter of an hour later we point out something to one another, which makes us bound with joy: the first French flag, floating in the air, at the stern of a steamer which is sailing down the river.

We come to the frontier near Agimont at 8.30. We should scarcely be aware of it if a Belgian customs officer, standing motionless upon the road, did not stop us, pointing to a side road, where is the customs-house. We go there and get quickly through the official formalities, and we start again.

'*République Française!*' There it is on a sign post, half hidden among the green. 'Halt!' We stop. Our hospitable Parisian colleagues wish to celebrate the moment of our entrance upon French soil. Champagne bottles put in an appearance, and glasses too, come from some country inn of the neighbourhood. In a moment the glasses are full and the bottles are empty, and the still fields echo with an '*Evviva!*' or rather with many '*Evvivas*' to France and Italy. We clink glasses; we shake hands; the wine is gone.

Quickly up again on to our cars. The French customs officers do not detain us long, and by 9.30 our four powerful cars are flying at high speed over the broad, wonderful French roads.

Paris is scarcely 200 miles away.

Now we come to Givet, surrounded by fortifications. On the grassy bastions the wallflower is abloom. The soldiers salute us from the windows of their large barracks. We pass over a drawbridge flanked by threatening loopholes, then all disappears.

We are out of that immense factory, Belgium. The sun seems

brighter. The blue seems bluer. A new kind of joy seems diffused over things. But perhaps this joy is in ourselves.

At ten o'clock we pass Fumay, the slate country. The *octroi* men stop us to look at our papers. Now we go up the gentle declivities of the Ardennes, shaded by woods, more like our woods at home. How glad we are to see again the beautiful disorderly vegetation which we love! Farewell, cool, regular, severe pine forests! The roads now seem avenues in a garden, even and flat. We feel as if we were scarcely running on them, only just skimming over them gently.

Rocroy, with its historic fortifications, appears before us at twenty minutes past ten, and we stop by the little square of the town to pick up a refill of fuel. The sharp-smelling liquid gurgles into our tanks, and the empty cans, which we call the 'carcasses', pile up upon the ground. The Italas have breakfasted. It is 10.40 when we start again in the direction of Rethel.

Paris is now 170 miles away.

While we are crossing a road, another *octroi* official suddenly bounds in front of us and commands us to stop, while another colleague appears behind him, brandishing a gun: ready to stop us, if need be, with more persuasive arguments. A further examination of our papers and inspection of our machine take place. At last, convinced that we are introducing no contraband merchandise on to the Republic's soil, the two watchful agents allow us to depart.

At twelve we see Rethel, whose shining slate roofs, half hidden among old elm trees, reflect the sunshine with gleams that look like steel. We pass one descending towards the plain of the Marne, all golden with ripe corn. At half-past twelve we enter Rheims. Rheims: on how many champagne labels have we not read this name! We think of all the toasts which we have drunk in the last few days, in a wine which invariably claimed the freedom of the City of Rheims, honorary, if not actual. A smell of food comes up to us, and in the smaller streets we can hear the clinking of the table silver and the sound of glass and china. It is dinner time in this quiet little provincial city. We decide to stop and have our dinner too.

On the principal road of the town some people run after us and salute us. Shopkeepers come out to their shop doors. A tram driver leans out over the platform of his car as we pass, and cries familiarly to Prince Borghese:

'Ca, c'est bien, mon petit!'

The passengers in the tram applaud.

We come out at the foot of the wonderful cathedral. We have scarcely time to admire its proportions with an ecstatic glance before the luminous vision disappears, and we find ourselves in the courtyard of an hotel 'with garage'. The yard is crowded, the guests of the hotel come down precipitately. An old gentleman, who looks like an artist, draws Prince Borghese aside and whispers solemn words into his ear. An American comes up to offer us champagne even while we are cleaning up; and all soapy and streaming as we are, we have to drink the toast. He gives us his congratulations and good wishes, but adds sincerely that he cannot understand what pleasure there can be in doing such a journey without making anything from it. Motorists arrive, the courtyard fills with people, smoke, and noise.

After lunch, as we are about to depart, some too-enthusiastic admirers, wishing to have a relic of our machine, throw themselves upon our 'guidon', the little triangular flag which we had affixed in front of our car. They tear it up and divide it among themselves. We have great difficulty in defending even our bigger flag at the rear. Then they start trying to cut splinters of wood from the body of the car, and the blades of their penknives are already at work. A little longer, and the car would be sacked, demolished, destroyed by all these sympathizers. But at the first touch of the pedal the good machine starts off as if she knew the danger, bounds forward and is safe. It is now three o'clock. The slender towers of the cathedral disappear from sight. We advance towards the Marne, among fertile vineyards.

Paris is now one hundred miles off.

We cross the Marne, calm and serene like the Meuse, at Vermeuil, and at last we cease from travelling southwards. From St Petersburg on we have scarcely done anything else: now we definitely turn our faces towards Paris, and we shall not swerve again from the straight line.

At a quarter-past four we stop at Château Thierry to drink a glass of beer without getting down from our car. We are surrounded by a crowd of good provincial people plunged into admiring and respectful silence.

'C'est la course!' we hear them exclaiming on all sides. La course: this is now the only name of our journey.

An old gentleman wearing decorations and looking like a retired officer hears the people's acclamations just as he is busy watering his little garden with a hose; he puts down his hose, quite forgetful of the destruction which it may bring about, and he comes to shake hands solemnly with the prince. Then he goes back with equal gravity to his watering business, satisfied with having fulfilled a duty.

We pass La Ferté at ten past five. The name of Paris is now beginning to appear on the sign posts which tell us the way.

Paris is fifty miles away.

Gradually as we approach it the welcome becomes more noisy, even in the country: more hearty, more lively; there is in it the open-heartedness of the people. The women come out to their doorsteps or look out of the window, smiling as soon as they hear the hooting of our horns; workmen leave their work to run and see, holding their hammers and other tools still in their hands. We decide to stop at Meaux and spend the night there. Our entrance into Paris is fixed for the next day, 10 August, at 4.30 in the afternoon; the committee of the race has settled it so. The point of our arrival, to be the office of *Le Matin*.

We are at Meaux. We reach it by a long avenue lined with trees. While we are about to enter among the first houses, an *octroi* guard from the middle of the road signals to us vigorously. Prince Borghese puts on the brake and asks:

'Are we to stop for the examination?'

'*Non, Monsieur, c'est pour la cinématographie.*'

And he smilingly points at a man who is working the cinematographic apparatus and who desires exactly the contrary of what his colleagues had desired at Berlin.

'Please, gentlemen, move, I beg you – move more – move very much! Again! *Il me faut du mouvement! Merci!*'

We do not wish to disappoint him. We turn to the right, to the left, we strain our necks, we twist ourselves about like bears in a cage; till the photographer, having had all the *mouvement* required, lets us go. And we come to the principal hotel, which is called La Belle Sirène.

Paris is now less than thirty miles away.

We get no sound sleep at Meaux. Early in the morning we go down to the garage almost as if we were to start and continue our advance endlessly towards some non-existing goal. We have formed a habit by now of travelling continuously, and at the hour of departure we instinctively leap out of our beds. To keep going – always to keep going – has become the object of our existence. To move on always like modern wandering Jews, condemned to perpetual restlessness.

No, we got no sleep during the last night of our pilgrimage across two continents. We slept better, more deeply and more heavily on the *kangs*, breathing bad, close, thick air, or in the fresh grass of the prairies, or on the wooden floors of the little Siberian *isbas*, wrapped in goatskins and with a camera by way of a pillow, than we can sleep now in the soft bed of the hotel at Meaux, thirty miles from Paris.

It is precisely this nearness of Paris that disturbs us. We seem to *feel* that great city. We seem to hear in the stillness of the night the powerful pulsations of its life, reaching to us out here. Several times I get up to go to the window, and look to the west, repeating to myself, '*Paris is there*', as if to convince myself of the truth of my statement, seized as I am by an unreasoning sense of doubt.

Day by day our journey has seemed to us quite reasonable, sometimes even easy. Events and episodes have succeeded one another slowly in a perfectly natural way. To reach Kiakhta after leaving Urga, to reach Verkhne-Udinsk after leaving Kiakhta, seemed a perfectly straight-forward process. We were passing from country to country, from people to people, by imperceptible degrees. Every change seemed to be dimmed by the long monotony of the hours which passed too slowly. But now, stopped as we are at the gates of Paris, with our minds no longer preoccupied by the road before us, we turn to look back upon the road we have covered, and in our minds it appears dramatically foreshortened.

We have been through the Peking gates crowned with pagodas; Chinese arms have helped this machine to traverse the rocks of Ki-mi-ni, where we have met palanquins drawn by mules and covered in blue silk; mandarins with the golden dragon embroidered on their tunics have been to look at this machine at Kalgan, while the gong of a neighbouring temple was striking the minutes one by one. This automobile has been pursued by tempestuous Mongolian cavalcades, and has in its turn pursued one morning on the threshold of the desert a great herd of tawny gazelles, mad with terror. It has forded the vast Iro, the last river of the Chinese Empire; it has been overturned on a little bridge in Trans-Baikalia; it has sped between the rails of the Trans-Siberian Railway; it has crossed the *taiga*, the vastest forest of the world; it has sunk in the mud at the gates of Tomsk . . . And now it is here, whole and strong, half an hour's run from the Vincennes Gate. We had not dared to hope, we had scarcely dared to think of the emotion of this moment when we left the Dochman Gate of Peking!

Prince Borghese has always made it his rule to impose upon himself short, easy tasks, and not to consider the difficulties lying beyond it. He often said to me during the trying, despairing days of slow, difficult advance:

'All I wish for is to reach the next village,' and he suppressed all the rest from his mind. Thus we laid all our forces, all the strength of our wills to the task of overcoming that short stretch of road, as if the next village was to be our last goal. And the next day we would begin again.

The huge, wonderful distance of our journey is, after all, only made up of a long series of short stages, each of them proportionate to our powers and to those of the machine. Our journey was, more than anything else, a long succession of victories of patience. We never reckoned up the distances before us, but always those behind. We tried to find the data which would encourage us, and yet we were so cautious in our reckoning that we have since become quite sure that we greatly underestimated the distances.

We almost certainly mistook our reckonings about the distances in Mongolia and in the Gobi desert, where we went at a good speed, from twelve to fourteen hours a day. We thought that we were travelling in that time, roughly, 150 miles. But in western Europe, in going at the same speed, we found that in the same length of time we covered nearly 300 miles. The exact total of the miles covered by our car remains, therefore, still unknown. We believe it to be over 8000. But we willingly allow the doubt to remain; we have certainly no intention to go back and take measurements!

The fact of being so near Paris moves us, surprises us, stuns us also because of the fantastic swiftness with which it has come upon us. During the last few days we have not had time to get accustomed to the idea of arriving. The furthest provinces of European Russia, Germany, Belgium, and France have passed by us like a dream. It took us twelve days to cover the first six hundred miles of our journey: we have flown over the last six hundred in two days and a half.

But the last few hours seem everlasting. They are hours of joy, but also of anguish – of a sudden, vague, inexpressible anguish, which makes us silent and gives us all the appearance of disappointed men.

On the morning of the 10th, Meaux is invaded by a small army of motor cars. More arrive at every moment. Large and small ones; some of them decked with flags, others covered with the names of newspapers written in large lettering; one bringing the Italian pressmen; several representing the French Automobile Club: there is a hooting of horns, cries like those of sea sirens. The engines are roaring and the people crowd upon the road, in the yard of the hotel, even in the garage. Our machine is not to be seen; it has been locked up in a room, and against the door of this room the curious crowd knocks in vain.

At a quarter past two the word of order is given, some of the cars set off, and there is a moment of excitement: we are about to start.

Ettore fastens the luggage on the case at the back of the car with the very special care he has bestowed upon this duty ever since we dropped the prince's portmanteau in the Gobi desert. He primes the carburettor. He gives a turn to the starting-handle, and the engine noisily starts into life. We sit down in our places; Prince Borghese starts the machine, engages the clutch, and slowly we go on to the road. All Meaux is gathered there to look at us.

The car passes with difficulty among the cheering spectators: all the windows are crowded with ladies who throw large bunches of flowers on to our machine. A long shout of 'hurrah!' runs by our side, and accompanies us to the exit of the town, where we head the line of advance. The first to follow us are the cars of the Paris correspondents, who have accompanied us from Berlin, and who will remain near us until our arrival.

We get up speed. In ten minutes we cover the ten kilometres which separate us from Couilly. We pass Crécy at 2.45, and shortly after we cross Lagny. At three we pass Chelles.

The prince will no longer slacken or swerve, not even when the road becomes less good. Why consider the machine now, when we are almost 'there'?

Paris is twenty miles off – now fifteen – now eight.

There is everywhere around us cheering, applause, the waving of handkerchiefs; Prince Borghese smiles no longer with his habitual enigmatical, ceremonious smile, but with spontaneity now. His admirably steady control of himself is not sufficient to repress the joy which is in him, and which opens itself a way in that smile.

The villages succeed one another without a break. They are beginning now to be truly suburbs of Paris. Many people who are waiting for us look up with a questioning expression as if to ask: 'Is it you?' not knowing which is the prince's carriage amongst so many others.

The greater part of the people make up their minds that the prince's carriage cannot certainly be the shabby-looking one that travels in front of all. And it is usually our travelling companions, our colleagues in the second carriage, who receive the clamorous demonstrations of the crowd. At Bry a fat woman of the people is waiting on the roadside with an enormous bunch of flowers, and with a beautifully aimed throw, she sends this bunch on the breast of our eminent colleague, Henri Des Houx, shouting to him:

'*A vous, Monseigneur!*'

As we approach Joinville there are people crowding, even in the open country, under the trees which border the roadside, they have come from the surrounding villas, and greet us with an ever growing, ever deepening enthusiasm. Cart drivers cry out: '*Bravo, mon gars!*' At St Maurice we find the gate shut at the level-crossing and have to stop for a few minutes until the train is past. The police are obliged to form a cordon round our car. We cross the Vincennes forest. Many cyclists have joined the procession, and precede our machine with real danger of being run over. We cry out to them to pay attention when they come too near the wheel. But the only reply they give is to wave their caps, shouting:

'*Vive le prince!*'

On all sides we hear the cries of '*Viva!*' The omnibuses and trams stop, and the passengers get up and clap as we pass. A storm is approaching; the sky now is covered with black clouds, chasing one another overhead; but the crowd does not grow less. As we reach St Mandé the rain begins to fall. It will henceforth not abandon us. We left Peking under rain; it is but right that we should arrive with the rain in Paris.

In the Cours de Vincennes we are stopped again; we are a whole hour before the time fixed for our entrance. The cyclists, who have formed themselves into a kind of improvised bodyguard, have grown in number to something like a hundred, and begin to describe fantastic figures before us. We are surrounded by an elaborate gymkhana.

At four o'clock a strange kind of car appears from Paris and puts itself at the head of our procession. It is one of those gigantic motor cars for twenty or thirty passengers, used to take tourists round Paris when they desire to see the town in a few hours. In this car are some bandsmen armed with trumpets and trombones, and the car is decked out with trophies and numerous French and Italian flags. It looks a little like a carnival show, but it seems indispensable to the due solemnization of our arrival. The band strikes up with the triumphal march out of *Aida*. This is the entry of Radamès, in Paris!

We continue our progress. It is now 4.15.

We come out on to the Avenue du Trône, between the two gigantic columns of Philip Augustus, half hidden by a crowd of people. Before us, veiled by the rain, we see the dim outline of the Tour Eiffel. It looks like some gigantic lighthouse – the great lighthouse of our journey's harbour.

The cheering becomes clamorous, intense, continuous. Whenever it abates for a moment we hear the ringing voices of the street vendors offering souvenir postcards for sale, with cries of: '*Le Prince Borghèse, quatre sous! Quatre sous, le Prince Borghèse!*'

The cordon of guardsmen along the Boulevard Voltaire are powerless to restrain the multitude, which surrounds us, advances by our side and behind us. Prince Borghese raises his hand courteously to make sign that we must be given a little room or an accident may occur: his hand is caught by a workman, who presses it effusively; then by another one;

it is held, it is pulled, everyone wises to shake it, and they do shake it with energetic friendliness. Not without a certain difficulty Prince Borghese succeeds in freeing that hand from the grip of the crowd, as dangerous as cog-wheeled machinery. He brings it back safely to the wheel.

On the Place de la République are standing in a line two mounted patrols of the Republican Guard; and they come to place themselves, one at the head and the other at the rear of our procession. We can see the shining of their helmets above the great waving crowd, as their horses gallop here and there.

At the entrance of the Boulevard St Martin, the cheering becomes one loud roar of applause. The cry, '*Vive Borghèse!*' is repeated and continuous. Prince Borghese is for one day the idol of Paris, of this generous city which loves so desperately when it loves at all.

The sight of the broad road before us is superb. The two high-railed pavements are black with people, and over the heads of the crowd is a great waving of hands, and hats, and handkerchiefs, and sticks, and even of umbrellas, for the relentless downpour still continues. Ettore is moved, intoxicated, and is waving his arms to return salutes with most excited gestures. The women of the people cry fond expressions to us in *argot*. At the corner of the Boulevard St Denis a woman comes forward carrying a little baby in her arms, and makes the baby clap.

We advance at a very slow pace, terribly afraid lest some mishap may occur. The crowd is grazing the wheels of the car. At the Boulevard Bonne Nouvelle the demonstration still continues fiercely. The clapping seems still louder, and the word *Borghèse*, with the two words *Vive* and *Bravo* supply henceforth the only cries that are heard.

We catch a glimpse of *agents de sûreté*, and of patrols of Republican Guards on the Boulevard Poissonière, keeping the road clear before a palace strangely coloured with red and adorned with flags: the office of *Le Matin*.

This is the winning-post.

Our long race is about to end. The Republican Guard on their excited horses go through rapid manoeuvres which sweep away the crowd, and the space deserted by the latter is immediately occupied by a number of photographers. They too go through manoeuvres in order to choose the best points of view, avoiding at the same time the hoofs of the horses. Some cinematographists now solemnly turn the handles of their machines, photographing the scene of our arrival, and shouting with all their might to us, 'Look up at the lens!'

The car, following the orders of a member of the Race Committee, describes a sweeping curve, and bounds softly on to the pavement before the entrance of *Le Matin* . . .

We have arrived!

Prince Borghese releases the clutch and puts on the brake.

The car stops.

The race is ended.

This is an indescribably solemn moment for us. The ovations of the crowd are loud and full. We remain seated in our places, confused, stunned.

I, who am sitting at the place on the step and should be the first to set foot aground, cannot make up my mind to get down. For a few moments I have a strange sensation that all I see is a hallucination, a dream. It all seems absurd and impossible; I cannot convince myself that we have come to the end, that we have really arrived. My limbs are inert, and with a mechanical gesture I continue smoking a cigarette which went out long ago. I turn round and look at Prince Borghese. He is still with his hands on the wheel, in the same eager attitude that he used to have at our short halts on the journey when he was ready to start.

'*Venez, venez!*' they cry to us from the buildings of *Le Matin*.

Then I jump down, as if just awakened. A shout of enthusiasm sweeps by like a hurricane; I am grasped and embraced, and suddenly I recognize in the effusive person who receives me thus, the solemn porter of *Le Matin* offices, unable any longer to contain his emotion, and who has thrown himself upon me.

We are dragged within the palace amid a deafening clamour. A band plays the Italian Royal March. I find colleagues and friends, and shake hands with them, unable to speak. I do not know how, but we find our arms full of bunches of roses; the crowd outside is shouting, and a tumultuous roar covers at times even the sound of the music. The people are asking to see '*Le prince*', and Prince Borghese is sent up to the balcony, looks out, bows repeatedly, holding a great bunch of flowers in his hand. Champagne bottles are opened, discourses are pronounced, toasts are drunk. We are photographed by flashlight with and without flowers . . .

And I don't know what happened next. I went off quietly, and had the happiness to mingle once again unknown among the crowd, leaving to the prince alone the onerous burdens of popularity.

A few hours later, on the Boulevards, which had reverted to their normal appearance, the street vendors were still selling the souvenir postcards. But now their cry was: '*Le Prince Borghèse – un sou!*'

No longer four sous, but one. What a solemn lesson lay in that fall of price! Fate conveys her pronouncements even through the cries of street vendors. Our popularity had fallen seventy-five per cent in two hours. *Sic transit gloria* . . .